Social Policy in a Development Context

The *Social Policy in a Development Context* series is an exciting, interdisciplinary contribution to the literature on economic development and social policy. Making the connection between economic development and social policy opens up new areas of scholarly inquiry while bringing pragmatic and actionable insights for policy design and implementation at the national and international levels. For further information on UNRISD work on social policy and development, visit www.unrisd.org.

More information about this series at
http://www.palgrave.com/gp/series/14480

Katja Hujo
Editor

The Politics of Domestic Resource Mobilization for Social Development

palgrave
macmillan

Editor
Katja Hujo
United Nations Research Institute for Social Development (UNRISD)
Geneva, Switzerland

ISSN 2662-6659 ISSN 2662-6667 (electronic)
Social Policy in a Development Context
ISBN 978-3-030-37594-2 ISBN 978-3-030-37595-9 (eBook)
https://doi.org/10.1007/978-3-030-37595-9

This Palgrave Macmillan imprint is published by the registered company Springer Nature Switzerland AG.
The registered company address is: Gewerbestrasse 11, 6330 Cham, Switzerland

Foreword

The international discourse on financing for development consistently emphasizes the foundational role of domestic resource mobilization in long-term sustainable finance. Many countries—typically those that are poorer and developing—require additional revenue mobilization and investment because they start from a low base in terms of infrastructure, institutions and service provision.

Official development assistance plays a critical role in supporting investments in many countries, and yet has high transaction costs associated with donor engagement and reporting, conditionality, the sporadic use of domestic systems and skewed accountability because of the absence of comprehensive citizen engagement. Foreign direct investment also ebbs and flows, depending on patterns of global growth and trade, and can present an additional challenge to governments when it is concentrated in certain sectors, especially those that deal in extracted commodities. Donors, for their part, have not been meeting their commitment—in the Addis Tax Initiative—to direct more of their assistance towards capacity building for revenue mobilization.[1]

Domestic resource mobilization has increased in the least developed countries since 2015, albeit from a low base. Improvements in tax

[1] Follow-up to and implementation of the outcomes of the International Conferences on Financing for Development, Report of the Secretary-General, United Nations, July 2019.

revenue-to-GDP ratios were seen in 60 per cent of the least developed countries in 2017. But domestic policy shifts have been insufficient, not only with regard to mobilizing additional resources, but most importantly in view of shifting the existing practice of development finance: progress towards the 2030 Agenda for Sustainable Development requires, first and foremost, a reallocation away from existing public and private spending patterns—expenditures and investments—that are incompatible with the Sustainable Development Goals, and towards those that are compatible. At the heart of this is moving towards renewable energy and away from consumption behaviours that are no longer sustainable within the natural bounds of this planet.

International support is also needed on the global tax environment. There must be further action to coordinate tax systems at the national level, in the light of increasing digitization of the economy and continued corporate tax avoidance and illicit financial flows. Pressure will be added in coming decades because of demographic shifts and climate change–related shocks. Universal social protection systems will be crucial for safeguarding populations, yet also require significant development and investment.

Drawing on a rich collection of country examples, this book highlights the importance of understanding the country-specific context for resource mobilization, including history and political complexion. It emphasizes the importance of more inclusive revenue and spending bargains, to ensure that priorities are accurately discerned and legitimacy is enhanced. Institutions that are strengthened along this more inclusive pathway can deliver greater social equity and cohesion and be a tool in tackling gender discrimination.

On behalf of UNRISD I would like to take this opportunity to thank the Swedish International Development Cooperation Agency (Sida) for their financial support of the project. As is the case with all UNRISD work, this important research would not have been possible without the core institutional support we receive from the governments of Sweden, Switzerland and Finland.

UNRISD, Geneva, Switzerland Paul Ladd
October 2019

Preface

Mobilizing the necessary financial resources for social and sustainable development is one of the key challenges policy makers are grappling with today. Scaling up domestic public revenues is crucial to meet international commitments, such as the Sustainable Development Goals, to implement national development priorities, and to anchor a country's social contract in a financially sustainable way.

The UNRISD research project on Politics of Domestic Resource Mobilization for Social Development (PDRM) received earmarked funding from the Swedish International Development Cooperation Agency (Sida). The project set out to answer questions about how to bridge existing funding gaps and increase fiscal capacity in the Global South, and how to improve understanding of the politics of revenue and social expenditure bargains and the accountability of governments to citizens. The research also sought to connect two scholarly literatures that had, until then, rarely spoken to each other: the politics of resource mobilization and the politics of social provision in developing countries. In-depth country-level research was undertaken by interdisciplinary teams in four countries: Bolivia, Nicaragua, Uganda and Zimbabwe. These studies, which are synthesized in four chapters in this book, were complemented with studies on aid, taxation and mineral rents, and their specific role in domestic resource mobilization strategies in different countries and regions.

The book aims to contribute a political economy analysis of the economic and political drivers of resource mobilization and its links with building nations and social contracts. It posits that finance debates cannot be separated from social policy and need to go beyond technical recommendations, shedding light on processes of contestation and bargaining, social relations and institution building. An integrated analysis of the politics of revenue and expenditure policies that takes account of the broader national and global contexts can improve our understanding of the obstacles and opportunities for designing transformative financing policies for inclusive and sustainable development—and, ultimately, make for more effective policy implementation and better outcomes.

Geneva, Switzerland
October 2019

Katja Hujo

Acknowledgements

I would like to take the opportunity to thank all researchers who participated in the PDRM project: Javier Arellano-Yanguas, Aniket Bhushan, Gloria Carrión, Cécile Cherrier, Gibson Chigumira, Enrique Delamonica, Guy Delmelle, Hilda Gutiérrez Elizondo, Wilson Jiménez Pozo, Jalia Kangave, Godfrey Kanyenze, Mesharch Katusiimeh, Anne-Mette Kjaer, Alan Martin, Rekopantswe Mate, Andrés Mejía-Acosta, René Mendoza, Thandika Mkandawire, Roberto Molina, Mick Moore, Jamee K. Moudud, Shamiso Mtisi, Santiago Oller Daroca, Verónica Paz Arauco, Esteban Pérez Caldentey, Wilson Prichard, Yiagadeesen Samy, Richard Saunders, Aaron Schneider, and Marianne Ulriksen.

Yusuf Bangura, who conceptualized this project before he retired from UNRISD, has been an inspiration and invaluable support throughout the project; I am especially grateful for his guidance and advice during the final book preparation phase. A special thanks also to all contributors to this volume, for their dedication to the research, for bearing with us during a period of institutional crisis which caused some delays in the project and for responding so patiently to our numerous requests and queries during the finalization of the manuscript. We are very grateful for the useful comments received from the two peer reviewers who read the whole collection, Jimi Adesina and Alexander Caramento. Thandika Mkandawire and Sarah Cook, former directors of UNRISD, as well as UNRISD Director Paul Ladd, encouraged and supported the research in many ways. Research Analysts Harald Braumann and Maggie Carter excelled in their multiple contributions to the project over several years, with Maggie managing the final production process with professionalism and eye for detail. My gratitude is also due to several research interns who have contributed to the project over the years, Martina Andrade, Nathalie Both, Jerome Patrick R. Cruz, Luisa Guerra, Inês Schjolberg Marques, Maudo Jallow, Tobias Lopez, Luisa Lupo, Ira Mataj, Alberto Parmigiani, Kidjie Saguin, Premila Sattiannayagam, Paul Scharfenberg, Tejal Shrikant Ambardekar, Sebastian Weishaupt.

And last but not least, thank you to our colleagues in the UNRISD Communications and Outreach Unit, Jenifer Freedman, Joannah Caborn Wengler and Sergio Sandoval Fonseca, and to Alexander Dénis for administrative support. This book is dedicated to Thandika Mkandawire, former director of UNRISD, who contributed Chap. 5. Thandika passed away on 27 March 2020, when we were in the final stages of producing this volume. He motivated us to explore the question of financing social policy, which was at the heart of the research project "Politics of Domestic Resource Mobilization".

Contents

Notes on Contributors

Javier Arellano-Yanguas is a research fellow and lecturer at the Centre for Applied Ethics at the University of Deusto (Bilbao, Spain). His research focuses on the political economy of natural resources–led development, social conflicts, social accountability, open government, and the interactions between religion and development. He has extensive work and research experience in India and across Latin America, especially in the Andean countries, and uses both quantitative and qualitative approaches. Arellano-Yanguas holds a PhD in Development Studies from the Institute of Development Studies (University of Sussex).

Yusuf Bangura was a research coordinator at UNRISD from 1990 to 2012 and lead author of the Institute's 2010 flagship report, *Combating Poverty and Inequality: Structural Change, Social Policy and Politics.* His most recent publications include *Developmental Pathways to Poverty Reduction* (editor, Palgrave Macmillan and UNRISD, 2015) and "Bargaining for Development: The World Bank's 2017 World Development Report, Governance and the Law" (*Development and Change*, March 2018).

Aniket Bhushan is an adjunct research professor at the Norman Paterson School of International Affairs (NPSIA) at Carleton University in Ottawa, Canada. He leads the Canadian International Development Platform (CIDP), a data analytics and policy research initiative on Canada's engagement with the developing world. His work sits at the intersection of data, technology and international development.

Gloria Carrión is a senior researcher in social policy and gender at the Fundación Nicaraguense para el Desarrollo Económico y Social (FUNIDES) in Managua, Nicaragua. She is also a research associate at the Centro de Investigación y Acción Social Educativa (CIASES) and at the Fundación Internacional para el Desafío Económico Global (FIDEG) in Managua. She has worked for UNRISD, the International Centre for Trade and Sustainable Development (ICTSD) and the Permanent Mission of Nicaragua in Geneva, Switzerland. She holds an MSc from the London School of Economics and a BA from Trent University.

Cécile Cherrier is a freelance consultant based in France and a research associate at the Overseas Development Institute. She specializes in social protection policies and programmes, with a specific focus on fragile, conflict-affected and disaster-prone contexts. Over the past 20 years, she has served as a humanitarian programme coordinator, technical advisor, policy analyst and researcher for a range of major donors, United Nations agencies, non-governmental organizations and research institutes. She holds an MSc in agronomy from Montpellier SupAgro and a PhD in governance and policy analysis from Maastricht University.

Enrique Delamonica is the senior advisor for Child Poverty and Gender Equality Statistics at the United Nations Children's Fund (UNICEF). He was previously UNICEF Social and Economic Policy Regional Advisor (Latin America and Caribbean) and Chief of Social Policy and Gender Equality (Nigeria). His publications cover child rights, social protection, socioeconomic disparities, financing social services, and the impact of macroeconomic trends on children. He taught economics, international development, policy analysis and research methods at, among other places, Columbia University, the New School and Saint Peter's College. He serves on the board of the Research Committee on Poverty, Social Welfare and Social Policy of the International Sociological Association.

Katja Hujo is a senior research coordinator in the Social Policy and Development Programme at UNRISD in Geneva, Switzerland. Hujo's academic work focuses on social policy, poverty and inequality, and socioeconomic development. She has published numerous papers and articles, one monograph, seven edited volumes and three journal special issues, and she was the coordinator and lead author of the UNRISD 2016 flagship report, *Policy Innovations for Transformative Change: Implementing the 2030 Agenda for Sustainable Development*. Hujo studied economics and political science at Eberhard Karls University Tübingen, Freie Universität Berlin (FUB) and National University of Córdoba, Argentina, and she holds a PhD in Economics from FUB.

Anne Mette Kjær is a professor in the Department of Political Science, University of Aarhus, Denmark. Her research focuses on African governance, politics and policy reforms. She has published widely, including her book *Governance* (2004), and co-authored *Politics of African Industrial Policy* (2015), as well as articles in *World Development*, *Public Administration*, *Commonwealth and Comparative Politics* and *Journal of Eastern Africa Studies*. She is the principal investigator for "Political Settlements and Revenue Bargains in Africa" (www.ps.au.dk/psrb), a research programme funded by Danida's Consultative Research Committee. She is also an affiliated researcher with ESID at the University of Manchester.

Andrés Mejía-Acosta is a senior lecturer in political economy of emerging markets at King's College London, United Kingdom. A political scientist by training, his work explores how formal and informal political coalitions advance or undermine the adoption of effective and inclusive public policies. He has published extensively on fiscal management of natural resource revenues, fiscal decentralization, nutrition policies, and transparency and accountability initiatives. His areas of expertise include Latin America, in particular the Andean region. He has worked as a country and thematic expert for the UK Department for International Development, the Inter-American Development Bank and the United Nations.

Thandika Mkandawire was a professor and Chair of African Development at the London School of Economics, United Kingdom. He served as the director of UNRISD and as the executive secretary of the Council for the Development of Social Research in Africa (CODESRIA).

Mick Moore was the founding chief executive officer of the International Centre for Tax and Development at the Institute of Development Studies (University of Sussex, United Kingdom), 2010–2020, and is now a senior fellow. He is a political scientist specializing in applied research on taxation, governance and public policy in poorer countries. His most recent book, with Wilson Prichard and Odd-Helge Fjeldstad, is *Taxing Africa* (2018).

Jamee K. Moudud is a professor of economics at Sarah Lawrence College in the United States. His research focuses on the intersection between legal theory, history and political economy. His current work focuses on the legal and political histories of central banks and of taxes, and the historical relationship between public finance, social protection, and public investment. He is on the Board of the Association for the Promotion of Political Economy and the Law (APPEAL) and is involved in launching the *Journal of Law and Political Economy*. He is also an associate editor of the *Review of Keynesian Economics*. He has a doctorate (with honours) in Economics from the New School for Social Research.

Verónica Paz Arauco a Bolivian economist, is the head of policy at Oxfam in Bolivia. She is also a research associate at the Commitment to Equity (CEQ) Institute at Tulane University in New Orleans. Previously, she has worked for UNICEF in Bolivia and has co-authored several National Human Development Reports for UNDP in Bolivia.

Esteban Pérez Caldentey heads the Financing for Development Unit within the Economic Development Division at the Economic Commission for Latin America and the Caribbean (ECLAC) in Santiago, Chile. He previously worked at ECLAC's sub-regional headquarters in Mexico City, and in Trinidad and Tobago. He is a member of the editorial board of the *International Journal of Political Economy*, co-editor of the *Review of Keynesian Economics*, co-editor-in-chief of the *Palgrave Dictionary of Economics*, and author of the first intellectual biography of Roy Harrod. Pérez Caldentey holds Master's and PhD degrees in Economics from The New School for Social Research.

Wilson Prichard is an associate professor of global affairs and political science at the University of Toronto, Canada, chief executive officer of the International Centre for Tax and Development, and research fellow at the Institute of Development Studies (University of Sussex, United Kingdom). His work focuses on the political economy of tax reform and connections between taxation, governance and development, particularly in Africa. He is the author of *Taxation, Responsiveness and Accountability in Sub-Saharan Africa* (2015), *Taxing Africa* (2018) and a variety of academic articles. He regularly engages with donors, civil society and governments about their tax reform programmes, particularly in sub-Saharan Africa.

Yiagadeesen Samy is a full professor of international affairs and the director of the Norman Paterson School of International Affairs (NPSIA) at Carleton University in Ottawa, Canada. He has published widely on issues related to international economics and economic development, and his most recent peer-reviewed work has appeared in *Politics and Governance*, *Canadian Journal of Development Studies*, *Third World Quarterly*, *International Interactions* and *Journal of Conflict Resolution*. He is a co-author of *African Economic Development* (2018) and of *Exiting the Fragility Trap* (2019).

Richard Saunders is an associate professor in the Department of Politics, York University, Canada, where he teaches African political economy and development, and a senior research associate at the University of Johannesburg, South Africa. His research focuses on the political economy of extractive resources, including issues of governance, participation and empowerment, and the potential for resource-fuelled "developmental states" in the Global South. His most recent book is the edited collection, *Facets of Power: Politics, Profits and People in the Making of Zimbabwe's Blood Diamonds* (2016).

Aaron Schneider is the Leo Block Chair of International Studies at the Josef Korbel School of International Studies at the University of Denver, United States. His work focuses on the intersection of wealth and power, and he has conducted research in Latin America, India and sub-Saharan Africa. In particular, he emphasizes the study of public finance as a window into the political economy of development and democracy.

Marianne S. Ulriksen is an associate professor at the Danish Centre for Welfare Studies (DaWS), University of Southern Denmark, and is also affiliated with the Centre for Social Development in Africa (CSDA) at the University of Johannesburg. Her research areas include comparative politics, political economy of welfare policy development, social protection, social justice, poverty and inequality, and resource mobilization and taxation. Her research work focuses primarily on Southern and Eastern Africa.

Abbreviations

AAC	AIDS Action Committee
AEA	Asociación Empresaria Argentina (Argentinian Enterprise Association)
AEO	African Economic Outlook
AFJP	Administradoras de Fondos de Jubilaciones y Pensiones (Pensions and Retirement Accounts Fund Managers)
AGP	Asom Gana Parishad (Assam Peoples Association)
AIDS	Acquired immunodeficiency syndrome
ALBA	Alternativa Bolivariana para los Pueblos de Nuestra América (Bolivarian Alternative for the People of our America)
ALBANISA	ALBA de Nicaragua Sociedad Anónima (ALBA of Nicaragua S.A.)
ALP	Arm's length principle
AMLAE	Asociación de Mujeres Nicaragüenses Luisa Amanda Espinoza (Nicaraguan Women's Association Luisa Amanda Espinoza)
ANDEN	Asociación Nacional de Educadores de Nicaragua (National Teachers' Association)
ANSES	Administración Nacional de Seguridad Social (National Social Security Administration)
ASM	Artisanal and small-scale mining
ATAF	African Tax Administration Forum
ATC	Asociación de Trabajadores del Campo (Rural Workers' Association)

AUGE	Acceso Universal con Garantías Explícitas (Universal Access with Explicit Guarantees)
BEAM	Basic Education Assistance Module
BEPS	Base erosion and profit sharing
BJP	Bharatiya Janata Party
BOB	Bolivian bolivianos (currency)
BRICS	Brazil, Russia, India, China, South Africa
BRL	Brazilian real (currency)
BSP	Bahujan Samaj Party (People in Majority Party)
CBGA	Centre for Budget and Governance Analysis
CIDA	Canadian International Development Agency
CIDE	Contribuição de Intervenção no Domínio Econômico (Contribution of Intervention in the Economic Domain)
CIT	Corporate income tax
CLP	Chilean peso (currency)
CMEs	Coordinated market economies
CNOOC	China National Offshore Oil Company
COFINS	Contribuição para o Financiamento da Seguridade Social (Contribution to Social Security Financing)
COINAGRO	Confederación Intercooperativa Agropecuaria (Intercooperative Agricultural Confederation)
COMIBOL	Corporación Minera de Bolivia (Bolivian Mining Corporation)
COSEP	Consejo Superior de la Empresa Privada (Supreme Council of Private Enterprise)
CPC	Confederación de la Producción (Production Confederation)
CPIA	Country policy and institutional assessment
CPMF	Contribuição Provisorio sobre Movimentação Financeira (Provisional Contribution on Financial Transactions)
CPSS	Contribuição para o Plano de Seguridade Social (Contribution to the Social Security Plan)
CRA	Confederaciones Rurales Argentinas (Argentinian Rural Confederations)
CRISSOL	Programa Cristiano, Socialista y Solidario (Christian, Socialist and Solidary Programme)
CRS	Creditor reporting system
CSLL	Contribuição Social sobre Lucro Líquido (Social Contribution on Net Profits)

CSO	Civil society organization
CSS	Contribuição Social para Saude (Social Contribution for Health)
CT-OVC	Cash Transfers for Orphans and Vulnerable Children
CUT	Centro Unico dos Trabalhadores (Unified Workers Central)
DAC	Development Assistance Committee
DFAT	Department of Foreign Affairs and Trade
DI	Development initiatives
DMK	Dravida Munnetra Kazhagam
DNP	Distribuidora Nicaragüense de Petróleo (Nicaraguan Oil Distributor)
DRM	Domestic resource mobilization
DT	Direct tax
EC	European Commission
EI	Extractive industries
ESAP	Economic Structural Adjustment Programme
EU	European Union
FAA	Federación Agraria Argentina (Argentinian Agrarian Federation)
FDI	Foreign direct investment
FETSALUD	Federación de Trabajadores de la Salud (Federation of Health Workers)
FGTS	Fundo de Garantia do Tempo de Serviço (Government Severance Indemnity Fund for Employees)
FIS	Fondo de Inversión Social (Social Investment Fund)
FISP	Malawi's Farm Input Subsidy Programme
FNT	Frente Nacional de Trabajadores (National Workers' Front)
FSE	Fondo Social de Emergencia (Social Emergency Fund)
FSLN	Frente Sandinista de Liberación Nacional (Sandinista National Liberation Front)
FTAA	Free Trade Agreement of the Americas
FTLR	Fast Track Land Reform Programme
FUNDAP	Fundação do Desenvolvimento Administrativo (Foundation for Administrative Development)
FY	Fiscal year
G20	Group of 20
G8	Group of 8
GBP	Pound sterling (currency)

GDP	Gross domestic product
GFS	Government financial statistics
GNI	Gross national income
GNU	Government of National Unity
GTZ	Gesellschaft für Technische Zusammenarbeit (German Technical Cooperation Agency)
HC-IDC	House of Commons International Development Committee
HDI	Human Development Index
HIPC	Heavily indebted poor countries
HIV/AIDS	Human immunodeficiency virus/acquired immune deficiency syndrome
HKND	HK Nicaragua Canal Development Investment Co., Limited
HNWI	High-net-worth individuals
HSNP	Hunger Safety Net Programme
IACHR	Inter-American Commission on Human Rights
IADB	Inter-American Development Bank
ICMS	Imposto sobre Circulação de Mercadorias e Serviços (Tax on the Movement of Goods and Services)
ICTD	International Centre for Tax and Development
IDA	International Development Association
IDH	Impuesto Directo a los Hidrocarburos (Direct Tax on Hydrocarbons)
IEE	Indigenisation and Economic Empowerment Act
IEHD	Impuesto Especial a los Hidrocarburos y sus Derivados (Special Tax on Hydrocarbons and their By-Products)
IFFs	Illicit financial flows
IFIs	International financial institutions
ILO	International Labour Organization
IMF	International Monetary Fund
INC	Indian National Congress
INE	Instituto Nacional de Estadísticas (National Statistics Institute)
ISAPRES	Instituciones de Salud Previsional (Private Health Insurance Institutions)
IT	Indirect tax
IT	Information technology
KPCS	Kimberley Process Certification Scheme
LEAP	Livelihood Empowerment Against Poverty

LGBTQ	Lesbian, gay, bisexual, transgender and queer or questioning
LMEs	Liberal market economies
MARENA	Ministerio del Ambiente y los Recursos Naturales (Ministry of the Environment and Natural Resources)
MAS	Movimiento al Socialismo (Movement for Socialism)
MCC	Millennium Challenge Corporation
MDC	Movement for Democratic Change
MDGs	Millennium Development Goals
MEFP	Ministerio de Economía y Finanzas Públicas (Ministry of the Economy and Public Finances)
MENA	Middle East and North Africa
MINESA	Sociedad Minera de Santander (Santander Mining Society)
MNCs	Multinational companies
MNR	Movimiento Nacionalista Revolucionario (National Revolutionary Movement)
MNREGA	Mahatma Gandhi Rural Employment Guarantee Scheme
MOFPED	Ministry of Finance Planning and Economic Development
MOHCW	Ministry of Health and Child Welfare
MP	Members of parliament
MST	Movimento dos Trabalhadores Sem Terra (Landless Workers' Movement)
NAC	National Advisory Council
NAC	National AIDS Council
NATF	National AIDS Trust Fund
NCC	National Chamber of Commerce
NDP	National Development Plan
NGO	Non-governmental organization
NIO	Nicaraguan córdoba (currency)
NRI	Non-resident Indian
NRM	National Resistance Movement
NSI	North-South Institute
NSSA	National Social Security Authority
OAP	Old Age Pension
OBC	Other backward classes
ODA	Official development aid
OECD	Organisation for Economic Co-operation and Development
PAF	Poverty Action Fund
PAYE	Pay As You Earn

PCdoB	Partido Comunista do Brasil (Communist Party of Brazil)
PDRM	Politics of domestic resource mobilization
PDT	Partido Democrático Trabalhista (Democratic Labour Party)
PEAP	Poverty Eradication Action Plan
PEFA	Public expenditure and financial accountability
PEPD	Petroleum Exploration and Production Department
PFL	Partido da Frente Liberal (Party of the Liberal Front)
PFM	Public financial management
PIS	Programa de Integração Social (Programme of Social Integration)
PISPPS	Partido Popular Socialista (Popular Socialist Party)
PIT	Personal income tax
PL	Partido Liberal (Liberal Party)
PMDB	Partido do Movimento Democrático Brasileiro (Brazilian Democratic Movement)
PP	Partido Progressista (Progressive Party)
PPB	Partido Progressista Brasileiro (Brazilian Progressive Party)
PPD	Partido Por la Democracia (Party for Democracy)
PPM	Policy and political mix
PR	Partido de la República (Party of the Republic)
PRA	Power resources approach
PRN	Partido de la Reconstrucción Nacional (National Reconstruction Party)
PRSP	Poverty Reduction Strategy Papers
PS	Partido Socialista (Socialist Party)
PSA	Production sharing agreement
PSB	Partido Socialista Brasileiro (Brazilian Socialist Party)
PSD	Partido Social Democrático (Social Democratic Party)
PSDB	Partido da Social Democracia Brasileira (Brazilian Social Democratic Party)
PSF	The Private Sector Foundation
PSM	Pensão Social Mínima (Minimum Social Pension)
PSNP	Productive Safety Net Programme
PSOL	Partido Socialismo e Liberdade (Socialism and Liberty Party)
PSSB	Programa de Subsídio Social Básico (Basic Social Subsidy Programme)
PT	Partido dos Trabalhadores (Workers' Party)
PTB	Partido Trabalhista Brasileiro (Brazilian Labour Party)

PV	Partido Verde (Green Party)
PwC	PricewaterhouseCoopers
RBZ	Reserve Bank of Zimbabwe
RJD	Rashtriya Janata Dal (National People's Party)
RN	Renovación Nacional (National Renewal)
RoU	Republic of Uganda
RSS	Rashtriya Swayamsevak Sangh (National Patriotic Organization)
SAGE	Social Assistance Grants for Empowerment
SAP	Stabilization and adjustment policies
SC	Scheduled caste
SCT	Social Cash Transfer
SDGs	Sustainable Development Goals
SEA	Servicio Estatal de Autonomías (Public Service for Autonomies)
SEMAPA	Servicio Municipal de Agua Potable y Alcantarillado (Municipal Service for Drinking Water and Sewerage)
SM	Minimum salary
SML	Special mining lease
SP	Samajwadi Party (Socialist Party)
SRA	Sociedad Rural Argentina (Argentinian Rural Association)
SSA	Sub-Saharan Africa
SSS	Sistema de Seguridade Social (Social Security System)
ST	Scheduled tribe
SUNAT	Superintendencia Nacional de Aduanas y de Administración Tributaria (National Superintendency of Customs and Tax Administration)
SWF	Sovereign Wealth Fund
TADAT	Tax Administration Diagnostic Assessment Tool
TDP	Telugu Desam Party (Party of the Telugu Land)
TNC	Transnational corporation
TNF	Tripartite Negotiating Forum
TPIN	Taxpayer identification number
TS&L	Tax, social and labour
TT	Total tax
UDI	Unión Democrática Independiente (Independent Democratic Union)
UGIETA	Uganda Import and Export Traders Association

UGX	Ugandan shilling (currency)
UIA	Unión Industrial Argentina (Argentinian Industrial Union)
UK	United Kingdom
UMA	Uganda Manufacturers Association
UN	United Nations
UNCTAD	United Nations Conference on Trade and Development
UNDP	United Nations Development Programme
UNICEF	United Nations Children's Fund
UNO	Unión Nacional Opositora (National Opposition Union)
UNRISD	United Nations Research Institute for Social Development
UPA	United Progressive Alliance
UPE	Universal primary education
URA	Uganda Revenue Authority
US	United States
USAID	United States Agency for International Development
USD	United States dollar (currency)
VAT	Value added tax
VoC	Varieties of capitalism
VUP	Vision 2020 Umurenge Programme
WDI	World Development Indicators
WFP	World Food Programme
WHO	World Health Organization
YPFB	Yacimientos Petrolíferos Fiscales Bolivianos (Bolivian National Hydrocarbons Company)
ZANU-PF	Zimbabwe African National Union—Patriotic Front
ZIM ASSET	Zimbabwe Agenda for Sustainable Socio-Economic Transformation
ZIMCORD	Zimbabwe Conference on Reconstruction and Development
ZIMPREST	Zimbabwe Programme for Economic and Social Transformation
ZIMRA	Zimbabwe Revenue Authority
ZINARA	Zimbabwe National Road Authority

List of Figures

List of Tables

1

The Politics of Domestic Resource Mobilization for Social Development: An Introduction

Katja Hujo and Yusuf Bangura

Introduction[1]

At a time when the development community is grappling with the challenge of raising the required investment—estimated in the trillions of dollars—for attainment of the Sustainable Development Goals (SDGs), countries' mobilization of their own domestic resources for development is receiving ever-increasing attention. Indeed, domestic resources are the most sustainable source of investment in national development priorities over the long term, and from an aggregated perspective, they are already the most important financing source in developing countries (Fig. 1.1).

[1] We thank Tejal Shrikant Ambardekar for updating the figures presented in this chapter.

K. Hujo (✉) • Y. Bangura
United Nations Research Institute for Social Development (UNRISD), Geneva, Switzerland
e-mail: katja.hujo@un.org

K. Hujo (ed.), *The Politics of Domestic Resource Mobilization for Social Development*, Social Policy in a Development Context,
https://doi.org/10.1007/978-3-030-37595-9_1

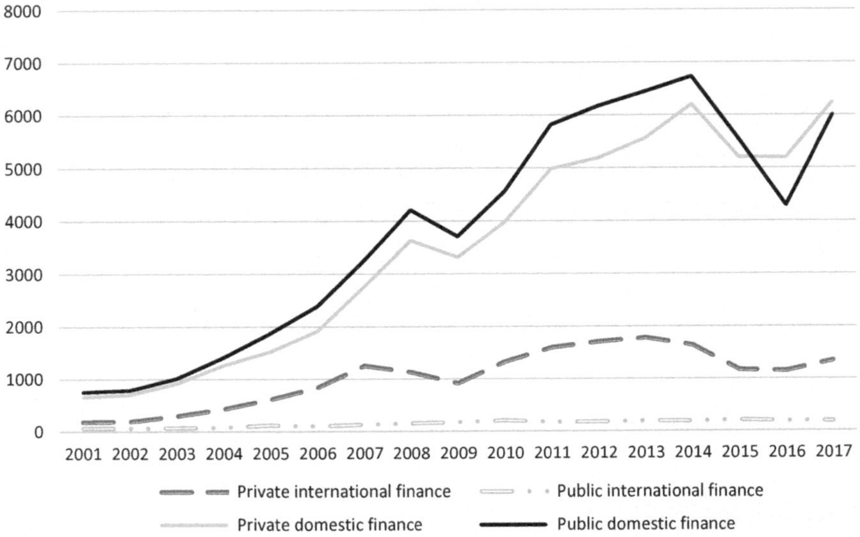

Fig. 1.1 Financing trends in developing countries (USD billions, constant prices) (2001–2017). (Source: Author elaboration based on data from ICTD and UNU-Wider (2018), OECD (2017, 2016), and World Bank (2019). Notes: Public domestic finance is defined here as total government revenue. Gross-fixed capital formation by the private sector was used as an indicator for private domestic finance. Private international finance is the sum of foreign direct investment (FDI), portfolio equity and bonds, commercial banking and other lending, and personal remittances. Public international finance equals the total official flows (official development assistance and other official flows). Data on private domestic finance: (1) for low- and middle-income countries in East Asia and the Pacific, data was not available; (2) for MENA countries, data was available for the period 2000–2007 only, with no figures available for 2001. Data on public domestic finance for 2000–2017 is the average of 137 countries classified as low- and middle-income countries by the World Bank. The figure illustrates the absolute increase in financing sources; in relative terms, financing sources have largely followed trends in GDP growth)

Nevertheless, financing gaps persist (Table 1.1), and different countries display different financing mixes and needs, with some countries continuing to be heavily aid-dependent (Fig. 1.2). Already in 2002, the Monterrey Consensus recognized that many poor countries have weak fiscal capacity and would require additional resources to transform their economies and meet the needs of their citizens. However, official

Table 1.1 Financing gaps as percentage of GNI (current USD) for country groups (2014)

Country groups	GNI (in current USD billion)	Financing gaps as percentage of GNI	
		Lower limit USD 1,500 billion	Upper limit USD 2,500 billion
World	78,203	1.9	3.2
High-income countries	53,268	2.8	4.7
Middle-income countries	24,584	6.1	10.2
Low-income countries	392	382.8	637.9

Sources: Author elaboration based on data from World Bank (2016), Oxfam and DFI (2015), and UNCTAD (2014)

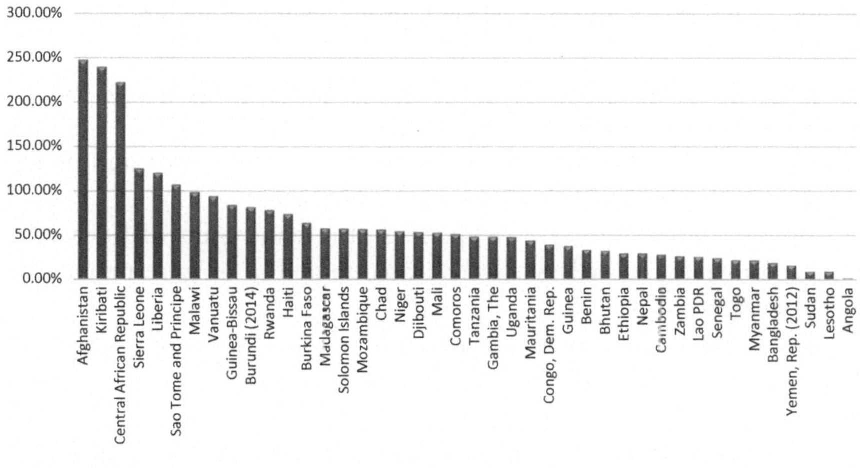

Fig. 1.2 Aid dependency in LDCs (2015): Country programmable aid (CPA) as percentage of tax revenue. (Source: Author elaboration based on data from OECD (2019b) and ICTD Government Revenue Dataset (2018). Notes: Used data from different years for Burundi (2014) and Yemen (2012). Outliers such as Somalia (880.71 per cent) and Tuvalu (782.70 per cent) were not included in the graph to preserve visible variation in the lower end of the range of Y-values. Social contributions are not included in tax revenues)

development aid (ODA) is failing to fill these gaps. This is due, for one, to donors' continued and systematic failure to deliver on aid commitments targeted at less developed countries. Additionally, the global economic and financial crisis in 2008, as well as mounting fiscal pressures in developed countries, has proved aid disbursement to be highly volatile, procyclical, and frequently determined by (geo-) political interests rather than recipient countries' needs.

While aid will continue to be crucial as an international instrument for redistribution (Ortiz 2009), and in particular for least developed and conflict-affected countries (Fig. 1.2), for the majority of countries, scaling up domestic public revenues is crucial to meet the SDGs and national development priorities and for anchoring their social contract in a financially sustainable way.

By focusing on domestic resource mobilization (DRM) as a promising pathway for financing policies for social development and transformative change, UNRISD designed a research project which aimed to:

- bridge the funding gaps for meeting key global development targets and social programmes in developing countries;
- enhance national ownership of development programmes and policy space, which is linked to improved fiscal capacity;
- improve understanding of the politics of revenue and social expenditure bargains, as well as effective accountability of governments to citizens; and
- connect the literatures on the politics of resource mobilization and the politics of social provision in developing countries.

The integrated analysis of financing and expenditure policies, as reflected in these objectives, has guided UNRISD social policy research over the last two decades, responding to a glaring research gap in contemporary social policy scholarship that exclusively focuses on the expenditure side, assuming a glass ceiling for state revenues (Hujo and McClanahan 2009; Kangas and Palme 2005). However, connecting financing issues with questions related to building sustainable welfare regimes and social contracts opens the door to a dynamic analysis which allows understanding of the feedback loops between resource mobilization and resource allocation. The question of who pays for and who benefits from public policies has a bearing on fiscal performance and on broader development goals such as economic growth, democratization, and institution building. It affects social relations and social institutions, constituting a key social development concern. In the context of the 2030 Agenda for Sustainable Development, the question of sustainable finance requires a new definition beyond mainstream economic approaches of debt sustainability or fiscal space (UNRISD 2016). Both revenue and spending policies should be sustainable in economic, social, environmental, and political terms; they should be conducive to a dynamic accumulation process within planetary boundaries so that more income can be created, redistributed, and allocated to public goods and social policy.

This introductory chapter will present key issues and trends related to DRM for social development, the conceptual framework and research questions that have guided the overall project, and an overview of the structure and contents of the volume.

The Issue

Implementing development strategies rests on the capacity of states to design policies, create political support, and mobilize the required financial and administrative resources. Domestic resources are key for financing the SDGs and national development priorities. Domestic resources, in particular public domestic resources, are already the most important source of development finance (ODI et al. 2015), exceeding private flows as well as international aid (Fig. 1.1).[2]

This challenges the popular belief that budgets in developing countries rely heavily on external funding and highlights the relevance of domestic resources. At the same time, average finance trends tend to hide

[2] The slumps in the graph are explained by the financial crisis of 2008 and the decrease in commodity prices post-2014. According to a joint report by Development Finance International and Oxfam, 77 per cent of spending on the Millennium Development Goals (MDGs) came from government revenues, with taxation accounting for around three-quarters of government revenue in all income groups. See Oxfam and DFI (2015) and Moore (2013: 7). Except for high-income non-OECD (Organisation for Economic Co-operation and Development) countries, which are largely oil-rich countries.

challenges for specific regions or countries, in particular if investment and spending needs are very high.

Estimates of the amounts needed to finance the 2030 Agenda are in the range of "trillions, not billions" (Development Committee 2015) to cover global financing gaps of between USD 1.5 trillion per year (Oxfam and DFI 2015) and USD 2.5 trillion or more (UNCTAD 2014: 140). While this amounts to 2 to 3 per cent of global gross national income (GNI), the costs of implementing the 2030 Agenda in proportion to the GNI of developing countries (low- and middle-income) are far higher (Table 1.1).

A recent IMF (International Monetary Fund) study (Gaspar et al. 2019) estimates the required additional spending in 2030 as 2.6 trillion US dollars (2.5 per cent of the 2030 world GDP) in 121 emerging market economies and low-income countries.

However, incentives to mobilize resources do not only come from countries' international development commitments. Governments have also come under pressure from citizens to provide more and better services and basic social protection. Demands for improved services and social security have been aided by the rights and freedoms unleashed by democratization processes, in which voters compel governments to show results in order to be elected (Bangura and Hedberg 2007).

However, it is increasingly clear that many low and lower middle-income countries have weak fiscal capacity and would require additional resources to honour their global and national commitments. Foreign aid plays a large role in the public finances of these countries (Fig. 1.2), and there have been strong calls on donors to scale up aid as part of the campaign to meet the SDGs. However, although aid has increased since 2007, reaching its all-time high in 2017, USD 146.6 billion (OECD 2018a), many donors have failed to honour their pledges. Some countries are increasingly benefitting from loans and foreign direct investment (FDI) from so-called new or emerging donors such as the BRICS countries (Brazil, Russia, India, China, South Africa), as well as oil-rich countries in different parts of the world, and regional South-South cooperation schemes such as ALBA (Bolivarian Alternative for the People of our America, see Chaps. 10 and 11 on Nicaragua and Uganda, respectively, in this volume). While these new aid partnerships offer access to finance based on different types of conditionalities compared to traditional donors and international financial institutions (IFIs), expanding policy space for some governments which have experienced rising tensions with some of their established donors, they also tend to display some volatility related to the economic situation (which can be highly dependent on international commodity prices) and political preferences in new donor countries.

Limitations regarding international finance are also associated with fiscal and political pressures in traditional donor countries in the aftermath of the financial crisis that struck the global economy in 2008 and in the context of the European refugee crisis. These pressures have recently led to significant cuts in ODA, or changes in aid allocation that have direct implications for resource flows to developing countries (ActionAid 2011), such as counting expenditures on refugees as aid (OECD 2015).

Against this backdrop, developing countries cannot rely only on donor transfers if they are keen to meet their global targets and respond to the needs of their citizens. They will have to increase efforts in mobilizing domestic resources. Indeed, the importance of DRM is becoming evident to both recipient and donor governments. From the perspective of recipient governments, even if ODA improves substantially, it often comes with conditions, such as buying donor goods and services, giving donors considerable space in the policy process, as well as delays and uncertainties in aid disbursement. Many of these countries, especially those whose governments have embraced a developmental approach to poverty reduction, have introduced measures to increase domestic revenues.

At the same time, donors increasingly hold the view that aid can be made more effective when linked to efforts by recipient governments to mobilize domestic resources.[3] In the Monterrey Consensus that followed the Conference on Financing for Development in 2002, donors pledged to increase aid in return for improved tax efforts by developing countries. In the face of persistent poverty and reports of aid mismanagement, critics of aid have become vocal, and sections of voters in donor publics are either weary of aid or insist on aid delivering clear results. A growing body of literature even sees aid as a curse that stifles development and

[3] United Nations (2003), Bhushan and Samy (2010), Chap. 2 in this volume.

democratic accountability of governments to citizens.[4] Furthermore, much of the wealth of poor countries—especially those that are resource-rich—is siphoned out as capital flight, raising questions about the value of aid in such settings.

Some estimates suggest that the amount of money that is channelled illicitly from poor to rich countries through tax havens is higher than ODA: in the case of sub-Saharan Africa (SSA), illicit financial flows (IFFs) were estimated at USD 100 billion per year, while ODA amounted to 52 billion in the same year.[5]

Discounting the more extreme calls for dismantling aid or handing donor funds directly to poor people, one interesting view in this debate is that of restoring aid to its original goal of complementing DRM and foreign investments, and for donors to demand that recipient governments take responsibility for their development, by controlling capital flight, improving domestic revenue yields, and being accountable for the aid they receive. It has been estimated that aid that targets DRM can lead to a ten-fold increase in domestic revenue yields in Africa (Bhushan and Samy 2010). From this perspective, if aid and DRM work in tandem, recipient governments will be more responsive to the constituencies that provide the resources, that is, citizens and donors. The growing literature on aid, taxation, and governance has tended to reflect this shift in focus on the financing of development.[6]

However, support for DRM does not guarantee that the desired amount of resources will be generated, let alone allocated to preferred programmes, or that the burden of resource extraction will be distributed fairly among different population groups. Issues of contestation and bargaining are bound to influence the extent to which governments can succeed in extracting resources from their populace. Bargaining may involve acceptance by citizens of governments' tax and savings plans in exchange for services, social protection, employment guarantees, and income support, inextricably linking the politics of domestic resource mobilization (PDRM) with the politics of social development.

[4] Easterly (2003), Moyo (2009), Collier (2007), Moore (2004).

[5] ECA (2014, 2018), OECD (2019a). See also Moore and Prichard, Chap. 4, in this volume.

[6] Brautigam et al. (2008), OECD and AFDB (2010), Culpeper and Bhushan (2008), Gupta and Tareq (2008), Di John (2010), African Economic Outlook (2010).

Resource Bargains

Resource extraction and expenditure are closely connected. In general, governments cannot spend what they do not have unless they can borrow or receive assistance from domestic and external sources. However, even for rich countries, excessive borrowing can lead to unsustainable debt, which may compromise future growth and well-being. At the same time, governments rarely borrow to finance social expenditures since repayment ultimately depends on the ability to generate revenue. Therefore, for most successful countries, the financing of social development—such as education, health, and social protection—often involves resource bargains as the money has to be raised from citizens. However, many low-income countries have been unable to fully finance social development since the 1980s and 1990s following far-reaching economic crises and adoption of stabilization policies recommended by the international financial institutions (IFIs). First with social services, and more recently with social protection, governments in poor countries increasingly depend on foreign donors to meet their social commitments and responsibilities.

Dependence on IFIs for macroeconomic policy reform, and on donors more generally for financing social development, has defined the politics of resource mobilization in two important ways. First, resource mobilization has been treated as a technical issue that does not require attention to politics and bargaining with citizens (Hujo and McClanahan 2009; Di John 2015). The primary goal has been to ensure that reforms facilitate trade liberalization by substituting import and export taxes with consumption taxes; producing neutral, simplified, and predictable tax systems; and weakening the redistributive role of taxation through discouragement of high marginal tax rates (Fjeldstad and Moore 2008; Stewart 2002). Independent revenue authorities, which have grown rapidly across regions, are expected to guide the transformation to a depoliticized and market-friendly tax regime.

At the same time, donor dependence has tended to free low-income governments from the responsibility of striking bargains with their citizens. Instead, rather perversely, resource bargains between aid-recipient governments and donors have gained more prominence in public policy.

Donor initiatives, such as the Highly Indebted Poor Countries (HIPC) programme (1996) that provided debt relief to indebted countries, and the Gleneagles commitments[7] to increase aid to poor countries in the context of the Millennium Development Goals (MDGs), have been increasingly framed in terms of bargains: poor countries that receive aid need to channel more resources towards social sectors, respect human rights, and demonstrate commitment to, and capacity for, improved governance. The United States' Millennium Challenge Account introduced by President Bush in 2002 used 16 indicators on governance, human development, and economic freedom to determine its aid allocation to low-income countries (White House Archive 2004). These kinds of bargains have led to more intensive donor involvement in the policy-making systems of low-income countries, a trend that has continued in the post-2015 era and partly accounts for the attractiveness of new emerging donors such as China, whose aid modalities lack these types of policy conditionality (see Chaps. 10 and 11 on Nicaragua and Uganda, respectively, in this volume).

It can be argued that largely because of these two developments, much of the literature on the politics of social development in poor countries has focused on the expenditure or demand side of development. This literature includes trade union resistance to public expenditure cuts or welfare state contraction; politics of expanding coverage to excluded groups and regions; campaigns to introduce new social programmes for certain categories of people; and political pressures to limit the negative effects that privatization of services or removal of subsidies from essential commodities have on the poor. Even when financial issues are addressed, such as user fees, the arguments are usually couched in terms of access and control of government expenditures and are less concerned about raising revenues to fund services. Indeed, the money saved from user fees is often so small that it hardly covers the administrative cost of collecting the fees (Oxfam 2016).

[7] The G8 summit at Gleneagles in July 2005 pledged dramatic increases in aid to get progress towards the Millennium Development Goals (MDGs) in Africa back on track by 2010. Africa was promised an additional USD 25 billion per year in aid.

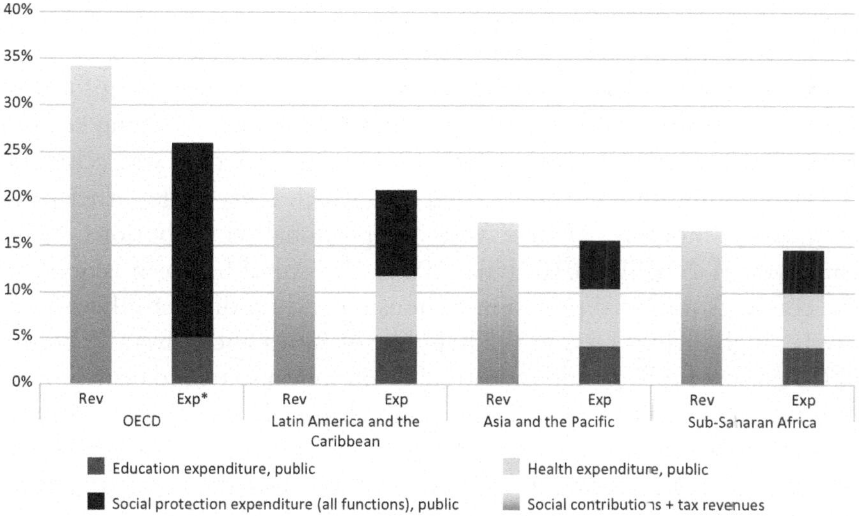

Fig. 1.3 Tax revenues and social spending in advanced and developing countries as percentage of GDP, latest available year (2012–2017). (Source: Author calculation based on data from World Bank (2019), ILO (2017), OECD (2018b), WHO (2019), and UNESCO (2019). Notes: *For OECD countries, public health expenditure is included in public social protection expenditure)

It is important to note, however, that the literature on established welfare states is not divorced from the issues of resource generation or taxation. Rich countries, on average, spend more on social development because they collect more taxes than low- and middle-income countries (Fig. 1.3). However, there are significant variations in tax efforts even among rich countries. Those that spend more on social development (e.g., Austria, Belgium, Denmark, Germany, Netherlands, Norway, and Sweden) collect more taxes than those that spend less (e.g., Australia, Ireland, Japan, United Kingdom, and United States) (Tanzi and Schuknecht 2000). Variations in social expenditure and the size of the welfare state are a product of competing values on rights and differences in power relations or bargains that shape tax regimes (Steinmo 1993). Countries with relatively universal social protection regimes do not only tax more but also tend to incorporate more people in the tax net (Steinmo 1993; Huber and Stephens 2001). Indeed, it has been shown that the redistributive effects of universal social policies become progressive only when taxes (in which the rich pay more than the poor) are factored into the analysis (Mkandawire 2005; Korpi and Palme 1998).[8]

However, it is crucial to note that resource bargains have also informed the development experiences of many developing and emerging economies. Singapore's high savings rate of about 50 per cent was achieved through setting up a provident fund into which every wage earner paid mandatory monthly savings with proportional contributions from employers (UNRISD 2010; Huat 2005). This fund has been central to the country's universal provision of housing and funding of other social needs. High savings rates in the Republic of Korea and Taiwan Province of China that funded rapid industrialization were also tied to provision of services, job security, and social insurance, especially for workers in state sectors and key industries. The universal provision of primary education in western Nigeria during the 1950s and 1960s was also based on a bargain between the regional government and farmers. The government used the surpluses generated by the cocoa marketing board to support its development programme as well as cushion the incomes of farmers and provide social services to the wider public (Helleiner 1964; Wheeler 1968). Mining companies in many poor countries also struck social bargains with governments and mining populations during the early period of independence in the form of health clinics, educational programmes, and community services (Ferguson 2006; Chap. 12 on Zimbabwe in this volume). In Bolivia, the hydrocarbon sector was nationalized in 2006 with the promise to channel more mineral rents into social development (see Chap. 9 on Bolivia in this volume). The Chilean Royalty for Innovation, or Specific Tax on Mining Activities, introduced in 2005, was politically justified with the aim to mobilize resources for the necessary productive transition once mineral resources are depleted (Guajardo Beltrán 2012). Similar bargains are being revived today as mineral extraction expands in many countries, and community groups, non-governmental organizations (NGOs), and informed citizens insist on

[8] Universal social provisioning has been criticized on the grounds of its supposed regressive distributional impact, suggesting that targeted transfers and services for poor people are more progressive. This partial view ignores the financing side of the equation, while not weighing off the multiple benefits of universal social policies against disadvantages of targeting such as exclusion errors and high administrative costs. For a discussion, see UNRISD (2010, 2016) and Mkandawire (2005).

environmental standards, economic diversification, and good social returns (Hujo 2012).

The concept of resource bargain implies negotiation and less use of coercion in extracting resources. This volume draws on the rich literatures on fiscal contract theory and state building in understanding the dynamics of bargaining around tax and social development issues. The large literature on taxation and state building in early modern Europe[9] focuses largely on what Moore (2008: 45–46) calls "the exchange of tax revenues (for the state) for institutionalized influence over public policy (for citizens)." In this bargain, European states wanted resources to finance wars and citizens wanted "representative, responsive and effective government." However, contemporary resource bargains address the provision of social benefits explicitly. With representative institutions already established in most countries that have experienced democratization, the process of meeting the social part of resource bargains may help to enhance the quality of representation and governmental responsiveness. Bargaining can be formal and direct, as well as informal, implicit, and indirect. Formal bargaining may take the form of fiscal pacts, insertion of fiscal issues in welfare and wage negotiations, and earmarked taxes that have gained prominence in the public finances of local governments. However, most resource bargains in poor countries are indirect, implicit, and informal, which may explain why they have not received much scholarly attention. They usually occur when tax systems are being reformed. For instance, value added taxes (VAT) that have been introduced in many poor countries often elicit much debate, claims, and counter-claims, and may lead to militant campaigns or tax boycotts. The process can stimulate formation of tax advocacy groups, governmental engagement with tax payers, and further reforms, which may set broad parameters on taxation and social services. In Sierra Leone, for instance, public resistance to the introduction of the Goods and Services Tax in 2009 (which is another name for VAT) forced the government and its key donors to link the new tax to improved provision of services. And in Tanzania and Uganda, for example, the abolition of taxes levied on the informal sector and the poor, such as the graduated tax and the

---

[9] Levi (1988), Brewer (1988), Tilly (1975), Braddick (1996), and Daunton (2001).

development levy, respectively, have been closely linked to electoral calculations (see Chap. 11 in this volume).[10] In Bolivia, a violent conflict broke out when the government tried to introduce a personal income tax on wage earners following advice from the IMF, prompting the leadership to withdraw the proposal (see Chap. 9 in this volume).

Resource bargains can also occur when governments sign agreements with business corporations, especially those in the mining sector. Many poor countries are resource-rich. During the 1980s and 1990s, as these countries experienced crises and conflicts, their ability to bargain effectively with corporations was eroded. Mining companies in particular enjoyed generous tax concessions and protections and had fewer links with communities. However, concerns for environmental and labour standards, citizen activism on resource extraction issues, and pressure by mining communities for a fairer share of mineral rents have produced a variety of resource bargains in many countries. Most of the bargains are still lopsided, and there is a lot of resource leakage out of the economy as companies exploit loopholes in the tax system and pressure or bribe government elites to relax controls on tax evasion (see also Chaps. 4 and 12 in this volume). However, public awareness and mobilization for better bargains, including higher returns to the national economy and social investments, have increased, as country examples in this volume demonstrate.

Pressures for resource bargains can also emanate from the social expenditure side when citizens demand more and better services. Governments are then forced to generate the necessary resources by asking citizens and corporations to pay more taxes, if other revenues cannot be mobilized or expenditure reallocations are insufficient. Social expenditure-driven resource bargains can be particularly important in the contemporary context of global target setting such as the SDGs or the social protection floor initiative, among others.

Three issues addressed in Margaret Levi's (1988) analytical framework on tax bargains and state formation in Europe are important for understanding resource bargains in poor countries. The first is that resource bargains are always imperfect in the sense that both governments and tax

[10] Kjaer and Therkildsen (2013), Kjaer and Ulriksen (2014), and D'Arcy (2012).

payers may not fully comply with the contracts. Especially when linked to provision of public goods, citizens may want to free-ride or evade tax payment while still enjoying the service that others have paid for; and governments may under-supply public goods once normal politics are resumed after the events that led to the bargains. The second is that citizens may comply with tax bargains when they are perceived as fair in terms of the level and progressivity of taxation, and when all tax payers honour their commitments. Tax evasion or revolt is likely to be high when each of these is compromised. The third is the credibility of governments to deliver their own part of the bargain in providing public services. This is especially important in low-income countries where the track record of governments in delivering services has been poor since the period of economic stabilization. How governments restore or signal credibility is therefore crucial in understanding the politics of resource mobilization.

Types of Domestic Resources and Recent Policy Trends

UNRISD research[11] has thrown light on a number of resources that can be generated to finance social development, ranging from domestic instruments such as taxation, mineral rents, social security contributions, profits generated by state-owned enterprises, savings, remittances, or internal debt to foreign instruments such as external debt, ODA, or FDI. Among this set of instruments, we will consider two types of public domestic resources, taxation and revenues from extractive industries (EI), presenting different challenges and opportunities. Generally speaking, public domestic resources have various social, economic, and political benefits compared to private or external funds. Among these are their linkages with domestic policy making and policy space, their potential for impacting positively on institution building and accountability, their ability to redistribute income and stabilize the economy, and their capacity to make production and consumption more sustainable in environmental,

[11] UNRISD (2016, 2010), Hujo and McClanahan (2009).

economic, and social terms. Public domestic resources are more likely than external resources to trigger transformative structural change of the economy and to sustainably finance redistribution, leading to higher equality, inclusion, and social protection (UNRISD 2010: chapter 8).

For most countries, tax income is the most important national revenue source, accounting for 83 per cent of government revenues in high-income countries of the OECD, and around 72 per cent in low and lower-middle income countries.[12] Low-income countries collect, on average, much fewer taxes than middle- and high-income countries (Fig. 1.3). Tax efforts in low-income countries have traditionally favoured international trade taxes, which are less costly to collect, rather than personal income, corporate, and property taxes (UNRISD 2010). Most people earn a living in the informal economy or in small-scale agriculture, sectors that are often difficult to tax; the corporate sector is very small, and property-owning groups are often powerful enough to evade taxes or influence tax policies.

In addition, revenue mobilization is also constrained by economic strategies and economic crises that result in low growth, increasing inequalities, and low employment creation. The turn towards neoliberal policies in the early 1980s resulted in lower public revenues and redistribution of the tax burden from corporations and higher-income groups to consumers and lower-income groups.

Trade liberalization, which has reduced tariff rates worldwide, is making it difficult for countries to rely on trade taxes to finance development programmes. Governments have been increasingly forced to raise consumption taxes (such as VAT), which, though regressive, reach a large section of the population, and thus have the potential to substantially increase state revenues. Consumption taxes have been complemented by user charges and increased levies on utilities and other services. The latter have assumed importance in local governments. Consumption taxes, charges, and levies have generated protests across a number of countries where they have been implemented. In some countries, governments have also come under pressure from citizen groups to raise the level of taxes paid by corporations and property owners.

---

[12] Author calculations based on data from ICTD Government Revenue Database 2018.

However, most developing countries have made little progress in more progressive instruments such as taxes on income and profits—which, on average, reach only 5.1 per cent of GDP in low-income countries (Akitoby et al. 2018) versus 33.6 per cent in OECD countries (OECD 2018c)—and few countries significantly raised property taxes as part of their fiscal consolidation efforts (IMF 2013). Carbon pricing and environmentally related taxes have also made little progress (IMF 2013), while reforms of corporate income tax (CIT) has led to mixed results, with some positive results in some countries, and declines in progressivity due to a race-to-the-bottom approach in others (UNRISD 2016; see also Chap. 7 on Argentina and Chile in this volume).

Many of the countries that managed to scale up domestic revenues over the last decade, including several of the case studies analysed in this volume, benefited from a booming natural resource sector and rising international prices for agricultural, mining, and fuel products, in particular between 2003 and 2010 (IMF 2012). Natural resource rents present opportunities for development, especially in contexts where financial and fiscal resources are otherwise scarce. Government revenues from EI can be substantial, although data tend to be poor. This holds true in particular for some developing countries (IMF 2014). Realistically, not extracting the resources is often not an option, despite the recognition that the sector is intrusive to the environment, has high risks for pollution and disasters, and fossil fuel production and consumption exacerbates the problem of climate change.

Therefore, the opportunities of the sector in terms of transformation lie in using it to kick-start longer term development processes through structural change of national economies, sustained economic growth, and overall improvements in the welfare of citizens. Yet, many countries that base their development models on the extraction of resources have not been successful in ensuring longer term development (UNRISD 2010). Indeed, there is research that sees mineral wealth as a "resource curse" (Sachs and Warner 1999; Auty 2001).

Resource abundance, however, need not be a curse (UNRISD 2012; Hujo 2012). Rather, it is the quality of political processes, policies, and institutions guiding decisions about whether and how to extract resources, and how to capture, distribute, and allocate natural resource revenues, that determines the economic and social yields from the sector, as well as the level of environmental costs society (both national and international) is willing to accept. As technical innovations are unlocking new natural resource stocks and driving new industries, the question of how mineral wealth can be harnessed for development that is sustained, socially inclusive, and minimizes the impacts extraction has on the environment is becoming more and more pressing.

Research Themes, Hypotheses, and Case Studies

Three themes shaped the country research of the PDRM project. The first addressed issues of **contestation, bargaining, and outcomes**. It examined the nature of resource bargains; types of resources and social programmes involved in bargains; trade-offs among competing programmes and resources; and resource yields. DRM generates conflicts over types of resources to be mobilized, who pays, who and what is exempted, how much should be paid, and how the resources collected should be allocated across sectors, groups, and communities. This suggests that issues of coverage, tax and premium levels, and outcomes in terms of resource yields, allocation, and benefits cannot be predetermined. The institutional contexts for contestation and bargaining may differ across countries depending on, for example, the extent to which basic rights for contestation exist; the structure of interest group and party formation around issues of resource generation and social provision; and institutions that exist for channelling claims and regulating conflicts in public policy.

The second theme is about changes in **key relationships**. It examined the extent to which the politics of resource mobilization led to a redefinition of state-citizen and state-business relations, and whether improvement in DRM led to more fiscal space and autonomy in policy making. It engaged the literature on taxation and governance, which emphasizes the importance of contractual relations between citizens and states for effective mobilization of domestic resources. Three types of relationships were examined:

- State-citizen relations. The history of resource extraction in many poor countries is associated with coercion and authoritarian rule. However, calls for generation of more revenues and social expenditure have coincided with greater openness of political systems and rights of independent organization and contestation. The key issue is whether citizen contestation of DRM policies and demands for improved services encouraged governments to opt for more consensual styles of policy making; resort to less use of coercion as an instrument of state policy; and engage citizens more constructively on tax and revenue mobilization issues.
- State-business relations. During the period of economic crises and structural adjustment, the ability of developing countries to bargain effectively with corporations was eroded. How can states strike a bargain with domestic elites such as domestic capital owners on tax policies? How can states negotiate successfully beneficial terms with multinational companies (MNCs), in particular EI?
- Donor-recipient relations. Although the studies focused largely on DRM, it is clear that donor-recipient relations were likely to be affected by changes in the domestic scene. The study engaged the literature on aid and governance that posits a link between DRM, fiscal space, and national ownership of programmes. It asked the following questions: does improvement in DRM lead to more fiscal space and autonomy in policy making? Does domestic success influence donor strategies in allocating aid, which in recent times has been geared more towards social services than infrastructure and productive activities? What is the role of emerging donors and South-South cooperation?

The third theme focused on **institutional development**—or capacities for revenue mobilization and service delivery. It examined the extent to which the politics of DRM generated pressures for upgrading the institutions entrusted to deliver services. Success in resource mobilization and service provision requires institutional development. To support stabilization policies and revenue mobilization, governments in low-income countries have, through the support of the IFIs, strengthened institutions in the financial sector: ministries of finance, tax offices, and central banks. Independent revenue authorities have been created in several countries that provide a set of incentives on careers, pay, and training, as well as granting of autonomous powers to officials tasked with revenue collection. However, institutions concerned with service provision have been neglected and are usually the first targets for retrenchment and cuts. To what extent do the politics of domestic resource mobilization generate pressures for improving the quality of service delivery institutions?

Research on the three themes was guided by the following hypotheses:

- Resource bargains that yield improved revenues to governments and social benefits to citizens require effective state engagement with citizens.
- Successful revenue bargains reduce donor influence in policy-making processes of recipient states. However, improved fiscal capacity in recipient states either reduces dependence on foreign aid or encourages donors to provide more aid to successful countries.
- Institutional development in revenue generation sectors has spillover effects on institutions in social sectors as the links between resource generation and social provisioning become established in the strategies of governments and citizens.

While guiding the overall project, this analytical framework was more consistently applied in four in-depth country case studies which were commissioned for the project, two in Latin America—Bolivia and Nicaragua—and two in sub-Saharan Africa—Zimbabwe and Uganda.[13] These countries comprise low-income economies (Zimbabwe and Uganda) and lower middle-income countries (Bolivia and Nicaragua), and represent different types of economies, as the structures of economies and development paths may have a bearing on tax strategies and resource mobilization in general.

In terms of economic structure, Bolivia follows a mineral-dependent growth path, with hydrocarbons and minerals driving growth rates and constituting the main revenue source for the state, while the agricultural and service sectors with low productivity still account for the bulk of employment. Nicaragua, the poorest country in Central America, is a

[13] In addition to applying the described analytical framework, contributing authors in this volume draw on a variety of conceptual and theoretical approaches, introduced in their respective chapters.

small commodity-exporting economy and financially dependent on ODA and remittances. Zimbabwe's crisis-ridden economy is built on agriculture and mining, with strong dependence on migrant remittances and aid (in particular, emergency and food aid), whereas growth in Uganda, one of the biggest aid recipients in SSA, is largely driven by the service sector, with industry and agriculture remaining important, the latter in particular in terms of exports and employment. Mineral rents are already highly important in Zimbabwe, and are likely to play an increasing role in Uganda following the discovery of oil.

Concerning the political context, selected countries represent a range of democratic/participatory and elite-dominated frameworks; post-conflict transitions play a role in Nicaragua, Uganda, and Zimbabwe. Regimes are relatively open in all four countries to allow for contestation and bargaining around revenue and expenditure policies, although the situation has temporarily worsened in Nicaragua and Zimbabwe. DRM is high on political agendas in all countries.

The case studies addressed the three research themes within their specific country contexts and through multidisciplinary teams, with particular attention paid to those domestic revenue sources that are considered most relevant for each case, for example mineral rents in the case of Zimbabwe and Bolivia, and taxation and aid in the case of Nicaragua and Uganda.

Overview of the Volume

This book is divided into two parts, apart from the introduction and conclusion chapters, with chapters in the first part drawing on thematic papers commissioned for the project, while the second part features the four country case studies.

The first part comprises chapters exploring the relationship between DRM and aid, taxation, and mineral rents.

In Chap. 2, Bhushan and Samy examine the interaction between fiscal performance and donor aid allocation based on three factors. First, since the 2002 Monterrey Consensus, attention to DRM has increased, an objective that was confirmed in the 2030 Agenda for Sustainable

Development and the Addis Ababa Action Agenda. Second, donors themselves have sought to explicitly link aid to taxation and tax effort in partner countries on the grounds that high reliance on aid undermines good governance by distorting domestic political accountability. Third, while the aid allocation literature has largely ignored taxation as an independent variable in explaining aid flows, the authors argue that the inability of countries to raise revenue through taxes because of their structural characteristics is also a reflection of recipient needs. Therefore, from an analytical perspective, taxation and fiscal performance variables can be a useful proxy for recipient needs. However, the analysis in the chapter reveals that that rhetoric fails to meet reality in terms of the role of fiscal performance in determining aid allocation as there is hardly any correlation between overall aid and fiscal performance and capacity. Furthermore, the authors point to gaps in terms of donors delivering on their commitments to align with recipient country priorities and providing aid through country Public Finance Management systems—despite promises to pay greater attention to DRM efforts of recipient countries. Based on these findings the authors recommend improving tax data collection and harmonization; to set up knowledge and information sharing platforms among various donors based on their experience in supporting tax capacity; to better coordinate donor interventions on DRM avoiding high transaction costs for recipient countries; and to broaden the stakeholder base involved in tax issues.

Chapter 3 by Cécile Cherrier analyses ODA in relation to social protection spending, a specific bargain between governments and donors. It explores whether foreign aid can have a catalytic effect on the expansion of basic social protection in low-income countries. Empirical evidence drawn from twelve social transfer schemes in SSA reveals a different picture from the views expressed by prominent scholars in the recent past. It confirms foreign aid actors as important players in the mobilization of resources for social transfers but shows that most schemes (also) have domestic origins—that is, the origins of the different schemes do not fall in any clear-cut categories, such as donor-driven versus nationally instigated processes. It also suggests that externally supported programmes may bring about sustainable policy change—all of the studied schemes, including those heavily supported by foreign aid actors, appear to have resulted in moves towards national ownership and investment of domestic resources. This might imply that accountability relations are shifting from external to national constituencies, and in the best case, social programmes are becoming more institutionalized. The author concludes that for social transfer schemes to help address poverty and inequality at a more transformative level across the SSA region, efforts are needed to strengthen citizen-state relations and ensure a human rights-based approach as a requirement for transformative change.

Chapter 4 by Mick Moore and Wilson Prichard provides a synthesis of lessons learned over years of research on how governments of low-income countries can collect more tax revenue. The approach Moore and Prichard take is to deconstruct the overarching question of how governments can increase the tax take into two smaller questions. First, what specific potential revenue sources do the governments of many developing countries tend to under-exploit? And second, what is the potential for increasing the tax take through national and global tax policies? Regarding the first question, the chapter posits that the potential additional revenue from more effectively tackling transfer mispricing seems significant, recognizing that it is a long-term endeavour and requires considerable resources, including knowledge, staff, and capacity to access information from commercial databases or from tax agencies overseas. Mining is also identified as a potential revenue source, which in low-income countries due to technical and deeply political reasons is generally grossly undertaxed. Taxing alcohol and tobacco, eliminating exemptions, reforming VAT, taxing the rich and property are also identified as "dangling fruit," areas that are currently under-exploited, though not to be confounded with low-hanging fruit. Finally, tax policy reform could consider the wider use of taxes levied on measures of company turnover or sales, especially in contexts when it is easy for companies to practice transfer mispricing; to opt more for regional tax coordination than for bilateral treaties; and to address political obstacles to tax the rich. The chapter concludes that tax issues need to advance both at the national and international level.

Chapter 5 by Thandika Mkandawire shows that in order to understand tax performance, historical legacies have to be taken into account. The so-called labour reserve economies of Southern Africa, for example, display higher tax takes based on direct tax, compared with, for example, Western African cash-crop economies with lower tax takes and reliance on trade taxes. A major explanation for high taxation in the labour reserve economies of Southern Africa was the racially exclusive welfare regimes that were set up for the white minority population, while the reliance on a large low-wage sector resulted in minimal social protection for the native population and reliance on communities and households (Mkandawire 2010). Based on these insights, the chapter explores the different kinds of welfare regimes in African countries, considering both the social expenditure and state revenue side. Mkandawire proposes a two-dimensional classification along the axes of tax effort and welfare effort, which generates four welfare regimes: High taxation effort/high welfare effort regimes (e.g., Botswana, South Africa, Namibia); high taxation effort/low welfare effort regimes (e.g., Gambia); low taxation effort/high welfare effort regimes (e.g., Cameroon, Democratic Republic of Congo); and low taxation effort/low welfare effort regimes (e.g., Uganda, Ghana, Senegal). The existence of these different welfare regimes is then analysed in terms of the policy and structural drivers behind the performance of the countries along the two axes drawing on available data on social expenditure and share of tax in GDP. The analysis shows that labour reserve economies are generally high taxation/high social expenditure regimes. Most cash crop economies fall into the low expenditure/low taxation categories. Gambia stands out among high taxation cash crop economies for reasons related to the importance of smuggling and transit of goods to Senegal. The low taxation/high social expenditure regime mostly belongs to the concession economies where mineral royalties played an important role. The chapter concludes by stating that "colonial legacies are not destiny. Indeed, the process of challenging such legacies can be a stimulus to efforts to redress the injustices of the past or to create new institutional arrangements appropriate to current conditions."

Another important structural factor impacting tax capacity are the types of citizenship regimes existing in a country, as analysed in Chap. 6

by Aaron Schneider. Citizenship regimes create links between governments and certain social actors or groups by establishing them as legitimate participants in political processes and claimants on public resources and authorities. These groups are more likely to be included in fiscal compacts and, using the terminology of resource bargains, establish themselves as actors in informal bargaining processes. Applying this concept to the cases of Brazil and India, it appears that India has expanded social rights in recent years without generating new revenues and keeping a low tax/GDP ratio, while Brazil expanded revenues both as part of fiscal adjustment and to expand social spending. The explanation for this difference lies in the incorporation of both middle classes and popular sectors in Brazil, in particular under the leadership of the Partido dos Trabalhadores (PT/Workers Party). This was achieved through expanded social and labour market policies that resulted in higher formal employment, social protection, and consumption, though the tax system remains fragmented and regressive. In the case of India, fragmented and shifting social coalitions have led to a fragmented tax system and to privileges for the dynamic economic sectors, while attempts to form cross-class coalitions and mobilize for greater redistribution have thus far failed. The chapter concludes that development occurs when both state capacity to stimulate broad collective action, as found in Brazil, as well as embeddedness in strategic sectors, as found in India, are present. However, both types of state capacity are vulnerable to economic downturns when elites are less inclined to support the inclusion of minorities or the poor.

Chapter 7 by Enrique Delamonica, Jamee K. Moudud, and Esteban Pérez Caldentey discusses the ways in which taxation, social, and labour market policies in Argentina and Chile have been shaped by state-business relations and capital-labour relations, relating this to varying degrees of cohesiveness of business organizations and associations. Departing from a fiscal sociology approach, the authors argue that the implementation and maintenance of such policies by the state over time is a contested process that has to constantly mediate between business pressures for pro-business policies and the larger society's demands for social justice. A key difference between Chile and Argentina is the higher level of business cohesiveness in Chile. This has allowed business-encompassing associations in Chile to effectively influence the policy-making process, thereby limiting the creation and extension of egalitarian fiscal and labour market policies. On the other hand, the greater level of inter-business rivalries in Argentina has enabled the state to push through important social policies. The study suggests that for both countries, the construction of an effective and stable tax base depends to a large extent on whether civil society deems taxes as coercive rather than contractual, which requires public services being perceived as fair and efficient. The authors conclude that the sustainability of progressive revenue and spending policies requires the design of a policy and political mix that can maintain robust business confidence, for example through incentives for private investment, in the presence of strong unions and a strong welfare state financed by a progressive tax system.

In Chap. 8, Javier Arellano-Yanguas and Andrés Mejía-Acosta review the criteria for distributing EI revenues between central and local governments and explain some of the underlying arguments behind the adoption of revenue-sharing formulas. The review (based on data from Bolivia, Brazil, Colombia, Ecuador, Ghana, Indonesia, Mexico, Nigeria, Papua New Guinea, and Peru) shows that although some institutional arrangements, like federal or unitary structures, matter, there is great variation in the nature and shape of EI revenue distribution. The overall tendency is that fiscal decentralization informs but does not determine the patterns of subnational redistribution of revenues. The analysis shows that countries with higher levels of fiscal decentralization (e.g., Brazil) tend to prioritize redistribution that benefits both producing and non-producing regions, whereas unitary countries with weak fiscal decentralization (e.g., Peru and Ecuador) tend to concentrate the transfers in producing jurisdictions. Countries with moderate to low levels of fiscal decentralization (e.g., Colombia and Mexico) tend to combine devolution to producing regions with formula-based distribution to all territories. Political dynamics and historical processes better explain distribution formulas and mechanisms across countries and territories. The relative strength of the subnational governments vis-a-vis the central government, the relative alignment of preferences between local and national governments, and the sequence of the adopted reforms are factors that influence the nature and magnitude of revenue-sharing formulas. The authors recommend discussing distribution formulas for EI transfers within broader fiscal decentralization debates; to combine earmarked and discretional allocations of revenues; to introduce subnational stabilization mechanisms; to reinvigorate budget transparency rules and procedures for the management of EI revenues; and to carefully monitor the development impacts of EI investment at subnational levels.

The second part of the volume comprises the four country case studies.

Chapter 9, the Bolivia case study, synthesized by Verónica Paz Arauco, examines the economic conditions and political process underlying the mobilization of domestic resources for social development in Bolivia. Drawing on the revenues from its rich mineral resources, the Bolivian state has managed to increase public revenue and improve performance on several social indicators, reducing poverty rates by 20 per cent and mitigating deeply entrenched inequalities. At the core of these changes towards greater social inclusion was the social mobilization that led to oil and gas sector nationalization in 2006 under the first indigenous president, Evo Morales, which resulted in growing fiscal space and a prioritization of social spending. Less dependence on external aid for funding public investment led to a change in relations between the Bolivian state and donors, the successful renegotiation of contracts with foreign companies in the hydrocarbon sector reflected the strengthened bargaining power of the new government, while the renewal of state-citizen relations was formalized by the approval of a new constitution in 2009 and a new Law on Autonomies and Decentralization. While the government has been most successful in making inroads into poverty and inequality through a new generation of cash transfer programmes for children, mothers, and elderly persons, challenges regarding social service delivery and local administrative capacity persist.

The Nicaragua case is synthesized by Gloria Carrión in Chap. 10, with a special focus on state-citizen relations. Nicaragua has gone through profound political, economic, and social transitions in recent decades.

Following a turbulent history of dictatorship (Somoza 1936–1979), the Sandinista revolution (1979–1989), and neoliberal adjustment (1990–2006), it remains one of the poorest countries in Latin America. Periods of high social tension and violence were followed by relative peace and democratic transitions. Social conflicts and contradictions, however, have continued to emerge, and have intensified during the third presidential term of Sandinista leader Daniel Ortega (who assumed power in 2007), with street protests and large-scale demonstrations demanding his resignation in 2018 in a context of violent state repression. As a consequence, state-society relations, which have historically fluctuated from stronger to weaker, have experienced a backlash. In terms of DRM, efforts to increase tax revenues over past decades have generated limited results. Despite frequent tax reforms, measures to attract FDI, and increasing mining revenues, the Nicaraguan government has not managed to provide a stable domestic resource base to underpin a social contract. Historically aid-dependent and a beneficiary of the HIPC initiative, Nicaragua has recently received less ODA due to a reconfiguration of aid governance at the global level, donor fatigue, and the global economic crisis in 2008. Nicaragua therefore sought new partnerships with the governments of Venezuela and China. However, these alliances are relatively fragile since they depend on partner governments' political priorities and the economic situation, which in the case of Venezuela has deteriorated significantly. Under Ortega, there has been talk of reinvigorating the role of the state in social provisioning, and the introduction of free healthcare and education. There have been advances in literacy, social security, and aspects of food security, but per-capita expenditure on health and education services remains low. Big challenges are also reflected in the fragmentation of services, limited cooperation with parts of civil society, and insufficient state capacity to implement social and economic programmes, including those aimed at empowering poor rural and urban women.

In Chap. 11, Anne-Mette Kjaer and Marianne S. Ulriksen synthesize the research findings from the Uganda case study. The Ugandan government has become gradually less dependent on aid, and the promise of oil revenues, in addition to increased loans and grants from Chinese partners, appears to have affected government priorities, becoming less accommodating to Western donors and focusing increasingly on energy and infrastructure provision to the detriment of social spending. However, in a context of increasing electoral competition, the Ugandan leadership continues to emphasize "prosperity for all," while patronage and political pressures on the public budget are preventing such policies from adequately addressing poverty and social exclusion. The case study finds that the need to maintain political power has led to reduced tax intakes as a result of abolishing taxes levied on rural voters and introducing tax exemptions for powerful supporters. On the spending side, social development concerns compete with other public policy areas as well as the pressure to allocate resources for political purposes. Regarding institution building, the Uganda Revenue Authority (URA) has built considerable institutional capacity and is making efforts to expand the tax base, which has been traditionally narrow against the backdrop of a slowly transforming economy. To the extent that it enjoys formal autonomy from political intervention, the URA has been able to take some initiatives in that direction, but political interference has steadily increased, with uncertain effects on long-term institution building. Domestic civil society actors influence tax policy decisions to a limited extent, even if there are signs that tax associations are being formed and are increasingly vocal. The findings suggest that one precondition for an expanded revenue base would be a gradual structural transformation of the economy. Combined with electoral pressures for public goods, this could lead to more public debate and higher prioritization of social spending.

Chapter 12, the case study on Zimbabwe, by Richard Saunders, examines evolving models and experiences of DRM in Zimbabwe since independence in 1980. While Zimbabwe has typically enjoyed a high tax effort and performance relative to many of its neighbours, it has also experienced multiple obstacles which have hindered the effective translation of revenue growth into improved social services and social protection. Constructive state-citizen relationships in the first years of independence were soon eroded by neoliberal stabilization and structural adjustment policies, worsening sharply in the 2000s during a period of heightened political contestation, economic crisis, and dramatically contracting fiscal space. As state transparency and accountability weakened in the context of elite state capture and increasing militarization of the political space, governance and state-citizen relations frayed and sharply undermined resource bargaining. The collapse of social protection in the early 2000s provoked a fiscal and social emergency, and set the stage for a new period of DRM innovation in a new political context. In 2009, a coalition government, the Government of National Unity (GNU), brokered by the international community and led by President Mugabe's ZANU-PF (Zimbabwe African National Union-Patriotic Front) and the opposition party MDC (Movement for Democratic Change), was actively supported by international donors and accompanied by greater openness of consultations between the state and domestic business and social stakeholders. Innovative financing instruments such as the AIDS Levy (1999) or the road tolls introduced in 2009 facilitated much needed public expenditure in health and infrastructure. After 2013 when ZANU-PF returned to unilateral power, the state budget was entirely financed by domestic resources; however, revenue yields were systematically undermined by interference by the political elite in state management processes, for example by the striking of special tax bargains with platinum miners and secretive management of alluvial diamond resources. The sudden ousting of President Mugabe in November 2017 was followed by a closely fought election which led to disputed results and state violence against opposition supporters recalling the strong-arm political tactics of the previous Mugabe government. For Zimbabwe to embark on a more transformative development pathway, the study suggests strengthening bureaucratic capacity and autonomy, reinstalling fiscal discipline, improving tax equity by lowering the disproportionate tax burden borne by poorer Zimbabweans, and strengthening the links between resource bargains and development outcomes through empowering civil society and social partners in democratic and transparent policy processes.

Chapter 13, by Katja Hujo, concludes that DRM is a political process of contestation and bargaining which is marked by differences and asymmetries of power at different levels, from the local to the global, which are in turn shaped by historical legacies and the economic and political context. The chapter further summarizes the changes in key relationships between state, civil society, donors and business actors in the different country case studies associated with DRM strategies, and shows that upgrading institutions for DRM and service delivery goes beyond technical approaches to capacity building, reflecting a deeply historical and political process of creating a social compact and the fiscal institutions underpinning it, as well as state capacity to strike sustainable bargains with key stakeholders and to build consensus on broad policy directions. Based on the studies presented in the volume, the chapter distills four policy recommendations: create inclusive resource bargains with links to social policy; diversify the financing mix in favour of sustainable instruments; support national bargains with global bargains; and create an enabling environment for DRM through public policies.

References

ActionAid. 2011. *Real Aid: Ending Aid Dependency*. London: Action Aid. Accessed 10 May 2016. http://www.actionaid.org/sites/files/actionaid/real_aid:3.pdf.

African Economic Outlook. 2010. *Public Resource Mobilization and Aid in Africa*. Report, African Development Bank. Paris: Organization for Economic Cooperation and Development Publications.

Akitoby, Bernardin, Anja Baum, Clay Hackney, Olamide Harrison, Keyra Primus, and Veronique Salins. 2018. *Tax Revenue Mobilization Episodes in Emerging Markets and Low-Income Countries: Lessons from a New Dataset*. IMF Working Paper, WP/18/234. Washington, DC: International Monetary Fund.

Auty, Richard M., ed. 2001. *Resource Abundance and Economic Development*. New York: Oxford University Press.

Bangura, Yusuf, and Carl-Johan Hedberg. 2007. Democracy and Social Policy Development: Introduction and Overview. In *Democracy and Social Policy*, ed. Yusuf Bangura. Basingstoke: Palgrave Macmillan and United Nations Research Institute for Social Development.

Bhushan, Aniket and Yiagadeesen Samy. 2010. *Enhancing Domestic Resource Mobilization for Effective Development: The Role of Donors*. The North-South Institute, Ottawa. Accessed 26 August 2019. http://www.nsi-ins.ca/wp-content/uploads/2010/04/Enhancing-Domestic-Resource-Mobilization-for-Effective-Development-DonorPaperFINALPOST.pdf.

Braddick, Michael J. 1996. *The Nerves of State: Taxation and the Financing of the English State, 1558–1714*. Manchester: Manchester University Press.

Brautigam, Deborah, Odd-Helge Fjeldstad, and Mick Moore. 2008. *Taxation and State-Building in Developing Countries: Capacity and Consent*. Cambridge: Cambridge University Press.

Brewer, John. 1988. *The Sinews of Power: War, Money and the English State, 1688–1783*. Cambridge, MA: Harvard University Press.

Collier, Paul. 2007. *The Bottom Billion: Why the Poorest Countries are Failing and What Can Be Done about It*. Oxford: Oxford University Press.

Culpeper, Roy, and Aniket Bhushan. 2008. *Domestic Resource Mobilization: A Neglected Factor in Development Strategy*. Background Paper Prepared for Workshop on Domestic Resource Mobilization in Sub-Saharan Africa. Entebbe, Uganda, 27–28 May. Accessed 17 October 2012. http://www.dfid.gov.uk/R4D/PDF/Outputs/ProPoor_RPC/60667_Background_Paper.pdf.

D'Arcy, Michelle. 2012. *Taxation, Democracy and State-Building: How Does Sequencing Matter?* Quality of Government (QoG) Institute, Working Paper Series No. 2012-4. Gothenburg: University of Gothenburg. Accessed 28 August 2019. https://qog.pol.gu.se/digitalAssets/1369/1369867_2012_4_darcy.pdf.

Daunton, Martin. 2001. *Trusting Leviathan: The Politics of Taxation in Britain—1799–1914*. Cambridge: Cambridge University Press.

Development Committee. 2015. *From Billions to Trillions. Transforming Development Finance Post-2015 Financing for Development: Multilateral Development Finance*. Joint Document by African Development Bank, Inter-American Development Bank, International Monetary Fund and World Bank. Accessed 28 August 2019. http://siteresources.worldbank.org/DEVCOMMINT/Documentation/23659446/DC2015-0002(E)FinancingforDevelopment.pdf.

Di John, Jonathan. 2010. *The Political Economy of Taxation and State Resilience in Zambia*. Working Paper No. 78, London: Crisis States Research Centre, London School of Economics.

———. 2015. Taxation, Developmental State Capacity and Poverty Reduction. In *Developmental Pathways to Poverty Reduction*, ed. Yusuf Bangura, 55–73. Basingstoke: Palgrave MacMillan and United Nations Research Institute for Social Development.

Easterly, William. 2003. Can Foreign Aid Buy Growth? *Journal of Economic Perspective* 17 (3): 23–48.

ECA (Economic Commission of Africa). 2014. *Illicit Financial Flows: Why Africa Needs to 'Track It, Stop It and Get It.'* Report, United Nations ECA. Accessed 28 August 2019. https://www.uneca.org/sites/default/files/PublicationFiles/illicit_financial_flows_why_africa_needs.pdf.

———. 2018. *Illicit Financial Flows Continue to Impede Africa's Development, Says ECA's Boko at HLPD 2018*. United Nations Communications Section, 11 July. Accessed 28 August 2019. https://www.uneca.org/stories/illicit-financial-flows-continue-impede-africa%E2%80%99s-development-says-eca%E2%80%99s-boko-hlpd-2018.

Ferguson, James. 2006. *Global Shadows: Africa in the Neoliberal World Order*. Durham, NC: Duke University Press.

Fjeldstad, Odd-Helge, and Mick Moore. 2008. Tax Reform and State-Building in a Globalized World. In *Taxation and State-Building in Developing Countries: Capacity and Consent*, ed. D. Brautigam, O.-H. Fjeldstad, and M. Moore, 235–260. Cambridge: Cambridge University Press.

Gaspar, Vito, David Amaglobeli, Mercedes Garcia-Escribano, Delphine Prady, and Mauricio Soto. 2019. *Fiscal Policy and Development: Human, Social, and Physical Investment for the SDGs*. IMF Staff Discussion Note 03/19. Washington, DC: IMF.

Guajardo Beltrán, Juan Carlos. 2012. Mineral Rents and Social Development in Chile. In *Mineral Rents and the Financing of Social Policy: Opportunities and Challenges*, ed. Katja Hujo, 185–222. Basingstoke: Palgrave Macmillan and United Nations Research Institute for Social Development.

Gupta, Sanjeev, and Shamsuddin Tareq. 2008. Mobilizing Revenue: Strengthening Domestic Revenue Bases is Key to Creating Fiscal Space for Africa's Development Needs. *Finance and Development* 45 (3): 469–482.

Helleiner, Gerald K. 1964. The Fiscal Role of the Marketing Boards in Nigerian Economic Development, 1947–61. *The Economic Journal* 47 (295): 582–610.

Huat, Beng Chua. 2005. Welfare Developmentalism in Singapore and Malaysia. In *Transforming the Developmental Welfare State in East Asia*, ed. H.J. Kwon, 98–118. Basingstoke: Palgrave Macmillan and United Nations Research Institute for Social Development.

Huber, Evelyn, and John Stephens. 2001. *Development and Crisis of the Welfare State: Parties and Policies in Global Markets*. Chicago: University of Chicago Press.

Hujo, Katja, ed. 2012. *Mineral Rents and the Financing of Social Policy: Opportunities and Challenges*. Basingstoke: Palgrave Macmillan and United Nations Research Institute for Social Development.

Hujo, Katja, and Shea McClanahan, eds. 2009. *Financing Social Policy: Mobilizing Resources for Social Development*. Basingstoke: Palgrave Macmillan and United Nations Research Institute for Social Development.

ICTD (International Centre for Tax and Development) and UNU-WIDER (United Nations University-World Institute for Development Economics Research). 2018. *Government Revenue Dataset*. September. Accessed 26 August 2019. https://www.ictd.ac/dataset/grd/.

ILO (International Labour Organization). 2017. *World Social Protection Report 2017–2019 Dataset*. Geneva: ILO. Accessed 29 August 2019. https://www.social-protection.org/gimi/gess/ShowWiki.action?id=594#tabs-3.

IMF (International Monetary Fund). 2012. *Fiscal Regimes for Extractive Industries: Design and Implementation*. Prepared by the Fiscal Affairs Department. Washington, DC: International Monetary Fund. Accessed 29 August 2019. https://www.imf.org/external/np/pp/eng/2012/081512.pdf.

———. 2013. *Fiscal Monitor: Taxing Times*. World Economic and Financial Surveys 0258-7440, October. Washington, DC: IMF. Accessed 29 August 2019. http://www.imf.org/external/pubs/ft/fm/2013/02/pdf/fm1302.pdf.

———. 2014. *Revenue Administration: Administering Revenues from Natural Resources—A Short Primer*. Technical Notes and Manuals Prepared by Andrea Lemgruber and Scott Shelton. Accessed 29 August 2019. https://www.imf.org/external/pubs/ft/tnm/2014/tnm1402.pdf.

Kangas, Olli, and Joakim Palme. 2005. *Social Policy and Economic Development in the Nordic Countries*. Basingstoke: Palgrave Macmillan and United Nations Research Institute for Social Development.

Kjaer, Anne Mette, and Ole Therkildsen. 2013. Elections and Landmark Policies in Uganda and Tanzania. *Democratization* 40 (4): 592–614.

Kjaer, Anne Mette, and Marianne S. Ulriksen. 2014. *From Consensus to Contention: Changing Revenue and Policy Dynamics in Uganda*. PDRM Working Paper No. 2014-21. Geneva: United Nations Research Institute for Social Development. Accessed 18 February 2016. http://www.unrisd.org/kjaer-ulriksen.

Korpi, Walter, and Joakim Palme. 1998. The Paradox of Redistribution and Strategies of Equality: Welfare State Institutions, Inequality, and Poverty in the Western Countries. *American Sociological Review* 63 (5): 661–687.

Levi, Margaret. 1988. *Of Rule and Revenue*. Berkeley: University of California Press.

Mkandawire, Thandika. 2005. *Targeting versus Universalism in Poverty Reduction*. Social Policy and Development Programme, Paper No. 23. Geneva: United Nations Research Institute for Social Development.

———. 2010. On Tax Efforts and Colonial Heritage in Africa. *Journal of Development Studies* 46 (10): 1647–1669. Accessed 23 February 2016. http://eprints.lse.ac.uk/31211/.

Moore, Mick. 2004. Revenues, state formation, and the quality of governance in developing countries. *International Political Science Review* 25 (3): 297–319.
———. 2008. Between coercion and contract: Competing narratives on taxation and governance. In *Taxation and State-Building in Developing Countries: Capacity and Consent*, ed. D. Brautigam, O.-H. Fjeldstad, and M. Moore, 34–63. Cambridge: Cambridge University Press.
———. 2013. *Obstacles to Increasing Tax Revenues in Low Income Countries*. International Centre for Tax and Development and PDRM Working Paper No. 15. Brighton: ICTD at IDS/United Nations Research Institute for Social Development. Accessed 28 August 2019. https://www.ictd.ac/publication/obstacles-to-increasing-tax-revenues-in-low-income-countries/.
Moyo, Dambisa. 2009. *Dead Aid: Why Aid is Not Working and How There is Another Way for Africa*. London: Penguin.
ODI (Overseas Development Institute), ECDPM (European Centre for Development Policy Management), GDI (German Development Institute), University of Athens and the Southern Voice Network. 2015. *European Report on Development 2015: Combining Finance and Policies to Implement a Transformative Post-2015 Development Agenda*. Brussels: ODI, ECDPM, GDI/DIE, University of Athens and the Southern Voice Network. Accessed 28 August 2019. http://ecdpm.org/wp-content/uploads/2015-European-Report-on-Development-English.pdf.
OECD (Organisation for Economic Cooperation and Development). 2015. *Financial Official Development Assistance Figures in 2014*. Accessed 16 March 2016. http://www.oecd.org/dac/stats/final-oda-2014.htm.
———. 2016. OECD.Stat: Deflators for Resource Flows (2016 = 100). Accessed 26 August 2019. https://stats.oecd.org
———. 2017. Total Official Flows by Country and Region (ODA + OOF). Accessed 26 August 2019. https://stats.oecd.org/Index.aspx?DataSetCode=REF_TOTALOFFICIAL.
———. 2018a. *Launch of ODA Figures 2017*. OECD Press Release, 9 April. Accessed 29 August 2019. https://www.oecd.org/development/launch-of-oda-figures-2017-france-april-2018.htm.
———. 2018b. OECD.Stat: Revenue Statistics—Comparative Tables. Accessed 29 August 2019. http://www.stats.oecd.org.
———. 2018c. *Revenue Statistics 2018: Tax Revenue Trends in the OECD*. Report. Paris: OECD.
———. 2019a. *Development Aid at a Glance: Statistics by Region (Africa)*. Report. Paris: OECD. Accessed on 29 August 2019. http://www.oecd.org/dac/financing-sustainable-development/development-finance-data/Africa-Development-Aid-at-a-Glance-2019.pdf.

———. 2019b. OECD.Stat: Country Programmable Aid (CPA). Paris: OECD. Accessed 29 August 2019. http://www.stats.oecd.org.

OECD and AFDB (African Development Bank Group). 2010. *Public Resource Mobilization and Aid Effectiveness*. Paris: OECD.

Ortiz, Isabel. 2009. Financing for Development: International Redistribution. In *Financing Social Policy: Mobilizing Resources for Social Development*, ed. Katja Hujo and Shea McClanahan, 53–85. Basingstoke: Palgrave Macmillan and United Nations Research Institute for Social Development.

Oxfam. 2016. *The Right Choices: Achieving Universal Health Coverage in Malawi*. Joint Agency Briefing Note, 7 June 2016. Accessed 26 August 2019. https://oxfamilibrary.openrepository.com/bitstream/handle/10546/611820/bn-right-choices-universal-health-coverage-malawi-070616-en.pdf?sequence=1.

Oxfam and DFI (Development Finance International). 2015. *Financing the Sustainable Development Goals: Lessons from Government Spending on the MDGs*. Government Spending Watch 2015 Report. Accessed 24 February 2016. https://www.oxfam.org/sites/www.oxfam.org/files/file_attachments/rr-financing-sustainable-development-goals-110615-en.pdf.

Sachs, Jeffrey D., and Andrew M. Warner. 1999. Natural Resource Intensity and Economic Growth. In *Development Policies in Natural Resource Economies*, ed. Jörg Meyer, Brian Chambers, and Ayisha Farooq, 13–38. Cheltenham: Edward Elgar Publishing.

Steinmo, Sven H. 1993. *Taxation and Democracy: Swedish, British, and American Approaches to Financing the Modern State*. London; New Haven, CT: Yale University Press.

Stewart, Miranda 2002. *Global Trajectories of Tax Reform: Mapping Tax Reform in Developing and Transition Countries*. Public Law and Legal Theory Research Paper No. 29. Melbourne: Faculty of Law, University of Melbourne.

Tanzi, Vito, and Ludger Schuknecht. 2000. *Public Spending in the 20th Century: A Global Perspective*. Cambridge: Cambridge University Press.

Tilly, Charles. 1975. *The Formation of National States in Western Europe*. Princeton, NJ: Princeton University Press.

UNCTAD (United Nations Conference on Trade and Development). 2014. *World Investment Report 2014: Investing in the SDGs: An Action Plan*. Geneva: UNCTAD. Accessed 29 August 2019. http://unctad.org/en/pages/PublicationWebflyer.aspx?publicationid=937.

UNESCO (United Nations Educational, Scientific and Cultural Organization). 2019. *Government Expenditure on Education as a Percentage of GDP Dataset*. Paris: UNESCO. Accessed August 2019. http://data.uis.unesco.org/index.aspx?queryid=3373.

United Nations. 2003. *Financing for Development: Monterrey Consensus on the International Conference on Financing for Development*. The Final Text of Agreements and Commitments. New York: United Nations.

UNRISD (United Nations Research Institute for Social Development). 2010. *Combating Poverty and Inequality: Structural Change, Social Policy and Politics*. Flagship Report. Geneva: UNRISD. Accessed 16 March 2016. http://www.unrisd.org/poverty.

———. 2012. *Mineral Rents and the Financing of Social Policy: Options and Constraints*. Research and Policy Brief No. 16. Geneva: UNRISD. Accessed 16 March 2016. http://www.unrisd.org/rpb16.

———. 2016. *Policy Innovations for Transformative Change. Implementing the 2030 Agenda for Sustainable Development*. Flagship Report. Geneva: UNRISD. Accessed 29 August 2019. http://www.unrisd.org/flagship2016.

Wheeler, A.C.R., ed. 1968. *The Organization of Educational Planning in Nigeria*. African Research Monographs No. 13. Paris: International Institute for Educational Planning, UNESCO.

White House Archive. 2004. The Millennium Challenge Account. Accessed 29 August 2019. https://georgewbush-whitehouse.archives.gov/infocus/developingnations/millennium.html#.

World Bank. 2016. Database: World Development Indicators. Accessed 29 August 2019. http://www.databank.worldbank.org/data/.

———. 2019. World Development Indicators. Accessed 26 August 2019. https://databank.worldbank.org/source/world-development-indicators.

World Health Organization (WHO). 2019. Global Health Expenditure Database. Accessed 29 August 2019. https://apps.who.int/nha/database.

Part I

Domestic Resource Mobilization Through the Lens of Aid, Taxation and Mineral Rents

2

Fiscal Capacity and Aid Allocation: Domestic Resource Mobilization and Foreign Aid in Developing Countries

Aniket Bhushan and Yiagadeesen Samy

Introduction

This study is concerned with the interaction between fiscal capacity and performance in developing countries on the one hand, and donor aid allocation on the other. We are interested in whether fiscal capacity and performance in developing countries have any impact on donor aid allocation decisions. Given that domestic resource mobilization (DRM) is now seen by the international community as an important component of financing for development, we attempt in this chapter to conduct an empirical analysis of whether (and the extent to which) donors consider tax performance in aid allocation decisions.

A. Bhushan (✉) • Y. Samy
Norman Paterson School of International Affairs, Carleton University, Ottawa, ON, Canada
e-mail: aniket@cidpnsi.ca; yiagadeesen.samy@carleton.ca

K. Hujo (ed.), *The Politics of Domestic Resource Mobilization for Social Development*, Social Policy in a Development Context,
https://doi.org/10.1007/978-3-030-37595-9_2

To answer this question, the chapter is divided into the following five sections. The next section sets out the rationale and motivation for the analysis in more detail. The section "Aid Allocation, Fiscal Capacity and Performance: What Does the Literature Say?" reviews the fiscal performance and aid allocation literature, pointing out the contributions and gaps in the literature. The section "Cross-Country Empirical Analysis and Discussion" presents our empirical framework and discusses the results of our large-N empirical analysis. The section "Overview of Country Cases" discusses recent fiscal performance data and donor involvement in taxation and public financial management (PFM) in four case study countries (Bolivia, Guatemala, Uganda and Zimbabwe).[1] An examination of different cases allows us to answer our main research question by looking more specifically at donor-recipient relationships, which the large-N analysis (due to data limitations at the individual donor level) cannot do. We are able to calculate a tax effort index for recipient countries and examine trends in various fiscal performance metrics. A concluding section highlights key messages and findings, and suggests areas that require further research, especially for further examination of the cases using local knowledge.

Rationale and Motivation

While there is already a significant literature on determinants of aid allocation and a growing literature on whether high levels of aid are a disincentive to greater tax effort, especially in highly aid-reliant countries, the rationale for examining fiscal performance from the perspective of donor aid allocation is not obvious at the outset. Hence, the main question here is *not* embedded in an established theoretical literature. However, even if donors are not using recipient tax performance as a factor determining their allocation of aid, it is still helpful to see whether the rhetoric and observations from independent evaluations show up in the data. Recipient

[1] These countries were selected for the UNRISD project on "The Politics of Domestic Resource Mobilization for Social Development" (UNRISD 2012), and Guatemala was replaced later by Nicaragua. In any case, the four cases discussed in this chapter are helpful for a better understanding of the relationship between fiscal capacity and aid allocation.

countries may also be interested to know whether and the extent to which they may be penalized if they increase DRM.

Therefore, the first issue we must confront is why such an analysis is still worth pursuing. We put forward three reasons why it is worth analysing fiscal performance from the perspective of donor aid allocation.

First, the international community has increasingly recognized the importance of DRM.[2] For example, the 2002 Monterrey Consensus served to highlight and focus attention on DRM even in the poorest regions. The 2030 Agenda for Sustainable Development and the Addis Ababa Action Agenda agreed in 2015 have also set high expectations for developing country DRM efforts and the contribution of DRM to financing the ambitious Sustainable Development Goals (SDGs). Second, as of late, donors themselves have sought to explicitly link aid to taxation and tax effort in partner countries. This argument stems from the thinking that the main reason to be concerned about high levels of aid dependence (defined as aid-to-gross national income ratios above 10 per cent) is that such high reliance on aid undermines good governance by distorting domestic political accountability. Third, while the aid allocation literature has largely ignored taxation as an independent variable in explaining aid flows, one could argue that the inability of countries to raise revenue through taxes because of their structural characteristics is also a reflection of recipient needs. Therefore, from an analytical perspective, taxation and fiscal performance variables can be a useful proxy for recipient needs.

The links between aid allocation and fiscal performance can go both ways. For instance, one might expect donors to "reward" countries making significant tax effort and/or reforms with more aid or better aid (e.g. aid on better terms).[3] On the other hand, one might also expect to see more aid going to countries with lesser fiscal capacity (thus filling in gaps in DRM), or certainly more aid specifically to taxation- and PFM-related

[2] For the purposes of the analysis in this chapter, domestic resource mobilization, or DRM, refers mainly to domestic *revenue* mobilization. While we recognize that private savings mobilization and banking and financial sector issues are an important component of DRM, these are outside the scope of the present analysis.

[3] By "better aid" we mean aid modalities that are associated with fewer conditions, and aid that is more aligned with recipient priorities.

issues going to countries that have greater needs in these areas. One of the few cross-country econometric analyses in this area found evidence that suggests donor PFM support is positively and significantly associated with the quality of recipient PFM systems (de Renzio et al. 2011). Moreover, the same study also finds that donors reward countries with better PFM systems by shifting more of their aid to directly support the government budget.

To sum up, despite the lack of a theoretical literature and established framework, it is worth analysing whether fiscal capacity and performance have any discernible impact on donor aid allocation. This is an issue that is important for the reasons discussed above and that has been largely ignored by the existing literature.

Aid Allocation, Fiscal Capacity and Performance: What Does the Literature Say?

Given that our central objective is to examine whether improvements in fiscal capacity in low- and middle-income developing countries have any impact on donor aid allocation decisions, we briefly review the existing literature on how aid *is* allocated,[4] namely, how much aid countries receive and why.

Aid allocation studies have not taken fiscal performance into consideration as an explanatory variable. There is now a broad consensus that aid allocation patterns are dictated by a combination of political, strategic, commercial and humanitarian factors; in other words, recipient needs and donor interests matter, and their relative importance varies across donors. Obviously, the type of aid being allocated matters, and this is indeed a major issue with earlier studies that have examined, possibly because of a lack of data, aggregate aid flows and thus failed to distinguish among aid types. In the empirical analysis that we conduct in the next

[4] There is a parallel, though prescriptive/normative literature, that examines how aid *should* be allocated. See Collier and Dollar (2002).

section, we face a somewhat similar problem in that we are not able to examine the behaviour of individual donors.

Empirical models of aid allocation going back to the 1970s make the implicit assumption that donors derive utility from the impact of their aid on recipient countries and/or provide aid because they care about the well-being of recipient countries; self-interest and developmental objectives are thus both present in those studies. More recent studies have included several variables that account for donor interests (e.g. trade openness, colonial history and United Nations voting patterns), political factors (level of democracy and civil liberties) and recipient needs (proxied by variables such as per capita income, the human development index and infant mortality) to explain aid allocation patterns.[5]

On a practical level, there are differences between donors in terms of their criteria for aid allocation. Multilateral agencies use explicit resource allocation formulas to determine their aid allocations to countries based on their global mandate. Formulas, such as those employed by the World Bank's International Development Association (IDA) and African and Asian development banks, typically incorporate both recipient needs and institutional performance metrics. For example, the World Bank resource allocation index considers factors related to economic management, structural policies, policies for social inclusion and equity, and public sector management and institutions. By accounting for both recipient need and institutional performance in allocation formulas, multilateral agencies ensure that poor countries, which tend to have lower institutional capacity than higher-income developing countries, continue to receive an adequate proportion of aid funds despite lower governance rankings (OECD 2012).

Bilateral donors generally do not explicitly use quantitative aid allocation formulas, but even here there are exceptions. The UK and Netherlands, for instance, use explicit aid allocation formulas in determining aid allocation (OECD 2012). We should thus expect to see different donors (bilateral vs. multilateral) react differently to taxation and fiscal capacity as a factor in their aid allocation strategies.

[5] For example, Alesina and Dollar (2000), Neumayer (2003a, b), Alesina and Weder (2002), Berthelemy and Tichit (2004), Dollar and Levin (2004) and Clist (2011).

Several studies have also assessed how different types of aid affect recipient fiscal systems. For instance, it has been shown that the composition of aid modalities can affect revenue mobilization. In a much-cited paper, Gupta et al. (2003) analysed the difference between the impact of loans versus grants. They find that net aid has a negative impact on government revenue, and that the relationship is primarily driven by the negative impact of grants on government revenue. The relationship is more pronounced in countries with high levels of corruption as grants seem to substitute domestic revenue effort (as opposed to loans—presumably because they must be serviced). There are also indications that donors are recognizing the importance of differences in aid modalities in the context of support for taxation and PFM more generally, namely, how different aid modalities contribute to better taxation systems and strengthen the links between taxation and governance (OECD 2013a). Although not the focus of the current study, the impact of aid on tax effort from large-N studies is far from conclusive,[6] and country case studies can contribute further evidence to this debate.

Cross-Country Empirical Analysis and Discussion

As discussed in the previous section, aid allocation studies have largely ignored fiscal capacity as an independent variable. Although a country's level of development (measured by per capita income) reflects its fiscal capacity, countries at similar levels of development differ in terms of revenue collection through taxes; it would therefore be appropriate to consider fiscal capacity as an additional explanatory variable for aid allocation. One could also interpret fiscal performance as a form of selectivity, whereby donors reward countries as domestic performance improves. Although we are agnostic about the net impact, we want to know whether the latter is significant or not, and how that varies between bilateral and multilateral aid.

[6] For a review of this literature, see Bhushan and Samy (2012).

We follow the approach taken by aid allocation studies such as Alesina and Dollar (2000) and focus on the aggregate, as opposed to individual, behaviour of bilateral and multilateral donors. We are aware that our approach does not consider the different behaviour of donors, and that this may affect our results. However, we believe this is a useful first step as it allows us to answer the question at the aggregate level from the perspective of recipient countries.

Our baseline specification for estimation takes the following general form:

$$\ln\left(AID_{it}\right) = f\left(GDPPC_{it-1}, POP_{it-1}, DEM_{it-1}, OPEN_{it-1}, GOV_{it-1}, FISCAL_{it-1}\right)$$

where *i* refers to countries and *t* refers to time. The dependent variable, *AID*, consists of bilateral and multilateral aid (official development assistance or ODA) in separate regressions; the data is from the OECD Development Assistance Committee (DAC). Since bilateral aid is typically more strategic, one would expect it to respond more to donor interests while multilateral aid is more responsive to the needs of recipient countries. By the same logic, multilateral agencies are expected to respond more to fiscal capacity than bilateral ones. A possible problem with these dependent variables (bilateral and multilateral aid), however, is the fact that they lump together various forms of aid, including, for example, humanitarian aid, which does not have anything to do with fiscal capacity. We thus also consider aid that goes towards PFM, obtained from the OECD DAC Creditor Reporting System (CRS), which includes fiscal policy and planning, support to ministries of finance, strengthening financial and managerial accountability, public expenditure management, improving financial management systems, tax policy and administration, budget drafting, and so on.

The only recipients' need variable considered here is the natural log of GDP per capita in constant 2005 USD from the World Development Indicators (WDI). Although many other studies have considered infant mortality—a measure of physical need—as an additional control variable, it was excluded because of its high correlation (at 0.8) with per capita incomes. Population, *POP*, is included to control for country size, and is also obtained from WDI. We include a measure of the level of democracy, *DEM*, as a proxy for civil and political rights. This variable is constructed by adding a civil liberties index to a political rights index, both of which are published annually by Freedom House. Another variable that is often used to measure democracy is from the Polity dataset, which varies from strongly autocratic (−10) to strongly democratic (+10); we will consider it to check for sensitivity. We consider two additional independent variables. Trade openness, *OPEN*, which is the sum of exports and imports as a percentage of GDP, is obtained from WDI and is a measure of economic/strategic interest. Government effectiveness, *GOV*, is included to control for the quality of institutions and policies. It comes from the Worldwide Governance Indicators research project by Kaufmann et al. (2019). This indicator varies from −2.5 to +2.5, with higher numbers corresponding to better outcomes.

For our main variable of interest, namely fiscal capacity, we consider two indicators. The tax/GDP ratio is the most commonly used variable in empirical studies. Tax data is available from the Government Financial Statistics (GFS) database from the International Monetary Fund (IMF), and has now been merged with WDI; we thus consider *TAX1*, the tax/GDP ratio from WDI, as one indicator. However, there are numerous gaps in the data, especially for developing countries. The African Economic Outlook (AEO) database also contains detailed data on taxation at the country level for all African countries but cannot be merged with WDI because it uses a different methodology. We will use the tax/GDP ratio, *TAX2*, from AEO when we examine sub-Saharan African (SSA) countries as a separate sample and then compare our results with *TAX1* (for SSA countries).

The above equation is estimated using panel data for the period 1992–2010. Although additional data are now available for more recent years, it is unlikely that these would have affected the results of our analysis because averaging over three years would yield only a few additional observations per country. Furthermore, it is only very recently, and as part of post-2015 discussions, that donors have started paying more attention to DRM. Changes in tax/GDP ratios would thus not be significant enough in our view to affect our results. All independent variables are averaged over three-year periods to smooth annual fluctuations, starting in 1992. The dependent variable is also averaged over three years but allows a time lag of one year for the effect of the independent variables on the dependent variable by starting from 1993 to reduce the likelihood of endogeneity. Regarding the specification of the above equation, to correct for skewness and produce a more normalized distribution, we took the natural logarithm of the aid variables, per capita income and population. Aid allocation studies typically introduce both linear and quadratic terms for per capita incomes and population to control for a middle-income or population bias. However, one main problem with this approach is the high level of collinearity between linear and squared terms. We thus follow the approach of Neumayer (2003a, b) who considers only linear terms in his analysis of bilateral and multilateral aid flows. We did, however, run some tests using squared terms and they were generally not significant.

Table 2.1 provides summary statistics for the (untransformed) variables that are used in the empirical analysis. The different estimated models will contain fewer observations as combinations of these variables are considered together in different specifications. We have fewer observations for the fiscal capacity variables because there are many gaps in taxation data. The average values for bilateral and multilateral aid are

Table 2.1 Summary statistics

Variable name	Number of observations	Mean	Median	Standard deviation
Bilateral aid (USD m)[a]	879	311.26	139.91	654.95
Multilateral aid (USD m)[a]	837	100.78	32.80	167.85
GDP per capita (USD)[b]	892	3590.00	1716.00	4828.00
Population (m)[b]	924	31.74	5.64	133.56
Democracy (Freedom House) [c]	924	7.25	7.00	3.97
Openness (per cent) [c]	871	85.79	78.84	43.33
Government effectiveness[c]	763	−0.35	−0.41	0.71
Tax/GDP (per cent)—TAX1[b]	452	16.13	15.11	8.48
Tax effort[e]	334	1.20	1.00	1.31
PFM[f]	334	14.93	5.47	24.87
Tax/GDP (per cent)—*TAX2*[g]	237	13.72	12.11	6.86

Source: (a) OECD (2013c), (b) World Bank (2013), (c) Freedom House (2013), (d) Kaufmann et al. (2009), Worldwide Governance Indicators Database (2013), (e) authors calculations based on World Bank (2013), (f) OECD (2013b) and (g) AEO (2013)

basically in line with what is typically observed, namely, that significantly more aid is allocated bilaterally than multilaterally (more than 3:1). We note in passing that a lot of aid that is coded as bilateral is in fact delivered through multilateral agencies. Although bilaterals or their ministries tend to make these decisions, they are only signing a cheque to a multilateral that will then be the executing agency. This so-called "bilateralization" of multilateral aid is often seen in the case of tax projects.

When *TAX1* is restricted to African countries only, the coverage is quite poor (see tables below). Although the tax/GDP ratio is widely used in empirical analysis, it can also be misleading. For instance, there is no simple association between the tax/GDP ratio and overall economic performance; as an example, resource-rich countries can report high tax ratios when resource-related revenues are counted in. Furthermore, the tax/GDP ratio can increase for reasons that have nothing to do with better performance and be extremely punitive when, for example, rapacious governments mobilize revenue in the face of instability or embargoes. Thus, one can use a tax effort measure, *TAXEFF*, which is the ratio of actual tax collection to taxable capacity (discussed in detail later in the chapter). The latter is estimated from *TAX1* as a predicted tax/GDP ratio that considers the country-specific characteristics that influence tax mobilization. Since *TAXEFF* is itself derived from some of the independent variables in the above equation, we cannot use it for estimation. However, a simple correlation of this variable with bilateral aid (Fig. 2.1) shows a very weak relationship between aid and tax effort.[7]

Table 2.2 presents the first set of estimates for the above equation with bilateral aid (in natural log form) as the dependent variable.[8] As expected, per capita income is significant across different specifications with the right sign; as countries develop, they receive less aid, other things remaining equal. The controls for the level of democracy and government effectiveness are also significant and with the expected signs. More democratic countries

[7] A similar result was obtained with multilateral aid.

[8] The equations are estimated with period dummies and fixed effects; panel-corrected standard errors are reported and account for both cross-section heteroskedasticity and autocorrelation. Using pooled estimates would have assumed that the intercept value and slope coefficients of different countries are the same and may produce biased estimates. Hausman tests provided strong evidence against the null hypothesis that there is no misspecification in the case of random effects; as a result, we report the fixed-effects estimation results.

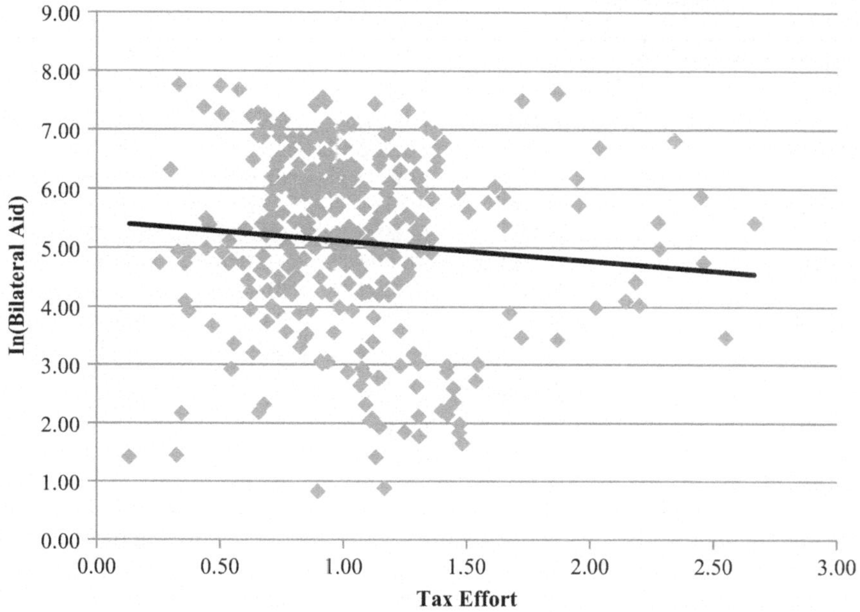

Fig. 2.1 Bilateral aid versus tax effort. (Source: Author elaboration and calculation using tax effort data and aid data from OECD 2013c)

are rewarded with more aid, and countries with better institutions and policies also receive more bilateral aid.[9] This is perhaps not surprising given that our analysis corresponds largely with debates about selectivity that started in the late 1990s. On the other hand, population and openness do not seem to be important factors. None of the fiscal capacity variables are significant, indicating that they are not important in explaining aid allocation decisions at the bilateral level. This is also true when SSA countries are considered separately (column (4) of Table 2.2, where *TAX1* is not significant when only SSA countries are considered).

In the case of multilateral aid (see Table 2.3), per capita income and the level of democracy are significant in a few cases but the fiscal capacity variables are generally not significant, except in the case of *TAX1* when the sample is restricted to SSA countries only. Given the small number of countries and observations for that variable, we cannot therefore

[9] The results do not change significantly when a different measure of democracy from Polity 2 (as noted before in the text) is considered.

Table 2.2 Allocation of bilateral aid and fiscal capacity, fixed effects

Explanatory variables	(1)	(2)	(3)	(4)
Constant	−6.683	7.430	6.221	42.56
	(7.299)	(10.647)	(16.787)	(35.833)
ln(GDPPC)	−0.313*	−0.902**	−0.315*	−2.754**
	(0.175)	(0.202)	(0.161)	(1.290)
ln(POP)	0.920**	0.263	0.127	−1.115
	(0.427)	(0.603)	(1.049)	(2.119)
DEM	−0.053**	−0.007	−0.086*	−0.096*
	(0.015)	(0.022)	(0.045)	(0.057)
OPEN	0.001	0.001	0.001	0.001
	(0.001)	(0.002)	(0.002)	(0.007)
GOV	0.313**	0.504**	0.447**	1.661**
	(0.119)	(0.147)	(0.154)	(0.513)
TAX1		0.018		
		(0.017)		
TAX2			0.015	
			(0.013)	
TAX1(SSA only)				0.022
				(0.023)
#Observations	673	359	233	96
#Countries	148	108	49	31
Hausman Test	127.34	54.10	48.12	33.46
(p-value)	0.000	0.000	0.000	0.000

Source: Author estimations

Notes: (1), (2), (3), (4) are the results of a different regression (each with different tax variables)

Except where indicated otherwise, the figures in parentheses are the robust standard errors

*(**) indicates 10(5) per cent level of significance. Coefficients on time dummies not reported

conclude that multilaterals are behaving any differently from bilateral donors when it comes to fiscal capacity. Finally, we examine what happens when we use aid that goes towards PFM as our dependent variable (results not shown here). Given its specific nature and purpose, as noted above, one would expect fiscal capacity to be better correlated with this variable. However, this is not the case. Contrary to expectations, we also find that countries that are more open tend to receive less aid towards PFM. Because of lower data coverage, we have fewer observations in the case of aid that goes towards PFM than bilateral or multilateral aid (Tables 2.2 and 2.3).

The preliminary results obtained here reinforce the view that donors—whether bilateral or multilateral—have paid little attention to fiscal

Table 2.3 Allocation of multilateral aid and fiscal capacity, fixed effects

Explanatory variables	(1)***	(2)***	(3)***	(4)***
Constant	5.668	26.752	−11.170	−3.759
	(8.379)	(16.816)	(20.353)	(31.864)
ln(GDPPC)	−0.369**	−1.182	−0.731**	−1.777*
	(0.119)	(0.781)	(0.222)	(0.903)
ln(POP)	0.054	−0.855	1.303	1.202
	(0.535)	(0.730)	(1.303)	(1.824)
DEM	−0.059*	−0.111**	−0.054	0.045
	(0.030)	(0.040)	(0.034)	(0.052)
OPEN	0.004**	0.000	−0.001	−0.001
	(0.002)	(0.003)	(0.003)	(0.005)
GOV	0.375	0.113	0.229	0.380
	(0.266)	(0.263)	(0.351)	(0.376)
TAX1		0.017		
		(0.015)		
TAX2			0.016	
			(0.014)	
TAX1(SSA only)				0.045**
				(0.045)
#Observations	616	324	228	95
#Countries	139	99	49	30
Hausman Test	100.06	83.95	51.44	70.34
(p-value)	0.000	0.000	0.000	0.000

Source: Author estimations

Note: Except where indicated otherwise, the figures in parentheses are the robust standard errors

*(**) indicates 10(5) per cent level of significance. Coefficients on time dummies not reported

*** (1), (2), (3), (4) are the results for a different regression (each with different tax variables)

capacity in their aid allocation decisions. It would be interesting in terms of future work to see whether different measures of aid and/or fiscal capacity yield different results, and whether there is a difference in behaviour across different bilateral donors when it comes to fiscal capacity. In particular, since donors have only recently begun to pay more attention to DRM, we should be able to examine whether fiscal capacity[10] is correlated with aid allocation in a few years.

[10] We should note that there is also now better data on taxation—the Government Revenue Dataset—that has become publicly available from the International Centre for Taxation and Development that could be correlated with aid allocation. See ICTD (2019).

Overview of Country Cases

Large-N analyses are useful in providing an overall sense of the relationship (or lack thereof) between fiscal performance and aid allocation. It is important, however, to assess the relationship further at the more specific donor-recipient level. A more limited and specific case study approach is useful in this regard. This section provides a descriptive overview of fiscal performance and donor involvement in supporting taxation and public financial management efforts in four countries: Bolivia, Guatemala, Uganda and Zimbabwe.[11] The discussion is divided into two subsections: (1) taxation and fiscal performance issues and (2) donor involvement.

Taxation and Fiscal Performance

How do the four case study countries compare with others in their respective regions and income groups? Table 2.4 provides a comparison from the perspective of the tax/GDP ratio. Bolivia and Guatemala are lower middle-income countries, while Uganda and Zimbabwe are low-income countries.

On the tax/GDP ratio, Bolivia fares better than the regional average for Latin America and for lower middle-income countries. This may be due to the inclusion of resource-related revenues, which may be significant in the case of Bolivia given the presence of natural gas, oil and minerals.[12] Guatemala on the other hand fares far worse than both the regional average and the average for lower middle-income countries. Guatemala's tax/GDP ratio is half that of its regional- and income-level

[11] These cases were selected by the UNRISD project leads. The case of Guatemala was eventually substituted by Nicaragua, see UNRISD (2015). For a more detailed description of country case studies of the PDRM project, see UNRISD (2013a, b, c), as well as Chaps. 9, 10, 11 and 12 in this volume.

[12] The main primary source of data for the USAID database is the IMF Article IV consultation. We suspect this includes resource-related revenues as other sources of revenue make up a small share. Please see Appendix for corporate tax (CITY), personal income taxes (PITY) and value added tax (VATY), all as a percentage of GDP for case study countries (Table 2.6) and income groups and regions (Table 2.8).

Table 2.4 Tax/GDP ratio

	2007–2008	2008–2009	2009–2010	2010–2011	2011–2012
Bolivia	23.80%	22.30%	23.36%	27.40%	26.40%
Guatemala	10.38%	12.22%	11.48%	10.40%	10.48%
Uganda	11.63%	12.53%	12.22%	6.95%	12.18%
Zimbabwe		4.00%		20.10%	27.90%
Central Europe and Central Asia	24.7%	23.5%	24.3%	23.1%	18.3%
Latin America and Caribbean	20.1%	20.3%	20.6%	18.4%	20.1%
East Asia and Pacific	19.1%	19.6%	17.8%	17.5%	18.4%
Sub-Saharan Africa	16.7%	16.2%	17.5%	16.2%	16.9%
Middle East and North Africa	17.0%	17.1%	14.6%	15.4%	12.7%
South Asia	10.1%	10.5%	10.6%	11.5%	11.0%
Low Income	14.3%	14.5%	14.8%	13.7%	14.7%
Lower Middle Income	20.4%	20.5%	19.5%	18.3%	18.2%
Upper Middle Income	21.9%	21.3%	21.6%	20.5%	18.3%

Source: Data from USAID (2013)

average, indicating very low collection levels.[13] While Uganda consistently fares worse than (the already low) regional average and low-income country average tax/GDP ratio, Zimbabwe fares better in both comparisons (except for 2008–2009).[14]

The tax/GDP ratio is useful in providing a general aggregate comparison. However, it does not provide a sense of the revenue sources contributing to the overall performance. Detailed breakdowns of the composition

[13] The main advantage of using the USAID (2013) database here is that it includes more recent data. While the USAID data is largely consistent with other sources such as the IMF GFS, World Bank and AEO data for Guatemala, Uganda and Zimbabwe, tax ratios for Bolivia reported here are higher, perhaps due to the inclusion of resource revenues, which are typically excluded from other sources. Data for Zimbabwe should be interpreted with caution. However, USAID has not updated this database since 2012–2013.

[14] Zimbabwe's poor performance in 2008–2009 can be attributed to the then ongoing economic crisis. Uganda's poor performance is the result of a very narrow tax base due to low compliance, poor enforcement and too many tax exemptions.

of international comparable revenue sources are hard to find. However, we can use USAID (2013) and AEO (2013) to shed light on the case study countries from a comparative perspective.

USAID (2013) provides data on three main tax types: corporate income taxes, personal income taxes and value added taxes (as a share of GDP). There is a reasonably clear pattern in terms of the relative importance of the three types of taxes and their relationship with levels of development. Personal income taxes and corporate income taxes tend to be the main tax revenue sources in higher income countries with more developed tax systems, while consumption taxes such as value added tax (VAT) are more important in less developed, low- and lower middle-income developing countries.

Corporate taxes in Bolivia in recent years have been similar to both the regional average for Latin America, as well as the average for lower middle-income countries. However, corporate tax collection in Guatemala lags both the regional average and lower middle-income country average. Corporate taxes in Uganda are far lower than both the already low average for SSA countries as well as low-income countries. Similarly, personal income tax collection levels as a share of GDP in both Guatemala and Uganda are a fraction of both their respective regional averages and the average for lower middle- and low-income countries.

Of the three tax types compared here, VAT is the most important in all four countries. This is consistent with the broader trend across low- and lower middle-income countries where VAT collection as a share of GDP is rising. VAT collection levels are comparable or higher than regional and income level averages in both Bolivia and Guatemala. While still lower than the regional and income group average, VAT collection in Uganda is approaching SSA and low-income country levels.

Drawing on AEO (2013) data we can analyse the revenue mix further for the two African countries. Over a longer period (2000–2010), the data indicates that while direct taxes are increasing as a share of the overall revenue mix in Uganda, they have been falling in the case of Zimbabwe. Another interesting pattern worth noting is that grants (foreign aid) made up the largest share of the revenue mix in Uganda as recently as in

2000. The share of grants since then has been declining and now stands lower than the share of domestic direct taxes. This indicates that Uganda is having some success in transitioning from its historically high reliance on foreign aid.

Beyond tax collection and composition, the data allows us to shed some light on the efficiency and effectiveness of tax systems. USAID (2013) includes structural data on the average cost of tax collection and the ratio of taxpayer staff to population. The average cost of tax collection is calculated as a ratio of the budget of the tax authority and the total revenue collected by the authority. The tax authority staff ratio is calculated as the number of tax authority staff members per 1000 persons in the country.

Data on cost of collection is available for three out of the four countries. At around 3.1 per cent, the cost of collection in Uganda is comparable with the regional average for sub-Saharan Africa at 2.9 per cent and for low-income countries, but the cost of collection in Zimbabwe at 7.4 per cent is far higher than the regional and income group average. The cost of collection in Guatemala at around 3.4 per cent is more than double that of the regional average at 1.3 per cent, as well as the average for lower middle-income countries. The tax authority staff ratios for Guatemala and Bolivia are similar to both the average for the Latin American region and lower middle-income countries. This pattern indicates that out of the four countries Guatemala is clearly the least efficient and effective at raising taxes. Tax collection ratios in Uganda are similarly low by comparison with reference groups; however, Uganda's efficiency metrics are in line with comparable countries.

As discussed elsewhere, the data for 2011–2012 show that SSA still has some of the most expensive tax collection systems of any developing region (Bhushan et al. 2013). The ratio of tax authority staff to population is one of the lowest and, despite significant recent reforms, most countries in the region still have inefficient tax collection systems. By comparison, Latin America has almost the same average tax authority staff ratio but is more than twice as efficient as SSA. Despite recent technological developments, including electronic filing, there is room for more donor investments in this capacity.

Tax Effort Index

While the tax/GDP ratio is the most widely used tax performance measure, it is not without weaknesses. A low tax/GDP ratio does not necessarily mean bad performance and a high ratio does not necessarily mean good performance. For example, Lesotho and Swaziland report atypically high tax ratios that are related to a revenue sharing agreement with South Africa, which arguably has little to do with domestic fiscal capacities. Moreover, the literature indicates that the tax/GDP ratio can increase for all sorts of reasons, including those that have little to do with better performance or a better state-citizen compact.

The tax effort index is a more sophisticated, yet still easy to interpret measure of tax performance, as it estimates a relative index controlling for the known factors affecting taxation. We calculate the index as a ratio between the share of actual tax collection and taxable capacity. For this we first need to compute *taxable capacity*. Following Le et al. (2012), taxable capacity is estimated to be the predicted tax/GDP ratio calculated using the estimated coefficients of a regression specification, considering the country-specific characteristics that influence tax mobilization. In other words, we control for factors such as income levels (GDPPC), openness (trade-GDP ratio) and the economic structure (agriculture share of GDP) that influence the tax/GDP ratio to predict what individual countries *should* be collecting, given their structural characteristics.

A tax effort index value above 1 indicates "high tax effort," whereas an index value below 1 indicates "low effort." The correct interpretation of the index is that high tax effort countries are utilizing their tax bases well to increase revenues, while low tax effort countries may have relatively substantial scope to increase revenue collection from existing tax bases.

Figure 2.2 shows the average tax effort over the period 1990–2012 on the horizontal axis while the average tax/GDP ratio over the same period range is given on the vertical axis.[15] In this way countries can be divided into four groups: (a) countries where tax effort is high, that is, above 1,

[15] All the data for this calculation is taken from the World Development Indicators database (World Bank) and covers the period 1990–2012. The tax effort index is calculated for each country for each year where data were available.

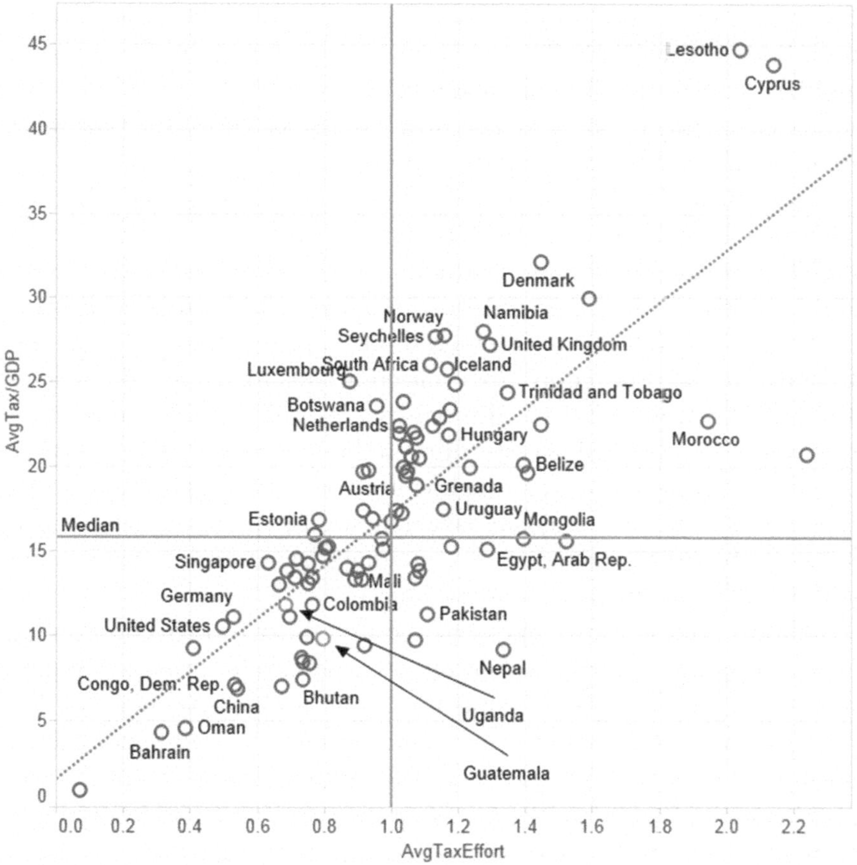

Fig. 2.2 Tax effort index (1990–2012). (Source: Author elaboration; AvgTaxEffort is based on authors calculations; AvgTax/GDP is based on World Bank World Development Indicators Database)

and tax/GDP is above the median level, (b) countries where tax effort is above 1, but the tax/GDP ratio is below median, (c) countries where tax effort is below 1, but the tax/GDP ratio is above median, and (d) countries where tax effort is below 1 and tax/GDP is below median.

Given data limitations we calculate average tax effort index scores over the 1990–2012 period for 94 countries. Forty-seven countries fall above the tax effort score of 1 and an equal number below 1. Data is only available for two of the four case study countries: Guatemala and Uganda.

The results of the tax effort index analysis reconfirm the earlier discussion. Both Guatemala (0.79) and Uganda (0.68) fall in the low tax effort and below median collection quadrant. Time series data for Guatemala shows a declining trend in the tax effort index since 2002. The time series trend for Uganda has been flat since 2000.[16]

Given their classification as low effort, and relatively low collection countries, both Guatemala and Uganda should be able to increase tax mobilization further without constraining other objectives such as growth and investment. In this regard our findings are consistent with other studies. Le et al. (2012), for instance, similarly place both Guatemala and Uganda in the low effort low collection quadrant (for the period 1994–2009). Le et al. (2012) also classify the other two case study countries: Bolivia is classified as high effort but low collection, and Zimbabwe is classified as high effort and high collection.[17] The implication is that Bolivia and Zimbabwe may not have significant room to increase tax collection substantially, given their structural characteristics, at least not without affecting broader economic objectives.

Political economy dynamics can certainly be a further constraining factor, beyond structural characteristics. Guatemala for instance has definite political economy constraints for raising further revenues. Political interference created instability in top management in the revenue agency during the early years of operation, leading to inconsistent policies and programmes. In addition, the Ministry of Finance allocated less funding than stipulated by law and revenue performance stagnated. The weak performance has also been attributed to outdated tax laws, tax expenditures, the effects of trade liberalization on customs revenue and widespread evasion (Mann 2004).

[16] When we initially conducted our analysis, the WDI data showed a spike in the tax ratio for Uganda in 2011, which implies a jump in the tax effort index. WDI data initially placed Uganda's tax/GDP ratio at 16.1 per cent in 2011. Two other sources we used, USAID (12.1 per cent) and AEO (12.7 per cent), indicate different figures, which were more consistent with each other than with WDI. Using these, the tax effort trend in Uganda is largely flat. However, in an updated version of WDI, Uganda's tax ratio for 2011 has been revised to 13.2 per cent, and the numbers in recent years to 2015 have been around 10–11 per cent. This would thus confirm our initial finding that the tax effort trend in Uganda has not changed a lot in recent years.

[17] We were unable to replicate these results despite using similar data. Results for Zimbabwe should be interpreted with caution as the data quality is likely to be questionable, and the ratios may be high due to the impact of inflationary and other economic crises on GDP.

Donor Involvement in Taxation and Public Financial Management

This section provides an overview of donor involvement in taxation and PFM efforts, including in the four case study countries. We complement data on donor involvement in taxation and PFM from the OECD-DAC Creditor Reporting System (CRS) with other, more contextual and qualitatively richer information sources. These include the Public Expenditure and Financial Accountability (PEFA) assessment framework, which assesses key elements of country PFM systems and scores the same on an ordinal scale (PEFA 2011). Additionally, we complement data from the Paris Declaration Monitoring Survey, which includes useful information gathered from both donor and recipient country sources (OECD 2011). The survey data provides insights into donor perceptions of country PFM systems, fiscal capacity and fiscal performance. The main limitation of both surveys (PEFA 2011; OECD 2011) is that they are relatively recent and are not carried out very frequently.[18]

As Fig. 2.3 shows, Uganda receives the largest amount in total ODA from all donors compared to the other three countries. Total ODA to Uganda exceeded the USD 2 billion/year mark in recent years or between USD 45 and USD 55 per capita (between 2009 and 2011). By comparison, the other case study countries, Bolivia, Guatemala and Zimbabwe, have never received even half the amount Uganda receives from donors, although on a per capita basis Bolivia and Zimbabwe display similar levels.[19] This trend coincides with the trend in aid to the PFM sector. As Fig. 2.4 shows, compared to the other countries, Uganda receives a large amount of aid targeted at taxation and PFM issues.

Which donors are important providers of PFM aid in the four case study countries?[20] Data from both the OECD-DAC CRS (2013b) and

[18] A new PEFA framework was introduced in 2016 to reflect reforms in PFM systems and good practices. The Paris Declaration Monitoring Survey, last conducted in 2011, has now been replaced by the 2014 Global Partnership Monitoring Framework.

[19] On a per capita basis, however, Bolivia received between USD 65 and USD 75; Guatemala around USD 27; and Zimbabwe around USD 55 over the same period.

[20] At the time of writing, data for Zimbabwe was not available for most years. However, more recent data from the OECD-DAC CRS database shows that ODA to the PFM sector in Zimbabwe for

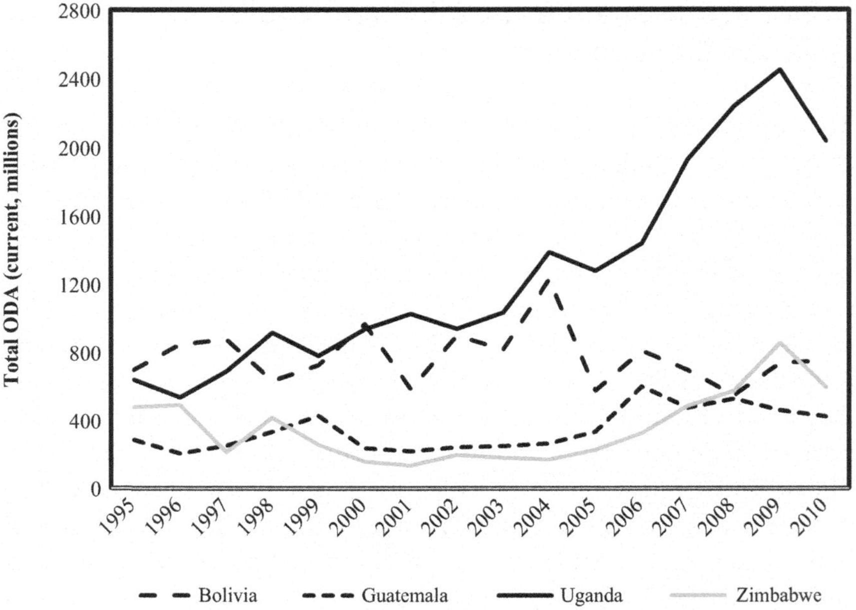

Fig. 2.3 Total ODA to Bolivia, Guatemala, Uganda and Zimbabwe (USD millions). (Source: Author elaboration using data from OECD (2013b))

the Paris Monitoring Survey (OECD 2011) indicate that the main providers of PFM assistance are multilateral agencies. In Uganda, the main provider of aid to the PFM sector in recent years has been the World Bank, through the IDA. Select bilateral donors such as the UK, Denmark, Norway, Netherlands, Ireland, Japan and Sweden have also been significant providers of PFM aid to Uganda. In contrast the main providers of PFM aid to Guatemala in recent years have been Japan, Germany, the Netherlands and the United States, whereas the main provider of PFM aid to Bolivia in recent years has been the Inter-American Development Bank.

What is the perception of donors of country PFM capacity and PFM systems? The Paris Monitoring Survey provides a sense of donor perceptions of country PFM systems and capacity, as Table 2.7 asks, "how

the period 2010–2017 was less than 1 per cent of total ODA, representing about USD 3.4 million, on average (OECD 2019).

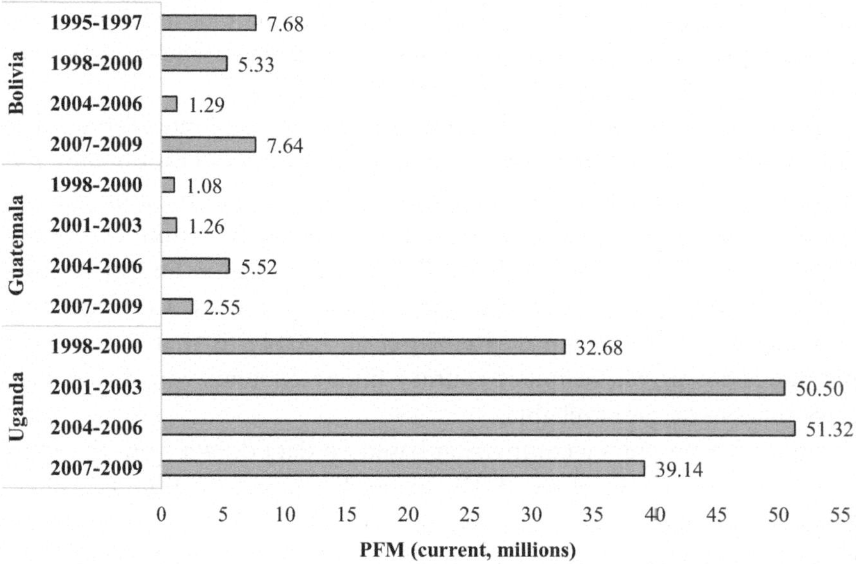

Fig. 2.4 ODA to the PFM sector in Bolivia, Guatemala and Uganda (USD millions). (Source: Author elaboration using data from OECD (2013b))

reliable are country PFM systems?" Donors rely on the World Bank's Country Policy and Institutional Assessment (CPIA) to rate the reliability of PFM systems from 1 (lowest) to 6 (highest) (OECD 2011). Bolivia's score remains at 3.5 in all three years of the survey (2005, 2007 and 2010). Uganda's score has deteriorated from 4.0 in 2005 and 2007 to 3.5 in 2010. Guatemala and Zimbabwe are not reported. It is interesting to note that despite providing significant support to building PFM capacity in Uganda over the years, donors perceive Uganda's PFM systems to have deteriorated in terms of reliability.[21]

The Paris Monitoring Survey allows further, albeit indirect, analysis of donor perception of country systems. The survey and related database comprise the results of separate but related questionnaires submitted to donor and recipient country representatives. Since the aim of the survey is to monitor compliance with the Paris Declaration on Aid Effectiveness,

[21] For some of the reasons (such as budget scandals) of this deteriorating donor perception, see Kjaer and Ulriksen (2014).

one of the key principles of which is the alignment of aid flows with national priorities, the survey and resultant database include data on indicators used to measure alignment (OECD 2011).

The donor questionnaire asks how much ODA the donor disbursed at the country level in 2010. In the recipient government questionnaire, the survey asks how much estimated ODA was recorded in the annual budget as grants, revenue or ODA loans. The closer the two numbers are the higher the share of aid that is channelled through country budget systems and thus aligned with national systems and priorities. Our tentative hypothesis here, following de Renzio et al. (2011), is that donors will provide more aid via recipient country budget systems where they perceive these to be more reliable.

Figure 2.5 provides a comparison based on data drawn from the Paris Monitoring Survey for three of the case study countries (OECD 2011).[22] Donors estimated they disbursed over USD 1.5 billion in ODA in Uganda; however, only around USD 900 million of this was recorded in Ugandan budget systems. The ratio for Uganda was around 60 per cent in 2010 and around 71 per cent as an average over the three years of the survey. By comparison, the ratio for Bolivia was only around 28 per cent in 2010 and around 37 per cent as an average over the three years of the survey. The ratio for Guatemala was only around 22 per cent in 2010 (Guatemala was not covered in the earlier years).

However, we should note that the monitoring survey and data have only been made available on three occasions (see also footnote 18). While they are useful in providing a sense of general trends, they do not go into detailed explanations in specific cases. One explanatory factor for the above trends could be the type of aid modality. Certain modalities (e.g. budget support) will be more reflected in country systems and on-budgets (i.e. disbursed through the government's budget) by definition and countries receiving this type of support may show higher percentages. Other types (such as technical support or direct support provided through local partners) may not be readily reflected on budget or in country systems.

[22] Differences between the Paris Monitoring Survey data and other OECD-DAC aid data may be because not all donors have participated in the Paris Monitoring Survey.

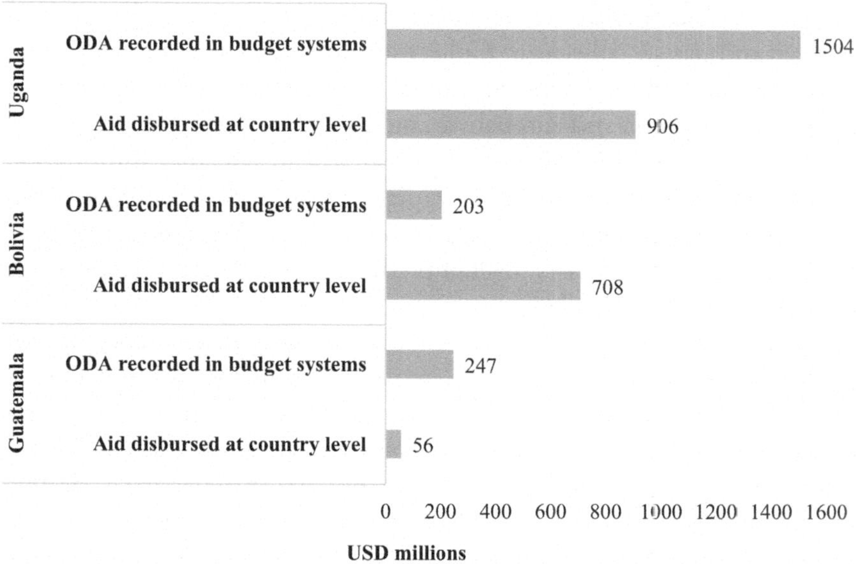

Fig. 2.5 Recipient assessment of ODA recorded in budget systems versus donor assessment of aid disbursed at the country level (USD millions). (Source: Author elaboration using data from OECD (2011). Note: Data based on USD 2010)

What do Public Expenditure and Financial Accountability PEFA assessments tell us about country PFM systems in the case study countries? The 2011 PEFA framework is based on individual country assessments. It provides information on 28 indicators that assess key elements of the PFM systems, including processes, institutions and legislature. There are four relevant tax indicators within the PEFA framework: aggregate revenue out-turn compared to the original budget (PI-3), transparency of taxpayer obligations and liabilities (PI-13), effectiveness of measures for taxpayer registration and assessment (PI-14) and effectiveness of collection of tax payments (PI-15). These indicators help provide more context around country fiscal capacity and performance.

Results of the PEFA assessments based on the 2011 PEFA framework (Bolivia, 2009; Guatemala, 2013; Uganda, 2012; Zimbabwe, 2012) are presented in Table 2.5. While Bolivia and Guatemala fare reasonably well on most measures, Uganda and Zimbabwe perform poorly by comparison. The main differences in performance result from discrepancies between revenue performance as predicted and reported in the national budget and actual collection. Collection on arrears and links between taxpayer registration systems and other systems have been identified as areas where Uganda and Zimbabwe could improve performance.

Furthermore, PEFA assessments provide useful reference information on donor involvement with the recipient country in the area of PFM, especially around budget support, and the predictability of donor engagement. Of the selected cases, overall predictability of budget support was only applicable in Uganda.

On providing financial information for budgeting and reporting on project and programme aid, completeness and timeliness of budget estimates by donors, frequency and coverage of reporting by donors on actual flows including the share of flows managed via national procedures, donors receive only a C grade in Bolivia. In Guatemala, donors receive an A grade on deviations from forecast budget support, but only D+ in providing financial information for budgeting, C in completeness and timeliness of budget estimates, D in frequency of reporting and coverage and C in the share of aid managed through national procedures.

Table 2.5 Taxation indicators in recent PEFA assessments in Bolivia, Guatemala, Uganda and Zimbabwe

	Bolivia (2009)	Guatemala (2013)	Uganda (2012)	Zimbabwe (2012)
Aggregate revenue out-turn compared to the original budget (PI-3)	A	B	D	D
Transparency of taxpayer obligations and liabilities (PI-13)	B+	B+	A	B
Effectiveness of measures for taxpayer registration and assessment (PI-14)	B+	B+	B	C+
Effectiveness of collection of tax payments (PI-15)	B+	B+	C+	D+

Source: Data from PEFA (2011)

Predictability of donor budget support in Uganda received a poor D grade. In two of the last three years, budget support fell short of forecast by more than 15 per cent and disbursement delays were commonplace. On most other areas, including the share of aid managed through national procedures, donors receive also a poor grade of D in Uganda (less than 50 per cent of aid funds are managed through national procedures in the years surveyed). In the case of Zimbabwe, there was no information on the predictability of donor budget support but donors also receive a poor grade of D on the share of aid managed through national procedures.

Despite calls for adherence with internationally agreed aid effectiveness principles, there seem to be significant gaps in recipient government estimates of promised donor support and actual support. PEFA assessments are largely consistent with other surveys such as the Paris Monitoring Survey, which have shown that there remains a significant distance between stated commitments to aid effectiveness principles and actual performance.

Conclusion

Expectations surrounding developing country DRM efforts continue to be high in the context of the 2030 Agenda for Sustainable Development. DRM is being emphasized as a self-sustaining development financing strategy, one that is preferable to foreign aid, increasingly even in the poorest countries. Our broad conclusion is that rhetoric fails to meet reality in terms of the role of fiscal performance in determining aid allocation. Donors are increasingly calling upon developing countries to improve fiscal performance. However, there is not much evidence to suggest that donors collectively pay requisite attention to fiscal performance when they make aid allocation decisions. As we pointed out earlier, this result may change when individual donors are considered.

The level of aid to strengthen tax systems at the aggregate level remains very low. Given the importance of taxation to state building, good governance and ultimately domestic accountability, not to mention the potentially high payoff in terms of aid resources invested, donors need to think of creative ways of stepping up such support. Increasing aid levels entirely unconditionally can create incentive problems; therefore, a graduated approach, linked for instance to revenue-related or institutional performance-related targets, could be worth considering in appropriate contexts. This is by no means a totally new idea given the extensive academic and policy literature on aid selectivity since the late 1990s. However, while the focus has been on providing aid to countries with good policies and institutions, we would argue that an additional dimension worth exploring is tying aid to tax and revenue performance.

Furthermore, taxation and DRM are as much about how revenue is collected as they are about how much is collected, a fact that was not always given much attention in post-2015 discussions leading to Agenda 2030. However, Agenda 2030 now contains goals related to inclusive societies and institutions (SDG 16) and means of implementation (SDG 17). That said, taxation needs its own data revolution to improve the availability and consistency of basic information. Donors have a role to play in this regard, as they have already done by investing in data initiatives (such as the setting up of the African Economic Outlook's fiscal performance database).

Several studies over the years have emphasized the importance of domestic ownership when it comes to progress in the area of taxation and development. One effective investment could be setting up knowledge and information sharing platforms among various donors on their experience in supporting tax capacity. Similarly, continued and increased support for south-south platforms, such as the African Tax Administration Forum and similar initiatives in Latin America and Asia, could have important longer term effects.

A key issue in terms of the role of donors in supporting DRM that rarely receives sufficient attention is the question of coordination versus fragmentation, and the high transactions costs associated with the same. Past research has shown that donors tend to herd into particular countries in terms of their support for DRM (Bhushan and Samy 2012; OECD 2012). Given the importance of country ownership, the burden of donor coordination for all practical purposes falls on the developing country partner. Donors would do well to both better coordinate their interventions and division of labour, as well as share their expectations in terms of payoffs more transparently.

Tax issues tend to be taken up purely from a technical capacity building perspective and issues like the importance of investing in independent policy research, public outreach, and engagement with the media, civil society and private sector groups get less attention. Broadening the stakeholder base involved in tax issues can have significant benefits, and remains an area donors could not only invest more in but also where they could share their own domestic experience (OECD 2013a).

Appendix

Table 2.6 Composition of tax revenue across case study countries

	Country	2007–2008	2008–2009	2009–2010	2010–2011	2011–2012
TAXY	Bolivia	23.80	22.30	23.36	27.40	26.40
	Guatemala	10.38	12.22	11.48	10.40	10.48
	Uganda	11.63	12.53	12.22	6.95	12.18
	Zimbabwe		4.00		20.10	27.90
CITY	Bolivia	2.30	2.90	0.50	3.90	4.10
	Guatemala	1.75	2.30	2.10	2.80	2.74
	Uganda	1.84	0.90	0.80	0.40	0.91
	Zimbabwe		0.60		1.00	3.40
PITY	Bolivia					
	Guatemala	0.28	0.10	0.30	0.30	0.37
	Uganda	1.51	2.80	1.90	1.10	1.91
	Zimbabwe		0.70		3.50	5.80
VATY	Bolivia	6.23	7.20	7.20	6.50	7.00
	Guatemala	5.20	6.60	6.10	4.90	5.09
	Uganda	3.67	4.00	4.30	2.30	3.85
	Zimbabwe		1.00		8.40	9.30

Source: Data from USAID (2013)

Note: *TAXY* tax-to-GDP, *CITY* corporate tax-to-GDP, *PITY* personal income tax-to-GDP, *VATY* value added tax-to-GDP

Table 2.7 Tax administration and capacity metrics (2011–2012)

	Avg cost	Avg tax staff
East Asia and Pacific	1.19	0.45
Central Europe and Central Asia	1.13	0.99
Latin America and Caribbean	1.26	0.33
Middle East and North Africa	3.17	0.46
South Asia	1.83	0.27
Sub-Saharan Africa	2.93	0.32
Western Europe	0.93	1.19
US and Canada	1.53	0.69

Source: Data from USAID (2013)

Table 2.8 Composition of tax revenue across income groups and regions

		Year				
		2007–2008	2008–2009	2009–2010	2010–2011	2011–2012
Low income	AvgCITY	2.42	2.16	2.12	2.23	2.44
	AvgPITY	1.70	1.79	2.02	2.32	3.70
	AvgVATY	3.65	4.07	4.52	4.33	5.09
	AvgTAXY	14.30	14.50	14.80	13.70	14.70
Lower middle income	AvgCITY	3.49	3.25	3.42	3.19	3.61
	AvgPITY	2.85	2.71	2.48	2.71	3.60
	AvgVATY	6.82	7.40	7.28	5.43	6.80
	AvgTAXY	20.40	20.50	19.50	18.30	18.20
Upper middle income	AvgCITY	3.61	3.43	3.45	3.40	3.11
	AvgPITY	3.39	3.43	3.37	2.75	3.85
	AvgVATY	7.09	6.94	6.81	6.34	7.02
	AvgTAXY	21.90	21.30	21.60	20.50	18.30
High income	AvgCITY	4.45	4.95	4.41	3.72	4.09
	AvgPITY	6.82	7.21	5.86	5.84	7.05
	AvgVATY	6.48	6.73	6.56	4.71	6.17
	AvgTAXY	26.00	24.30	23.80	25.40	20.00
		2007–2008	2008–2009	2009–2010	2010–2011	2011–2012
East Asia and Pacific	AvgCITY	5.51	5.53	4.20	4.01	4.77
	AvgPITY	3.61	4.20	3.58	3.60	6.46
	AvgVATY	4.90	5.21	5.26	3.40	5.51
	AvgTAXY	19.10	19.56	17.85	17.53	18.40
Central Europe and Central Asia	AvgCITY	2.75	2.64	2.74	2.20	1.72
	AvgPITY	3.40	3.42	3.21	2.56	3.00
	AvgVATY	8.40	9.06	8.63	8.17	8.71
	AvgTAXY	24.71	23.48	24.32	23.08	18.30

(continued)

Table 2.8 (continued)

		2007–2008	2008–2009	2009–2010	2010–2011	2011–2012
Latin America and Caribbean	AvgCITY	3.99	3.14	3.86	3.39	4.06
	AvgPITY	2.65	2.13	2.11	2.22	4.43
	AvgVATY	6.09	6.28	6.36	5.64	6.69
	AvgTAXY	20.14	20.32	20.64	18.41	20.06
Middle East and North Africa	AvgCITY	3.12	4.44	4.03	4.70	4.23
	AvgPITY	2.98	2.31	2.34	1.75	2.72
	AvgVATY	6.82	7.07	7.58	2.90	5.43
	AvgTAXY	16.97	17.08	14.64	15.37	12.69
South Asia	AvgCITY	1.65	2.42	2.42	2.18	2.20
	AvgPITY	0.65	0.87	1.35	1.38	1.52
	AvgVATY	4.06	3.75	3.58	1.79	2.74
	AvgTAXY	10.13	10.45	10.60	11.50	11.05
Sub-Saharan Africa	AvgCITY	2.84	2.51	2.66	2.65	2.96
	AvgPITY	2.38	2.48	2.61	2.98	4.06
	AvgVATY	3.77	4.00	4.32	5.17	5.34
	AvgTAXY	16.72	16.23	17.46	16.23	16.90
Western Europe	AvgCITY	3.47	3.96	3.51	2.98	2.85
	AvgPITY	7.46	8.16	7.06	8.46	6.92
	AvgVATY	6.98	7.43	7.30	6.77	6.53
	AvgTAXY	29.11	28.26	27.84	30.20	21.71
US and Canada	AvgCITY	2.32	2.85	1.35	2.30	3.00
	AvgPITY	8.00	9.40	6.65	9.55	12.60
	AvgVATY	2.27	2.00	1.70	0.85	1.70
	AvgTAXY	15.49	16.40	13.83	18.99	16.45

Source: Data from USAID (2013)

References

AEO (African Economic Outlook). 2013. Database on African Fiscal Performance. Accessed 15 April 2014. http://www.africaneconomicoutlook.org/en/database-on-african-fiscal-performance.

Alesina, Alberto, and David Dollar. 2000. Who Gives Foreign Aid to Whom and Why? *Journal of Economic Growth* 5 (1): 33–63.

Alesina, Alberto, and Beatrice Weder. 2002. Do Corrupt Governments Receive Less Foreign Aid? *American Economic Review* 92 (4): 1126–1137.

Berthelemy, Jean-Claude, and Ariane Tichit. 2004. Bilateral Donors' Aid Allocation Decisions—A Three-Dimensional Panel Analysis. *International Review of Economics and Finance* 13 (3): 253–274.

Bhushan, Aniket, and Yiagadeesen Samy. 2012. *Aid and Taxation: Is Sub-Saharan African Different?* North-South Institute Research Report (May). Accessed 19 May 2020. http://www.nsi-ins.ca/wp-content/uploads/2013/02/2012-Aid-and-Taxation.pdf.

Bhushan, Aniket, Yiagadeesen Samy, and Kemi Medu. 2013. *Financing the Post-2015 Development Agenda: Domestic Revenue Mobilization in Africa*. The North-South Institute (September). Accessed 15 April 2014. http://www.nsi-ins.ca/publications/financing-the-post-2015-development-agenda-domestic-revenue-mobilization-in-africa/.

Clist, Paul. 2011. 25 Years of Aid Allocation Practice: Whither Selectivity? *World Development* 39 (10): 1724–1734.

Collier, Paul, and David Dollar. 2002. Aid Allocation and Poverty Reduction. *European Economic Review* 46 (8): 1475–1500.

Dollar, David, and Victoria Levin. 2004. *The Increasing Selectivity of Foreign Aid, 1984–2002*. Policy Research Working Paper No. 3299. Washington, DC: World Bank.

Freedom House. 2013. *Freedom in the World Comparative and Historical Data*. Accessed 8 September 2013. http://www.freedomhouse.org/report-types/freedom-world#.U2zbO2pOXV8.

Gupta, Sanjeev, Benedict Clements, Alexander Pivovarsky, and Erwin R. Tiongson. 2003. *Foreign Aid and Revenue Response: Does the Composition of Aid Matter?* IMF Working Paper No. 03/176: Washington, DC: International Monetary Fund.

International Centre for Tax and Development (ICTD) and United Nations University-World Institute for Development Economics Research (UNU-WIDER). 2019. Government Revenue Dataset. Accessed 25 September 2019. https://www.wider.unu.edu/project/government-revenue-dataset.

Kaufmann, Daniel, Aart Kraay, and Massimo Mastruzzi. 2009. *Governance Matters VII: Aggregate and Individual Governance Indicators, 1996–2008*. World Bank Policy Research Working Paper No. 4978. Washington, DC: World Bank.

———. 2019. The Worldwide Governance Indicators (WGI) Project. Accessed 18 July 2019. http://info.worldbank.org/governance/wgi/#home.

Kjaer, Anne-Mette, and Marianne Ulriksen. 2014. *From Consensus to Contention: Changing Revenue and Policy Dynamics in Uganda*. PDRM Working Paper No. 2014-21. Geneva: United Nations Research Institute for Social Development.

Le, Tuan Minh, Blanca Moreno-Dodson, and Nihal Bayraktar. 2012. *Tax Capacity and Tax Effort: Extended Cross-Country Analysis from 1994 to 2009.* Policy Research Working Paper No. 6252. Washington, DC: World Bank.

Mann, Arthur. 2004. *Are Semi-Autonomous Revenue Authorities the Answer to Tax Administration Problems in Developing Countries? A Practical Guide.* Fiscal Reform in Support of Trade Liberalization Project. Washington, DC: USAID.

Neumayer, Eric. 2003a. Is Respect for Human Rights Rewarded? An Analysis of Total Bilateral and Multilateral Aid Flows. *Human Rights Quarterly* 25 (2): 510–527.

———. 2003b. Do Human Rights Matter in Bilateral Aid Allocation? A Quantitative Analysis of 21 Donor Countries. *Social Science Quarterly* 84 (3): 650–666.

Organisation for Economic Co-operation and Development (OECD). 2011. *Survey on Monitoring the Paris Declaration.* OECD Publishing. (See Also Related Database, Data Annexes and Country Tables).

———. 2012. *Identification and Monitoring of Potentially Under-Aided Countries.* Background study for DAC High Level Meeting (December).

———. 2013a. *Tax and Development: Aid Modalities for Strengthening Tax Systems.* Paris: OECD Publishing.

——— 2013b. Creditor Reporting System (CRS) Database. Accessed 29 November 2013. http://stats.oecd.org/Index.aspx.

———. 2013c. QWIDS (Query Wizard for International Development Statistics) Database. Accessed 8 September 2013. http://stats.oecd.org/qwids/.

———. 2019. Creditor Reporting System (CRS) Database. Accessed 24 September 2019. http://stats.oecd.org/Index.aspx.

Public Expenditure and Financial Accountability (PEFA). 2011. *Public Financial Management Performance Measurement Framework.* Washington, DC: PEFA Secretariat. Accessed 15 April 2014. http://www.pefa.org/sites/pefa.org/files/attachments/PMFEng-finalSZreprint04-12_1.pdf.

———. 2016. *Framework for Assessing Public Financial Management.* Washington, DC: PEFA Secretariat. Accessed 12 August 2017. https://pefa.org/content/pefa-framework.

de Renzio, Paolo, Matt Andrews, and Zac Mills. 2011. *Does Donor Support to Public Financial Management Reforms in Developing Countries Work? An Analytical Study of Quantitative Cross-Country Evidence.* Working Paper No. 329. London: Overseas Development Institute (ODI).

UNRISD (United Nations Research Institute for Social Development). 2012. *The Politics of Domestic Resource Mobilization for Social Development*. Project Brief No. 1. Geneva: UNRISD.

———. 2013a. *An Anti-Development Model? Overcoming Obstacles to Domestic Resource Mobilization in Zimbabwe*. UNRISD Project Brief No. 6. Geneva: UNRISD.

———. 2013b. *Contestation and Social Change. The Politics of Domestic Resource Mobilization in Bolivia*. UNRISD Project Brief No. 7. Geneva: UNRISD.

———. 2013c. *Mobilizing Domestic Revenues in Aid-Dependent Uganda*. UNRISD Project Brief No. 8. Geneva: UNRISD.

———. 2015. *New Alliances for Social Development. Mobilizing Resources in Nicaragua*. UNRISD Project Brief No. 13 (December 2015). Geneva: UNRISD.

USAID. 2013. *Collecting Taxes Full Data Source*. Washington, DC. Accessed 12 August 2017. https://www.usaid.gov/data/dataset/cdeb8a1b-3440-4e88-b6cb-81b2428f8cea.

World Bank. 2013. World Development Indicators Database. Accessed 8 September 2013. http://data.worldbank.org/data-catalog/world-development-indicators.

Worldwide Governance Indicators Database. 2013. Accessed 8 September 2013. http://info.worldbank.org/governance/wgi/index.aspx#home.

3

Domestic Resource Mobilization for Social Transfers in Sub-Saharan Africa: Can Foreign Aid Act as a Catalyst?

Cécile Cherrier

Introduction

Sub-Saharan African has recently broken with a historical trend of limited economic growth, but this has yet to translate into massive improvements in human development outcomes. Low-income African countries experienced an annual growth rate of real per capita GDP above 3.5 per cent in the early 2010s (IMF 2015). After slowing sharply in 2016, economic growth in sub-Saharan Africa continues to recover steadily and is forecasted to firm to an average of 3.6 per cent in 2019–2020 (World Bank 2018). Yet, the vast majority of these countries continue to show low human development according to the composite Human Development Index (UNDP 2013). Social transfers offer great potential for helping the continent rise to its major development challenge:

C. Cherrier (✉)
Overseas Development Institute, London, UK
e-mail: c.cherrier@odi.org.uk

K. Hujo (ed.), *The Politics of Domestic Resource Mobilization for Social Development*, Social Policy in a Development Context,
https://doi.org/10.1007/978-3-030-37595-9_3

sustaining the pace of economic growth and making it more inclusive. The term "social transfers" shall refer here to a specific subset of social policy and social protection instruments. As understood in this chapter, social transfers are non-contributory,[1] publicly financed, direct, regular and predictable resource transfers (in cash or in kind) to vulnerable individuals.[2] Thus defined, social transfers can take many different forms, ranging from school feeding to food vouchers to cash transfers.

Providing direct resources to poor and vulnerable people in a predictable and regular manner has a proven track record of effectiveness in fighting poverty and inequality, as well as supporting inclusive socioeconomic development. Brazil saw a massive reduction of poverty and hunger following the introduction of Bolsa Família, its national social transfer programme.[3] Could similar success stories spread all over sub-Saharan Africa? Nothing could be less certain. In low-income African countries, public investments in social transfers, and social protection in general, remain relatively small; non-contributory social protection measures tend to be ad-hoc and temporary (AU 2008; ILO 2014). In environments where social transfers are most needed, such as low-income countries where poverty is widespread, national policy makers are often reluctant to introduce them. This has to do with a general reserved attitude towards the innovation that such a pro-poor policy instrument still represents in these countries. One common apprehension also concerns the significant budgetary commitment that such a policy represents over the long run.[4]

---

[1] Meaning no direct personal financial contribution is required from individuals as a condition of entitlement to receive benefits—in contrast with the contributory benefits of social insurance schemes.

[2] Such a definition differs with that of the ILO, which considers all social protection benefits to represent social transfers (Behrendt et al. 2014), but is consistent with the way the term is used in various countries and international organizations—see, for instance, Devereux and Sabates-Wheeler (2004), DFID (2005) and Grosh et al. (2008).

[3] Bolsa Família reaches almost a quarter of the population—transferring an average of BRL 167 (USD 49) per family per month to over 14 million families in January 2015, as long as they fulfil education and health conditionality (Lavinas et al. 2017). It has contributed to decreasing hunger from 22.8 million people in 1992 to 13.6 million in 2012 (FAO 2013), and the poverty rate from 36 per cent in 2001 to 11 per cent in 2011—social assistance schemes, including Bolsa Família, are estimated to have accounted for 15 per cent of this reduction in poverty (Lavinas 2013; Lavinas et al. 2017).

[4] See, for instance, Barrientos and Hulme (2008), Niño-Zarazúa et al. (2010) and Samson et al. (2006).

The international evidence base on the multidimensional impacts of social transfers is growing quickly, in particular for social cash transfers.[5] Reviewing the evidence base on the impact of cash transfers, Bastagli et al. (2016: 13) conclude:

> Clear and significant impacts are especially well documented for intended outcomes, such as expenditure on food and other household items, access to schooling or use of health services. Importantly, cash transfers are shown to have impacts on a range of outcomes simultaneously, for instance greater school attendance is consistently accompanied by a reduction in child labour. There is also robust evidence that cash transfers can affect first- and second-order outcomes that are generally not the immediate focus of many programmes, such as savings, productive investments and diversification of livelihood strategies. Positive impacts on investment in livestock and agricultural inputs are consistently found across [conditional cash transfers] in Latin America and [unconditional cash transfers] in sub-Saharan Africa, suggesting that cash transfers can not only play a role in reducing poverty by redistributing resources to the poor, but can also foster their economic autonomy and self-sufficiency.

Empirical evidence from seven cash transfer schemes in sub-Saharan Africa reveals that all of them generate significant spillovers in the local economy. The nominal programme income multipliers range from 1.27 to 2.52—that is, each US dollar transferred to a poor household adds more than a US dollar to total income in the local economy (Thome et al. 2016). Using rigorous evaluations conducted on large-scale government unconditional cash transfers in sub-Saharan Africa, Handa et al. (2017) refute six common negative perceptions associated with cash transfers: cash transfers would induce higher spending on alcohol or tobacco, be fully consumed (rather than invested), create dependency (reduce participation in productive activities), increase fertility, lead to negative community-level economic impacts (including price distortion and inflation) and be fiscally unsustainable. Many other studies have shown that

[5] See, for instance, Arnold et al. (2011), Barrientos and Niño-Zarazúa (2010) and Bastagli et al. (2016).

basic social protection not only can be made affordable in low-income countries, but can also be a pathway to development.[6]

Encouraged by this evidence, foreign aid actors have been allocating resources to promote and support the expansion of social transfers in low-income countries as a key driver for inclusive development. Donor-funded social transfer pilot projects flourished throughout sub-Saharan Africa in the 2000s in an attempt to demonstrate the value of the approach and convince national decision makers to adopt and finance pro-poor social transfer policies. This trend accelerated in the aftermath of the 2008 global food, fuel and financial crisis, notably with the launch by the United Nations system of the global Social Protection Floor initiative, a conceptual catalyst for the international community to advocate for the development of a "set of basic social rights, services and facilities that the global citizen should enjoy" (CEB 2009; ILO and WHO 2009: 4). A new turning point was reached at the 2012 International Labour Conference with the adoption of Recommendation 202, which calls for the establishment of "nationally defined sets of basic social security guarantees which secure protection aimed at preventing or alleviating poverty, vulnerability and social exclusion" (ILC 2012: 2; ILO and IMF 2012). For over a decade now, aid actors have conducted a range of activities to promote the use of social transfers in low-income countries, such as capacity-building events, feasibility studies, pilot projects to generate context-specific evidence of social transfer effectiveness, and direct financial support to nascent social transfer schemes. The objective has been to provide incentives for national governments to eventually establish domestically funded, permanent social protection schemes, which are governed by national administrations, enshrined in national law and monitored by beneficiaries and civil society.

But at the beginning of the 2010s, after a decade of such aid efforts in sub-Saharan Africa, a number of prominent scholars voiced concerns about the likelihood of such aid initiatives to translate into sustainable policy change.[7] They alerted on what they perceived as serious limitations in the capacity of aid actors to promote local ownership around social

[6] See, for instance, ILO (2008, 2010), OECD (2009) and Townsend (2009).

[7] See Devereux et al. (2010), Hickey et al. (2009), Holmqvist (2010) and Niño-Zarazúa et al. (2010).

transfers, and encourage a shift away from time-bound foreign aid grants towards sustainable domestic funding.[8] Where do we stand today? Has foreign aid had any catalytic effect on the mobilization of domestic resources for social transfers in low-income African countries? This chapter investigates this question, assessing the critiques expressed a few years ago in the light of recent empirical evidence drawn from 12 African case studies. Interestingly, the evidence points to alternative conclusions, suggesting aid can have a catalytic effect.

Prominent Views on Aid for Social Transfers

The main critiques expressed at the beginning of the 2010s revolved around the view that aid had remained the main direct trigger for the introduction of social transfer schemes in sub-Saharan Africa, and that such externally driven processes were unlikely to bring about sustainable policy change. By granting sufficient resources to make programmes possible, aid actors managed to implement social transfer schemes in contexts where there was little government support or initiative for this, even if only reluctantly accepted by a recipient government "as a necessary price to pay to access financial aid in spite of conflicting policy preferences" (Whitfield and Fraser 2009: 4). In 2010, Devereux and White argued that, with some notable exceptions, much of the impetus for social protection in Africa still actually came from foreign aid actors. The critical question was thus whether such aid-triggered social transfer schemes could be transformed into nationally owned, domestically financed, sustainable schemes.

Devereux et al. (2010) underlined that foreign aid actors also tended to be directly in charge of the implementation of these (pilot) schemes, and they suggested a low degree of national ownership of these schemes. Devereux and White (2008: 10) further advanced that foreign aid actors' pilot projects "create temporary islands of access to internationally financed social welfare. […] but they are unlikely ever to scale up into national programmes, because they are not 'government owned' from

[8] See, in particular, Devereux et al. (2010) and Niño-Zarazúa et al. (2010).

inception". Niño-Zarazúa et al. (2010) also claimed that these new (and small) social transfer schemes were almost entirely funded by foreign aid. These scholars concluded that with low degrees of national ownership, there was little prospect for externally driven processes to encourage a subsequent mobilization of domestic financial resources.

In a recent study, Ortiz et al. (2015) indicate reasons as to why it may be difficult for such schemes to transition to national ownership. They conclude that fiscal space[9] for social protection exists in all countries, even the poorest ones, but budgetary decisions are ultimately political decisions, which prioritize certain expenditures over others. Every country has to follow its own political process and define, through its own budgeting and planning process, which resources to mobilize to finance which type of social transfers (Wildavsky and Caiden 2004). A decisive element is thus the political will[10] of a government to allocate domestic resources to social transfers; and the politics around this are complex.

Unlike some other forms of social protection, such as contributory social health insurance, social transfers need to be fully funded by public resources. A government willing to finance a new social transfer scheme may consider a number of financing options, notably: reallocating spending; increasing revenues by raising taxes; tapping into newly discovered or exploited natural resources; obtaining aid grants; and/or borrowing.[11] Each of these options would mobilize different types of revenue (such as income taxes, mineral rents or aid grants). For each type of revenue, decisions would be made by a different set of actors in different bargaining spheres, and social transfer policies can be expected to be determined by both those who benefit from them and those who pay for them (Ulriksen 2013).

A common feature of most low-income countries is that they mobilize only a small share of their revenues through taxation, and face many tax

[9] Fiscal space can be defined as "the availability of budgetary room that allows a government to provide resources for a desired purpose without any prejudice to the sustainability of a government's financial position" (Heller 2005: 3).

[10] Political will can be defined as "the determination of an individual or a group of political actors to do and say thing that will produce a desired outcome" (Manor 2004: 1).

[11] See, for instance, Cichon et al. (2004), Durán-Valverde and Pacheco (2012), Grosh et al. (2008), Ortiz et al. (2015) and Ulriksen (2013).

policy challenges (Moore 2013). Many low-income countries remain dependent on commodity exports and rely heavily on easy-to-collect taxes such as international trade taxes (UNRISD 2010: chapter 8). This makes them vulnerable to price volatility and deterioration in terms of trade observed over the past decades, and tends to crowd out other types of taxation. Trade liberalization, in particular tariff reduction, which has been a condition for countries to access loans by international financial institutions (IFIs), has made it difficult for low-income countries to rely on trade taxes to finance social policies. This has made tax replacement crucial, but many low-income countries have struggled to replace the easy-to-collect sources of revenue with the hard-to-collect ones (value added tax, income tax, property tax). The context of high economic informality that prevails in most low-income countries generates a taxation trap—a vicious circle where a low taxation level weakens state credibility and capacity in providing public goods, further weakening the justifications for the citizens to pay taxes, and contributing to maintaining high poverty levels (Sindzingre 2009).

Meanwhile, the high level of aid dependency of many low-income countries may make them particularly sensitive to international influence (Monchuk 2014)—for instance, having large aid-funded projects implemented by non-governmental organizations (NGO) can shape local practices and inform future policies. But Devereux et al. (2010: 4) observed that aid-supported social transfer projects were "rarely fully integrated into local and national policy processes, so they generate little political traction". Taking stock of progress towards the expansion of social protection in Africa, they concluded, "there is still a long way to go in many countries, while in others progress appears to have stalled, with no clear consensus among domestic and external stakeholders on the way forward" (Devereux et al. 2010: 1). Niño-Zarazúa et al. (2010: 17) further deplored that "donors have not engaged productively with the politics of social protection" in Africa towards shifting away from time-bound foreign aid grants towards sustainable domestic funding. They concluded:

> there is a pressing need for donors to become more attuned to the politics of social protection in Africa and to align their efforts more adroitly in support of forms of social protection that are likely to foster the growth of

> political constituencies (elite or mass or combined) that will support the evolution and public financing of long-term social protection policies. (Niño-Zarazúa et al. 2010: 24)

Looking at the first years of social protection promotion, Hickey (2011: 2) suggested that aid actors are unlikely to be able to "promote progressive social contracts around social protection without significant reforms to the way in which aid currently works". In a rather provocative article, Freeland (2013) implied that social protection works where there is a strong government (as in Ethiopia, Rwanda, Botswana or South Africa) and/or a strong civil society (as in South Africa or Bangladesh), but does not work where there are strong donors (as in Malawi or Zambia).

A few years later, does the evidence still support these views? Can foreign aid actors be found to have successfully enabled the emergence of a permanent, scaled-up and nationally owned social transfer scheme in a low-income African country context?

Methodology

The approach adopted to look into this question has been to examine cases of (at least partial) success in terms of policy uptake, and investigate the degree of involvement of foreign aid actors, if any, and the effect that this has had on the sustainability of the schemes. This methodology implied the selection of cases meeting all the following criteria (without prejudging the involvement of aid actors in their early development): the social transfer scheme was introduced in a sub-Saharan African country with a low-income economy (context of the research)[12]; it operates on a multi-year or long-term basis; it is domestically (co-)funded; and it benefits a sizable portion of the population.[13] For this last criterion, the threshold was arbitrarily set at 1 per cent of the total population, a

[12] We used the World Bank's classification based on estimated gross national income per capita at the time the scheme was introduced—the country's classification may have changed since.

[13] This had to hold true as of September 2013 when the case selection process took place.

threshold that proved empirically relevant (setting the threshold much higher would have resulted in a very small set of eligible cases, too small for a meaningful study; setting the threshold much lower would have resulted in including all sorts of small initiatives, including isolated pilot projects) but shows how little significance social transfer schemes have at present, except for some large ones. Lastly, since recent experiences with social transfers (and foreign aid actors' influence) were of primary interest for this study, an additional selection criterion was used: the scheme was introduced in the 1990s or 2000s (Cherrier 2016).

Based on global and regional reviews of social transfer schemes,[14] a long list of cases meeting all these different criteria was established in September 2013. Using maximum variation sampling, 12 cases were purposively selected from this long list[15]: Cabo Verde's Pensão Social Mínima (PSM); Ethiopia's Productive Safety Net Programme (PSNP); Ghana's Livelihoods Empowerment Against Poverty (LEAP) programme; Kenya's Cash Transfers for Orphans and Vulnerable Children (CT-OVC); Kenya's Hunger Safety Net Programme (HSNP); Lesotho's Old Age Pension (OAP); Malawi's Farm Input Subsidy Programme (FISP); Mozambique's Programa de Subsídio Social Básico (PSSB); Rwanda's Vision 2020 Umurenge Programme (VUP); Uganda's Social Assistance Grants for Empowerment (SAGE); Zambia's Social Cash Transfer (SCT) scheme; and Zimbabwe's Basic Education Assistance Module (BEAM).

A simple framework was developed to guide data collection and analysis through a retrospective process tracing approach aimed at tracking the pathways that led to the mobilization of public resources—domestic revenue and/or official development aid—to introduce the selected social transfer scheme.[16] The starting point for within-case analysis was the introduction of the selected social transfer scheme at scale, or in its current form if it was still at an early development stage. While some social

[14] Devereux and Cipryk (2009), Ellis et al. (2009), Garcia and Moore (2012), Grosh et al. (2008).

[15] Twelve was estimated to be the right number to achieve a balance between depth and breadth, that is, to have a sufficient number of cases to establish patterns while keeping the set small enough to allow a detailed analysis of each case within the resources available for this research.

[16] The proposed framework builds on the Drivers of Change approach adopted by DFID (2004), as well as Hickey's work to conceptualize the politics of social protection (Hickey 2006, 2008, 2009, 2011).

transfer schemes will have been introduced at scale, others will have been developed in a progressive manner, through successive phases of testing and refining, until they reach their intended full scale. The policy-making dynamics are likely to differ within each phase—new actors may get involved; new ideas, for instance, in regard to the result of an initial pilot phase, may inform decisions; etc. In such a case, the framework was used to guide phase-specific analyses. A major change in funding arrangements and/or design would mark the transition from one phase to the next, within the broader conception phase.

Through this phase-specific analytical approach, the framework invited to examine the following key aspects of the adopted policy (*policy outcome*[17]): funding arrangements; technical and institutional design; and level of national ownership. National ownership can be considered a continuous rather than discrete variable. In an initial attempt to define clear parameters that could guide a comparative analysis and approximate the notion of national ownership, we identified a set of indicators easily measurable from any set of basic project data. In line with the discussion above, we focus on three dimensions: the legal dimension, the budgetary dimension and the operational (or policy) dimension.[18] The proposed set of indicators and related thresholds is presented in Table 3.1. In this first approach, the thresholds for the budgetary commitment indicator were arbitrarily set—their appropriateness was however subsequently empirically confirmed.[19] Using this simple tool, an aid-driven pilot project funded by a bilateral donor and implemented by an international NGO would rank very low, and a fully institutionalized scheme would rank very high. Whenever possible, additional indicators were considered for a sharper analysis, as suggested in Cherrier (2016).

Proceeding with the retrospective process tracing analysis, the framework was intended to help organize the different triggers and conducive factors that have led to this policy outcome (*policy process*), categorizing

[17] Here, the term "policy outcome" refers to the resulting shape of the social transfer policy/scheme, and not to the impact of that policy.

[18] This choice of dimensions echoes the three prerequisites to the introduction of a social transfer scheme Samson et al. (2006) distinguish: political will, fiscal space, and technical and administrative capacity.

[19] The different co-funded schemes reviewed could be distributed between the suggested low, moderate and high categories.

Table 3.1 A first approach to assessing the degree of national ownership

Dimension	Indicator	Thresholds	Values
Legal commitment	Nature of the document setting eligibility & operational rules	• Law/decree • Adopted national policy only • Project document only	High Moderate Low
Budgetary commitment	Percentage of scheme budget covered by domestic resources	• 100%—Fully domestically funded • > 60%—Mainly domestically funded • 40–60%—Domestically & aid funded • < 40%—Largely aid funded • 0%—Fully funded by aid resources	Very high High Moderate Low Very low
Operational commitment	Profile of the main bodies responsible for the delivery & oversight of the scheme	• National bodies only • Both national & international bodies • International bodies only	High Moderate Low

Source: Cherrier (2016)

them into events, actors, ideas, institutions and structural features. Doing so, it focused on distinguishing, as much as possible, between influencing factors of a national, regional or global nature. Integrating deductive and inductive approaches, the framework was refined in parallel to the first steps of the empirical research.

Three methods were used to collect a mix of secondary and primary data. Secondary data was drawn from an extensive review of white and grey literature—academic publications, evaluation reports, strategy papers, activity reports, media articles, etc. This in-depth documentary analysis was complemented and triangulated with primary data collected through an online survey (66 complete responses collected) and key informant interviews (17 persons interviewed) with individuals directly involved in the development of one (or more) of the selected schemes.[20]

[20] See Cherrier (2016) for details on how this multiple-case study was conducted between December 2013 and February 2015.

For each of the selected cases, data analysis was conducted in successive steps. The purpose of the initial descriptive phase was to: (1) depict the salient *policy features* of the scheme at scale, or in its current form if it is still at an early development stage; and (2) establish a chronology of events, that is, outlining the *pace of development* and its different phases. This provided the necessary basis for moving on to a more analytical phase. This second phase required phase-specific analyses to: (3) isolate and classify the main *triggers and conducive factors*, distinguishing among them those related to foreign aid actors; and (4) relate the latter to resulting policy features. This enabled determining the influence, if any, of foreign aid on the emergence and features of the selected scheme.

Empirical Evidence from Twelve African Cases

Findings drawn from this multiple-case study reveal a different picture from the views expressed by prominent scholars only a few years ago. First, they show that a number of recent large-scale social transfer schemes in fact have (also) domestic origins—that is, the origins of the different schemes do not fall in any clear-cut categories, such as donor-driven versus nationally instigated process. Second, recent evidence suggests that all of these schemes, including those heavily supported by foreign aid actors, have resulted in moves towards national ownership and investment of domestic resources.

Influence of Foreign Aid in the Origins of the Selected Schemes

Unravelling the origins of the 12 selected schemes establishes foreign aid actors as important players in the mobilization of resources for social transfers. Influential aid actors have included international financial institutions recommending the reform of costly subsidy policies,[21] agen-

[21] Price subsidies, pervasive in low-income countries, came under renewed scrutiny during the sharp increases in food and fuel prices in 2007–2008, when many countries increased or planned

cies specialized in social protection advocating for coverage extension and humanitarian actors calling for more cost-effective ways to provide assistance in protracted crises. Eventually, four broad types of origin stories have emerged in regard to the role played by foreign aid actors. This typology is summarized in Table 3.2. They reflect various degrees of involvement of aid actors in the policy process, from no involvement in Type I to a very high involvement in Type IV. Also, while Types I and III would tend to represent the introduction of a new initiative, Types II and IV would tend to emerge from the restructuring of an existing measure—a government-led programme in the case of Type II, and recurrent aid-funded emergency transfers in the case of Type IV.

The origins of Lesotho's OAP and Malawi's FISP fall into what is here qualified as Type I. These cases illustrate a situation where a scheme emerges out of domestic political dynamics in the absence of specific support by development partners, or even against the advice of international financial institutions. In regard to foreign actors' involvement, these two cases differ slightly. While Lesotho's OAP has remained a fully domestically funded initiative, Malawi's FISP has received direct donor support later in its development, although accompanied by recurrent government-donor disagreements.

In contrast to the two cases above, a social transfer scheme may grow out of rather smooth cooperation between a government and its development partners. In what we qualify as Type II origins, foreign aid actors act in support of domestic efforts to restructure existing assistance programmes for more efficiency and financial sustainability, often with the idea to progressively consolidate a nascent national social protection system. Three of the selected schemes fall in this category. In Mozambique, the PSSB was born in a context of civil war as a measure to mitigate the adverse consequences of structural adjustment and was expanded to accompany the reform of a subsidy system that was deemed unsustainable. In Cabo Verde, the PSM arose from the desire to streamline disparate, embryonic social pension schemes. In both cases, donors have played

to increase them. Unsustainable fiscal burdens, along with negative spillover effects, encouraged discussions about reforming these policies. Social transfers were promoted to shield the poor from subsidy cuts.

Table 3.2 A typology of origin stories of social transfers in Sub-Saharan Africa

Type	Storyline	Main characteristics of the initial phase	Illustrative cases
I	Domestic initiative to expand benefits rooted in national historical, geographical, political and cultural factors	• Process initiated by ruling elites, not necessarily within a social protection agenda • Initial design defined within state bodies • Measure funded out of general revenues, at least initially without direct aid support	• Lesotho's OAP • Malawi's FISP
II	Restructuring of a domestically funded social policy measure as a process of retrenchment, economic restructuring or system consolidation	• Process initiated by ruling elites as part of efforts to sustain the assistance system • Initial design defined within state bodies, possibly with foreign aid support • Measure funded out of general revenues, with possible aid co-funding	• Cabo Verde's MSP • Mozambique's PSSB • Zimbabwe's BEAM
III	Aid-supported initiative to expand antipoverty or social protection provisions informed by global poverty reduction and social protection agendas	• Context of PRSP-framed development • Process supported by aid actors and ministry in charge of social protection • Initial design defined between government and aid actors • Measure funded with substantial levels of aid support	• Ghana's LEAP • Kenya's CT-OVC • Rwanda's VUP • Uganda's SAGE • Zambia's SCT
IV	Aid-supported initiative to restructure recurrent aid-funded emergency transfers in a context of protracted crises	• Context of recurrent large-scale food crises • Process promoted by aid actors, possibly with ministry in charge of rural development • Initial design largely influenced by aid actors • Measure primarily funded by foreign aid	• Ethiopia's PSNP • Kenya's HSNP

a supportive role through technical and financial assistance, primarily through budget support. In Zimbabwe, the BEAM results from the redesign of a poorly performing targeted school fee waiver programme.

The cases of Kenya's CT-OVC, Zambia's SCT, Rwanda's VUP, Ghana's LEAP and Uganda's SAGE exemplify how, when Poverty Reduction Strategy Papers (PRSP)[22] strongly influence development strategies in low-income countries, a social transfer scheme may emerge out of specific aid-supported initiatives informed by global poverty reduction and social protection agendas. These schemes, here qualified as Type III, emerged in the 2000s at a time of growing interest among development partners and, progressively, African governments, in social protection. Whereas the Type II schemes reviewed above that began in the 1990s were largely designed in dialogue with one main donor around practical considerations to make an existing programme more efficient, Type III schemes grew against a backdrop of a multiplicity of aid actors and were largely motivated by a desire to introduce a seemingly successful instrument for poverty reduction, as momentum around social cash transfers was fuelled by reported success stories from Latin America and pioneering African countries. Each case reviewed, however, reflects particular dynamics of policy formation. One important explanatory factor for these differences appears to be the institutional level at which domestic ownership and oversight are initially found—from a small unit within a technical ministry in the case of Zambia's SCT up to the president of the republic and a cabinet minister in the case of Rwanda's VUP.

In contexts of protracted crises with large-scale donor investment in humanitarian assistance, a fourth type of origin of social transfers can be identified. Both Ethiopia's PSNP and Kenya's HSNP arose out of concerns over emergency food aid and the desire to evolve towards more predictable, multi-year, cash-based assistance. These two cases differ, however, in the degree of donor involvement over time. While the PSNP was established out of long discussions between the Ethiopian government and foreign aid actors, the HSNP started as a stand-alone aid-funded project conceived outside national policy-making processes, with

[22] PRSPs are documents required by the International Monetary Fund and the World Bank, as well as other major donors and lenders, before low-income countries can receive aid.

a view to streamline and improve recurrent humanitarian interventions. For several years, it remained a separate initiative primarily driven by a donor agency and its implementing partners. Remarkably, it is today likely to achieve full domestic funding in the medium term.

Contrary to the popular perception that most of these schemes have been donor-instigated and donor-driven, it was often not possible to establish whether the initial impulse (the very first idea to consider a social transfer policy instrument) came from foreign aid actors or domestic players. In the case of Ghana's LEAP, for instance, foreign aid actors appear to have given weight to national proponents within the ministry of social affairs that had been weak in the intragovernmental competition for resources. Forming both formal and informal alliances, aid actors are found to have contributed to convincing other decisive entities within governments, such as ministries of finance. Hence, findings highlight the fragmented nature of government commitments and national ownership. Within the same government, one entity might be in favour of social transfers, while another might oppose it. Insights brought by this multiple-case study actually challenge the perspective developed in the literature on global social policy and development that tends to identify two competing strands of argumentation regarding social policy making in developing countries, one emphasizing global influence and the other domestic drivers.[23] Instead, the national social transfer policies reviewed here appear to emerge out of complex interactions between groups of international and national policy actors with their different views on social protection, mainly on the share a state is to take financial responsibility for.[24]

Social, Political and Financial Sustainability of the Schemes

In terms of resulting policy features, evidence challenges the view that a strong involvement of foreign aid actors in the origins of a scheme would jeopardize its long-term social, political and financial sustainability. The

[23] See, for instance, Collier and Messick (1975) and Deacon (2007).

[24] Studying the case of Cambodia, Kwon et al. (2015) reach a similar conclusion.

overall picture emerging from this multiple-case study reveals an interesting evolution over the recent years and suggests a few nascent remarkable dynamics. A progressive appropriation phenomenon, with more and more governmental actors (including ministries of finance) supporting social transfers, is observed across different cases. Government decisions to support a sizable social transfer scheme tend to occur within broader strategies of state-led social protection and pro-poor policy extension, possibly as part of deliberate moves to put the state in a role of primary welfare provider. Related social assistance bills were passed into law in Lesotho (Type I), and in Cabo Verde, Mozambique and Zimbabwe (Type II). In Lesotho, the OAP appears today as one of the initial steps in what seems to be a nascent social protection system, which also includes the aid-supported Child Grants Programme. But in Kenya, too, cash benefits targeted to the poorest children under the CT-OVC scheme (Type III) are becoming a part of the fabric of the Kenyan social system, notably with the passing of the social assistance bill in 2013. This occurs in a broader context of social protection expansion, which includes several other cash-based schemes. Such efforts towards building systems, and no longer just individual programmes, are observed across the different cases.

Another notable pattern stems from the rising degree of government's appropriation and concerns budgetary commitments. Table 3.3 provides an overview of the funding arrangements of the selected schemes. In most cases, donor funding remains high, but two notable trends are observed: the predictability and reliability of aid tend to improve thanks to multi-year commitments and pooled funding mechanisms; and the share of domestic contribution is on the rise. For schemes with Type I or II origins that have later received donor contributions, such as Mozambique's PSSB and Malawi's FISP, government revenue remains the main funding source. In the case of Cabo Verde's PSM, the consolidation of the scheme did benefit from technical and financial support from aid actors, through budget support, but PSM spending has been on budget and it has remained entirely funded out of central revenues. More interestingly, an upward tendency is observed in the mobilization of domestic resources for Type III or IV schemes, for which the involvement of foreign aid actors has been greater. There are even plans for some

Table 3.3 Resulting features of selected social transfer schemes

Origin	Case	Funding arrangements	Level of national ownership
Type I	Lesotho's OAP	Domestic resources only • Government (100%)	Very high • Legal basis (Old Age Pensions Act) • Fully domestically funded • Delivered by national bodies
	Malawi's FISP	Domestic and aid resources 2005/06–2006/07: • Government (100%) 2007/08 onwards: • Government • Donors (13% on average over the 2007/08–2011/12 period with a peak at 41% in 2011/12)	High • No legal basis • Largely domestically funded • Delivered by national bodies
Type II	Cabo Verde's MSP	Domestic resources only • Government (100%)	Very high • Legal basis • Fully domestically funded • Delivered by national bodies
	Mozambique's PSSB	Domestic and aid resources As of 2014: • Government (over 70%) • DFID • Netherlands	High • Legal basis (Law on Social Protection) • Largely domestically funded • Delivered by national bodies
	Zimbabwe's BEAM	Domestic and aid resources 2001–2008: • Government (100%) 2009 onwards: • Government • Donors (45% over 2009–2011) through a multi-donor funding mechanism	Very high • Legal basis (Social Welfare Assistance Act) • Largely domestically funded and initially fully domestically funded • Delivered by national bodies

Type III	Ghana's LEAP	Domestic and aid resources Pre-pilot, 2006: • UNICEF Pilot, 2008–2012: • Government (HIPC initiative funds) Rollout, 2014 (indicative): • Government (63%) • DFID (26%, grant, 2012–2016) • World Bank (10%, credit, 2010–2016)	High • Weak legal basis • Largely domestically funded • Delivered by national bodies
	Kenya's CT-OVC	Domestic and aid resources Pre-pilot, 2004: • Government (tax) • UNICEF and SIDA Rollout, 2013 (indicative): • Government (31%, tax) • Trust Fund: UNICEF and DFID (30%, grant, until 2016), World Bank (39%, loan and grant, until 2016)	High • Legal basis (Social Assistance Bill) • Increasing domestic funding • Delivered by national bodies
	Rwanda's VUP	Domestic and aid resources As of 2010/11: • Government (over 65%) • Donors (incl. DFID, EU, UNICEF, World Bank, SIDA)	High • No legal basis • Largely domestically funded • Delivered by national bodies
	Uganda's SAGE	Domestic and aid resources Pilot, 2010–2015: • Government (5%) • DFID (85%) • Irish Aid (10%) Rollout, 2016–2020: • Government (34%) • DFID & Irish Aid (66%)	Moderate • No legal basis • Largely aid-funded but increasing domestic funding • Delivered by national bodies

(continued)

Table 3.3 (continued)

Origin	Case	Funding arrangements	Level of national ownership
Type III (cont.)	Zambia's SCT	Domestic and aid resources Pre-pilot, 2003: • GTZ Rollout, as of Dec 2013: • Government • DFID • UNICEF • Irish Aid • ILO	Moderate • No legal basis • Largely aid-funded but increasing domestic funding • Delivered by national bodies
Type IV	Ethiopia's PSNP	Domestic and aid resources • Trust Fund: World Bank, USAID, CIDA, DFID, Irish Aid, EC, WFP, etc. • Government (8% in 2008, exp. 14% over 2015–2020)	Moderate • No legal basis • High aid-dependency • Delivered by national and international bodies
	Kenya's HSNP	Domestic and aid resources Pilot phase (2008–2012): • DFID (100%) Scale-up phase (2013–2017): • Government (32% of core caseload, as of 2015) • DFID and DFAT	Moderate • No legal basis • High aid-dependency • Delivered by national and international bodies

of them, in Ghana and Kenya for instance, to achieve full domestic funding in the medium term.

Securing such financial support from governments and encouraging an upward trend in their budgetary commitments over the years to come appears to be a key focus today for foreign aid actors. In the case of Kenya's HSNP, domestic funding has now exceeded 30 per cent of the regular caseload and is expected to increase further in the coming years (DFID 2015b). Donors increasingly push for the inclusion of the mobilization of domestic resources as a benchmark for continued support—as in the cases of Uganda's SAGE, Ethiopia's PSNP and Kenya's HSNP. Meanwhile, aid funding allows a faster expansion of the schemes. In the case of Uganda's SAGE, the government has committed UGX 149 billion for the Senior Citizen's Grant roll-out over the period 2015–2020. This financial commitment was made "on the basis of matching [development partners'] support"—conversely, the mobilization of domestic resources was a benchmark for DFID's continued support beyond the initial five-year period ending in June 2015 (DFID 2016).

While Type III or IV schemes remain dependent on aid, which covers at least one-third of their budget, it is hard to imagine that donors would suddenly withdraw their support and let them fail. Major donors, notably the World Bank and DFID, have funding in the pipeline to maintain their support over the years to come. Ethiopia's PSNP, for instance, is today one of the largest targeted social transfer schemes in Africa, the primary instrument of social protection in the country and an international flagship programme. The Ethiopian government has committed to ramp up its contribution from 8 per cent of annual costs in the first year to 22 per cent in the fifth year of the new phase of the programme. This means doubling its funding from GBP 190 million over the last five years to GBP 323 million over the next five (DFID 2015a). From the perspective of donors, this incremental increase in domestic funding is expected to "allow the Government to become comfortable with the idea of on-budget financing and will be continued in the future until the programme is largely or entirely domestically financed" (DFID 2015a: 9) Meanwhile, there is recognition that this requires long-term efforts and "continued donor support to the next phase of the programme;" [...] "with per capita [gross national income] a third of the sub-Saharan African average, and limited scope for reallocation from other sectors (Ethiopia already has one of the highest rates of pro-poor spending), it does not yet have the fiscal space to cover the whole PSNP budget" (DFID 2015a: 2).

Overall, empirical evidence suggests a catalytic effect of aid, which can be observed even when the involvement of foreign aid actors in the origins of a scheme has been strong. Foreign aid actors not only had an enabling role in the emergence of most of the selected schemes; they have also played a significant role in mobilizing additional national efforts for social transfers.[25] The conclusion that aid can have a catalytic effect, rather than a crowding out or substitution effect, on social transfer policies and spending, contrasts with previous studies on social transfers in sub-Saharan Africa.[26] But today, there are good prospects to see most of these schemes fully domestically funded in the future. All of the sizable schemes reviewed here can in fact be qualified as being, to differing degrees, nationally owned, even in contexts of strong aid actor engagement (Table 3.3). Government's support for the reviewed aid-supported schemes has been increasing. Ensuring citizen's support and ownership might be the next area for attention towards long-term sustainability of the schemes. There are early signs indicating that in some cases such a social appropriation process has started. Social transfer-related issues receive increased attention in the national media, and the schemes tend to enjoy a fair level of social acceptance. In some cases, such as Ghana's LEAP and Mozambique's PSSB, foreign aid actors have encouraged this by supporting public campaigns to raise awareness among society at large about the need for poverty-targeted social transfers (Cherrier 2016: 218).

Ways Forward for Transformative Change

Insights uncovered by this multiple-case study invite reflection to inform current and future efforts by foreign aid actors towards the expansion of basic social protection in low-income countries. The catalytic role of

[25] See chapter 4 in Cherrier (2016) for more details on the interactions between foreign aid actors and national stakeholders throughout the development of the selected schemes.

[26] This conclusion, however, echoes Morrissey's (2009) econometric analyses that show that aid increases social spending.

foreign aid actors towards the adoption of social transfers may have perverse effects. For social transfer schemes to help address poverty and inequality at a more transformative level across the sub-Saharan African region, critical issues still need to be addressed. In particular, efforts are needed towards strengthening citizen-state relations and ensuring a human rights-based approach, as a requirement for transformative change.

Strengthening Citizen-State Relations

In all the cases reviewed, policy decisions around social transfers have been primarily taken in closed policy spaces, in the executive branch, often in dialogue with donors (or creditors). National uptake and budget commitment may result from asymmetrical power relations between actors, as illustrated by the Kenyan case where the allocation of domestic resources has been a condition for continued donor support.[27] In the case of basic social protection in low-income countries, one may argue that aid actors promoting social transfers can be seen as playing the role of needy citizens' advocates, giving a voice to the powerless in policy spaces. However, their legitimacy and capacity to do so is open to debate.

As Devereux et al. (2010) deplored, there tends to be little consultation with beneficiaries (let alone, citizens more broadly) on project selection, design choices, and implementation modalities. The multiple-case study uncovers that for most schemes with Type III or IV origins there has been only limited consultation with citizens (or future beneficiaries) on the initial design of the schemes. Even when a donor agency is willing to support predictable social transfers as a form of social protection, internal procedures may hamper the capacity of field teams to conceive a scheme through a genuine participatory process. This played out, for example, in the case of a DFID-funded social transfer scheme introduced with the intention that national counterparts would progressively take it over and fund it. The project needed to be approved in headquarters, on

[27] Studying the case of Kenya, Ouma and Adésínà (2019) found that within social relations in the policy space, agents exercised power in three ways: first, by controlling the policy agenda by insertion of experts; second, by excluding other actors through a process of depoliticization; and third, by influencing the preference of domestic actors through social learning.

the basis of a business case,[28] before any extensive consultations with state officials and targeted communities could take place. But the business case already set two important parameters—unconditional transfers and categorical targeting. Implementing NGOs eventually discovered that local stakeholders were not at ease with such an approach, but they felt they had little room for manoeuvre. Yet, this was possibly a poor start for an initiative concerned with generating national ownership and ensuring sustainability. This echoes another situation reported by practitioners involved in the initial phase of the DFID-funded HSNP in Kenya, who admit that consultations with beneficiary communities were limited to informing people of what was going to happen, rather than inclusive design (Cherrier 2016: 221). An enthusiasm for cash transfer instruments, for instance, along with a focus on international best practices, may have led foreign aid actors to neglect longstanding national social policies and ignore historical and cultural contexts of society vis-à-vis social protection.

A catalytic effect of elections is observed at some point in all the reviewed cases. In Kenya, discussions that led to the introduction of the CT-OVC scheme started in the run-up to the 2002 parliamentary elections, encouraged by a UNICEF-supported lobbying strategy (Pearson and Alviar 2009). In Ghana and Ethiopia, the scheme was launched a few months before general elections. Ghanaian President Mahama re-launched an expanded LEAP programme prior to the 2002 general elections with a promise that the benefit level would be tripled. In Lesotho, the OAP benefit value was increased every election year (Cherrier 2014; Ellis et al. 2009). However, in most cases, citizens do not appear to have actively sought the introduction of a social transfer scheme, participated in the initial decision to opt for a social transfer policy or played a significant role in its initial design choices. This may change in the future as the schemes become increasingly domestically funded and discussed in mass media and during election campaigns. Increasingly, civil society representatives are invited to take part in policy consultation processes. Citizens

[28] A business case is the core internal proposal document DFID uses to assess and approve programmes before any funding can be released (DFID 2011). These business cases appear to be the only written documents where the scope, scale, objectives and outputs of the programme are formally articulated.

(taxpayers or people in need of assistance) might play a role in the subsequent development phases of the schemes. In the meantime, however, donor-supported initiatives will possibly have engendered path dependency.

Ensuring a Human Rights-Based Approach

Financing and spending decisions associated with the introduction of a social transfer scheme may modify the nature of state-society relations. Predictable transfers constitute a social contract that binds a state to its citizens; and introducing a new scheme can be seen as a means of extending this pact to vulnerable citizens (Hickey 2011). In countries with an existing social contract between the state and (sub-groups of) citizens, the challenge lies in sustaining the contract while including new beneficiaries and keeping costs down (Monchuk 2014). In Lesotho, the introduction of the universal old age pension scheme at scale and the adoption of the Old Age Pensions Act within a few months after first payments were made elevated OAP benefits to the status of a right. The case of Lesotho's OAP shows the value of universal benefits from a rights-based perspective.[29] Eligibility criteria are clear and transparent. Pensions have fostered a sense of citizenship among beneficiaries by allowing them to contribute to their community; they are seen as an entitlement in the eyes of beneficiaries and other citizens (Pelham 2007).

Contrasting with the case of Lesotho's OAP, Ghana's LEAP design (largely developed during discussions between governments and donors around poverty reduction strategies) includes tight poverty-based targeting, conditionality and a progressive rollout strategy. A rationing mechanism is used where beneficiaries are accepted until a given caseload that exhausts a fixed budget is reached—as opposed to an entitlement design, as is that of Lesotho's OAP, where any citizen meeting eligibility criteria

[29] The intended tasks for different schemes differ and so are the norms that undergird them. A universal social transfer scheme, such as Lesotho's OAP and Cabo Verde's MSP, runs on a significantly different normative framework than schemes such as Malawi's FISP (focused on raising the productive capacity of farming communities) and Zimbabwe's BEAM (focused on human capital development and school attendance improvement).

can claim his/her benefits. The LEAP case illustrates options frequently promoted to make a scheme more affordable and politically acceptable, as well as to account for limited implementation capacities—options that include gradual expansion strategy, narrow eligibility criteria, limited enrolment campaigns, restrictive conditions and absence of indexation for inflation. Such a gradual approach demonstrates policy makers' awareness that benefits provided within a social transfer scheme are not simply ad hoc handouts that can be terminated any time, but that they tend to become de facto (if not *de jure*) entitlements in the eyes of beneficiaries. Still, while understandable in the context of low-income countries, such an approach is not (yet) in line with an entitlement design.

The rights-based perspective is at the core of the Social Protection Floor initiative, which advocates for the development of a "set of basic social rights, services and facilities that the global citizen should enjoy" (ILO and WHO 2009: 4). Signatories of the International Covenant on Economic, Social and Cultural Rights are committed to ensure the realization of human rights to their "maximum available resources" (UNGA 1966: Art. 2). Measures need to be put in place to gradually improve the rights-based design of social transfer schemes, and eventually move towards universal social guarantees.[30] In that respect, the recent launch of the Global Partnership for Universal Social Protection marks a commitment by the ILO and the World Bank to "use their individual and collective resources and influence" to support "countries to design and implement universal and sustainable social protection systems" as part of efforts to implement the United Nations Sustainable Development Goals (ILO and World Bank 2016: 5).

Contributing to a Broader Transformative Agenda

For social transfer schemes to be transformative, they need to be embedded in a larger system which addresses deeper causes of poverty and inequality. A narrow focus on social transfer instruments by the international community may have directed resources away from policies

[30] For instance, following the concrete guidelines developed by Sepúlveda and Nyst (2012).

addressing deeper causes of poverty and marginalization, such as quality social services, decent work, land rights and access, doing a disservice to the transformative agenda development partners claim to defend. The prevailing emphasis of foreign aid actors on social cash transfers may generate a "rob-Peter-to-pay-Paul" effect, with significant increase in domestic budgets for social cash transfers funded through a reduction in other pro-poor expenditures. In Zambia, Hickey et al. (2009) stress that over-focusing on social cash transfers distracted resources and attention from other viable social protection measures, such as the Public Welfare Assistance Scheme, without achieving (at least then) the goal of a national scale-up. In Ethiopia, the PSNP does contribute to counter failing agricultural policies, but Lavers (2013) warns that a narrow focus on social transfers has distracted attention and resources away from the deeper causes of poverty and marginalization, such as the sensitive land issue. He questions whether the social transfer approach promoted in Ethiopia is genuinely tackling the power imbalances in society that encourage, create and sustain vulnerabilities, or whether it simply represents a means of increasing consumption and basic welfare outcomes among the poorest, without significantly addressing the dynamics of marginalization. Harland (2014) makes a similar point in the case of Zambia's SCT. This underlines the importance for foreign aid actors of better understanding (and better addressing) the power imbalances in society that create and sustain poverty and vulnerability.

Some authors, such as Adésínà (2010) and Deacon (2010), have raised more fundamental questions around what they perceive as an hegemonic ideology behind aid actors' efforts to expand social protection systems in developing countries. They argue that, generally speaking, development partners' approaches to social transfers have built on the following paradigm: a strong focus on poverty reduction and on providing support to the poorest; a focus on risk and vulnerability; cash transfer as the policy instrument of choice; a preference for means-testing; and a disconnection between the social and the broader economic aspects of development policy making (Adésínà 2010; Barrientos 2010). Adésínà (2010: 4) denounces what he calls an "aggressive policy-merchandising" by development partners in the African context, and calls for a return to a "wider vision of society that embeds social policy with a wider development strategy". This critique points to the importance of conceptualizing social and economic policies in tandem, and of moving away from approaches that target the poor exclusively towards more universal and integrative approaches, as exemplified by Lesotho's OAP.

References

Adésínà, 'Jìmí O. 2010. *Rethinking the Social Protection Paradigm: Social Policy in Africa's Development*. Paper Prepared for the Conference on 'Promoting Resilience Through Social Protection in Sub-Saharan Africa', Organized by the European Report of Development in Dakar, Senegal, 28–30 June.

Arnold, Catherine, Tim Conway, and Matthew Greenslade. 2011. *Cash Transfers: Evidence Paper*. London: Department for International Development.

AU (African Union). 2008. *Social Policy Framework for Africa*. First Session of the AU Conference of Ministers in charge of Social Development, Windhoek, Namibia, 27–31 October 2008. CAMSD/EXP/4(I). Addis Ababa: African Union.

Barrientos, Armando. 2010. *Social Protection and Poverty*. Social Policy and Development Programme Paper No. 42. Geneva: United Nations Research Institute for Social Development.

Barrientos, Armando, and David Hulme, eds. 2008. *Social Protection for the Poor and Poorest: Concepts, Policies and Politics*. Basingstoke: Palgrave Macmillan.

Barrientos, Armando, and Miguel Niño-Zarazúa. 2010. *Effects of Non-Contributory Social Transfers in Developing Countries: A Compendium*. Working Paper. Geneva: International Labour Office.

Bastagli, Francesca, Jessica Hagen-Zanker, Luke Harman, Valentina Barca, Georgina Sturge, Tanja Schmidt, and Luca Pellerano. 2016. *Cash Transfers: What Does the Evidence Say? A Rigorous Review of Programme Impact and of the Role of Design and Implementation Features*. London: Overseas Development Institute.

Behrendt, Christina, Krzysztof Hagemejer, and Sven Nef. 2014. *Introduction: Social Transfers*. International Labour Organization. Accessed 27 September 2019. http://www.social-protection.org/gimi/gess/ShowTheme.action?th.themeId=11.

CEB (United Nations System Chief Executives Board for Coordination). 2009. *The Global Financial Crisis and Its Impact on the Work of the UN System*. CEB Issue Paper. Geneva: CEB.

Cherrier, Cécile. 2014. *The Politics of Revenue Mobilisation for Social Transfers in Sub-Saharan Africa*. Paper Presented at the 14th General Conference of the European Association of Development Research and Training Institutes (EADI) on 'Responsible Development in a Polycentric World: Inequality, Citizenship and the Middle Classes' Held on 23–26 June 2014 in Bonn, Germany.

———. 2016. *The Expansion of Basic Social Protection in Low-income Countries: An Analysis of Foreign Aid Actors' Role in the Emergence of Social Transfers in Sub-Saharan Africa*. PhD Thesis. Maastricht University: Boekenplan.

Cichon, Michael, Wolfgang Scholz, Arthur van de Meerendonk, Krzysztof Hagemejer, Fabio Bertranou, and Pierre Plamondon. 2004. *Financing Social Protection*. Report. Geneva: International Labour Office/International Social Security Association.

Collier, David, and Richard E. Messick. 1975. Prerequisites versus Diffusion: Testing Alternative Explanations of Social Security Adoption. *American Political Science Review* 69 (4): 1299–1315.

Deacon, Bob. 2007. *Global Social Policy and Governance*. London: Sage.

———. 2010. *Global Social Floor or Global Social Investment: From the 'Global Politics of Poverty Alleviation' to 'the Global Politics of Welfare State (Re)Building'*. Paper Presented at the ERD Conference on Experiences and Lessons from Social Protection Programmes across the Developing World: What Role for EU?, European Report on Development, Paris, France, 17–18 June.

Devereux, Stephen, and Rachel Cipryk. 2009. *Social Protection in Sub-Saharan Africa: A Regional Review*. Report Prepared as Part of a Social Protection Scoping Study Funded by the Ford Foundation. Brighton: Centre for Social Protection, Institute of Development Studies.

Devereux, Stephen, and Rachel Sabates-Wheeler. 2004. *Transformative Social Protection*. Working Paper 232. Brighton: Institute of Development Studies.

Devereux, Stephen, and Philip White. 2008. *Social Protection in Africa: Can Evidence, Rights and Politics Converge?* Paper Presented at the Conference on Social Protection for the Poorest in Africa: Learning from Experience, Chronic Poverty Research Centre, Development Research & Training and Brooks World Poverty Institute, Entebbe, Uganda, 8–10 September.

———. 2010. Social Protection in Africa: Evidence, Politics, and Rights. *Poverty and Public Policy* 2 (3): 53–77.

Devereux, Stephen, Mark Davies, Anna McCord, Rachel Slater, Nicholas Freeland, Frank Ellis, Philip White, and Rachel Sabates-Wheeler. 2010. *Social Protection in Africa: Where Next?* Brighton: Centre for Social Protection

(CSP) at the Institute of Development Studies (IDS), Social Protection Programme at the Overseas Development Institute (ODI), School of International Development at the University of East Anglia (UEA-DEV), and Regional Hunger & Vulnerability Programme (RHVP).

DFID (Department for International Development). 2004. *DFID Drivers of Change Public Information Note*. London: DFID.

———. 2005. *Social Transfers and Chronic Poverty: Emerging Evidence and the Challenge Ahead*. London: DFID.

———. 2011. *Writing a Business Case, How to Note*. London: DFID.

———. 2015a. *Business Case and Summary: Ethiopia Productive Safety Net Programme Phase 4 (PSNP 4)*. London: DFID.

———. 2015b. *Hunger Safety Net Programme—Annual Review*. London: DFID.

———. 2016. *Expanding Social Protection in Uganda: Annual Review—Summary Sheet*. London: DFID.

Durán-Valverde, Fabio, and Francisco Pacheco. 2012. *Fiscal Space and the Extension of Social Protection: Lessons learnt from Developing Countries: Bolivia, Botswana, Brazil, Costa Rica, Lesotho, Namibia, Thailand and South Africa*. ESS (Extension of Social Security) Paper No. 33. Geneva: International Labour Office.

Ellis, Frank, Stephen Devereux, and Philip White. 2009. *Social Protection in Africa*. Cheltenham: Edward Elgar Publishing.

FAO (Food and Agriculture Organization of the United Nations). 2013. *The State of Food and Agriculture 2013: Food Systems for Better Nutrition*. Rome: FAO.

Freeland, Nicholas. 2013. Social Protection and the Four Horsemen of the Donor Apocalypse. In *Social Protection in Developing Countries: Reforming Systems*, ed. Katja Bender, Markus Kaltenborn, and Christian Pfleiderer, 226–236. Abingdon: Routledge.

Garcia, Marito, and Charity M. T. Moore. 2012. *The Cash Dividend. The Rise of Cash Transfer Programs in Sub-Saharan Africa*. Report. Washington, DC: World Bank.

Grosh, Margaret, Carlo del Ninno, Emil Tesliuc, and Azedine Ouerghi. 2008. *For Protection & Promotion: The Design and Implementation of Effective Safety Nets*. Report. Washington, DC: World Bank.

Handa, Sudhanshu, Silvio Daidone, Amber Peterman, Benjamin Davis, Audrey Pereira, Tia Palermo, and Jennifer Yablonski. 2017. *Myth-busting? Confronting Six Common Perceptions about Unconditional Cash Transfers as a Poverty*

Reduction Strategy in Africa. Innocenti Working Paper 2017-11. Florence: UNICEF Office of Research.

Harland, Charlotte. 2014. Can the Expansion of Social Protection Bring About Social Transformation in African Countries? The Case of Zambia. *European Journal of Development Research* 26 (3): 370–386.

Heller, Peter S. 2005. *Understanding Fiscal Space*. IMF Policy Discussion Paper No. 05/4. Washington, DC: International Monetary Fund.

Hickey, Sam. 2006. *The Politics of What Works in Reducing Chronic Poverty: A Synthesis Report for the Ministry of Foreign Affairs, The Netherlands*. Working Paper No. 91. Manchester: Chronic Poverty Research Centre.

———. 2008. Conceptualising the Politics of Social Protection in Africa. In *Social Protection for the Poor and Poorest: Concepts, Policies and Politics*, ed. Armando Barrientos and David Hulme, 247–264. Basingstoke: Palgrave Macmillan.

———. 2009. The Politics of Protecting the Poorest: Moving Beyond the 'Anti-Politics Machine?'. *Political Geography* 28 (8): 473–483.

———. 2011. *The Politics of Social Protection: What Do We Get from a 'Social Contract' Approach?* Working Paper No. 216. Manchester: Chronic Poverty Research Centre.

Hickey, Sam, Rachel Sabates-Wheeler, Bruce Guenther, and Ian Macauslan. 2009. *Promoting Social Transfers: DFID and the Politics of Influencing*. Working Paper No. 32. London: Department for International Development.

Holmqvist, Göran. 2010. *External Financing of Social Protection—Opportunities and Risks*. Paper Prepared for the Conference on 'Promoting Resilience Through Social Protection in Sub-Saharan Africa', Organized by the European Report of Development in Dakar, Senegal, 28–30 June.

ILC (International Labour Conference). 2012. *R202—Social Protection Floors Recommendation, 2012 (No. 202): Recommendation Concerning National Floors of Social Protection*. 101st ILC Session, 14 June. Accessed 27 September 2019. http://www.ilo.org/dyn/normlex/en/f?p=NORMLEXPUB:12100:0::NO::P12100_INSTRUMENT_ID:3065524.

ILO (International Labour Office). 2008. *Can Low-Income Countries Afford Basic Social Security?* Social Security Policy Briefings, Paper No. 3. Geneva: ILO.

———. 2010. *World Social Security Report 2010/11: Providing Coverage in the Time of Crisis and Beyond*. Geneva: ILO.

———. 2014. *World Social Protection Report 2014/15: Building Economic Recovery, Inclusive Development and Social Justice*. Geneva: ILO.

ILO (International Labour Office) and IMF (International Monetary Fund). 2012. *Towards Effective and Fiscally Sustainable Social Protection Floors*. Preliminary Report Prepared for the Meeting of the G20 Labour and Employment Ministers in Guadalajara, Mexico, 17–18 May.

ILO (International Labour Office) and WHO (World Health Organization). 2009. *The Social Protection Floor: A Joint Crisis Initiative of the UN Chief Executives Board for Co-ordination on the Social Protection Floor*. Geneva: ILO and WHO.

ILO (International Labour Office) and World Bank. 2016. *A Shared Mission for Universal Social Protection*. Concept Note. Geneva: ILO and World Bank.

IMF (International Monetary Fund). 2015. *Sub-Saharan Africa: Navigating Headwinds*. Report. Washington, DC: IMF.

Kwon, Huck-ju, Sarah Cook, and Yusun Kim. 2015. Shaping the National Social Protection Strategy in Cambodia: Global Influence and National Ownership. *Global Social Policy* 15 (2): 125–145.

Lavers, Tom. 2013. Food Security and Social Protection in Highland Ethiopia: Linking the Productive Safety Net to the Land Question. *Journal of Modern African Studies* 51 (3): 459–485.

Lavinas, Lena. 2013. 21st Century Welfare. *New Left Review* 84: 5–40.

Lavinas, Lena, Denise Gentil, and Barbara Cobo. 2017. *The Controversial Brazilian Welfare Regime*. Working Paper 2017-10. Geneva: United Nations Research Institute for Social Development.

Manor, James. 2004. *Politicking for the Poor—Appendix 3: Understanding 'Political Will'*. Brighton: Institute of Development Studies, University of Sussex.

Monchuk, Victoria. 2014. *Reducing Poverty and Investing in People: The New Role of Safety Nets in Africa*. Report. Washington, DC: World Bank.

Moore, Mick. 2013. *Obstacles to Increasing Tax Revenues in Low Income Countries*. UNRISD-ICTD Working Paper No. 15. Geneva: United Nations Research Institute for Social Development/International Centre for Tax and Development.

Morrissey, Oliver. 2009. Aid and Financing of Public Social Sector Spending. In *Financing Social Policy: Mobilizing Resources for Social Development*, ed. Katja Hujo and Shea McClanahan, 141–163. Basingstoke: Palgrave Macmillan and United Nations Research Institute for Social Development.

Niño-Zarazúa, Miguel, Armando Barrientos, David Hulme, and Sam Hickey. 2010. *Social Protection in Sub-Saharan Africa: Will the Green Shoots Blossom?*

Brooks World Poverty Institute Working Paper No. 116. Manchester: University of Manchester.

OECD (Organisation for Economic Co-operation and Development). 2009. *Promoting Pro-Poor Growth: Social Protection*. Report. Paris: OECD.

Ortiz, Isabel, Matthew Cummins, and Kalaivani Karunanethy. 2015. *Fiscal Space for Social Protection: Options to Expand Social Investments in 187 Countries*. ESS (Extension Social Security) Working Paper No. 48. Geneva: International Labour Office.

Ouma, Marion, and Jìmí O. Adésínà. 2019. Solutions, Exclusion and Influence: Exploring Power Relations in the Adoption of Social Protection Policies in Kenya. *Critical Social Policy* 39 (3): 376–395.

Pearson, Roger, and Carlos Alviar. 2009. *Cash Transfers for Vulnerable Children in Kenya: From Political Choice to Scale-Up*. Social and Economic Policy Working Paper. New York: United Nations Children's Fund.

Pelham, Larissa. 2007. *The Politics behind the Non-Contributory Old Age Social Pensions in Lesotho, Namibia and South Africa*. Chronic Poverty Research Centre Working Paper No. 83. Manchester: University of Manchester.

Samson, Michael, Ingrid van Niekerk, and Kenneth Mac Quene. 2006. *Designing and Implementing Social Transfer Programmes*. Cape Town: Economic Policy Research Institute.

Sepúlveda, Magdalena, and Carly Nyst. 2012. *The Human Rights Approach to Social Protection*. Helsinki: Ministry for Foreign Affairs of Finland.

Sindzingre, Alice. 2009. Financing Developmental Social Policies in Low-Income Countries: Conditions and Constraints. In *Financing Social Policy: Mobilizing Resources for Social Development*, ed. Katja Hujo and Shea McClanahan, 115–141. Basingstoke: Palgrave Macmillan and United Nations Research Institute for Social Development.

Thome, Karen, J. Edward Taylor, Mateusz J. Filipski, Benjamin Davis, and Sudhanshu Handa. 2016. *The Local Economy Impacts of Social Cash Transfers: A Comparative Analysis of Seven Sub-Saharan Countries*. Report. Rome: Food and Agriculture Organization of the United Nations.

Townsend, Peter, ed. 2009. *Building Decent Societies: Rethinking the Role of Social Security in Development*. London: Palgrave Macmillan and the International Labor Organization.

Ulriksen, Marianne. 2013. The Politics of Social Protection Expenditure and Financing in Southern Africa. *Development Southern Africa* 30 (1): 39–53.

UNDP (United Nations Development Programme). 2013. *Human Development Report 2013. The Rise of the South: Human Progress in a Diverse World.* New York: UNDP.

UNGA (United Nations General Assembly). 1966. *International Covenant on Economic, Social and Cultural Rights*. General Assembly Resolution 2200A (XXI). 16 December. Accessed 27 September 2019. http://www.ohchr.org/EN/ProfessionalInterest/Pages/cescr.aspx.

UNRISD (United Nations Research Institute for Social Development). 2010. *Combating Poverty and Inequality: Structural Change, Social Policy and Politics*. Geneva: UNRISD.

Whitfield, Lindsay, and Alastair Fraser. 2009. Introduction: Aid and Sovereignty. In *The Politics of Aid: African Strategies for Dealing with Donors*, ed. Lindsay Whitfield and Alastair Fraser, 1–27. Oxford: Oxford University Press.

Wildavsky, Aaron B., and Naomi Caiden. 2004. *The New Politics of the Budgetary Process*. 5th ed. New York: Pearson.

World Bank. 2018. Africa's Pulse, April 2018: An Analysis of Issues Shaping Africa's Economic Future. No. 17. Washington, DC: World Bank.

4

How Can Governments of Low-Income Countries Collect More Tax Revenue?

Mick Moore and Wilson Prichard

Introduction

There is currently something of an international consensus that the governments of low-income countries should be aiming to tax more to increase the proportion of gross domestic product (GDP) that they collect in taxes. This consensus is embodied in the immediate outcomes of the 2015 Third International Conference on Financing for Development—the Addis Ababa Action Agenda and the Addis Tax Initiative—and in a range of subsequent statements and programmes. A proposal that

M. Moore (✉)
IDS, University of Sussex, Brighton, UK
e-mail: mickm@ids.ac.uk

W. Prichard
IDS, University of Sussex, Brighton, UK

Munk School of Global Affairs and Public Policy, University of Toronto, Toronto, ON, Canada
e-mail: wilson.prichard@utoronto.ca

K. Hujo (ed.), *The Politics of Domestic Resource Mobilization for Social Development*, Social Policy in a Development Context,
https://doi.org/10.1007/978-3-030-37595-9_4

governments should raise revenues equivalent to at least 20 per cent of GDP was formally defeated at the Addis Ababa meeting. But the notion that there should be some target for the minimum acceptable level of national revenue collection has not gone away, with the figure of 15 per cent of GDP now widely cited. Whatever one's views on such targets, there is now a widespread view that those lagging behind in the revenue collection business should raise their game.[1] A range of reasons are given, the most tangible being the need to finance the public spending programmes required to achieve the Sustainable Development Goals by 2030. At a more theoretical level, there are claims that increases in tax collection might generate beneficial by-products in the form of improvements in the quality of governance, while also addressing economic inequality. There is also a vision of traditional aid donors bowing out gracefully and constructively from the era of "big aid" by supporting a push to raise substitute domestic revenue sources in formerly aid-dependent countries. The most recent statistics indicate that low-income countries are already moving in this direction. Since about 2010 in particular, average tax take has increased quite markedly in low-income countries in general, and in sub-Saharan Africa in particular, while changing little in other parts of the world.[2]

We have reservations about an uncritical consensus in favour of higher revenue collections. Above all, the public benefits of expanded taxation are unlikely to be realized without an equal or greater focus on (a) improving the equity of tax collection, which is frequently characterized by corruption, extractions that fail to reach state budgets and a failure to consistently and adequately tax the wealthy and politically connected, and (b) ensuring that taxpayers get better value for their money through improved public spending. The push to expand revenue collection is sometimes motivated by the idea that paying taxes is not a routine

[1] Generally speaking, governments that collect unusually low proportions of GDP in revenue tend to be concentrated in South Asia and Central America. There are few in Africa. For statistics, see ICTD/UNO-WIDER (2019).

[2] So that the conclusions will be unaffected by changes in global market prices for oil, gas and minerals, we have used figures for non-resource revenues, that is they exclude governments' royalty and tax incomes from the extractives sector. The detailed figures are available at ICTD/UNO-WIDER (2019).

practice for citizens of low-income countries. The reality, however, is that while some taxpayers may escape paying their fair share, others pay more. In particular, in some countries, poorer citizens sometimes bear especially heavy burdens of both formal and informal taxes (Jibao et al. 2017; Paler et al. 2017). Without an equivalent focus on how tax is collected, from whom and how the revenues are spent, a simple emphasis on increasing collections risks exacerbating problems.[3]

How can we begin to answer the question of how governments of low-income countries can collect more tax revenue? There is no obviously correct procedure. We have deconstructed the overarching question of how governments can increase the tax take into two smaller questions:

- What specific potential revenue sources do the governments of many developing countries tend to under exploit (*Dangling fruit*)?
- What is the potential for increasing the tax take through changing domestic and international tax policies?

Because in most low-income countries central government agencies collect nearly all revenues harvested by the state, this is the focus of our inquiry. We do not deal here with the important question of enhancing subnational revenues. Neither do we discuss what seems in many contexts to be the most obvious and direct way to increase the tax take: to increase the rates on existing taxes—income, profits and withholding taxes, value added tax (VAT), customs and the like.

By presuming to indicate how governments of low-income countries might raise additional revenue, we risk being accused of promoting "one-size-fits-all" policies. While we are suggesting some specific, potentially large revenue sources which we believe are, on average, under exploited in low-income countries, we also develop a strategic approach to increasing the tax take that can be adapted and applied to various contexts. Our menu is not fixed, but does contain some recommended items.

[3] See also UNRISD (2016).

Dangling Fruit

Dangling fruit is not necessarily *low hanging*, that is gains that can be harvested with little effort. The term refers rather to those specific potential sources of large additional tax revenues that seem generally to be under exploited in many low-income countries. While they are ripe for attention, exploiting them successfully may require a great deal of political and organizational effort that may not necessarily pay off in the short term. In the longer term, these dangling fruits, of which we've identified seven, are too tempting and potentially too large to ignore. Their rank in terms of potential revenues will vary according to context. To give a sense of the magnitudes involved, we estimate that, over a period of five to ten years, each has the potential to increase the tax take by 1–2 per cent of GDP, and perhaps significantly more.

For convenience of exposition, we discuss first those dangling fruits where the international dimension is most evident.

Transfer Mispricing in International Economic Transaction

More than a half of international trade occurs between what lawyers term "related parties," that is agents that are not independent of one another, but connected through ownership or influence. The most important related parties for present purposes are companies that comprise part of the same transnational corporate group. The prices at which related parties trade goods and services between themselves across international borders are unlikely to be set through competitive market bidding. They are set partly or wholly through administrative decisions about what price levels would most benefit the larger corporation to which the related parties belong. Indeed, since the typical transnational corporation (TNC) exists precisely to manage a set of operations that are integrated internationally or globally, it may be very difficult even for its best accountants to accurately calculate a market-like price for transactions between two of its subsidiary companies.

Imagine a transnational corporation called HydroEng that manufactures state-of-the-art electronically controlled pumping equipment in Germany. It also invests heavily in research and development operations in the Netherlands. A subsidiary incorporated in Nigeria, HydroEngNigeria, has a 30-year contract to build, manage and maintain a large drainage and water management facility in Lagos. HydroEngNigeria regularly dispatches motors, pumps and other complex items of equipment to a specialized facility in South Africa, owned by HydroEngDurban, where they are serviced and repaired, often by specialist engineers who fly in from Germany. Even HydroEng's own accountants are challenged to estimate the real cost to the company of providing this maintenance and repair service. In addition to many other variables, they have to factor in the high research and development expenditures that underlie the corporation's competitiveness. This situation is so much more challenging for the Nigerian tax authorities, who have no access to HydroEng's internal management accounts to verify the validity of the price that HydroEngDurban charges HydroEngNigeria for this service. According to the standard procedures of the international tax system, they should seek a few *comparators*—that is other cases of companies providing similar maintenance services for electronically controlled pumping equipment in Nigeria—where prices are not administratively controlled, but set in competitive markets. Some average of the prices of comparators would provide a benchmark for the appropriate price for this transaction. In reality, appropriate comparators are often scarce or absent.

That is the essence of the transfer pricing and mispricing problem. Given the basic structure of HydroEng—with locally incorporated subsidiary companies, taxable locally, responsible for local operations in Nigeria, South Africa and perhaps dozens of other countries—someone has to set a transfer price so that the accounts of HydroEngNigeria and HydroEngDurban can be closed at the end of the year and tax returns submitted. If the companies involved deliberately set that price in order to shift profits among jurisdictions, then we say that they are practicing *transfer mispricing*. We know that (a) transfer mispricing is widespread; (b) it is used mainly to transfer profits from higher tax to lower tax jurisdictions; and (c) these transfers are especially likely to be made from low-income countries. This reflects a combination of biases in existing laws and international tax treaties and agreements, the lesser capacity of government institutions in low-income countries to control abuses and a reluctance on the part of companies and wealthy individuals to hold large amounts of capital in politically fragile countries.

A key policy question for developing countries is how much effort to invest in auditing—that is, challenging and interrogating—the tax accounts presented by TNCs for potential transfer mispricing? On this point there is significant disagreement. Part of it centres on the question of *how much* revenue is available to be collected by improved enforcement. Widespread international attention to these issues has been driven in part by very large estimates of *illicit financial flows*, with implications that these imply very large tax losses.[4] However, it is increasingly clear that the larger estimates of the size of these illicit flows are substantially inflated (Forstater 2017b), as are guesses about the amount of revenue loss this implies for governments of low-income countries (Forstater 2017a). More credible, but still very rough, estimates seem to point towards revenue losses on the scale of perhaps 2 per cent of GDP—certainly significant but also not a limitless pot of gold. The second source of disagreement relates to the capacity of government institutions in developing countries to actually tap these potential additional revenues. TNCs typically employ large numbers of skilled lawyers and accountants to help minimize their tax bills. Tax administrations in many low-income countries are, by comparison, very poorly resourced. At the very least, it is clear that they face major challenges. Finally, there are questions about whether, by leading to increases in effective corporate tax rates, better enforcement of transfer pricing rules could have negative effects on investment levels. Again, evidence is limited, but it is inadvisable for governments of low-income countries to be much concerned about this possibility. Research on low-income countries suggests that tax levels are much less of a constraint on investment than a range of other investment

[4] "Illicit financial flows" is not a technical term in economics or accounting. While there is no agreed definition, broadly, the concept represents the sum of (a) the profits that transnational and other companies move abroad through the use of transfer mispricing and other profit-shifting techniques and (b) the capital that wealthy, influential people transfer abroad using illegal or illicit channels. The "taxes foregone" are the taxes that might have been collected on these profit and capital transfers in the country from which they are made (Reuter 2012).

climate concerns, including the quality of public infrastructure (roads, ports, electricity, water, broadband) and public institutions (the legal system) and the predictability of the tax system (Kinda 2014). However, a poorly executed programme of auditing for potential transfer mispricing could discourage investment by increasing the perceived unpredictability of the tax system.

On balance, there are good reasons to believe that, for most low-income countries—indeed for most countries in the world—challenging corporate accounts for potential transfer mispricing is either a sensible strategy for today or an appropriate aim for tomorrow, once capacity is developed:

- The evidence suggests that, when tax administrations mount serious challenges to transfer mispricing, they tend to be rewarded by substantial additional revenues. This is true even in countries that have historically not been tolerant of transfer mispricing. As in many rich countries, the British tax authority has in recent years invested additional resources in challenging TNCs, especially through strengthening its transfer pricing team. The authority sees this as a major reason why corporate income tax revenue increased by 12 per cent in 2016–2017 compared to the previous year.[5] In recent years the OECD has been providing expertise to the tax administrations of some low-income countries, specifically to enable challenges to apparent transfer mispricing. They report substantial additional revenues.[6]
- Many low-income countries now have transfer pricing laws and regulations, based principally on OECD guidelines, but many do not. Where these laws and regulations are in place, they are mostly new. For example, in 2000, only two countries in Africa—South Africa and

[5] The British tax authority also reports that, following a transfer pricing challenge, the additional tax collected is typically around a half of the figure that the authority initially suggests (Financial Times, 30 August 2017).

[6] Over a two-year period 2015–2017, a joint programme between the OECD (2013) and the African Tax Administration Forum (ATAF) (2017) to provide technical assistance support to transfer pricing audits in Africa has generated additional revenues of more than USD 120 million. For one West African country, in a single year, these audits led to a 12-fold increase in the revenues earned from challenging for transfer mispricing. This information was provided by Lee Corrick, an OECD/ATAF transfer pricing expert, in a personal communication on 12 September 2017.

Zambia—had these laws and regulations in place. This number increased to 7 by 2005 and 14 by the end of 2014 (EY 2014). An increasing amount of training on how to deal with transfer mispricing is available internationally. The quality of staff in tax administrations in low-income countries is rising. Most tangibly, there has been great progress in recent years in establishing global institutions through which tax administrations can (more or less easily) exchange information about "taxpayers-of-interest" with one another.[7]

The potential additional revenue from more effectively tackling transfer mispricing seems significant.[8] That said, we need to recognize that not all tax administrations in low-income countries are in a position to significantly increase revenue through transfer pricing audits within the next few years. Some countries as yet have no transfer pricing legislation or regulations. In others, like Nigeria, there are contradictions between the legislation and the regulations. Other countries have legislation and regulations in place, but in practice do not use them. There are a range of reasons for this. Effectively challenging transfer mispricing can be difficult. It requires considerable resources, including knowledge, staff and capacity to access information from commercial databases or from tax agencies overseas. It is often a long-term game, with individual investigations taking months or years, while tax administrations are focused on meeting annual revenue collection targets. The legislation is not always watertight. Transfer pricing cases are typically so complex that it is too costly to take them to court. The Kenya Revenue Authority is one of the most effective tax administrations in sub-Saharan Africa and an acknowledged leader in transfer pricing issues. However, recent research shows that it still has a way to go to be effective (Waris 2017).

The OECD approach to transfer pricing is virtually the global standard. It was originally designed for the institutional and economic

[7] We refer to the Global Forum on Transparency and Exchange of Information for Tax Purposes (OECD 2018).

[8] For a brief summary of some recent research, see Forstater (2017a). A recent estimate from the IMF, that includes other sources of revenue loss through *base erosion and profit shifting*, in addition to transfer mispricing, mentions a figure possibly as high as 1 per cent of GDP for developing countries generally (IMF 2014).

conditions of rich OECD countries: relatively deep and competitive import and export markets; extensive recording of economic transactions; and well-equipped tax authorities. Many tax administrations in low-income countries find themselves unable to deploy it effectively. They are seeking simpler, more effective tools to curb transfer mispricing. There is work to be done to support them.[9]

Mining[10]

The economic importance of mining varies significantly from one country to another and changes over time as global prices for minerals fluctuate. Recent decades have seen the (re)emergence of mining in particular—and resource extraction in general (i.e. oil, gas and minerals)—as a major activity, especially in sub-Saharan Africa. This seems set to continue as extractives are a dominant source of export revenues. While some minerals, like coal, may face a long-term price decline, others, including rare earths, have buoyant market prospects.

In low-income countries, mining is generally grossly under-taxed, and to a much greater extent than the other main components of the extractive sector, oil and gas. The reasons are both technically complex and deeply political. Almost all mine operators are large TNCs. Few other entities can generate the very high levels of capital that mining requires, or bear the high risks involved. The rents—the financial return over and above "normal profit"—extracted from mining can be vast. Debates around the taxation of mining are fundamentally about how these rents will be distributed between transnational investors, government treasuries and, via corruption of many kinds, the political elites who enjoy effective control over access to the right to mine mineral resources. Significant chunks of the revenue from mining that should be paid into public treasuries are often siphoned off through a combination of collusion between

[9] Transfer pricing methods and issues become very complex. The OECD approach is based on the arms' length principle (ALP), estimating what transfer prices should be used by using data from other comparable (market, non-administered) transactions.

[10] There is a large literature on this topic. See in particular Aarsnes and Lundstol (2013), Africa Progress Panel (2013), Collier (2010), Daniel et al. (2010, 2016), Durst (2016), Laporte and de Quatrebarbes (2015), Lundstøl et al. (2013).

mining companies and various political operators and more straightforward forms of tax evasion (see also Chap. 12 in this volume). The main channels through which revenue is lost are:

- Mining contracts: these are often overly generous to investors, and are in effect private deals between them and a few people who control the host government. Open and honest auctions of mining rights are a widely advocated potential antidote, but rarely practiced.
- Transfer pricing: because almost all mining is conducted by locally incorporated subsidiaries of large TNCs, and because almost all mining products from low-income countries are exported, there is wide scope to use transfer mispricing to shift profits out of the host country. The operating companies typically purchase most of their equipment and expertise from related parties, and sell all their products to other related parties.[11]
- The tax regime: a high degree of reliance on corporate income taxes is very risky from the government perspective because transfer mispricing can be used to grossly understate the profits of the local mine operator. One feasible alternative is for governments to focus more on obtaining revenues through *royalties*, that is the charges that mining companies pay for the national assets (copper, coal, titanium, gold, etc.) that they are removing and selling.[12]
- Capital gains: mining projects frequently undergo one or more changes of ownership at a relatively early stage. A "junior" company with a low public profile and a limited concern for its corporate reputation organizes the exploration and the securing of land and extraction rights. The operation is then sold to one of the larger transnational mining companies that are more concerned about reputational issues. The sale typically takes place "offshore" between companies domiciled in tax havens. The question of whether the company making the sale should

[11] They may also manipulate information on the quantity, and quality, of mineral exports in order to reduce reported revenues (Durst 2016; Readhead 2016, 2017).

[12] Because market prices for minerals fluctuate widely, an excessive reliance on royalties risks pushing mining companies into operating losses when commodity prices are low. The risk can however be ameliorated through the use of *variable rate royalties*, that is royalties that are pegged to world market prices for the product (Durst 2016).

be liable to capital gains tax in the host country has been the subject of high-profile law cases because much national legislation is ambiguous or silent on the issue. To date, companies have more frequently been the winners.[13] This particular piece of dangling fruit may be low hanging for many countries.

Tobacco and Alcohol[14]

Governments of most richer countries collect useful amounts of revenue from excise taxes levied on specific commodities, especially on tobacco and alcohol. Governments of low-income countries generally under-tax these products. The IMF concludes that "Tobacco excise revenues are generally low: 0 to 0.2 percent of GDP in most sub-Saharan countries, 0.2 to less than 1 percent of GDP in the OECD countries and many large developing markets such as Vietnam or the Philippines, and slightly more in some large middle-income markets such as Egypt (1 percent of GDP) and Turkey (1.4 percent of GDP)" (IMF 2016: 1). A major reason is that the large TNCs that dominate the production and supply chains in most poor countries invest significant resources in lobbying and other political activities to persuade governments not to tax tobacco or alcohol.

In low-income countries, consumer spending on commercial tobacco and alcohol products is still relatively low. It is however increasing fast, especially in Africa. The analysis of experience from elsewhere suggests that, for tobacco in particular, levying significant taxes only curbs consumption in the long term. In most poor countries, doubling excise taxes on tobacco could increase revenues immediately while reducing long-term consumption. In the case of tobacco in particular there is potential political support for raising taxes—domestically from health professionals and ministries of health, and internationally from global networks of

[13] In 2015, Tullow Oil, having lost a case in the Uganda High Court, finally accepted that it owed the Uganda Revenue Authority USD 50 million in relation to an offshore sale of this nature. However, this is not the norm.

[14] There is a very large literature on this topic. This section is based in particular on IMF (2016), National Cancer Institute (2017), Savedoff and Alwang (2015), Van Walbeek et al. (2013).

tobacco control organizations, most of them connected to the World Health Organization.

Exemptions

There is widespread agreement among tax specialists that governments in general, and especially governments of low-income countries, give away too much revenue by granting excessive tax exemptions to investors, both foreign and domestic. The specialists have been arguing that case for many years. The IMF, the OECD, the United Nations and the World Bank have recently produced a joint statement on this issue.[15] But it seems likely that exemptions are being used more rather than less frequently in low-income countries (Keen and Mansour 2009). Estimating the scale of these exemptions is difficult as data is often imperfect and most published studies include both corporate tax benefits and exemptions aimed at reducing tax burdens on low-income groups, and other broadly social purposes—while disentangling the two is often impossible. That said, there is broad consensus that corporate exemptions are often substantial.

Tax exemptions for investors are unlikely to disappear. There are valid cases for exemptions, provided they are used carefully and strategically. If exemptions were being used strategically, whether to attract investment in general or to focus it on certain sector and activities, the process would involve:

- Granting exemptions only on the basis of clear criteria and agreed, transparent procedures.
- Placing time limits on all exemptions.
- Monitoring their use and effects.
- Ensuring that all exemptions and their beneficiaries are registered with the tax administration, so that the enterprise could be taxed after the expiry of exemptions.

[15] IMF et al. (2015).

In practice, these procedures are often not followed. Attracting and steering investment are not the only reasons that governments grant exemptions. They are also widely used to reward political allies, to provide leverage over potential political opponents and to raise money, both for private pockets and to fund elections and other political activities (Moore 2015).[16] Foreign investors in particular are often quite skilled at persuading governments of poor countries that tax exemptions are required, even if they have already decided to invest anyway. The threat that the investment will go instead to a neighbouring country can panic governments. For this reason, the harmonization of incentive arrangements on a regional level could be very useful in shifting the balance of bargaining power in favour of governments.

Poor institutions, weak governance, inadequate infrastructure and uncertainty about taxation regimes are typically much bigger disincentives to investment than corporate tax levels in low-income countries. It is unlikely that lowering the tax rate can compensate for a bad investment climate. In surveys of investors conducted in seven African countries between 2009 and 2012, an average of 84 per cent of respondents said that the availability of tax exemptions had not affected their investment decisions (IMF et al. 2015). Before giving tax exemptions, governments should focus on improving the investment climate by tackling such issues as excessive regulation and red tape (e.g. for registering a business, or for construction permits); the quality of roads, ports, electricity, telecoms and other infrastructure; and the predictability of the tax and legal systems. If taxes were not waived and some of the revenue were used to help dissolve these obvious obstacles to investment, almost everyone would stand to benefit.

[16] Therkildsen and Bak (2019) argue that the increasing competitiveness of elections has been a major driver for the multiplication of tax exemptions in Tanzania.

Implementing VAT[17]

VAT has steadily become more important, and is now the largest single source of revenue for governments of low-income countries. It is however collected inefficiently. There is a standard measure, known as C-efficiency. In 2010, C-efficiency for VAT averaged about 60 per cent in high-income countries, meaning that 60 per cent of potential VAT revenue was being collected. By contrast, the figure for low-income countries was less than 40 per cent, although increasing steadily over time. The dominant reason for the VAT gap in Europe is that governments choose to exempt consumers from paying VAT on basic consumption items, notably food and clothes. We have much less consistent data for low-income countries. However, a wide range of observational evidence suggests that the (much bigger) VAT gaps are due in large part to a combination of (a) the use of a wide range of VAT rates for different products and services, (b) organizational failures in collection and (c) the success of lobbying by business for VAT exemptions at some intermediate point in the production chain, that is exemptions for sports facilities and local production of motor tyres, rather than for final consumer items like food. These causes are mutually reinforcing: the greater the complexity of the VAT regime, the wider the scope for evasion. There is considerable scope to increase revenue collections by simplifying the structure of VAT systems and more closely monitoring compliance. The impact on income distribution is unclear, but the burden would certainly not fall entirely on final consumers. Businesses benefit in various ways from complex, "leaky" VAT systems.

Taxing the Rich

Rich people in poor countries typically pay low taxes on both their assets and their incomes. Sometimes, as for example in much of Latin America, this is because they have long experience of dealing with populist or leftist governments who have tried to tax them, and have developed

[17] The research underlying this paragraph is summarized in Keen (2013). Note that there is an overlap between the exemptions discussed in the previous paragraph and VAT exemptions.

sophisticated avoidance techniques that often involve keeping assets offshore. In contemporary sub-Saharan Africa, the more common story is that tax collectors have generally not come after them in a determined way because, it appears, of the power of political connections, patronage and collusion. This results in an increasingly obvious inequity in the distribution of the tax burden between rich and poor. In many African countries, and in other low-income regions, the numbers of the wealthy and the super-wealthy seem to be growing fast (McCluskey 2016).

Research conducted by the Uganda Revenue Authority (2016) gives some idea of the scale of the problem. For example, researchers found that in 2013–2014, among a sample of the 60 top lawyers in the country, only 35 per cent paid any personal income tax; only 5 per cent of company directors did so; and among 71 top-ranking government officials, who owned enormous assets, including hotels, private schools and media houses, only one had ever paid personal income tax (Kangave et al. 2016). The same phenomenon is visible (though somewhat disguised) in public revenue statistics. The average personal income tax collection in sub-Saharan African countries—outside of South Africa—is about 2 per cent of GDP, still a far cry from the 10 per cent of GDP found in wealthier countries.[18] Less often noted is that much of the revenue from personal income taxes comes from withholding taxes on formal sector salaries. This reflects the fact that tax revenues based on incomes from professional self-employment and from property and other investments—the main income sources of the rich—are generally very limited.

Meanwhile, there is mounting evidence that a very large share of African financial wealth is held offshore in tax havens. The best estimates, from Gabriel Zucman, suggest that at least 30 per cent of all African financial wealth is held offshore (Zucman 2015). This is higher than any global region other than Russia and the Gulf States. It implies that *wealthy* Africans, who are the only ones with wealth offshore, almost certainly hold significantly more than *half* of their financial wealth overseas. Zucman estimates tax losses of at least USD 15 billion annually based on the failure to tax investment returns on those funds—about 0.5 per cent of GDP. Treating this as a lower bound, and considering other forms of

---

[18] For the data, see ICTD/UNU-WIDER (2019).

wealth held abroad (property, art, jewellery, etc.), it is easy to imagine annual revenue losses of more than 1 per cent of GDP on average, quite apart from taxes foregone when the funds were first stashed offshore.

Some of these tax losses reflect the logistic and organizational difficulties in taxing the rich. International cooperation remains inadequate for low-income countries, and some domestic administrations struggle to verify incomes from self-employment and from investment. However, if tax administrations could overcome some of the political barriers to action, significant increases in revenue would be quickly attainable. Meanwhile, the status quo risks becoming increasingly strained as poorer citizens continue to bear heavy tax burdens, and come to recognize the tax privileges enjoyed by the comparatively wealthy.

Property Taxes[19]

Land and property are among the most visible indicators of personal wealth. Because they are easily identified and immovable, they are potentially easy to tax. And in many low-income countries, urban-centric economic growth and continued urbanization mean that urban real estate values have grown fast, generating enormous unearned income and wealth for property owners. Despite being widely recognized as an economically efficient and progressive revenue source, property taxes are much underused in virtually all low-income countries. This is perhaps the most glaring example of the failure of governments to tap potential revenue collection, particularly from the wealthy.

In most OECD countries, property taxes account for 1–2 per cent of GDP, while in the fast growing states of East Asia they are sometimes larger. Reliable figures on property tax collection in sub-Saharan Africa are rare. In most countries for which we have reliable figures, collections

[19] We focus here on the most common kinds of property taxes: recurrent charges on the owners or occupiers of real estate. There are however two other ways of taxing property that might be equally useful, according to circumstances: (a) income taxes on the income earned from renting out property, and (b) taxes on the sale or legal transfer of property ownership. See Bahl et al. (2008) and Bird (2010, 2011).

amount to only 0.1–0.2 per cent of GDP. It seems likely that levels are lower in countries where no data is available.

The weakness of property taxes has sometimes been attributed to the technical difficulty of maintaining complete and up to date registers of property values. This is certainly a challenge, but a small one when compared to the difficulties of tracing the incomes and wealth of rich people or deconstructing the tax accounts of transnational corporations. There are two deeper reasons for the poor performance of property taxes. The first is that systems of property taxation inherited from the colonial period involve unnecessarily complex valuation methods and fragmented administrative arrangements. The second stems from the simple logic of politics. Effective property tax systems bear relatively heavily on economic and political elites, who have used their power to frustrate reform. Perhaps the best evidence on the nature of these barriers is a growing number of local success stories where property tax revenues have expanded rapidly—albeit from extremely low bases—as a result of concerted political and administrative commitment.[20] Underpinning many of these successes has been a common theme: simplifying recruitment of staff, property identification and valuation, and tax billing to better reflect local realities and ease effective administration.

Changing Tax Policies

Our central question is: how can governments of low-income countries increase the tax take? We have just presented one answer: through focusing on developing specific, under exploited revenue sources. We now present another: by trying to change tax policies, both nationally and internationally, to better adapt them to the taxation circumstances of low-income countries. Our goal here is not to review the entire range of tax policy questions facing low-income countries, nor to enter into contested debates about whether tax rates should be higher or lower in particular domains. This is in part because these issues are well addressed elsewhere. It is equally because we prefer to highlight a series of areas in

[20] Cheeseman and de Gramont (2017), de Gramont (2015) and Jibao and Prichard (2016).

which we believe there could be significant payoffs from shifting policy in meaningful new directions.

Tax Companies More on Turnover, and Less on Reported Profits

It is one of the core features of contemporary tax systems that company contributions to the public treasury should as far as possible be levied on their profits, and not on measures of turnover or sales. The simplified economic argument for this is powerful: the more that companies are taxed on turnover, the more likely it is that they will be obliged to pay taxes even when their profits are low or they are making losses. That in turn would lead to reductions in overall levels of investment and economic activity, leaving everyone worse off.

There are, however, potential trade-offs between economic efficiency and governments' need to raise revenue. Profit-based taxes are more attractive to firms, but are significantly more difficult for governments to enforce than taxes on turnover. This is especially true when companies are part of a transnational group, and tax administrations have limited capacity. As we explained above, in these circumstances companies are better able to artificially reduce locally declared profits through transfer mispricing or by inflating costs. Where governments are able to enforce them relatively effectively, profit-based taxes are preferable because they improve economic efficiency. However, where enforcement capacity is weak, the efficiency benefits of profit-based taxes may be significantly outweighed by their impact in reducing public revenue. This is the conclusion of a recent empirical study from Pakistan, which provides evidence that shifting from profit-based taxes to turnover-based taxes could reduce evasion by almost 70 per cent without reducing economic efficiency (Best et al. 2015).

There is therefore a good case for governments to consider the wider use of taxes levied on measures of company turnover or sales. This is especially likely to make sense when it is easy for companies to practice transfer mispricing, for example large telecommunications companies that have operations in adjacent countries. In some countries they are already taxed in this way (Durst 2015). The argument for taxing mining companies more through royalty-like arrangements (see section on mining above) is a special case of the same general argument. None of these variants of turnover taxes are without problems and arrangements may need to be made to deal with loss-making situations. But all taxes in practice are adapted for special cases and unusual situations. Indeed, turnover taxes are becoming more common even in higher-enforcement OECD countries as governments struggle with the problem of taxing the (elusive and mobile) profits of large IT companies.

Beware of Tax Treaties

Until recently, it was common for governments to sign bilateral tax treaties in the belief that this was essential to encourage investment. It was argued, for example, that Belgian companies would not invest in Morocco unless there was a bilateral tax treaty between Belgium and Morocco to ensure that Belgian investors would be adequately treated in tax terms. In recent years, the term "abusive tax treaties" has become increasingly common. It has become more evident that tax treaties are often not needed to ensure foreign investment, and that those in place—around 4000 in all—are often quite disadvantageous to the country receiving investment.[21] In many cases, governments have signed away the rights to levy taxes on inward investors, including capital gains taxes and a range of withholding taxes, while in some cases these treaties have also opened up avenues for aggressive strategies for shifting profits into tax havens. Through the Multilateral Convention to Implement Tax Treaty Related Measures to Prevent Base Erosion and Profit Shifting, the OECD is currently organizing a process to try to remove abusive clauses from existing tax treaties. The best general advice for low-income countries is to actively review existing tax treaties, while being very careful before signing any new ones.

[21] Action Aid (2016), Hearson and Kangave (2016), IMF (2012).

Act Regionally on Tax Exemptions and International Tax Rules

A defining feature of many of the tax challenges facing low-income governments is that they cannot be effectively confronted by countries acting independently, but demand more concerted regional action. The most striking example is tax exemptions, a classic beggar-thy-neighbour policy problem (see section on exemptions above). International investors frequently pit neighbouring countries against one another, placing each under pressure to offer bigger exemptions in order to attract investment. In the short term, countries are persuaded that providing tax exemptions will bring them additional investment. In the long term, however, this process drives effective tax rates down everywhere. All countries are left with reduced public revenues. The potential solution lies in regional coordination around the terms and processes through which any tax exemptions can be awarded. Though politically daunting, this is not impossible. The European Union, for example, has rules limiting the use of exemptions by its members to compete for investment, while the East African Community has made significant progress in advancing broader tax cooperation. Meanwhile, regional cooperation could also bear dividends in other areas, including common rules on transfer pricing and cooperative approaches to taxing telecoms, tobacco and alcohol. For example, if all countries in a region harmonized their transfer pricing rules, this would reduce the transactions costs of the taxation process for both tax administrations and investors.[22]

There is a similar case for more regional cooperation in relation to the reform of international tax rules. The negotiation of international rules is dominated by the OECD. Relative to the UN Tax Committee, the OECD has the great advantage of being authoritative. It is able to get things done relatively quickly if there is adequate agreement among its members. But those members are all rich countries. Non-members may be consulted extensively and invited into meetings, but they ultimately

[22] The African Tax Administration Forum, the OECD and the World Bank are currently working to harmonize transfer pricing rules within the Economic Community of West African States (ECOWAS).

have no votes. However, we believe that a significant shift is underway in global tax politics. In 2013, the G20 charged the OECD with the task of taking control of what was known as the BEPS (*base erosion and profit-shifting*) process and gave them two years to come up with solutions to transnational tax evasion and avoidance. In historical terms, this appeared to be a rather regressive step—charging rich industrial countries to come up with an action plan for the world. This has elicited enormous and consistent criticism. Yet in practice, the OECD—sensing a threat to its long-term position due to the growing power of non-OECD countries—has been unexpectedly proactive in integrally involving non-members in its tax-related debates, and, after reporting on BEPS in 2015, has taken the lead in stimulating collective international action to revise abusive tax treaties and to improve the exchange of tax information among national tax administrations.

The status quo undoubtedly remains far from perfect. But threats to the institutional dominance of the OECD have resulted in low-income countries enjoying more bargaining power in relation to the international tax system than they have ever known. If they act collectively, they have the possibility of using it to push for reforms that are more appropriate to their taxation circumstances. These might include, among other possibilities, greater openness to alternatives to traditional approaches to transfer pricing, expanded transparency of country-by-country financial accounts of TNCs, greater transparency about the beneficial ownership of shell corporations, improved access for low-income countries to information of wealth held abroad by citizens, and greater legal cooperation in taxing this wealth.

Improve the Tools for Taxing the Wealthy

We noted above that perhaps the most important step towards more effectively taxing the wealthy is technically the simplest: improve the sharing of data *within* tax administrations to identify avoidance and evasion. The next step is likely to also lie in accessing data from parallel organizations that can be used for tax enforcement. This is in part a question of organizational performance, but it is likewise a question of policy reform: in many countries, laws either prevent the sharing of such information or are ambiguous about its legality (thus offering a convenient scapegoat for a lack of action). While not a silver bullet, simple legal changes to facilitate the sharing of *third party data*, coupled with organizational commitment to use the data, could yield significant gains in revenue and equity.

Some data sharing should take place among government agencies. This would likely include data from property and motor vehicle registries, utility companies, business registrations or government contracts (particularly where withholding taxes are not applied on those contracts). Access to such information on income, assets and spending can offer useful clues about potential tax evasion. Meanwhile, other information should come from third party actors outside of government, including stock exchanges, company registrars, banks and credit card companies. Access to such data is the norm in OECD countries, but has only slowly been introduced in lower-income countries, either owing to worries about data privacy, simple oversight or as an indirect way of preventing effective taxation of the wealthy. As with data sharing within tax agencies, progress in this area not only holds significant potential but may also act as a litmus test for broader commitment to tax reform.

Politics

The most obvious objection to the preceding discussion is that it is hopelessly naïve, as the greatest barrier to improved taxation is not a lack of knowledge but a lack of political commitment to reform. Certainly, politics lies at the root of most taxation challenges. But political barriers are not insurmountable, and governments are in general rather good at capturing income flows—every year they transfer something like a quarter of global income into public treasuries without generating much conflict. Yet the belief that political barriers are insurmountable can become a convenient excuse for inaction. Indeed, it is likely that the potential for revenue-raising through the measures discussed here—notably, the taxation of the rich—have been under-rated by reformers because they are believed to be politically too difficult. But if governments fail to tackle high profile and visible areas of tax non-compliance they risk reinforcing a lack of trust in tax systems, and thus further raise the political barriers to reform.

In seeking to confront political challenges, there are some general features of tax politics that any potential reformer might bear in mind:

- Most of the time, there is some kind of implicit social contract underpinning successful expansion of taxation (see Chap. 1 in this volume). This may include public services, policies favoured by particular groups, or complicity in the under-taxation of some kinds of people and activities. Being able to provide benefits to taxpayers can encourage grudging compliance, while also building the kinds of political coalitions needed to overcome resistance to reform.
- There is also mounting evidence that taxpayers value perceived fairness in the assessment and collection of taxes. We can think of three broad dimensions of fairness: redistributive fairness (tax burdens are distributed fairly among taxpayers); procedural fairness (taxes are collected according to the law); and retributive fairness (penalties for non-compliance are fair, and fairly applied). Improvements in fairness potentially play an important role in mobilizing support for reform, and increasing voluntary tax compliance.
- Historically in many low-income countries, tax reform has been the preserve of experts. It is often believed that discouraging public debate allows new taxes to be introduced without permitting sufficient time or space for significant opposition to arise. This has often worked well: large-scale changes to tax systems, led by the introduction of the VAT, were often carried out with limited public opposition in the 1980s and 1990s. However, this approach appears decreasingly effective. While secretive processes may forestall broad public opposition, they also rule out the possibility of broad popular support from those who would benefit from broader taxation and expanded public spending programmes. Without such support, little progress has been made in overcoming resistance to taxing economically and politically powerful individuals and interest groups. Opening up tax debates—and more clearly linking tax to visible benefits—is likely to be more effective.

- Significantly increasing the tax take typically involves a long slog, as well as significant opportunism in taking advantage of favourable moments for reform. Major initiatives may sometimes lead to significant breakthroughs, but most often they are blunted, thwarted and perhaps reversed. Big, sustained changes in the balance of power are rare. Tax policies and patterns of tax collection tend to be sticky: they normally change only incrementally from year to year.
- Confronting political resistance to reform often depends on building strong tax institutions. Tax authorities that suffer low organizational capacity find it very hard to brush aside political objections to their attempts to do their job. Conversely, those tax authorities that have a reputation for competence have some autonomy from political pressures. They are likely to obtain more generous operating and capital budgets and be able to retain and train good staff (Strauss 2008). The existence of institutions that practice sensible tax policies and collect revenue effectively and efficiently helps to shift the balance of political forces in favour of better taxation. It is not helpful to pose "getting the politics (of tax reform) right" or building up institutional tax capacity as alternatives. They are likely to be mutually reinforcing.

The very political character of taxation does not mean that increasing the tax take and reforming the revenue system are unusually challenging tasks. Doing it successfully will typically involve a great deal of hard and steady work, and the gradual and iterative construction of popular trust and (grudging) support for reform. A capable tax administration can be just as valuable an ally as a political party, social movement or lobbying group.

Conclusion

The suggestions presented here are not intended as a checklist for reformers, or as an exclusive guide to sensible reform priorities. Our hope is that they may nonetheless offer a useful conceptual approach to thinking about reform by pointing towards potential opportunities and potential strategies. With these potential targets in mind, reform programmes can then seek to combine creative administrative and policy reforms for expanding the tax take. These reform strategies are likely to be diverse, but recent research and experience has pointed towards some potentially underexploited options, which we have tried to highlight here.

In concluding, it seems useful to address a question that—often implicitly—looms large within recent reform debates: when seeking additional revenues, to what extent should the governments of low-income countries aim to increase collections by reforming domestic tax policies and administration, and to what extent should they be focused on reform of international tax rules and the taxation of transnational firms and individuals? The past decade has witnessed an upsurge in attention to the reform of international tax issues, driven by growing—though sometimes overstated—evidence of significant tax evasion and avoidance of TNCs and wealthy individuals (see sections above). The problem is substantively important and morally galling. The wealthiest and most powerful members of society are among the main beneficiaries. They have been knowingly aided and abetted by the governments, corporations, banks and professional organizations of some of the wealthiest countries. There are good reasons why advocacy has focused on these tax justice concerns. Contrary to the initial pessimism of many observers, the campaigners have helped stimulate important reforms in the international tax system.

The question is thus not whether this experience has been valuable, as it clearly has. It is rather: what to do next? On one hand, there are good reasons to continue to focus on international tax issues. While recent reforms have helped, the international tax rules remain far from optimal for low-income countries: transfer pricing rules remain extremely difficult to enforce, access to country-by-country corporate accounts is imperfect and access to information of wealth held abroad by citizens remains difficult, or impossible, for tax authorities with limited capacity. Continued effort on the international front is essential. But there is also a risk of allowing the moral outrage around international evasion and avoidance to pull attention away from the more banal, but perhaps ultimately more important, work of building domestic tax systems. In aggregate revenue terms, it is difficult to avoid the conclusion that the largest dangling fruits are largely domestic. The best estimates of revenue losses from transfer mispricing and the failure to tax individual wealth held offshore are each on the scale of 1–2 per cent of GDP, hugely important, but still only a small portion of the potential additional revenue. Revenue lost due to a simple lack of enforcement of income taxes on the wealthy, ineffective property taxation, overly generous tax exemptions, collusion and poor enforcement in the mining sector—not to mention basic questions around enforcement of the VAT and customs duties—is much larger in the long term. As important, building robust and broad-based revenue systems domestically is likely to be an essential ingredient to fully confronting international sources of evasion. While stronger international tax units, basic policy reforms and the adjustment or repeal of tax treaties are able to capture low-hanging fruit in confronting the most egregious of abuses, more systematic gains—and the prosecution of high-net-worth individuals (HNWIs) with wealth held abroad—will depend on strengthening revenue systems generally. The choice between an international versus a domestic focus is to a large extent beside the point: progress in one domain is dependent on advances in the other.

References

Aarsnes, Frian, and Olav Lundstol. 2013. *The Case for Windfall Taxes. A Guide to Optimal Resource Taxation*. PWPY Norway Report (November).

Action Aid. 2016. *Mistreated. The Tax Treaties That are Depriving the World's Poorest Countries of Vital Revenue*. Report. Johannesburg Action Aid. Accessed 25 September 2019. https://actionaid.org/publications/2016/mistreated#downloads.

Africa Progress Panel. 2013. Africa Progress Report 2013. *Equity in Extractives: Stewarding Africa's Natural Resources for All*. Flagship Report. Geneva: Africa Progress Panel.

African Tax Administration Forum. 2017. *African Tax Outlook 2017*. Pretoria: African Tax Administration Forum.

Bahl, Roy W., Jorge Martinez-Vasquez, and Joan Youngman, eds. 2008. *Making the Property Tax Work. Experiences in Developing and Transitional Countries*. Cambridge, MA: Lincoln Institute of Land Policy.

Best, Michael Carlos, Anne Brockmeyer, Henrik Jacobsen Kleven, Johannes Spinnewijn, and Mazhar Waseem. 2015. Production versus Revenue

Efficiency with Limited Tax Capacity: Theory and Evidence from Pakistan. *Journal of Political Economy* 123 (6): 1311–1355.

Bird, Richard M. 2010. *Subnational Taxation in Developing Countries. A Review of the Literature*. Working Paper No. 5450. Washington, DC: World Bank.

———. 2011. Subnational Taxation in Developing Countries. A Review of the Literature. *Journal of International Commerce, Economics and Policy* 2 (1): 139–161.

Cheeseman, Nic, and Diane de Gramont. 2017. Managing a Mega-City: Learning the Lessons from Lagos. *Oxford Review of Economic Policy* 33 (3): 457–477.

Collier, Paul. 2010. Principles of Resource Taxation for Low Income Countries. In *The Taxation of Petroleum and Minerals: Principles, Problems and Practice*, ed. Philip Daniel, Michael Keen, and Charles McPherson, 75–86. Oxon: Routledge.

Daniel, Philip, Michael Keen, and Charles McPherson. 2010. *The Taxation of Petroleum and Minerals: Principles, Problems and Practice*. London: Routledge and International Monetary Fund.

Daniel, Philip, Michael Keen, Artur Swistak, and Victor Thuronyi, eds. 2016. *International Taxation and the Extractive Industries*. London: Routledge.

de Gramont, Diane. 2015. *Governing Lagos. Unlocking the Politics of Reform*. Washington, DC: Carnegie Endowment for International Peace.

Durst, Michael. 2015. *Limitations of the BEPS Reforms: Looking Beyond Corporate Taxation for Revenue Gains*. Working Paper No. 50. Brighton: International Centre for Tax and Development.

———. 2016. *Improving the Performance of Natural Resource Taxation in Developing Countries*. Working Paper No. 60. Brighton: International Centre for Tax and Development.

EY. 2014. *Complexities, Challenges and Opportunities of Supply Chain Management in Africa*. Presentation made at the EY Africa Tax Conference, Johannesburg, 18–19 September. Johannesburg: EY.

Forstater, Maya. 2017a. *How Big Is the Transfer Pricing Prize for Development?* Center for Global Development. Accessed 25 September 2019. https://www.cgdev.org/blog/how-big-transfer-pricing-prize-development.

———. 2017b. *Illicit Financial Flows and Trade Misinvoicing: Time to Reassess*. Center for Global Development. Accessed 25 September 2019. https://www.cgdev.org/blog/illicit-financial-flows-and-trade-misinvoicing-time-reassess.

Hearson, Martin, and Jalia Kangave. 2016. *A Review of Uganda's Tax Treaties*. Working Paper No. 50. Brighton: International Centre for Tax and Development.

ICTD (International Centre for Tax and Development) and United Nations University-World Institute for Development Economics Research (UNU-WIDER). 2019. Government Revenue Dataset. September. Accessed 25 September 2019. https://www.wider.unu.edu/project/government-revenue-dataset.

IMF (International Monetary Fund). 2012. *Mongolia: Technical Assistance Report—Safeguarding Domestic Revenue—A Mongolian DTA Model*. Country Report No. 12/306 (November). Washington, DC: IMF.

———. 2014. *Spillovers in International Corporate Taxation*. Staff Report (May). Washington, DC: IMF.

———. 2016. *How to Design and Enforce Tobacco Taxes (3)*. Report Published by the Fiscal Affairs Department (November). Washington, DC: IMF.

IMF (International Monetary Fund), OECD (Organisation for Economic Co-operation and Development), UN (United Nations) and World Bank. 2015. *Options for Low Income Countries' Effective and Efficient Use of Tax Incentives for Investment*. Report to G-20 Development Working Group (October). Washington, DC: IMF.

Jibao, Samuel, and Wilson Prichard. 2016. Rebuilding Local Government Finances After Conflict: Lessons from a Property Tax Reform Programme in Post-Conflict Sierra Leone. *Journal of Development Studies* 52 (12): 1759–1775.

Jibao, Samuel, Wilson Prichard, and Vanessa van den Boogaard. 2017. *Informal Taxation in Post-Conflict Sierra Leone: Taxpayers' Experiences and Perceptions*. Working Paper No. 66. Brighton: International Centre for Tax and Development.

Kangave, Jalia, Susan Nakoto, Ronald Waiswa, and Patrick Zzimbe. 2016. *Boosting Revenue Collection Through Taxing High Net Worth Individuals: The Case of Uganda*. Working Paper No. 45. Brighton: International Centre for Tax and Development.

Keen, Michael. 2013. *The Anatomy of the VAT*. IMF Working Paper No. 13/111. Washington, DC: International Monetary Fund.

Keen, Michael, and Mario Mansour. 2009. *Revenue Mobilization in Sub-Saharan Africa: Challenges from Globalization*. IMF Working Paper No. 09/157. Washington, DC: International Monetary Fund.

Kinda, Tidiane. 2014. *The Quest for Non-Resource-Based FDI: Do Taxes Matter?* IMF Working Paper No. 14/15. Washington, DC: International Monetary Fund.

Laporte, Bertrand, and Céline de Quatrebarbes. 2015. *What Do We Know About the Mineral Resource Rent Sharing in Africa?* Working Paper No. 39. Brighton: International Centre for Tax and Development.

Lundstøl, Olav, Gael Raballand, and Fuvya Nyirongo. 2013. *Low Government Revenue from the Mining Sector in Zambia and Tanzania: Fiscal Design, Technical Capacity or Political Will?* Working Paper No. 9. Brighton: International Centre for Tax and Development.

McCluskey, Rhiannon. 2016. *Why African Governments Should Tax the Rich*. International Centre for Tax and Development. Accessed 25 September 2019. https://www.ictd.ac/blog/why-african-govs-should-tax-the-rich/.

Moore, Mick. 2015 July. *Tax and the Governance Dividend*. ICTD Working Paper No. 37. Brighton: International Centre for Tax and Development.

National Cancer Institute. 2017. *The Economics of Tobacco and Tobacco Control*. NCI Tobacco Monograph No. 21. Bethesda, MD: U.S.: Department of Health and Human Services, National Institutes of Health, National Cancer Institute; and Geneva: World Health Organization.

OECD (Organisation for Economic Co-operation and Development). 2013. *Analysis of Tax Expenditures in Ghana*. Paris: OECD.

———. 2018. *Global Forum on Transparency and Exchange of Information for Tax Purposes*. Paris: OECD. Accessed 25 September 2019. http://www.oecd.org/tax/transparency/automaticexchangeofinformation.htm.

Paler, Laura, Wilson Prichard, Raul Sanchez de la Sierra, and Cyrus Samii. 2017. *Survey on Total Tax Burden in the DRC*, Final Report (April). London: Department for International Development.

Readhead, Alexandra. 2016. *Preventing Tax Base Erosion in Africa: A Regional Study of Transfer Pricing Challenges in the Mining Sector*. London: Natural Resource Governance Institute.

———. 2017. *Toolkit for Transfer Pricing Risk Assessment in the African Mining Industry*. Eschborn/Bonn: Deutsche Gesellschaft für Internationale Zusammenarbeit.

Reuter, Peter, ed. 2012. *Draining Development? Controlling Flows of Illicit Funds from Developing Countries*. Washington, DC: World Bank.

Savedoff, William, and Albert Alwang. 2015. *The Single Best Health Policy in the World: Tobacco Taxes*. CGD Policy Paper No. 62. Washington, DC: Center for Global Development.

Strauss, Julia. 2008. Rethinking Institutional Capacity and Tax Regimes: The Case of the Sino-Foreign Salt Inspectorate in Republican China. In *Taxation and State-Building in Developing Countries: Capacity and Consent*, ed. Deborah Brautigam, Odd-Helge Fjeldstad, and Mick Moore, 212–234. New York: Cambridge University Press.

Therkildsen, Ole, and Ane Karoline Bak. 2019. *Democratisation in Tanzania: No Elections Without Tax Exemptions*. ICTD Working Paper No. 98. Brighton: International Centre for Tax and Development.

Uganda Revenue Authority. 2016. *Annual Report 2015/2016*. Annual Report. Kampala: Uganda Revenue Authority.

UNRISD (United Nations Research Institute for Social Development). 2016. Mobilizing Domestic Resources for Sustainable Development: Toward a Progressive Fiscal Contract. In *Policy Innovations for Transformative Change. Implementing the 2030 Agenda for Sustainable Development*, 167–195. Geneva: UNRISD.

Van Walbeek, Crone, Evan Blecher, Anna Gilmore, and Hana Ross. 2013. Price and Tax Measures and Illicit Trade in the Framework Convention on Tobacco Control: What We Know and What Research Is Required. *Nicotine & Tobacco Research* 15 (4): 767–776.

Waris, Attiya. 2017. *How Kenya Has Implemented and Adjusted to the Changes in International Transfer Pricing Regulations: 1920–2016*. Working Paper No. 69. Brighton: International Centre for Tax and Development.

Zucman, Gabriel. 2015. *The Hidden Wealth of Nations. The Scourge of Tax Havens*. Chicago/London: University of Chicago Press.

5

Colonial Legacies and Social Welfare Regimes in Africa: An Empirical Exercise

Thandika Mkandawire

Introduction[1]

The central purpose of this chapter is to engage the literature on welfare regimes with the aim of identifying any systematic variations and reasonably coherent clusters of regimes within Africa. Observers of social policy and welfare regimes in developing countries have noted how theoretical and descriptive the work is or how little has been done to identify commonalities among developing countries.[2] On the one hand, this is attributable to neglect of the literature on welfare regimes inspired by Esping-Andersen's seminal work *The Three Worlds of Welfare Capitalism* (Esping-Andersen 1990), which has produced a rich literature mainly around member countries of the Organisation for Economic Co-operation and

[1] The author would like to thank the two anonymous referees for the chapter for their comments.

[2] Mares (2004), Rudra (2007), Mkandawire (2011).

T. Mkandawire (deceased)
London School of Economics, London, UK

K. Hujo (ed.), *The Politics of Domestic Resource Mobilization for Social Development*, Social Policy in a Development Context,
https://doi.org/10.1007/978-3-030-37595-9_5

Development (OECD). On the other hand, until recently the social policy experiences of developing countries have hardly featured in comparative analysis of social policies. There is, however, a new interest in the role of social policy in the process of development which has led some taxonomy of historical or current policy regimes. This new literature has sought to widen the number of countries involved, to examine the applicability of Esping-Andersen's methodology and classificatory approach to developing countries and to modify the variables included. We now find a growing comparative literature on Latin America and East Asia.[3]

The literature on social policy in Africa has been slow in engaging with this literature in a systematic way. This can be attributed to many factors. One is the point that the funding of the welfare state has been generally neglected: "A relative indifference to the funding base and the exclusive concern with the redistribution is closely related. … The importance of the funding capacity of the state is overshadowed by an overwhelming concern for redistribution through welfare programmes and taxation" (Kato 2003: 2). In addition, the attention to aid has overshadowed the question of the domestic funding of social policy, although in most African countries this is the most significant source of funding. And where there is interest in the fiscal base of social policy in Africa, much of the work remains focused on, or descriptive of, a single country or specific sector and is not explicitly related to welfare regimes. This said, there have been useful contributions to the comparative analysis of African welfare regimes.

This study is also a follow-up to a previous one on taxation (Mkandawire 2010) which suggests that one could identify social welfare regimes in Africa closely allied to tax regimes which, in turn, could be traced to forms of a country's incorporation into the colonial economy (Mkandawire 2010). The conjecture drew on two ideas about social policy. The first was that welfare regimes—defined as "the combined, interdependent way in which welfare is produced and allocated between state, market and family" (Esping-Andersen 1999: 34–35)—are fundamentally inseparable from fiscal regimes so that, running concurrently or symbiotically with the inherited tax regimes, there are social spending patterns and institutions. It is the combination of these tax regimes and social expenditure

[3] For examples, see Mkandawire (2016), footnotes 2 and 3.

patterns that substantially indicate the features of the welfare regimes of individual countries. In the words of Gilbert and Moon, "the size of tax revenues has a direct bearing on a government's ability to spend on social welfare as well as on other items of public expenditures" (Gilbert and Moon 1988: 330). This is not to suggest that high tax efforts, even when associated with high social expenditure, result in better delivery of welfare services (Gough and Abu Sharkh 2011). The second idea was about the saliency of path dependence in contemporary analysis of social policy, suggesting that the pre-existence of certain institutions could facilitate the adoption of new social policy agendas both institutionally and ideationally (Blyth 2001; Pierson 1993). The origins and age of welfare systems create institutional inertia, political lobbies and institutional interests that favour their maintenance or expansion. In the African case, the colonial legacies of ideas, institutions and social stratification, operating on both sides of the revenue-expenditure balance sheet, play a significant, albeit formally deracialized, role almost half a century after independence.

The chapter is organized as follows. In the first section, it brings out the forms of colonial incorporation of African economies into labour reserve and cash crop economies and the colonial welfare policies and practices associated with the incorporation. I leave out concession economies due to lack of data in the post-colonial era. The second section demonstrates that, using data from the 1990s and after, these colonial legacies produced two clusters of welfare regimes in line with the colonial strategies discussed in the first section. The third section shows how this classification is a significant determinant of levels of social expenditure. The fourth section demonstrates the relevance of the comparative classification on one specific set of social policies—health expenditure.

The Initial Conditions: Colonial Legacy and Social Policy

In an earlier paper on taxation (Mkandawire 2010), I used a classification of African tax regimes along the lines suggested by the work of economic historians Samir Amin (1972) and Oliver and Atmore (1967). I suggested that the tax regimes in Africa could be classified according to the economic forms of colonial incorporation which had produced three major types: (1) the labour reserve economies (predominantly found in Southern Africa), in which "the 'white economy' drew on labour reserves for its labour requirements and used them for the disposal of unwanted labour"; (2) the cash crop economies, characterized by significant peasant control over the systems of production; and (3) the concession economies, where vast resources were managed by private companies (Mkandawire 2010: 1649–50).[4] I have slightly amended the classification to include Burundi and Rwanda, which provided labour to the British colony of Uganda and later, under Belgian labour recruitment schemes, to the mines in Congo.

Labour reserve economies tended to be high tax economies, relying more on direct taxes. In contrast, cash crop economies were low tax economies that relied on trade taxes (Frankema 2010). In the paper on taxation (Mkandawire 2010), I argued that an explanation for high taxation in the "labour reserve economies" was the racially exclusive welfare regimes that were set up for the white population. In this chapter, I seek to establish that in Africa, one can identify distinct welfare regime patterns that are closely associated with the "labour reserve economy" defined below and that differs in some substantial characteristics from the "non-labour reserve economies". Although there are some similarities between this classification and that of Acemoglu et al. (2001), it is important to bear in mind that the latter classification was ultimately focused on property rights, while the Amin classification (Amin 1972) considers labour and commodity market conditions, differential access to inputs such as human capital and differences in access to property rights. It focuses not only on the securing of property rights of the colonialists but the dispossession and proletarianization of the indigenous populations and their incorporation into world markets, which are much more institutionally demanding tasks.

There is a considerable amount of literature quantitatively examining the effects of colonialism on contemporary economic performance.[5] The colonial legacy can express itself through various channels: in the form of durable institutions that condition or constrain post-colonial ideas;

[4] See Table 5.1 for the classification of the countries. This chapter will focus on the first two types.

[5] For examples, see Mkandawire 2016 (footnote 5).

through ideas borrowed from or imposed by the erstwhile colonial masters; through pressures of incipient social interests that have become more pronounced in the post-colonial era; through the colonial ties that survive decolonization and the economic and political leverage that the erstwhile colonial masters continue to exercise; or due to "mundane administrative reasons" and the force of habit (Midgley 1984: 28).[6] Although it might seem that there is an overemphasis on the colonial legacy and on copying and continuity and much less on contestation and rupture, not all aspects of the colonial legacy are simple replications of what has been bequeathed by the past. They also involve contestation through resistance to the colonial order and the imagining of alternative futures. Colonialism impacted nationalist agendas and forms of mobilization and resistance, and the ideological progression and "social pacts" that emerged. There was also the reaction and attempts to rectify the injustice of the past. In the words of Patel, "the demands and struggles of opposition social movements account for the normative thrust in post-apartheid social policies with their focus on social justice and social rights, state intervention and the role of civil society in social developments" (Patel 2011: 81).

Colonial social policy was circumscribed by what Crawford Young refers to as the "the twin exigencies of hegemony and revenue" (Young 1988: 29). In the early years of colonial rule, active social policy was simply not on the agenda and the social protection schemes that existed were exclusively for citizens of the metropolis working in the colonies or for white settler populations. The assumption was that traditional forms of social protection would take the place of social security provided by the state. In his influential African Survey, Lord Acton stated that, "it is clear that by treating the native reserves as reservoirs of man-power, there is, in effect, a saving in that outlay on social services which in other circumstances might have to be incurred on behalf of industrialized labour" (Eckert 2004: 473).

[6] It should be stressed here that the existence of colonial institutions does not mean they serve the same purpose as they used to. See Midgley's reflections on social assistance schemes as an example (1984: 208).

The wave of protests by peasants against merchant capitalists in the 1930s, the growing assertiveness of African labour, the growing urban population and the social demands of demobilized African soldiers after the Second World War led to some reconsideration of social policy which culminated in the Colonial and Welfare Development Act in the British colonies.[7] However, the new initiatives were quite limited in their reach. They were also profoundly shaped by the mode of incorporation of the colonies and their fiscal base.

The Cash Crop Economies

One feature of the cash crop economy that had significant implications for social well-being was that the indigenous people's access to land was maintained and the control over the system of production was left in their hands. As Bowden et al. (2008: 1055) argue, this form of colonization "placed in the hands of lower-income groups a cluster of assets, not only permanent export crops but also the infrastructure and training required to produce and export them, which were to be important in determining the dynamics of poverty reduction processes in later years". This had huge implications on labour markets. For one, access to land and commodity markets raised the reservation price of labour and improved the bargaining power of Africans in the labour market. And thus for Ghana and Uganda, the real wage began to rise from its 1911 level in the 1920s and 1930s respectively, and never fell back to that floor.

The second feature was access to human capital and finance, both related to access to income through cash crop production. The booming exports provided peasants with income to pay for their education. In addition, the process of cash crop production and marketing required a semi-skilled indigenous labour force. Bowden et al. (2008: 1069) observe:

> From the beginning, the peasant-export economies had a greater propensity to invest in the human capital of the poor. This had various dimensions, of which the easiest to measure is the level of investment in African

[7] Seekings (2011), Cooper (1996), Eckert (2004), Midgley and Piachaud (2011).

> education. As one measure, in 1950, at a time when Southern Rhodesia (Zimbabwe) had only one African secondary school, and Kenya only three, Ghana (the Gold Coast) had 20 (together with three teacher-training colleges and a university college), and Uganda six (together with one teacher-training college and university college). Investment in the African labour force was, until the middle of the twentieth century, not part of the settler-colony vision.[8]

Social policies in these cash crop economies were often pursued through informal or community-based systems, which were seen as supplementing the "traditional" systems of social welfare in the community (Maclean 2002). The emphasis was on local leadership, self-help and voluntary effort, an aspect of "indirect rule" in such economies.[9] The access to incomes through direct participation in commodity markets, rather than through wage labour, set the stage for the out-of-pocket expenditures on social services that characterize cash crop economies to this day. One consequence of this informal provision of social welfare was a lack of strong and sustainable institutional bases that has undermined new initiatives in low-income countries (Niño-Zarazúa et al. 2012).

The more formal means of social policy came in roundabout ways in cash crop economies. In such economies, the new "social question" arose out of peasantization and commercialization of African crop production which immediately exposed peasants to new social vulnerabilities stemming from greater reliance on markets. These vulnerabilities became most acute during the Great Depression where price instability for cash crops led to riots. Colonial authorities were obliged to introduce measures for the stabilization of commodity prices and incomes of peasants through marketing boards (Eckert 2004; Cooper 1996). It is important to note that although marketing boards served the function of surplus extraction, they also responded to pressures on the government to mitigate domestic social conflict caused by volatility in the world economy (Alence 2001). Interestingly, the British colonial government saw the

[8] In a similar vein, Frankema (2012) shows a high correlation between social enrolment and subsequent literary levels with cash crop economy.

[9] Indirect rule refers to situations where the colonial governments ruled through "traditional rulers".

marketing boards as an instrument of social protection by shielding peasants from the vagaries of the market.[10] They thus became what Mishra (2004) would refer to as "social policy by other means".

Labour Reserve Economies

If in the cash crop economies the problem was that of peasantization, in the labour reserve economies it was that of proletarianization, which placed more complicated demands on state structures. I noted above how the cash crop economies allowed room for self-improvement by the indigenous population and developed skills for some level of self-management, as well as to meet the mercantile and administrative needs of the cash crop economy. This was in sharp contrast with the labour reserve economies where the imperative of producing cheap wage labour denied Africans the opportunity to work outside the white settler-dominated labour reserve economy, compelling them "to adopt a way of life in which they derived an increasing portion of their sustenance from land and equipment owned legally by others" (Richard Wolff 1973, cited in Good 1976: 600). Related to this was the myth that Africans had a backward-bending labour supply curve. The myth was that "[t]he more you gave Sambo the less he worked" (Palmer and Parsons 1977: 14), a racist myth sustained by increasing labour supplies even as wages fell. Thus a South African black's real wage was closely aligned to its subsistence floor of the labour reserve until the 1970s (Bowden et al. 2008). The effect of these policies was to reduce the "labour reserves" into dumping grounds of exhausted, injured or diseased labour (Meillassoux 1981; Palmer and Parsons 1977). Indeed the "pure settler" economies, South Africa and Zimbabwe, are the only ones where Bowden et al. (2008) observed a decline in African rural living standards over long periods (more than 15 years) within the twentieth century. They find that "settler economies" have had much worse poverty and income distribution outcomes than peasant export economies.

This is not to suggest that the labour reserve economies were devoid of social policies targeted to the indigenous population. They were not and

[10] For an explanation of the differences between the British and French colonial attitudes, see MacLean (2010: 125).

for a number of reasons. One function of social policy in a capitalist society is the reproduction of labour as a means of production, which was a central preoccupation in these economies. The aim was to achieve exploitation of labour without actually undermining its reproduction.[11] The solution was to transfer the burden of social security onto rural communities, most of whom were living at the subsistence level deliberately maintained to force peasants into the capitalist labour market.[12] The social question thus took on an entirely different turn from that of the cash crop economies, and the labour reserve economies developed certain features that have had a lasting impact on social policy and institutions.

The first had to do with management of labour migration. This included policy measures that inhibited migration to urban areas, ironically through the use of the "Pass system" which required "natives" to carry a passport endorsed by their employers. Closely related to this problem was the question of managing indigent labour in the urban areas through social assistance laws and programmes which were introduced to address the repatriation of redundant labour to the native reserves. Later there were also measures to reproduce more stable labour as demanded by industrialization that eventually included education, health and housing measures. Many of the social policies were based on the English Poor Laws and were targeted specifically at the urban indigent.

The second feature was the extractive capacity of the state. As argued in Mkandawire (2010), labour reserve economies tended to collect relatively more tax (when controlled for other features of the economy) than the cash crop economies. The third feature was the high regulatory capacity of the state designed to protect and service a racial minority in power and to ensure the regimentation and reproduction of a highly migrant labour force. The fourth feature was the establishment of racially segmented welfare regimes, which, with their high taxation capacity, required institutional arrangements that blocked the leakage of the benefits of tax

[11] These concerns are captured in a report by the Southern Rhodesia government, Report of the Native Production and Trade Commission (1944: 9–19). Sharon Stichter (1982: 27–28) has also aptly summarized this attitude for Kenya.

[12] Arrighi et al. (2010), Wolpe (1972, 1980), Burawoy (1976), Meillassoux (1981), Mhone (2000) and Phimister (1974).

to indigenous populations (Mkandawire 2010).[13] Settler economies produced extensive welfare states, which, when deracialized, provided substantial benefits to those included in this welfare world, with South Africa eventually emerging in the post-apartheid era as "probably the developing world's largest and most generous welfare state" (Ann Bernstein cited in Hassim 2006: 109).

The fifth feature was the pattern of urbanization that led to much more thorough forms of labour commodification than in the cash crop economies, in the sense that livelihoods in the highly regimented urban areas were dependent on formal employment. The result was lower levels of informalization and reliance on the formal sector employment for the provision of welfare benefits (Mkandawire 1986, 2005). The sixth feature was the high levels of horizontal inequality in which the most striking aspect of inequality was along racial lines. This has had huge implications on the incidence of both tax and public expenditure. In the advanced capitalist countries, much of the progressive welfare spending is funded through regressive taxes.[14] Such a process was not allowed in labour reserve economies. Progressive taxes were premised on regressive expenditure.

The final feature was the forms of resistance and the ideologies they spawned and which have had a profound influence on thinking about social policies in labour reserve countries. The nationalists' contestation of the racial order meant that one fundamental aspect of policy in the post-colonial period would be deracialization and extension of key aspects of the racialized welfare state. This contestation and resistance was to place a number of social policies, such as racial inequality or land reform and many labour laws, on the agenda of key regional movements and, through the labour migration process, to have contagious impacts on the region.

These factors had two consequences for social policy. The first is the political pressure to correct historical injustices. Unlike the case of the

[13] This was particularly the case in countries with large white working-class populations. For elaboration on the South African case, see Patel (2011) and Hassim (2006).

[14] Kato (2003), Lindert (2004) and Shaikh (2003).

cash crop economy where there was little political urgency to implement welfare policies pronounced by the colonial government, the labour reserve economies produced high levels of labour militancy for ending racial inequality and were driven by the logic of industrialism's need for a stable labour force. One consequence of this might be a reduction in horizontal inequality while vertical inequality, although partially deracialized, remains the same or even worsens, partly because the ensemble of fiscal measures is ultimately insufficiently redistributive.

The second is the pre-existence of social welfare programmes within the region, albeit highly racialized, which provided the foundations of new initiatives.[15] The legacy of extreme economic inequality plays an important role in marking the boundaries of social policy concern and has been suggested as a driving force behind social protection policies in Southern Africa (Devereux and White 2010; Hickey 2007). Indeed, it has been pointed out that it is precisely in the former settler economies with high levels of inequality that we see the most concerted efforts at broader social protection policies (Devereux and White 2010; Hickey 2007) and where the extension of grant-based social protection has emerged as a domestic and largely tax-funded initiative (Barrientos et al. 2009). One should also bear in mind the political mobilization that accompanied the end of the racial order and the subsequent organized pressure for change.[16] The political discourse was bound to be infused with concerns of horizontal inequality. In labour reserve economies, there was a tendency to undertake intra-group comparisons suggesting a focus on horizontal rather than vertical inequalities.[17]

---

[15] This is most obvious in South Africa. See Patel for a reflection on the "positive human development benefits" this has had in the country (2011: 81).

[16] Schüring and Lawson-McDowall (2011) argue that South Africa has "the most vibrant and motivated civil society on the continent", which has resulted in the wide application of rights, a trend they identify in several neighbouring countries as well.

[17] Stewart (2009), Devereux and White (2010) and Hickey (2007).

Social Welfare Regimes in Africa: The Problem of Classification

This chapter seeks to identify contemporary welfare regimes in Africa that are traceable to their colonial origins discussed earlier. A standard procedure for classifying social policy regimes is cluster analysis,[18] which has become the workhorse of comparative social policy. Cluster analysis is a way of inductively grouping data into few and meaningful categories. This statistical technique is ideal for the purpose of this chapter, as groupings are identified without any theoretical predispositions on the data.

The choice of variables included has been determined by availability and their inclusion in earlier studies. Following Gough and associates,[19] I include a broad spectrum of variables to capture a wide range of aspects relevant to welfare regimes in Africa. In the process of using this comprehensive list, one or two countries were lost from Table 5.1. Countries that were not colonized or did not exist on their current geographical form in the colonial days were excluded, as were small island countries (Table 5.2).

The clustering shown in the dendrogram in Fig. 5.1 was obtained using the variables indicated above and the countries for which data was

Table 5.1 Forms of colonial incorporation

Type	Countries
Cash crop economies (enlarged West Africa)	Benin, Burkina Faso, Cameroon, Côte d'Ivoire, Gambia, Ghana, Guinea, Guinea-Bissau, Mali, Mauritania, Niger, Nigeria, Senegal, Sierra Leone, Tanzania, Togo, Uganda
Africa of the concession companies (Congo Basin)	Central African Republic, Democratic Republic of Congo, Gabon, Republic of Congo
Africa of the labour reserves (East and Southern Africa)	Angola, Botswana, Burundi, Kenya, Lesotho, Madagascar, Malawi, Mozambique, Namibia, Rwanda, South Africa, Swaziland, Zambia, Zimbabwe

Source: Author elaboration from the classification by Oliver and Atmore (1967) and Samir Amin (1972)

[18] For a detailed explanation of cluster analysis and the methods I have used, see Mkandawire (2016).

[19] Gough and Abu Sharkh (2011), Gough et al. (2004), Abu Sharkh and Gough (2010).

Table 5.2 Description of variables

	Variables
Commodification	Health expenditure, private (% of GDP)
Global environment	Net ODA received (% of GNI) External debt stocks (% of GNI) Foreign direct investment, net inflows (% of GDP) Interest payments on external debt (% of GNI)
Economic structure	Industry, value added (% of GDP) Log of GDP per capita (constant 2000 USD) Urban population (% of total)
Social stratification	Literacy rate, adult female (% of females ages 15 and above) Total enrolment, primary, female (% net) Gini index Income share held by highest 10% Primary education, pupils (% female)
Other welfare outcomes	Military expenditure Literacy rate, adult total (% of people ages 15 and above) Total enrolment, primary (% net) Immunization, DPT (% of children ages 12–23 months)

available. Visual inspection of the dendrogram shows that there are two clusters of African economies, with the cluster on the right consisting of labour reserve economies and the other of non-labour reserve economies, with only a few misclassified. As often happens with cluster analysis, there are "rogue" countries that stray from the postulated historical affinities, especially given the passage of time (e.g. Angola and Tanzania).

Relationship with Other Studies and Literature

We start with Ian Gough and associates (2004) who have made the most ambitious attempt in using cluster analysis to identify welfare regimes in non-OECD countries. They identify two "meta-welfare regimes" in developing countries: an informal security regime and an insecurity regime. Under the latter, they identify a subcategory applicable to Africa, namely "failing informal security regimes" under which "public social policy has expanded in both expenditures and outreach and literacy levels are high, but these improvements are swamped by rising mortality and

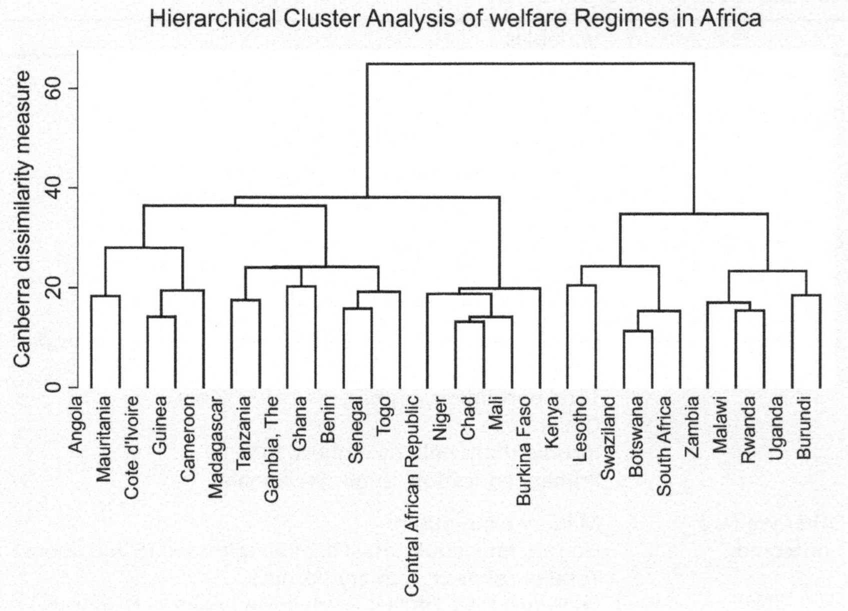

Fig. 5.1 Hierarchical cluster analysis of welfare regimes in Africa. (Source: Author elaboration from World Bank data)

morbidity due to HIV/AIDS". Comprising Botswana, Kenya, Namibia, South Africa and Zimbabwe, these countries interestingly belong to the "labour reserve economies". The "insecurity regime", on the other hand, "describe[s] institutional arrangements which block the emergence even of stable informal security mechanisms, and thus generate gross levels of insecurity and poor welfare outcomes" (Abu Sharkh and Gough 2010: 29). The remaining sub-Saharan countries (most of the cash crop economies) belong here.

Niño-Zarazúa et al. (2012) and Barrientos et al. (2009) identify two "models". The Southern African model includes Botswana, Lesotho, Mauritius, Namibia, Seychelles, South Africa and Swaziland. The analysis (in the dendrogram in Fig. 5.1) suggests that all these countries are in the "labour reserve category" and they may indeed constitute a subgroup of higher middle-income countries in the cluster. Their Middle Africa Model corresponds to our Cash Crop Economy model. The differences with the classification of Barrientos et al. (2009) is that while all the countries in the Southern African model belong to our labour reserve economy category, some of the countries we would include in the labour reserve economy are classified with many cash crop economies in the Middle Africa model. Barrientos and associates identify a number of factors to account for the extension of social assistance within these countries. In South Africa, the extension is attributed to deracialization and equity considerations, while in Namibia electoral politics play an important role. Barrientos et al. (2009: 7) observe: "There is a sub-regional underpinning for the 'model', as the countries involved have interlocking economies, and large-scale labour migration". They also note that these are higher middle-income countries. The fact that Botswana—another sub-Saharan Africa country with an unusually unequal society—is one of the few countries to have introduced a pension system adds further weight to this level of income argument and may suggest that many African countries have simply not reached the point of economic development and inequality whereby the impulse for social protection becomes pervasive.

However, we should bear in mind that there are other middle-income countries in Africa that have not embarked on such social policies. The Middle Africa model is a more heterogeneous model, involving programmes with different orientation and design. Nonetheless, many of the basic characteristics are shared: a focus on extreme poverty and food insecurity; a strong involvement by community organizations in the management and implementation of the programme; and precarious institutionalization and financing. These features are reminiscent of the colonial model of welfare for rural Africa discussed in the earlier parts of the chapter. Seekings (2005), who considers Esping-Andersen's classifications "less useful in the South", divides welfare regimes in developing countries into three categories: an agrarian world, an inegalitarian corporatist and a redistributive one:

> Agrarian regimes are defined by the private provision of welfare, dependent on access to land and/or kin; such access to land and/or kin is itself dependent on a set of supportive state policies. Inegalitarian corporatist regimes are defined by achieving income security through forms of risk-pooling

> and/or saving that are dependent on employment. … Finally, there are redistributive regimes which are defined by their recognition of citizens' rights to income security through, especially, non-contributory social assistance. (Seekings 2005: 16)

Seekings does not explicitly classify African countries, although one can surmise from what he says about Kenya, Mauritius and South Africa (labour reserve economies) that the rest of Africa would be placed in the agrarian regime category which is close to our cash crop economies.

These classifications, while contributing to the comparative study of social policy in Africa, have lacked historical narrative that would incorporate the elements discussed above. Much of the acknowledgement that colonial legacies would still have a bearing on the classification of social regimes is ad hoc and tentative. The comparative social policy on Africa has even been slower in relating social policy to the fiscal regime. To address some of the ambiguities and inconsistencies in these classifications, I make recourse to classifications above, suggesting the existence of welfare regimes that fall along the line of colonial incorporation captured in an earlier study on taxation (Mkandawire 2010). The question addressed here then is whether the past political practices, economic structures and social welfare institutions still have an impact on contemporary variations in social policy in Africa. In other words, using a number of standard socio-economic indicators, would the classification posited above have any predictive value?

The Social Expenditure Effect

Having identified two clusters of welfare regimes, we now turn to the question of whether there is a relationship between the welfare and the tax regimes, as conjectured in an earlier paper (Mkandawire 2010). This will be done through the lens of social expenditure, "the proverbial gold standard of welfare state development" (Kim 2010: 423). Social expenditure consists of basic assistance to families, unemployment compensation, public non-contributory pensions, public health, housing subsidies and public housing (Lindert 2004). Even if there were available data on these variables in the studies of welfare regimes in OECD countries, there would still be the question of the adequacy of these measures and the Eurocentric basis of the weights attached to them. It is clear that the measures exclude public social expenditures that may be more important in national budgets of developing countries than those of developed ones. More specifically, we should consider expenditures on measures that somehow capture "surrogate social policy" (Chang 2004: 252) or "social protection by other means" (Mishra 2004: 68). These may include price stabilization for farmers through marketing boards, subsidies for food, fertilizers or transport to poor farmers, which can all be quite substantial.[20] The political salience of these subsidies are often highlighted by "rice riots" when the subsidies are removed, often as part of liberalization policies. Unfortunately, such data is not available in a comparative form. And even for the basic data used in OECD studies, adequate data is available only for public expenditure on education and health.

A consequence of the labour reserve economy has been the creation of social conditions that have fanned the spread of HIV/AIDS in the regions—patterns of migration, separation of families and so on.[21] As a consequence, the labour reserve economies have been hit hard by the HIV/AIDS pandemic. Governments have had to significantly increase their expenditure on health, thus inflating social expenditure.

Rather than simply use total social expenditure I have to adjust my analysis by eliminating the part of expenditure that is not accounted for by HIV/AIDS. This is done by regressing SOCEXP on HIVPREV. The residual (SOCEXADJ) is then used as the adjusted social expenditure.

The generic form of the model is:

$$S_{t,i} = \alpha_{i,t} X_{i,t} + \beta_{t,i} Z_{i,t} + \partial R_{i,t} + \mu_{i,t} + \varepsilon_{i,t}$$

Where

[20] For instance in Malawi, the fertilizer subsidies to smallholders took up 6.4 per cent of the budget in 2006–2007 farming season as compared to around 8 per cent for social expenditure as measured by education and health expenditure (Government of Malawi 2006/2007).

[21] Sawers and Stillwaggon (2010), Lurie et al. (2003), and Brummer (2002).

$S_{t,i}$ is the adjusted share of social expenditure in GDP
$X_{i,t}$ is a matrix of independent variables
$Z_{i,t}$ is a matrix of control variables
$R_{i,t}$ is a matrix of the dummy variables

μ_i is the group effect for each county, and $\varepsilon_{i,t}$ is the error for each country, where $i = 1, 2, \ldots$ N are the cross-section units (in this case countries) and $t = 1, 2,$ T are the period.

As is standard in this literature, I use panel data for my analysis using an unbalanced pooled time-series analysis for 36 sub-Saharan countries for the period 1990–2011. Such panel data violate a number of assumptions in the standard ordinary least square analysis, such as the independence of errors across observations because of heteroskedasticity, spatial contemporaneous autocorrelation and serial autocorrelation. Consequently "determinants of social expenditure" literature resort to panel corrected standard errors and other tools to address these problems (Kim and Zurlo 2009; Rudra and Haggard 2005). I use panel corrected standard errors method in my analysis to address some of these problems.[22]

My core regressors are standard in social expenditure; I thus use log of per capita income (LOGCAP), share of INDUSTRY in GDP and URBANIZATION as indicators of Wilensky's "industrialism".[23] Industry and urbanization would be expected to have a positive effect on social expenditure, as organized labour and the "social question" in the urban areas pushes towards increases in welfare effort by the state. For some, the fact that urbanization tends to have a positive effect on welfare transfers "reveals that the welfare system serves the urban areas more than the countryside … rural residents tend to fall outside welfare transfers in poor countries", not least because urban dwellers are considered more politically valuable by governments (Feng and Gizelis 2002: 228). This is the "Urban Bias" thesis (Lipton 1977). DEPENDENCY measures the population under 15 and over 65. It is generally expected that the larger the population under 15, the more the state will spend on education and

[22] I use XTPCSE in Stata.

[23] According to Wilensky (1975), economic growth and its demographic and bureaucratic outcomes were crucial drivers behind emergence of the welfare state.

childcare, while the larger the population over 65, the greater the political pressure to allocate more for the care of the elderly. From these hypotheses a positive relationship between dependence and social expenditure could be posited.

The variable of interest will be the dummy variable RESERVE, which takes the value of 1 when the country belongs to labour reserve economy and 0 otherwise. My hypothesis is that it has a positive coefficient. LOGCAP is expected to have a positive coefficient. The three indicators AID, TRADE, DEBT and FDI are measures of globalization whose effect on welfare state expenditure has been the subject of considerable analyses on globalization and welfare. In aid-dependent economies, aid is bound to play a significant role with respect to resource allocation. Where it is simply additional to state expenditure on social policy, the relationship between aid and social expenditure will be positive. However, there are factors that might work in the opposite direction. Aid may "crowd out" domestic resources in the social sector as governments shift their resources elsewhere or reduce their overall budgetary efforts. Two opposite hypotheses are advanced with respect to integration in the world system. One is the "competition thesis" which suggests that in order to be competitive, a country may have to retrench welfare measures. The approach is to lower social expenditure by lowering tax revenue (Reuveny and Li 2003). A contrary view is that in order to avoid social conflict, countries may have to compensate the losers with social measures. Thus trade openness may lead to greater social expenditure as the state seeks to protect its citizens from the vagaries of globalization or compensates the losers. For similar reasons, FDI is theoretically ambiguous. DEBT is included as a proxy for the state's fiscal well-being. It would be expected to be negatively related to social expenditure.

The results of the analysis are presented in Table 5.4. Wilensky's relationship seems to be slightly true for African countries, unlike for developing countries in general.[24] URBANIZATION is negative, somehow contradicting what one would expect in light of the much vaunted "urban bias" of African governments. The most relevant result of the analysis is that the coefficient for the variable RESERVE is positive and significant (Table 5.3).

---

[24] For Latin America, see Haggard and Kaufman (2008).

Table 5.3 Variables used in all regressions

Variable	Description
TAXSHARE	Share of tax revenue in GDP
AGRI	Share of agriculture in GDP
DEBTSERVICE	Share of debt in total exports
SOCEXP	Share of social expenditure in GDP
SOCEXPHAT	Adjusted SOCEXP lagged
INDUSTRY	Share of industry in GDP
LOGCAP	Logarithm of per capita income
TRADE	(Export = import)/GDP
L.AID	Aid as percentage of GNI (lagged)
RESERVE	Equals 1 if country belongs to labour reserve and 0 if it does not
FDI	Foreign direct investment, net inflows (% of GDP)
DEPENDENCY	Population under age 15 and over 65
URBAN	Urban population as percentage of total population
HIVPREV	HIV/AIDS prevalence

Table 5.4 Determinants of social expenditure in Africa

Variables	Model 1	Model 2
L.SOCEXPHAT	0.967**	0.950**
	[57.04]	[59.93]
RESERVE	0.208**	0.153**
	[4.767]	[5.179]
LOGCAP		0.132**
		[7.279]
L.AID		
		[3.437]
INDUSTRY		0.00186*

Notes: Standard errors in parentheses: *$p < 0.1$, **$p < 0.01$

The variations in tax and social expenditure provide a two-by-two matrix which yields an interesting classification of African countries. We see that labour reserve economies are generally high taxation, high social expenditure. Most cash crop economies fall into the low expenditure, low taxation categories. Gambia stands out among high taxation cash economies for reasons related to the importance of smuggling and transit of goods to Senegal. The low taxation and high social expenditure mostly belong to the concession economies where mineral royalties played an important role (Table 5.5).

Table 5.5 Classification of African countries by taxation and social expenditure

	Share of social expenditure in GDP	
Share of tax in GDP	Greater than 5%	Less than 5%
Greater than 17%	Botswana South Africa Zambia Namibia Kenya Lesotho Swaziland	Gambia
Less than 17%	Guinea Cameroon Central African Republic Congo, Dem. Rep.	Burundi Sierra Leone Togo Senegal Niger Uganda Mali Burkina Faso Ghana Madagascar Rwanda Congo, Rep. Benin

Source: Author elaboration from World Bank data

To further understand the contributions of individual or group variables to the model's total explanatory value, the countries are divided into two categories: labour reserve and non-labour reserve. The R-squared is then decomposed into contributions of (groups of) regressor variables (Table 5.6).[25] The variables are grouped into four categories: (1) internal demand factors; (2) internal structural factors or the "Wilensky" structural factors as proxied by INDUSTRY and levels of per capita income (LOGCAP); (3) globalization factors represented by AID, DEBT, FDI and TRADE; and (4) political regime proxied by the Polity Index on democratization. In both cases, factors associated with demand for social services are high, accounting for 40.1 per cent in cash crop economies and 66 per cent in the labour reserve economies. This may be a reflection of high reliance on informal provision of social welfare in the cash crop

[25] The Stata module used is REGO whose decomposition of R^2 is based on Shapley or Owen values.

Table 5.6 Decomposition of social expenditure determinants

		Cash crop economies		Labour reserve economies	
	Regressor	Coefficient	Shapley decomposition	Coefficient	Shapley decomposition
Demand	DEPENDENCY	−0.0341037	40.7074	−0.2280898***	65.5244
	URBAN	−0.0434556***		−0.2007965***	
	HIVPREV	−0.1536005**		0.128587*	
Structure	INDUSTRY	−0.0538554***	24.6706	0.0761155	3.4682
	LOGCAP	−0.0602261		0.0321674	
Global	AIDGNI	0.0367939**	32.5364	0.0640404	28.3927
	TRADE	0.0206705***		0.0063561	
	FDI	−0.0584297***		0.1972561***	
	DEBTSERVICE	−0.0090271		−0.0072235	
Political regime	POLITY	−0.0037563	2.0856	0.0172673	2.6147
	INTERCEPT	10.50931		28.36521	

Notes: Standard errors in parentheses: *p <0.1, **p <0.05, ***p < 0.01

economies. Structural factors play a much more important role in the cash crop economies than in labour reserve economies. In both types, global factors play a significant role, although which factors matter differs, with AID being a more significant determinant in the cash crop economy than in the labour reserve economies where foreign direct investment is significant.

Social Protection Policies: The Case of Health Expenditure

Overall welfare regime type does not, of course, tell us what exactly happens at every social policy level, a point that some have used to criticize welfare regime classification (Kasza 2002). Kasza notes that although no one contends that every detail of every policy conforms to the same logic, there is often the implicit presumption that most of the key policies will indeed reflect a similar approach to issues of public welfare. Against this view, critics have pointed to certain inconsistencies in the behaviour of, or affinities across, regime types. Thus, although at high levels of aggregation, the British welfare regime differs from the Nordic "social democratic" one, it shares the same traits in the health sector with its universalistic National Health System.

We do not have detailed data on social policies at sector levels. However, we have data on the health sector at most disaggregated level for social expenditures data available on Africa. I have used this data to further underline the differences in the welfare regimes along the lines of my classification. Following Bonnoli's suggestion that welfare regimes can be captured by two dimensions of "how much" and "how" (Bambra 2007; Bonnoli 1997), I plotted two variables—total health expenditure as share of GDP for the level of health expenditures, and out-of-pocket expenditure as percentage of total health expenditure—for the way in which such a level of services is provided (Fig. 5.2). The quadrants are derived from the mean values of the two variables. We can identify four "health regimes" in Africa according to levels of expenditure and lack of health

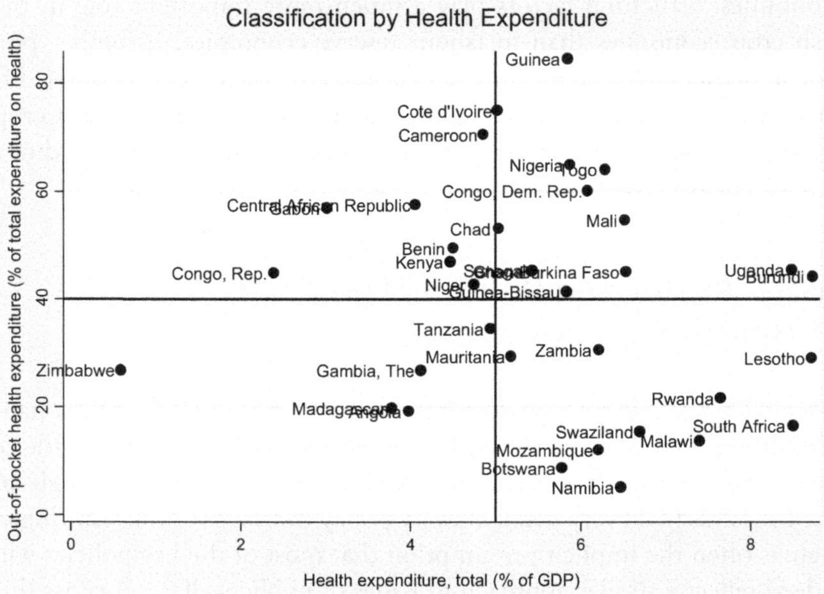

Fig. 5.2 Classification by health expenditure. (Source: Author elaboration from WHO Data)

insurance. Most of the labour reserve economies are in the bottom right quadrant with low out-of-pocket expenditure and high health expenditure.

Labour reserves economies have much higher levels of payments from prepaid private plans than non-labour reserve economies, and hence have much less out-of-pocket expenditure as percentage of private expenditure on health. In other words, there is much more private insurance in the labour reserve economies. In sharp contrast, non-labour reserve economies rely on out-of-pocket payments, which often involve informal arrangements. This is partly in line with the much larger share of the informal economy in these countries than in the labour reserve economies (Mkandawire 2010). It also fits with the larger issue of welfare regimes of the respective clusters of countries. In the words of Poullier et al. (2002: 12):

> Private insurance tends to be a luxury of either high-income countries or high-income households within low-income countries. The importance of private insurance in total health spending depends significantly on the health system's structure. In some countries private insurance is viewed as an integral part of the health system, subject to regulation. In other countries, private insurance is viewed as a luxury good, and either tolerated or encouraged. However, in most countries, private insurance is simply one more segment of a fragmented health system. The importance of private insurance, then, depends on the domestic level and distribution of income, as well as on public policy.

In the literature on OECD countries, the evidence is that the bulk of health expenditure is progressive (Lindert 2004). However, while the labour reserve economies spend more resources on health, one has to bear in mind that the inequality suggested by Gini coefficients permeates the entire social system. Thus, while South Africa spends 8.5 per cent of GDP on health (the World Health Organization/WHO recommendation is over 5 per cent), this is inequitably distributed among the population. People who belong to private medical schemes form 16 per cent of the population and consume over 50 per cent of total health care funds.

In South Africa, the portion of the population that purchases private health insurance is only about 15 per cent, while "the bulk of the population … is dependent on an underfunded public sector" (Eme Ichoku et al. 2013: 305). In Zimbabwe, only 8 per cent of the population is estimated to have private health insurance (Campbell et al. 2000: 2) whereas private health insurance expenditure accounts for 19 per cent of total health care spending.

Table 5.7 shows the different patterns of public health expenditure. These expenditure patterns underlie the health inequalities in Southern Africa. Thus in South Africa, infant mortality rates for African children were more than 10 times those of their white counterparts (Lund 1995).

In Table 5.7 we have the means for all the variables for the economy types. It also shows the result of an independent *t-test* to determine whether the mean difference between two groups is statistically significantly different to zero. We see that labour reserves economies have much higher levels of payments from prepaid private plans than non-labour

Table 5.7 Patterns of health expenditure in Africa

Indicator	All	Non-labour reserve economy	Labour reserve economy	Significance of difference of means (*t*-statistics), $H_0 = 0$
External resources for health as a percentage of total expenditure on health	16.9	14.4	22.0	−6.1
General government expenditure on health as a percentage of total expenditure on health	45.8	41.7	54.2	−9.0
General government expenditure on health as a percentage of total government expenditure	9.6	9.0	10.7	−5.1
Out-of-pocket expenditure as a percentage of private expenditure on health	73.0	85.3	48.2	24.9
Private expenditure on health as a percentage of total expenditure on health	54.2	58.3	45.8	9.0
Private prepaid plans as a percentage of private expenditure on health	9.5	2.8	24.1	−14.5
Social security expenditure on health as a percentage of general government expenditure on health	3.7	3.1	4.8	−2.9
Total expenditure on health as a percentage of gross domestic product	5.6	5.4	6.2	−3.7

Source: Author elaboration from WHO database

reserve economies, and hence have much less out-of-pocket expenditure as percentage of private expenditure on health. They also have higher public health expenditure. In other words, there is much more private insurance and public provision of health services in the labour reserve economies. In sharp contrast, non-labour reserve economies rely on out-of-pocket payments, which often involve informal arrangements. This is partly in line with the much larger share of the informal economy in these countries than in the labour reserve economies (Mkandawire 2010). It is also in line with the larger issue of welfare regimes of the respective clusters of countries.

Conclusion

This chapter sets out to achieve two things: first to identify welfare regimes in Africa that match the classification of African economies according to their incorporation into the colonial system. The "labour reserve economies" emerge as a fairly consistent welfare regime cluster that is distinct from the rest of Africa. The chapter has shown that labour reserve economies not only have high "tax effort" regimes but high social expenditure regimes as well, both attributes drawing legacies of colonialism. We have also seen that this classification has a bearing on the health sector level, suggesting the same normative principles at the macro level operate at the sectoral level as well. This implies that the suggested classification of social policy regimes may give a much more consistent and historically grounded classification than other accounts that have used per capita income or geographical location to classify African countries. The chapter also provides an answer to the puzzling behaviour of the "Southern African region" alluded to in the literature in terms of the high taxation-social expenditure nexus, the persistence of inequality, the wide range of social protection reforms in these countries and the unusual outcomes of what elsewhere would be progressive policies.

It is striking that 50 years of colonial legacies can be the basis of classifying African welfare regimes. However, colonial legacies are not destiny. Indeed, the process of challenging such legacies can be a stimulus to efforts to redress the injustices of the past or to create new institutional arrangements appropriate to current conditions. As noted above, many of the new social welfare reforms are taking place in the labour reserve economies and are generally internally rather than aid-driven. These responses and the welfare policies they entail are part of that historical legacy.

The main focus of the chapter is not about continuity of the practices but about the historical basis of both the old and new practices. In policy terms, the analysis allows us to understand the structural constraints on policy. It cautions against "one size fits all" in approaching social policies in Africa. Read in conjunction with work on "tax effort regimes" (e.g. Mkandawire 2010), the study points to the importance of thinking of social expenditure in relationship to domestic resource mobilization, as this volume sets out to do. The focus on aid and social expenditure has tended to obscure this important aspect of welfare regimes in Africa.

Finally, the chapter points to the need for more refined research of welfare regimes that draws on some of the significant conceptual gains in understanding welfare regimes elsewhere while broadening the scope of measures beyond the Eurocentric focus on social protection. It also underscores the value of historically grounded taxonomic exercises on social policy regimes in trying to understand the diversity of African economies. However, as the chapter suggests, data availability remains a major challenge in the classificatory exercises on welfare regimes in Africa.

References

Abu Sharkh, Miriam, and Ian Gough. 2010. Global Welfare Regimes: A Cluster Analysis. *Global Social Policy* 10 (1): 27–58.

Acemoglu, Daron, Simon Johnson, and James Robinson. 2001. The Colonial Origins of Comparative Development. *American Economic Review* 91 (5): 1369–1401.

Alence, Rod. 2001. Colonial Government, Social Conflict and State Involvement in Africa's Open Economies: The Origins of the Ghana Cocoa Marketing Board, 1939–46. *The Journal of African History* 42 (03): 397–416.

Amin, Samir. 1972. Underdevelopment and Dependence in Black Africa-Origins and Contemporary Forms. *Journal of Modern African Studies* 10 (4): 105–120.

Arrighi, Giovanni, Nicole Aschoff, and Ben Scully. 2010. Accumulation by Dispossession and Its Limits: The Southern Africa Paradigm Revisited. *Studies in Comparative International Development* 45 (4): 410–438.

Bambra, Clare. 2007. 'Sifting the Wheat from the Chaff': A Two-Dimensional Discriminant Analysis of Welfare State Regime Theory. *Social Policy & Administration* 41 (1): 1–28.

Barrientos, Armando, David Hulme, and Miguel Nino-Zarazua. 2009. *Will the Green Shoots Blossom? A New Wave of Social Protection in Sub-Saharan Africa.* Report. Manchester: Brooks World Poverty Institute, University of Manchester.

Blyth, Mark. 2001. The Transformation of the Swedish Model: Economic Ideas, Distributional Conflict, and Institutional Change. *World Politics* 54 (1): 1–26.

Bonnoli, Giuliano. 1997. Classifying Welfare States: A Two-Dimension Approach. *Journal of Social Policy* 26: 351–372.

Bowden, Sue, Blessing Chiripanhura, and Paul Mosley. 2008. Measuring and Explaining Poverty in Six African Countries: A Long-Period Approach. *Journal of International Development* 20 (8): 1049–1079.

Brummer, Daan. 2002. *Labour Migration and HIV/AIDS in Southern Africa.* Pretoria: International Organization for Migration Regional Office for Southern Africa. Accessed 30 September 2019. http://www.sarpn.org/documents/d0000587/Labour_migration_HIV-AIDS.pdf.

Burawoy, Michael. 1976. Functions of Reproduction of Migrant Labour: Comparative Material from Southern Africa and the United States. *American Journal of Sociology* 81 (5): 1050–1087.

Campbell, Paul, Karen Quigley, Pano Yeracaris, and Chaora MacDonald. 2000. *Applying Managed Care Concepts and Tools to Middle- and Lower-Income Countries: The Case of Medical Aid Societies in Zimbabwe.* Publication 84, Data for Decision Making Project. Boston: School of Public Health, Harvard University.

Chang, Ha-Joon. 2004. The Role of Social Policy in Economic Development: Some Theoretical Reflections and Lessons from Asia. In *Social Policy in a Development Context*, ed. Thandika Mkandawire, 246–261. Basingstoke: Palgrave Macmillan and United Nations Research Institute for Development.

Cooper, Frederick. 1996. *Decolonisation and African Society: The Labour Question in French and British Africa.* Cambridge: Cambridge University Press.

Devereux, Stephen, and Philip White. 2010. Social Protection in Africa: Evidence, Politics and Rights. *Poverty and Public Policy* 2 (3): 516–540.

Eckert, Andreas. 2004. Regulating the Social: Social Security, Social Welfare and the State in Late Colonial Tanzania. *The Journal of African History* 45 (3): 467–489.

Eme Ichoku, Hyacinth, William M. Fonta, and John E. Ataguba. 2013. Political Economy and History: Making Sense of Health Financing in Sub-Saharan Africa. *Journal of International Development* 25 (3): 297–309.

Esping-Andersen, Gøsta. 1990. *The Three Worlds of Welfare Capitalism*. Princeton: Princeton University Press.

———. 1999. *Social Foundations of Postindustrial Economies*. Oxford: Oxford University Press.

Feng, Yi, and Theodora-Ismene Gizelis. 2002. Building Political Consensus and Distributing Resources: A Trade-Off or a Compatible Choice? *Economic Development and Cultural Change* 51 (1): 217–236.

Frankema, Ewout. 2010. *Colonial Taxation and Government Spending in British Africa, 1880–1940: Maximizing Revenue or Minimizing Effort? Explorations in Economic History.* Corrected Proof. Published in 2011 in *Explorations in Economic History* 48 (1): 136–149, January.

———. 2012. The Origins of Formal Education in Sub-Saharan Africa: Was British Rule More Benign? *European Review of Economic History* 16 (4): 335–355.

Gilbert, Neil, and Ailee Moon. 1988. Analyzing Welfare Effort: An Appraisal of Comparative Methods. *Journal of Policy Analysis and Management* 7 (2): 326–340.

Good, Kenneth. 1976. Settler Colonialism: Economic Development and Class Formation. *The Journal of Modern African Studies* 14 (4): 597–620.

Gough, Ian, and Miriam Abu Sharkh. 2011. Financing Welfare Regimes: Mapping Heterogeneous Revenue Structures. *International Journal of Social Welfare* 20 (3): 280–291.

Gough, Ian, Geof Wood, Armando Barrientos, Philippa Bevan, Peter Davis, and Graham Room. 2004. Welfare Regimes in Development Contexts: A Global and Regional Analysis. In *Insecurity and Welfare Regimes in Asia, Africa and Latin America: Social Policy in Development Contexts*, ed. I. Gough, G. Wood, A. Barrientos, P. Bevan, P. Davis, and G. Room, 15–48. Cambridge: Cambridge University Press.

Government of Malawi. 2006/2007. *Budget Statement*. Lilongwe: Government of Malawi.

Haggard, Stephen, and Robert Kaufman. 2008. *Democracy, Development and Welfare States: Latin America, East Asia, and Eastern Europe*. Princeton: Princeton University Press.

Hassim, Shireen. 2006. Gender Equality and Developmental Social Welfare in South Africa. In *Gender and Social Policy in a Global Context: Uncovering the*

Gendered Structure of "the Social", ed. S. Razavi and S. Hassim, 109–129. Basingstoke: Palgrave Macmillan and United Nations Research Institute for Social Development.

Hickey, Samuel. 2007. *Conceptualising the Politics of Social Protection in Africa*. Manchester: Brooks World Poverty Institute, University of Manchester.

Kasza, Gregory J. 2002. The Illusion of Welfare 'Regimes'. *Journal of Social Policy* 31 (2): 271–287.

Kato, Junko. 2003. *Regressive Taxation and the Welfare State: Path Dependence and Policy Diffusion*. Cambridge: Cambridge University Press.

Kim, Pil Ho. 2010. The East Asian Welfare State Debate and Surrogate Social Policy: An Exploratory Study on Japan and South Korea. *Socio-Economic Review* 8 (3): 411–435.

Kim, Tae Kuen, and Karen Zurlo. 2009. How Does Economic Globalisation Affect the Welfare State? Focusing on the Mediating Effect of Welfare Regimes. *International Journal of Social Welfare* 18 (2): 130–141.

Lindert, Peter H. 2004. *Growing Public: Social Spending and Economic Growth since the Eighteenth Century*. Cambridge: Cambridge University Press.

Lipton, Michael. 1977. *Why Poor People Stay Poor: A Study of Urban Bias in World Development*. London: Temple Smith.

Lund, Francis. 1995. Changing Social Policy in South Africa. *Social Policy Review* 7.

Lurie, Mark N., Brian G. Williams, Khangelani Zuma, David Mkaya-Mwamburi, Geoff P. Garnett, Adriaan W. Sturm, Michael D. Sweat, Joel Gittelsohn, and S.S. Abdool Karim. 2003. The Impact of Migration on HIV-1 Transmission in South Africa: A Study of Migrant and Nonmigrant Men and Their Partners. *Sexually Transmitted Diseases* 30 (2): 149–156.

Maclean, Lauren Morris. 2002. Constructing a Social Safety Net in Africa: An Institutionalist Analysis of Colonial Rule and State Social Policies in Ghana and Cote d'Ivoire. *Studies in Comparative International Development* 37 (3): 64–90.

———. 2010. *Informal Institutions and Citizenship in Rural Africa: Risk and Reciprocity in Ghana and Côte d'Ivoire*. Cambridge: Cambridge University Press.

Mares, Isabela. 2004. Economic Insecurity and Social Policy Expansion: Evidence from Interwar Europe. *International Organization* 58 (4): 745–774.

Meillassoux, Claude. 1981. *Maidens, Meal and Money: Capitalism and the Domestic Community, Themes in the Social Sciences*. Cambridge: Cambridge University Press.

Mhone, Guy C.Z. 2000. *Enclavity and Constrained Labour Absorptive Capacity in Southern African Economies*. Harare: International Labour Organization (ILO) Southern Africa Multidisciplinary Advisory Team (SAMAT).

Midgley, James. 1984. Poor Laws Principles and Social Assistance in the Third World: A Study of the Perpetuation of Colonial Welfare. *International Social Work* 27 (1): 19–29.

Midgley, James, and David Piachaud. 2011. *Colonialism and Welfare: Social Policy and the British Imperial Legacy*. Cheltenham: Edward Elgar.

Mishra, Ramesh. 2004. Social Protection by Other Means: Can It Survive Globalisation? In *A Handbook of Comparative Social Policy*, ed. P. Kennett, 68–88. Cheltenham: Edward Elgar.

Mkandawire, Thandika. 1986. The Informal Sector in the Labour Reserve Economies of Southern Africa, with Special Reference to Zimbabwe. *Africa Development* 11: 61–82.

———. 2005. Towards a Development, Democratic and Socially Inclusive Africa Once Again. *Codesria Bulletin*, No. 3.

———. 2010. On Tax Efforts and Colonial Heritage in Africa. *Journal of Development Studies* 46 (10): 1647–1669.

———. 2011. Welfare Regimes and Economic Development: Bridging the Conceptual Gap. In *Overcoming the Persistence of Poverty and Inequality*, ed. V. Fitzgerald, J. Heyer, and R. Thorp. Basingstoke: Palgrave.

———. 2016. *Colonial Legacies and Social Welfare Regimes in Africa: An Empirical Exercise*. PDRM Working Paper No. 2016-4. Geneva: United Nations Research Institute for Social Development.

Niño-Zarazúa, Miguel, Armando Barrientos, Samuel Hickey, and David Hulme. 2012. Social Protection in Sub-Saharan Africa: Getting the Politics Right. *World Development* 40 (1): 163–176.

Oliver, Roland Anthony, and Anthony Atmore. 1967. *Africa since 1800*. Cambridge: Cambridge University Press.

Palmer, Robin H., and Neil Parsons. 1977. *The Roots of Rural Poverty in Central and Southern Africa*. Berkeley: University of California Press.

Patel, Leila. 2011. Race, Inequality and Social Welfare. In *Colonialism and Welfare: Social Policy and the British Imperial Legacy*, ed. J. Midgley and D. Piachaud, 71–84. Cheltenham: Edward Elgar.

Phimister, Ian. 1974. Peasant Production and Underdevelopment in Southern Rhodesia. *African Affairs* 73 (291): 217–218.

Pierson, Paul. 1993. When Effects Become Cause: Policy Feedback and Political Change. *World Politics* 45 (4): 595–628.

Poullier, Jean-Pierre, Patricia Hernandez, Kei Kawabata, and William D. Savedoff. 2002. *Patterns of Global Health Expenditures: Results for 191 Countries*. Discussion Paper No. 51. Geneva: World Health Organization.

Reuveny, Rafael, and Quan Li. 2003. Economic Openness, Democracy, and Income Inequality: An Empirical Analysis. *Comparative Political Studies* 36 (5): 575–601.

Rudra, Nita. 2007. Welfare States in Developing Countries: Unique or Universal? *The Journal of Politics* 69 (2): 378–396.

Rudra, Nita, and Stephan Haggard. 2005. Globalization, Democracy, and Effective Welfare Spending in the Developing World. *Comparative Political Studies* 38 (9): 1015–1049.

Sawers, Larry, and Eileen Stillwaggon. 2010. Understanding the Southern African 'Anomaly': Poverty, Endemic Disease and HIV. *Development and Change* 41 (2): 195–224.

Schüring, Esther, and Julie Lawson-McDowall. 2011. Social Protection in Zambia—Whose Politics? In *IDS Bulletin* 42 (6): 21–27. Brighton: Institute of Development Studies.

Seekings, Jeremy. 2005. *Prospects for Basic Income in Developing Countries: A Comparative Analysis of Welfare Regimes in the South*. Cape Town: Centre for Social Science Research.

———. 2011. British Colonial Policy, Local Politics and the Origins of the Mauritian Welfare State, 1936–50. *The Journal of African History* 52 (02): 157–177.

Shaikh, Anwar. 2003. Who Pays for the Welfare in the Welfare State? A Multicountry Study: Papers by and about New School Graduate Faculty Members. *Social Research* 70 (2): 531–550.

Southern Rhodesia Government. 1944. *Report of the Native Production and Trade Commission*.

Stewart, Frances. 2009. Horizontal Inequality: Two Types of Trap. *Journal of Human Development and Capabilities* 10 (3): 315–340.

Stichter, Sharon. 1982. *Migrant Labour in Kenya: Capitalism and African Response, 1895–1975*. London: Longman.

Wilensky, Harold L. 1975. *The Welfare State and Equality: Structural and Ideological Roots of Public Expenditures*. Berkeley: University of California Press.

Wolpe, Harold. 1972. Capitalism and Cheap Labour-Power in South Africa: From Segregation to Apartheid. *Economy and Society* 1 (4): 425–456.

———. 1980. Capitalism and Cheap Labour-Power in South Africa: From Segregation to Apartheid. In *The Articulation of Modes of Production: Essays from Economy and Society*, ed. H. Wolpe. London: Routledge and Kegan Paul Books.

Young, Crawford. 1988. African Colonial State and its Political Legacy. In *The Precarious Balance: State and Society in Africa*, ed. D. Rothchild and N. Chazan, 25–67. Boulder, CO: Westview Press.

6

Democratic Deepening and State Capacity: Taxation in Brazil and India

Aaron Schneider

Introduction

While Brazil and India have emerged as important global players, they display key differences in the way their democracies have deepened and what this means for their state capacities. Since the liberalization of the economy in the early 1990s, Brazil pursued incorporation of previously excluded lower- and middle-class groups, creating a kind of state capacity equipped for broad sacrifices to provide universal public goods, what might be called state capacity for broad collective action. In India, by contrast, incorporation of previously excluded regional, ethnic, and communal groups created state capacity to work with elites atop strategic sectors, what might be called embedded capacity. These differences appear in tax regimes as Brazil has increased its tax take significantly, and to some

A. Schneider (✉)
Josef Korbel School of International Studies, University of Denver, Denver, CO, USA
e-mail: aaron.schneider@du.edu

K. Hujo (ed.), *The Politics of Domestic Resource Mobilization for Social Development*, Social Policy in a Development Context,
https://doi.org/10.1007/978-3-030-37595-9_6

degree progressively, while India has structured its tax system to favour the most dynamic and globally integrated sectors.

To explain these differences in state capacity, as expressed in tax, this chapter focuses on the political economy of democratic deepening. The concept of democratic deepening refers to the ever-broader incorporation of excluded groups into public, political processes. While both countries have deepened their democracies, the groups excluded in Brazil have largely defined themselves and mobilized around class identities while in India excluded groups have largely defined themselves and mobilized around ascriptive identities, such as region, caste, and religion.

Distinct patterns of democratic deepening connect to tax through the mechanisms of incorporation by which previously excluded groups engage with politics and the state. By articulating demands for protection against neoliberal adjustment and institutionalizing links to a party system organized around left-right cleavages, class-based democratic deepening in Brazil produced a social base in support of raising revenues to provide universally distributed social policies. By contrast, with demands articulated to expand participation in the benefits of neoliberal expansion, ascriptively based democratic deepening in India produced coordination among domestic capital to use tax incentives and subsidies to strategically upgrade exports.

This chapter evaluates changes to state capacity in Brazil and India by looking at the political economy of democratic deepening. The first section outlines the main concepts that orient the argument: democratic deepening and state capacity as viewed through tax. The second section applies these concepts to Brazil and India, analysing state capacity and taxation. The third section links tax capacity with democratic deepening, focusing on the type of incorporation of new groups and the particular coalitions that have been built in the two countries and how this affects revenue mobilization.

Analytical Framework

Deepening Democracy

A crisis of representation and participation in developed countries (Putnam 1994) and new democracies (Roberts 1998) has provoked debate about the quality of democracies. Weaknesses in democracy are evidenced by declining voter participation, feeble political associations, and limited social mobilization in the aftermath of transitions to democracy (O'Donnell 1996), while democratic practice is constrained by economic inequality, traditional relations of clientelism, and state fragility. These shortcomings truncate citizenship, diminishing the full range of individual rights and responsibilities and excluding social groups (Goldfrank 2011).

Deepening democracy requires the recognition of excluded social actors as legitimate participants in politics and the establishment of new mechanisms of institutionalized interaction with public authority. This has been referred to by some in the context of citizenship regimes, which "define who has political membership, which rights they possess, and how interest intermediation with the state is structured" (Yashar 2004: 6). One implication is that deepening democracy is a never-ending process in which new identities are constantly constructed, leading to the formation of new social groups and new mechanisms of linkage between state and society (Held 1995). This allows for constant innovation as collective actors engage in "insurgent citizenship" and mobilize for incorporation into democratic practice as excluded actors (Holston 2009).

Collective actors can emerge from a variety of ideologies and patterns of exclusion. One pattern defines exclusion along class and sectoral lines, such as working class, middle class, and rural and urban popular sectors. Alternative bases for mobilization include ascriptive ethnic, religious, and regional identities. While the intensity of different types of cleavages within societies may vary, the most important determinant of mobilization is the political dynamic by which groups come to view themselves as excluded, the strategies they choose to gain inclusion, and the outcomes of their struggles for inclusion, including the response of existing members of the polity.

Given the turn of events in Brazil and India in recent years, the concept of deepening democracy must also consider the possibility for its opposite—shifts towards authoritarianism. Just as excluded groups can mobilize for access and struggle to deepen democracy, they can be blocked or re-excluded in revanchist efforts by existing elites. There is no single arc of history that always and forever bends towards justice; political struggles between those who seek inclusion and those who seek to exclude are uncertain and contingent. This is especially the case in developing countries where advanced productive and social actors adapted to contemporary international trends coexist in multiple and overlapping relations with actors entrenched in prior patterns of international and domestic activity (Rosenberg 1996).

State Capacity

Deepening democracy has implications for state capacity. Elitist theories argue that excessive mobilization threatens to overwhelm state capacity for institutionalization and lead to breakdown. Such approaches presume a trade-off between social mobilization and state capacity for order (Huntington 1968). When considering episodes of state capacity increase, elitist approaches at best seek explanations in accommodations among elites, especially business groups and state elites (Mahon 2004; Fairfield 2015), regional and national elites (Schneider 2019), and globally-oriented, national capitalist, and oligarchic elites (Schneider 2012).

Alternatively, perspectives that emphasize the role of social coalitions in support of the state note the potential for deepening democracy to strengthen capacity in the sense of Michael Mann's notion of "infrastructural power." Infrastructural power is the ability of the state to penetrate and implement policies across a territory. In contrast to the "despotic power" that authoritarian regimes use to limit social mobilization, democratic deepening offers infrastructural power for states to work through society, engaging citizens in national projects (Mann 1984).

The incorporation of new social groups into an institutionalized relationship with the state buttresses infrastructural power in two relevant ways. First, it allows the state to stimulate greater sacrifice on the part of the citizenry to generate public goods. Typically, public goods are underprovided, as they face problems of free-riding and time-inconsistency that prevent sufficient contributions from self-interested individuals and groups (Olson 1965). States that have incorporated a broader range of social actors can draw on a wider selection and greater quantity of public contributions to pursue national projects. For example, Eugene Weber describes how the French revolution allowed the state to construct a common identity and set of institutions to incorporate previously scattered rural peasants, turning "peasants into Frenchmen," who were willing to contribute soldiers and taxes in support of national development (1976).

A useful indicator of state capacity to stimulate collective action appears in public finance. Tax payments are "unrequited and compulsory" contributions of private wealth to the state (Buchanan 1963), in which increases in taxation can be seen as a collective action problem of getting individual taxpayers to sacrifice their resources in pursuit of social ends (Lieberman 2005). While every contributor might like others to contribute more, no revenues will be gathered if everyone puts the burden on someone else. Contributions can be conceived even more explicitly as examples of collective action when they are closely linked to spending policies allocated on a universal basis of social provision and protection (Sanchez-Ancochea and Martinez Franzoni 2016). While every beneficiary might prefer benefits allocated privately to them, this would lead to far fewer social benefits overall. In sum, broad-based collective action requires individuals and groups to accept collective sacrifice in pursuit of a common good, and strong public finance indicators for such collective action can result from an increase in tax capacity linked to expanded social spending and broader social protection.

The second kind of infrastructural power relevant here refers to "embeddedness," the ability of the state to engage strategic sectors through specialized relationships and policies. This close relationship allows the state to engage in "husbandry" to modernize leading actors and cultivate their international competitiveness (Evans 1995). This draws on the Polanyian observation of the state role in creating and "governing" markets (Wade 1990), and fits with studies of global integration, in which the state helps fit national economic actors into global value chains (Kaplinsky 2005), and to move them into higher value activities of international scale and scope (Mazzucato 2015). This also includes government fiscal, regulatory, and financial efforts to attract foreign capital and technology.

Capacity for embeddedness has its reflection in tax regimes, as elite actors negotiate fiscal bargains in exchange for shifting into riskier dynamic sectors. Especially in developing countries, where domestic capitalist classes tend to be weaker and lack access to capital and technology, government tax policy can be especially important. For such policies to be effective, however, they cannot devolve into rent-seeking and protection; rather they must be oriented towards pushing economic actors into ever-new markets and higher value activities (Kurtz and Schrank 2005). Capacity for embeddedness can be indicated by tax policies that offer inducements to competitiveness, such as export-processing zones, often with sunset clauses or other incentives that wean domestic producers off protection and stimulate dynamism. Such incentives are especially indicative of capacity for embeddedness when they are connected to outlays to build the infrastructure for high-value exports.

State Capacity and Tax in Brazil and India

Both Brazil and India have undertaken important changes to their tax regimes in the past two decades, but those changes have produced quite different results. In Brazil, changes to the tax regime have expanded revenues, with particular expansion in direct taxes and taxes drawn from newly incorporated social groups linked directly to social programmes. In India, reforms targeted the most dynamic and internationally integrated sectors with exemptions and incentives, promoting privately-held high-value exports, but limiting increases in revenues.

Brazil: Expanded Capacity for Broad-Based Collective Action

Following a concerted effort to increase tax capacity from the mid-1990s to the present, Brazilian taxes are today among the highest in the developing world.[1] Tax revenue increased steadily, with notable reforms to the tax system including an increase in income taxes and the implementation of numerous contributions linked to social spending. These increases more than compensated for decreases in tariffs as Brazil liberalized international trade.

Figure 6.1 shows the increase in tax as a percentage of gross domestic product (GDP) between 1991 and 2017. Taxes increased from 23.7 per cent to more than 32 per cent. These revenues were necessary as the country faced fiscal insolvency during the 1980s and had to muster revenues to balance the budget. In addition, the government needed additional income to support expanded social spending mandated in the 1988 Constitution and to respond to demand pent up during the 20-year military regime that ended in 1985.

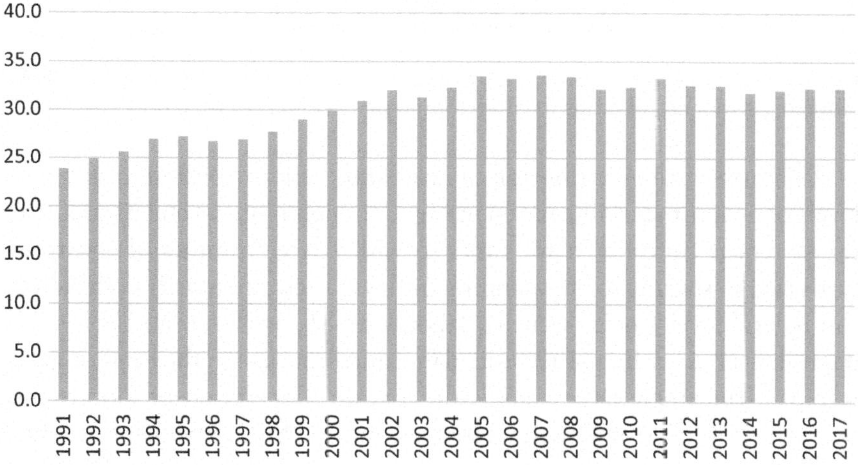

Fig. 6.1 Tax as percentage of GDP in Brazil (1991–2017). (Source: Author calculations from CEPALSTAT 2015)

[1] Calculations by Fenochietto and Pessino (2010) estimate Brazil taxes 98 per cent of what would be possible given its level of development and other characteristics.

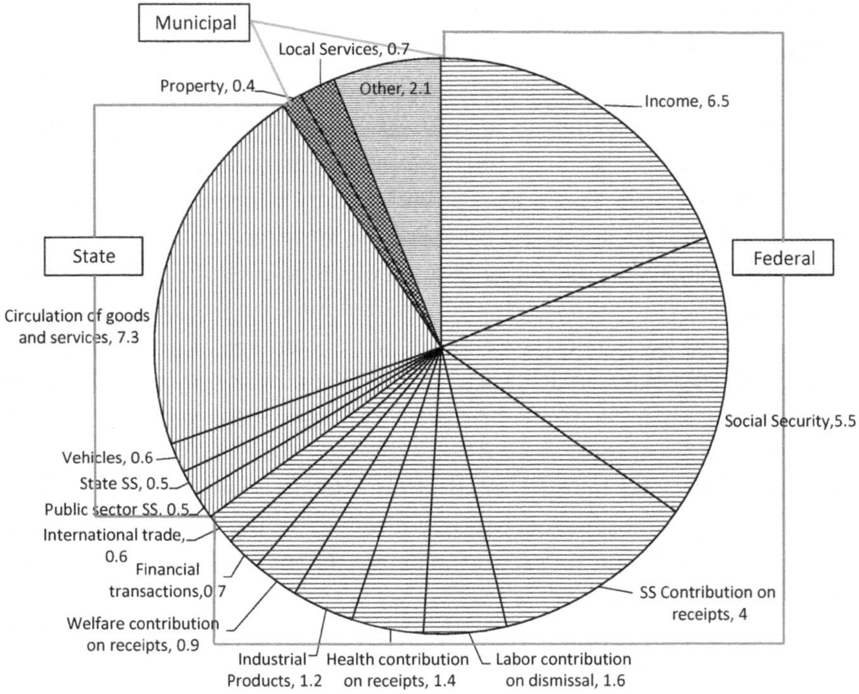

Fig. 6.2 Tax as percentage of GDP, by base and level of government, Brazil (2009). (Source: Author calculations from Secretaria de Receita Federal n.d.)

A glimpse at the distribution of taxes and their attribution to different levels of government, illustrated in Fig. 6.2, highlights several details. The tax system is complex, made more so with a large number of contributions tied to specific social spending outlays. These are mostly collected at the federal level (social security, labour, health, welfare), and some use payroll as a base, while others calculate contributions on the basis of gross receipts. The single largest tax is the Tax on Circulation of Goods and Services (ICMS) levied by the states, accounting for 7.3 per cent of GDP.

With the most important tax on consumption—the ICMS—controlled by state governments, the federal government was forced to exchange trade taxes lowered by liberalization for income taxes. This replacement was reasonably effective, as federal taxes stood at 7.97 per cent of GDP in 1994 and 7.67 per cent in 2010. The effort to raise

Table 6.1 Changes in direct tax and indirect tax incidence within total tax, Brazil (1996–2004)

Family income (SM)	DT % 1996	DT % 2004	IT % 1996	IT % 2004	TT % 1996	TT % 2004	% Increase
<2	1.7	3.1	26.5	45.8	28.2	48.8	20.6
2–3	2.6	3.5	20	34.5	22.6	38	15.4
15–20	5.5	6.9	9.4	21.6	14.9	28.4	13.5
20–30	5.7	8.6	9.1	20.1	14.8	28.7	13.9
>30	10.6	9.9	7.3	16.4	17.9	26.3	8.4

Source: Author adaptation from Afonso et al. (2013) based on Zockun et al. (2007)
Notes: *SM* minimum salary, *DT* direct taxes, *IT* indirect taxes, *TT* total taxes

income taxes resulted in an increase in direct taxes in the 2000s. By 2009, direct taxes were almost 60 per cent of the total, up from barely 44 per cent in 2000. As a percentage of GDP, this represented an increase from 13.59 per cent to 17.83 per cent (Afonso et al. 2013).

To increase revenues further, the federal government made use of earmarked taxes, known in Brazil as contributions. The use of earmarks is a good indicator of the type of fiscal contract offered to citizens, with revenues collected tied explicitly to social spending. These increased from 8.95 per cent of GDP in 1994 to 12.94 per cent of GDP in 2010. Federal contributions included social security, a social security contribution on business receipts (COFINS), a contribution to unemployment benefits for dismissed workers (FGTS), a health contribution on receipts (CSS), a welfare contribution on receipts (PIS), a public sector social security contribution (CPSS), a contribution on profits towards social security (CSLL), a contribution on fuel towards education and health (CIDE), and a temporary contribution towards education and health on financial transactions (CPMF).

In addition to considering changes in the levels and structure of revenues, it is also possible to evaluate the incidence of tax in terms of impacts on distribution. For example, while the increase in direct taxes is likely to have positive impacts on vertical equity, indirect taxes (IT), which continue to account for about half of all taxes, are likely to have negative impacts on vertical equity (DIEESE 2009). A more precise way to explore the equity impact of changes to the tax system is in terms of the relative burden on income groups. The chart (Table 6.1) is taken from a study that uses household surveys to calculate the incidence of tax and displays the change from 1996 to 2004 in direct, indirect, and overall taxes. First, the change from 1996 to 2004 shows an increasing burden for all deciles. People pay more of their incomes in tax. Second, the increase is steadily greater for poorer deciles than it is for richer deciles (except a portion of the upper middle class), and the increase weighs heavier on the poor. Still, though they appear to have become less progressive over time, the burden of direct taxes continues to increase with wealth.

India: Capacity for Embeddedness

In India, tax capacity has largely held steady since the onset of neoliberal reforms in the early 1990s, as is shown in Fig. 6.3. The figure displays total revenue as a percentage of GDP in the upper line, with the amount collected by central government and states below.

In fiscal year 1991, taxes stood at 15 per cent of GDP while the measure for 2017 was 18.16 per cent of GDP. Within this relatively steady

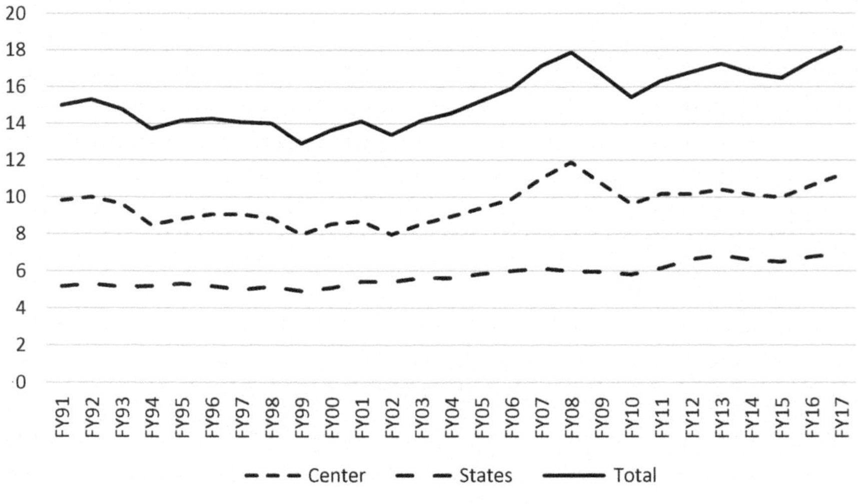

Fig. 6.3 Tax as percentage of GDP, India (1991–2017). (Source: Author calculations based on data from Indian Ministry of Finance 2014–2015. Notes: FY: fiscal year)

overall trend, there were some fluctuations, as taxes trended downwards most years between 1991 and 2001 and again during the international slowdown in 2008–2009. A combination of reforms and rapid growth offered reasonable upward movement that made up for drops in revenues between 2001–2002 and 2006–2007, and revenues have fluctuated around the 16–18 per cent level since then.

It may not be surprising to observers that levels of tax capacity in India are lower than in Brazil, bearing in mind the country's economic structure, poverty, and other characteristics that typically predict tax effort. Recent studies of tax effort however show that, even taking into account typical determinants of tax burden, India's tax capacity is quite low. According to the International Monetary Fund (IMF), India's actual tax effort is only 52.2 per cent of the predicted level when controlling for income per capita, economic openness, agriculture as a share of GDP, spending on education, income inequality, corruption, and inflation (Fenochietto and Pessino 2010).

In terms of distributional impact of tax, there have not been the same studies of incidence in India as in Brazil, but some conclusions can be drawn from the relative burden of direct and indirect taxes. Direct taxes on income, wealth, property, and capital gains tend to fall more heavily on those who are wealthier, and in India there would appear to have been a shift in the tax structure towards direct taxes, from 16 per cent of total revenues to a peak of 43 per cent in 2009–2010. Since 2009–2010, direct taxes have fallen a bit, steady at around 37 per cent over the past few years. The changing relative proportion of direct and indirect taxes is displayed in Fig. 6.4. Still, the low overall burden of taxes and the ongoing dependence on indirect taxes suggest that there is significant room to expand direct taxes and increase the progressivity of the tax regime.

More worrying still is that most of the direct taxes come from corporate income tax, which reflects the rapid growth in the country and the degree to which profits, as opposed to wages, have absorbed that growth (Sood et al. 2014). Further, reforms to the Income Tax Act of 1961 and the Wealth Tax Act of 1957, which were initially advanced in the 2009–2010 budget, caused revenue losses, drops in marginal rates on corporate income tax, and shifts in personal income tax brackets upwards such that most people fell into the lowest bracket. These changes had

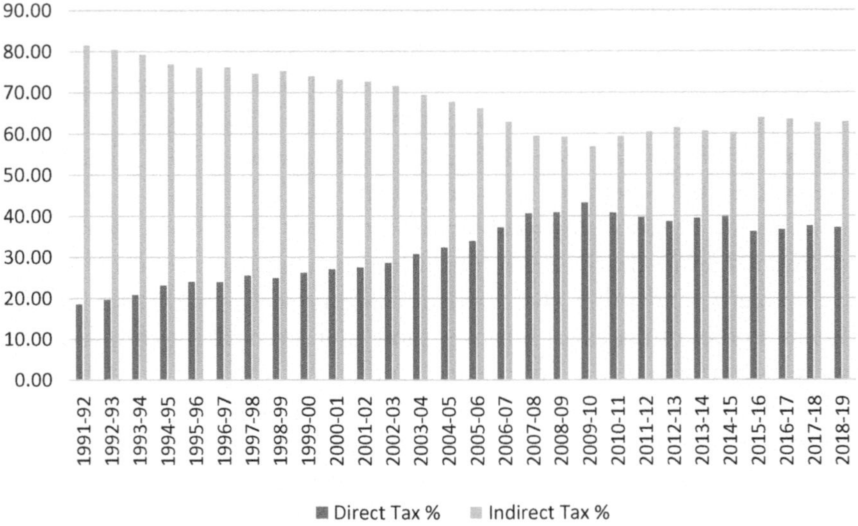

Fig. 6.4 Direct and indirect tax as percentage of total tax, India (1991/1992–2018/2019). (Source: Author calculations based on data from the Reserve Bank of India n.d.)

regressive impacts overall, as seen in an upward movement in the share of indirect taxes in total revenues to 61.6 per cent in 2012–2013.[2]

A number of specific differences emerge when exploring the role of social contributions in the fiscal revenues of the two countries. Brazil, as discussed earlier, gathers a significant portion of its revenues in contributions, 34.8 per cent in 2017 according to World Bank Development Indicators. By contrast, only 0.19 per cent of central government revenues in India came from social contributions in 2013,[3] whereas labour taxes as a percentage of commercial profits are nearly twice as high in

[2] Without incidence data from both countries, it is difficult to compare the degree of progressivity in the overall fiscal impact. Still, some trends are evident. Gini coefficients in Brazil were relatively flat during the 1990s at around 60 and fell to 54.69 in 2009 and to 51.3 by 2015. In 2016, they began to rise again, to 53.7, settling at 53.3 in 2017. In India, while data is less complete, they began at 30.82 in 1994 and have risen ever since, reaching 33.38 in 2005, 33.9 in 2010, and 35.7 in 2011 (World Bank).

[3] Neither the OECD nor the World Development Indicators (WDI) database show figures for India anymore, though they used to indicate that 0.32 per cent of revenues came from social contributions. The most recent available data can be found at https://tradingeconomics.com/india/social-contributions-current-lcu-wb-data.html.

Brazil (39.4 per cent in 2018) compared to India (20.3 per cent in 2018) (World Bank n.d.). This is explained on the one hand by the lack of mobilization of social contributions in India and the large size of the informal sector, hovering around 88.2 per cent in India according to the International Labour Organization (ILO 2018).[4]

While in India the capacity for broad-based collective action is limited, the state has instead cultivated its ability to engage with leading market actors. The estimated revenues foregone by India from incentives reached 5.9 per cent of GDP in 2011–2012 and 5.7 per cent in 2012–2013, more than a third of total revenues (CBGA 2013). Incentives are oriented to boost the fortunes of the wealthiest and most dynamic sectors; corporate tax incentives provide proportionally greater benefit to companies with larger profits, who pay lower tax rates than firms with smaller profits. Also, most exemptions apply to indirect taxes, customs, and excise duties, with 80 per cent of total taxes foregone occurring in these categories.

In addition, Indian exemptions are particularly oriented towards dynamic sectors deeply integrated in the international economy. In total, India has over 170 special economic zones in which tax incentives, among other benefits, are offered, often in the form of a deduction from corporate income of export profits (India Ministry of Commerce and Industry 2015). Software technology parks also enjoy special incentives, and Information and Technology enabled services and Business Process Outsourcing providers have seen tax rates as low as 7.4 per cent in 2006–2007, averaging 15.98 per cent, far lower than the 33.21 per cent statutory rate (CBGA 2013).

The difference between capacity for broad-based collective action and embeddedness appears starkly in Brazilian and Indian public finance. While Brazil has greatly expanded its revenues, especially through direct taxes and the use of earmarked contributions tied to social outlays, India has allowed revenues to stagnate while using the fiscal regime to favour exporters and dynamic, internationally integrated sectors. An explanation for these differences in capacity can be found in patterns of democratic deepening.

---

[4] Some estimates place the number as high as 93 per cent of non-farm employment in India (Kumar 2017), as compared to 42.2 per cent in Brazil in 2009, a rate that has fallen considerably since 2000, when it was over 60 per cent.

Deepening Democracy and Tax Capacity in Brazil and India

In India and Brazil, struggles for political access during the 1970s and 1980s legitimated excluded groups as collective actors, and in the 1990s they consolidated their organizational and partisan strategies and articulated demands in the context of neoliberal adjustments. With renewed growth during the 2000s (slightly earlier in India), previously excluded groups sought policies and institutions that would provide them with stable linkages to the state. This incorporation of excluded groups deepened democracy in both countries, but the results have been quite different with regard to state capacity as expressed in tax. In Brazil, popular sectors and middle classes formed a social coalition in support of efforts to expand tax revenues, make them more progressive, and connect them to universal social policies. In India, efforts to sustain internationally competitive leading sectors focused on targeting publicly financed benefits to urban middle classes and caste, regional, and other identity-based groups in shifting social coalitions. The countries differ in terms of which excluded groups mobilized, what demands they articulated, and the mechanisms of incorporation that linked them to the state.

Brazil: Cross-Class Coalitions

The following paragraphs trace the extension of citizenship regimes in Brazil that occurred with the mobilization of certain excluded groups, their articulation of demands, and linkage to the state during the period from the 1970s to the 2000s. The military leaders who governed Brazil from 1964 to 1985 promoted industrial deepening at the same time as they shut down democratic politics and brutalized opponents. Middle classes, including public sector workers and private urban professionals, had originally been a privileged segment within Brazilian state-led development, but certain segments, such as students and intellectuals, were among the most repressed by the military. Middle-class struggles for human rights brought them together with a wide range of social movements addressing citizenship and quality of life issues, including

Afro-Brazilian rights, women's rights, environmental protection, neighbourhood services, and public health movements, among others (Escobar and Alvarez 1992). Their efforts came to be understood as the struggle for the "right to have rights" (Dagnino 2007).

Working classes also mobilized in opposition to the military. They bore the brunt of both repression and regressive growth strategies, even as deepening import-substitution industrialization expanded their role in the economy. Gradually, urban formal sector workers created a space for autonomous organizing and struggle, convened on the shop-floor to avoid the reactionary control of sector-wide unions, and expanded their workplace gatherings to include community demands for public services.[5] Strike waves in the late 1970s were especially vigorous in the manufacturing belt around São Paulo, where an alternative national federation of unions, Unified Workers Central (CUT), formed in 1983.

The urban formal sector was joined also by other groups, such as informal sector workers and especially the rural landless population, which swelled in number and particularly suffered from political repression and biased growth strategies. Available land dwindled as national policy prioritized large-scale surplus production for export and industrial requirements of power and natural resources. Politically, the rural poor experienced renewed subjugation, as the military responded to faltering electoral support with dependence on rural elite allies and their clientelist networks in the poorest regions of the country (Hagopian 1996). Rural workers resisted, and with the help of the progressive Catholic Church (Houtzager 2000), developed a rural landless workers' movement with a series of occupations in 1979, becoming one of the largest social movements in Latin America, the Landless Workers' Movement (MST) (Woolford 2010).

These popular-sector and middle-class movements increasingly established their legitimacy as collective actors supporting democratization, as the military regime offered a unified target. Strikes and protests accelerated over the course of the 1970s, and the gradual opening of electoral

[5] The articulation of such demands and organizational efforts eventually birthed a New Union Movement joining urban worker struggle to neighbourhood and other popular movements (Seidman 1994).

competition after 1973 oriented at least part of the democratization struggle into the party system, with the main aggregator of opposition in the Democratic Movement of Brazil (MDB later PMDB), later joined by the Workers' Party (PT), formed in 1980. The PT was a new kind of partisan organization in Brazil, considered an "anomaly" compared to previous political formations, as it emerged from a "solid base in labour and social movements," with much of "its leadership drawn from the labour movement" (Keck 1992). As a party that emerged "from the bottom up" (Nylen 1997) with "extra-parliamentary" origins (Meneguello 1998), the PT was committed to the autonomy of its movement and union allies.

Once the military finally exited power in 1985, the 1988 Constituent Assembly included many of the demands of social movements and popular sectors. These demands called for expanded welfare state policies, including mandates for universal provision in health and education, expanded funding for housing and sanitation, as well as greater decentralization and participation (Draibe 2003). These policies would require greater resources, but the first priority of the candidate who entered office in 1990, Fernando Collor, was to stabilize an economy facing runaway inflation. Though he was eventually removed for corruption in 1992, Collor began the liberalization of trade and deregulation of the Brazilian economy that would accelerate under Fernando Henrique Cardoso's Party of Brazilian Social Democracy (PSDB) government from 1994 to 2002.

For those who had mobilized for democratization, the battleground shifted to the struggle over neoliberal adjustment. Cardoso earned convincing electoral victories on a base of middle- and upper-class supporters attracted by the technocratic and social democratic credentials of PSDB party founders, and defeating inflation extended his support to popular sectors who could finally begin consuming again (Baker 2010). Backed by this coalition, he took advantage of expanded contributions tied to social policy outlays, fulfilling some of the demands of the 1988 Constitution and securing resources for macroeconomic stabilization.[6]

[6] Fund for the Maintenance and Support of Basic Education (Fundef) and Unified Health System (SUS) and conditional cash transfer—Bolsa Escola.

Yet, many previously excluded actors were increasingly repelled by neoliberal elements of stabilization. Social movements that had fought for democratization opposed Cardoso's efforts at centralization, as well as the extensive use of decrees and other executive privileges that removed aspects of policy from public debate. Formal sector and manufacturing workers opposed privatization and the deindustrialization that followed trade liberalization (Hunter 2010), and those who had supported expanded social policies objected to the prioritization of macroeconomic stabilization.

Increasingly, the coalition of working classes, social movements, and middle-class actors who had mobilized for democratization articulated their demands in opposition to neoliberal adjustment. In the process, they drew closer to the PT, which remained in opposition to the adjustment strategy of the Cardoso government (Roman 2012). As an indicator of the articulation of demands around neoliberal adjustment, shifts in the party system showed an increasing left-right orientation and polarization (Hagopian et al. 2009). From 1990 to 1998, the PT steadily increased its support from 35 to 49 to 58 Congressional representatives, while Cardoso's PSDB increased from 37 to 67 to 99. Right-wing parties associated with the military regime disappeared and were absorbed into right-wing supporters of the PSDB's neoliberal stabilization strategy.

When Luiz Inácio Lula da Silva, a union leader and founding member of the PT, finally won the presidency in 2002, it was not clear that he would be able to successfully institutionalize linkages to working classes, social movements, and middle classes. To win the presidency, he had signalled that he would moderate, and the government maintained Cardoso's inflation targeting regime. Yet, a rebounding economy allowed the PT to pay off IMF obligations early and provided much-needed policy space. The government adopted an expansionary macroeconomic stance beginning in 2006, as Lula won re-election to a second term. During the 2008 international financial crisis, the government embarked on counter-cyclical fiscal expansion, led by the Growth Acceleration Programme inaugurated that year that spent a total of Brazilian reals (BRL) 1.7 trillion (USD 817 billion) (Ministerio de Fazenda 2014).

The expansionary fiscal strategy targeted precisely those previously excluded groups who had mobilized for democratization, articulated demands against neoliberalism, and now achieved policy and institutional linkage to the state through the PT. Middle-sector professionals benefited from employment and increased salaries and pensions, and government banking institutions further expanded consumer and housing credit to reach lower middle classes. The middle class increased to 55 per cent of the population, 105.5 million people (Barbosa 2010).

Even more significant were the efforts to expand the incomes and consumption of working classes and popular sectors. Successive increases in the monthly minimum wage, from BRL 350 in 2002 to BRL 560 in 2012[7] have improved conditions across the board, as many low-income jobs and pensions are indexed to minimum wages. Further extending the impact is the extension of pensions to informal sector workers, reaching 28 million people, as well as small farmer credits and agricultural extension that reached almost two million small producers (Melo 2008).

The flagship social policy, an income transfer programme called Bolsa Família, has absorbed and expanded various social programmes to extend income support, education, and health to low-income families. At its peak, Bolsa Família reached more than 40 million Brazilians and was credited with cutting poverty, improving health outcomes, and improving education attainment (Castiñeira et al. 2009; Hall 2006). According to World Bank data, the percentage of the population in poverty fell from 22.4 per cent in 2002 to 6.9 per cent in 2014, and the Ministry of Finance reports the incomes of the poorest three deciles had annual average rates of growth of 7.2, 6.3, and 5.9 per cent (as compared to 1.4, 2.5, and 3.3 per cent for the highest deciles) (2012). This has produced a fall in the Gini coefficient from 0.596 in 2001 to 0.519 by 2012 (Ministry of Finance 2012).[8]

The PT scaled up participatory innovations it had experimented with while governing at the local level during the 1990s (Lavalle et al. 2005). Participatory institutions had been mandated in the 1988 Constitution, and the PT had developed local-level participatory budgeting into a

[7] USD 150 in 2002 to USD 300 in 2012.

[8] Though there has been a slight increase to 53.7 in 2016, settling at 53.3 in 2017 (World Bank n.d.).

global reference.[9] With national power after 2002, the PT significantly expanded participatory councils for public policy. In 2010 they operated in 31 different policy areas, included 1350 members—with slightly more civil society (55 per cent) than government (45 per cent) representation—and undertook both deliberative and advisory tasks (Lopez and Pires 2010). As of 2005, there were over 300,000 registered civil society organizations, and by 2009, they were receiving over BRL 14 billion (USD 8 billion) in government transfers.

In targeting working class, social movement, and middle-class actors, policies and institutions stabilized linkages to the state for previously excluded groups. This once again shows up in the party system. While class-based voting patterns had been somewhat muddied by the anti-inflation consensus of the 1990s, a class cleavage consolidated in which the PT polled better among poorer voters and in poorer regions (Roman 2012). Voting intention for the PT was higher at lower income levels, with average support over the four elections from 2002 to 2014 at 57 per cent for those in the lowest income bracket and 42 per cent for those in the highest income bracket. Further, support from those with only primary education averaged 61 per cent over the same four elections, while support from those with tertiary education averaged 43 per cent (Datafolha 2014; IBOPE 2013).

PT support for social spending sought to institutionalize linkages to the cross-class coalition that had formed in democratization and which had articulated its opposition to neoliberalism in the 1990s. The counterpart to these social spending expansions was tax increases, including efforts to increase progressive taxation.

Two puzzles require further explanation. The first is the failure of the PT to construct more embedded forms of capacity in terms of forging alliances with elements of the national bourgeoisie and cultivating them into internationally competitive positions such that Brazil was not locked into a dependence on commodity exports. The second puzzle was revealed

---

[9] These institutions included allocation mechanisms that targeted working-class neighbourhoods in the redistribution of resources, "inverting priorities" that had long been dominated by elites (Avritzer et al. 2003), and participation among the poor tended to be higher than among the wealthy (Goldfrank 2011).

in the 2016 removal of the Workers' Party from power and rapid disintegration of their incorporation project by right-wing leadership.

At the heart of both puzzles is the historical dependence of the government on oligarchic factions of Brazilian capital, whose economic base rested on commodity exports and whose social base rested on clientelist links to voters. Dependence on oligarchic elites was in part a function of the party system, which was characterized by high levels of fragmentation and volatility, resulting in minorities in Congress for the party of the president (Kinzo 2004). To survive defections during legislative battles, executives built super-majority coalitions, a practice labelled "presidential coalitionism" (Abranches 1988). The most easily attracted partners for such coalitions were oligarchic and clientelist politicians whose need for patronage made their price relatively cheap.

Critical in such coalitions has been the PMDB, always among the top-three holders of seats in the legislature and an anchor of coalitional presidential strategies since the 1980s (Abranches 1988). From its origins as a partisan umbrella for a wide range of opponents against the military regime, the PMDB evolved into a catch-all vehicle dependent on oligarchic elites based in commodity-exporting states (Nobre 2010). The PMDB, and other conservative parties such as the Partido Republicano Brasileiro (PRB), Partido Progressista (PP), and Partido da Republica (PR), offered support for the government, but their leading actors were relatively uninterested in diversifying away from a commodity-export economy (Bresser-Pereira 2015).

This dependence on oligarchic factions of local elites also helps explain the 2016 impeachment of PT President Dilma Rousseff and the rapid roll back of universal social provision. The impeachment paved the way for explicit efforts to de-incorporate exactly the sectors incorporated since democratization, including a 20-year spending cap that will greatly reduce social spending and protection, a labour reform that stripped rights existing since the 1930s, and a proposed pension reform that would weaken coverage, lower benefits, and raise the age of retirement.

What sealed the fate of the inclusionary project was the sudden defection of middle classes to an alliance with oligarchic interests (Souza 2015). While the Workers' Party was unable or unwilling to manipulate judicial and legislative tools to escape an onslaught of corruption allegations, oligarchic elites showed no such restraint. Middle-class acceptance, and even encouragement, of a witch-hunt against leftist politicians while leaving oligarchic interests unscathed, exposed their essential suspicion of popular sectors and leftist projects as well as their essential weakness as political actors, unable to drive an agenda and able only to support those projects offered to them by other class actors.

In sum, the policies and institutions introduced since democratization stabilized linkages between the state and previously excluded groups such as working classes, social movements, and middle classes in support of expanded revenue mobilization and greater progressivity, especially when linked to social outlays. Yet, there was limited ability to coordinate dynamic sectors and escape commodity dependence, and the project was ultimately undermined when oligarchic elites turned on the Workers' Party and middle classes abandoned the cross-class coalition, restoring a neoliberal agenda to national politics.

India: Cross-Group Coalitions

In India, the Congress Party led the struggle for independence gained in 1947 and dominated politics until the 1970s, during which time it built a support base buoyed by a nationalist and developmentalist consensus. In the heavily populated and therefore electorally crucial north of India, Congress cohered a social coalition that combined a largely upper-caste leadership with a mass base among lower caste and Dalit (those who were previously labelled "untouchable" and officially labelled Scheduled Caste/SC)—a "coalition of extremes" as described by Brass (1984). To delay and deter potential rivals, Congress leaders were adept at absorbing "aspiring social groups" (Weiner 1967), preserving an elite coalition of political-bureaucratic state actors, large farmers, and industrial elites benefiting from state-led development (Bardhan 1984).

This was labelled the "Congress system" by Kothari (1964), and it left room at its margins for alternative groups to mobilize around identities not incorporated in the coalition of extremes. The "Congress system … (is) a party of consensus and parties of pressure. … These groups outside the margin do not constitute alternatives to the ruling party. Their role is to constantly pressurize, criticize, censure and influence it" (Kothari 1964: 1162). Such groups grew in strength as the Congress organization decayed and emerged especially in regions where the social and political coalition undergirding Congress dominance was already weaker (Jaffrelot 2003). The alternative to Congress's upper- and lower-caste/class coalition has been labelled a "sandwich coalition" (Swamy 2010), uniting Other Backward Classes (OBC), regional interests, middle classes, and Hindu nationalists left out of the Congress system.

The breakthrough for alternatives to Congress dominance happened in the North a decade later. Indira Gandhi was able to win a landslide election for Congress in 1971 with aggressive efforts to target the poor, symbolized by the slogan "garibi hatao" (abolish poverty). Yet, her strategy weakened the large-scale farmers that brokered Congress control in the countryside, opening space to increase mobilization among middle-peasant groups who had seen increases in resources and leverage as a result of the Green Revolution (Varshney 1998).

Eventually, the anti-Congress opposition united and won elections in 1977 led by the Janata Party (Kohli 1987). The Janata coalition included Hindu nationalist Bharatiya Jan Sangh, the market-oriented Swatantra Party, the middle-peasant-dominated Bharatiya Lok Dal, and the OBC-oriented Samyukta Socialist Party. This marked the arrival of a previously excluded middle class, OBC, medium-sized farmers, and regional interests as collective actors, and they formed a similar anti-Congress coalition in the 1989 election of the National Front.

For several reasons, previously excluded groups articulated demands in opposition to the Congress system by demanding recognition and benefits targeted on the basis of caste, regional, and other ethnic identities (Frankel 2004). One reason can be traced to the decision of the National Front to implement the recommendations of the 1980 Mandal Commission, reserving 27 per cent of government jobs for OBCs (Jayal 2005). This fulfilled one demand of the OBC movements but "divided the 'backward' from the 'forward' segments of the middle-peasant/backward-caste coalition, pitting peasant castes from different regions against each other" (Swamy 2010). Allocations of reservations depended on regional balances of caste demographics and conditions, producing regionally specific polarities of competition among different OBC, SC, and other identity-based movements, many of which formed caste-specific political parties to campaign for recognition and benefits (Jaffrelot 2003).

This identity-based orientation of demands received further impetus as Hindu nationalists in the Bharatiya Janata Party (BJP) stimulated controversy around the destruction of a Muslim shrine at Ayodhya, wooing upper classes that opposed protections for minorities and upper castes that opposed reservations. With the fragmentation of the party system preventing any outright majorities, partisan competition stimulated efforts by both the BJP and Congress to prime identity-based cleavages to patch together governing majorities of shifting, regionally specific, caste-based partisan allies (Yadav and Palshikar 2006).

The final factor focusing demands on identity-based issues was the essential agreement of Congress and BJP on the strategy of economic adjustment. Both parties pressed liberalizing reforms, starting with the Congress government of 1991 and deepening under the BJP governments of 1996 and 1998. Their implicit agreement kept debates over stabilization out of the public eye and reforms passed by "stealth," meaning through bureaucratic regulations and easily passed parliamentary measures (Jenkins 2000). At the same time, more difficult reforms were pushed to state governments, whose chief tools included market liberalization and export promotion (Sinha 2005), frequently emphasizing tax privileges and incentives for investment.

Over time, the BJP appeared to be more capable of forming alliances on a state-by-state basis, and its 1998–2004 government at times included as many as 24 parties. The BJP developed an "elite revolt" of Hindu nationalism and neoliberal market promotion with a base in upper castes and middle classes (Corbridge and Harriss 2000). Middle classes rejected what they perceived as corrupt and populist policies of Congress attempts to appeal to poor voters, and upper caste Hindus rejected preferential policies targeted at lower castes as a result of the Mandal Commission.

The BJP party cadre structure and its mass organization, the Rashtriya Swayamsevak Sangh (RSS), operate within a broader network of Hindu social organizations, the Sangh Parivar (Jaffrelot 1996). They have displayed the capacity to cultivate an internationally oriented middle class who blend Hindu nationalist and pro-business agendas, as evidenced by the deep ties between Sangh Parivar and non-resident Indians (NRI). NRI international success is taken as an indication of "Hindus' world historic mission," and the donations they send home sustain the RSS and similar organizations (Gopalakrishnan 2006).

Interestingly, the RSS has also proved sufficiently effective at penetrating poorer districts to balance efforts by other actors, especially Congress, in advancing a pro-poor agenda. While Congress reverts to its Congress-system practice of depending on local elite brokers, the RSS sends campaigners and charitable enterprises into poor districts, generating information about local political dynamics, stimulating Hindu supremacist cleavages, and neutralizing class-based opposition among urban and rural working classes and poor (Thachil 2011).

The 2014 election landslide expresses the electoral potential of the BJP coalition of middle classes, upper castes, and subaltern groups. Such a combination had been successfully exhibited by new Prime Minister Narendra Modi during his term as chief minister of the state of Gujarat, as he overcame the traditional Congress coalition to oversee a period marked by both rapid growth and anti-Muslim programmes.

Despite the dexterity of BJP alliance strategies and its potential coalition, it was the Congress government that attempted to institutionalize mechanisms of incorporation for previously excluded groups from 2004 to 2014. Congress's 2004 victory came somewhat as a surprise, as the Indian economy had already begun to achieve high rates of growth under the BJP, but the Congress-led United Progressive Alliance (UPA) won with allies such as the OBC-led Samajwadi Party (SP) and Dalit-led Bahujan Samaj Party (BSP), along with the Left Front of Communist Parties. With a mandate to respond to those ignored during neoliberal stabilization, the coalition partners agreed a Common Minimum Programme that stabilized linkages to previously excluded groups through institutions, policy, and legislation (Saez and Singh 2012).

The chief institutional innovation was the National Advisory Council (NAC), formally outside government, led by Sonia Gandhi, and composed of notable civil society activists with a mandate to provide policy advice to the government (Hasan 2012). As an autonomous and appointed body, the NAC appealed to the cohort of middle-class activists eager to provide input to public policy. On the other hand, when NAC initiatives stalled with the first UPA government, the council had to be reconstituted for the second UPA government starting in 2009, and its lack of governmental authority or civil society mobilization meant that it could be easily disbanded when the BJP returned to power in 2014 (Arora and Kailash 2015).

Still, a number of NAC policy innovations stabilized linkages to previously excluded groups. The most important was MNREGA, the Mahatma Gandhi National Rural Employment Guarantee Act, targeting small farmers and landless workers, many of whom had provided the support base to Dalit or OBC movements. Passed in 2005, MNREGA provided up to 100 days of work to each rural household at a minimum wage rate, and the average wage across all states has increased 180 per cent between 2005 and 2019. By 2010–2011, it had been rolled out in all districts that were not completely urban, reaching over 110 million people in 2019. On average, households received 50.85 days of work per year, and 19.48 per cent of beneficiaries were scheduled caste and 16.31 per cent scheduled tribe, well above their population percentage. As a result of the programme, which displayed 54 per cent women beneficiaries (Money Control 2018), rural wages increased an estimated 4.3 per cent, and households began to receive up to 8 per cent of their annual income from the programme.[10]

What distinguished the social policy regime pursued under the UPA governments was the legislation of social policy as rights, including legislation, covering rights to information, food, education, compensation for land acquisition, and forest rights. Rights-based legislation offered a justiciable mechanism by which individuals could hold the state to account, meeting one of the chief demands of middle-class activists hoping to weaken the control of local elites and corrupt or inefficient state bureaucrats (Jenkins and Goetz 2005).

Yet, Congress efforts at incorporation failed to unite a cross-class alliance in favour of mobilizing revenues to support its ambitious agenda. Segments of the middle class were unconvinced by the rights-based approach, especially as Congress's reputation was undermined by

[10] See Desai et al. (2015), Ministry of Rural Development (2012) and NIC (2019).

corruption scandals related to telecommunications licensing, coal, and construction for the 2010 Commonwealth Games, among others. It became increasingly difficult to expect middle classes to support mobilizing greater revenues from leading sectors, especially as they were the core of the urban, educated sector that was leading Indian emergence in international exports of technology and services (Fernandes and Heller 2006). Middle-class Indians oppose transfers for poor citizens as examples of "vote-buying" and efforts to target lower castes as "populism" (Kapur 2010).

Mechanisms of incorporation initiated by the UPA governments remained targeted to identity-based ethnic groups, with variable impacts across regions depending on political and caste configurations. For example, the UPA adopted what some labelled Mandal II by extending reservation of 27 per cent of seats to the premier federal government university system, including Indian Institutes of Technology, Indian Institutes of Management, and the All India Institute of Medical Sciences. As before, membership in an OBC category remained defined by states (Thorat 2005). Such targeting is cheaper than universal policies but reinforces divisions among subaltern groups and failed to generate a stable majority cross-class coalition in favour of progressive expansions of state capacity. Those policies that passed as universal rights, such as rights to information, education, and food, putatively altered the relationship between state and society, but were not supported with fiscal resources that made such rights a reality.

The result for India is a citizenship regime in which regional, caste, and ethnic actors have secured access to politics, but the targeted mechanisms of incorporation allow cycling among different combinations of support groups. The resulting instability limits the potential for collective projects such as increasing tax capacity, and progressivity in revenues is blocked by the elite consensus around neoliberal strategies of growth and middle-class opposition to redistribution. Decentralizing authority to states has intensified rivalry among different identity-based actors and across regions, producing incentive regimes that compromise both progressivity and universality in the tax system.

Conclusion

This chapter explored the nature of democratic deepening in Brazil and India and their relationship to state capacity. More specifically, India and Brazil differ in developing state capacity to raise revenue and channel these into social programmes or provide incentives to economic actors to support efforts at economic diversification.

In Brazil, middle-class and popular-sector actors legitimated themselves as collective actors in the struggle for democratization and constructed demands around opposition to neoliberalism. Their linkage to the state was institutionalized through social policies, state institutions, and left-right partisan competition. Cross-class democratic deepening built state capacity for broad-based collective action for social policies.

In India, ascriptive groups legitimated themselves in opposition to the Congress system and constructed demands for inclusion into the benefits of neoliberalism. Their linkage to the state was institutionalized through symbolic and targeted appeals channelled through bi-polar competition between national partisan coalitions led by the Congress and BJP. Cross-group democratic deepening built state capacity for embeddedness in local elites and cultivated international upgrading.

The patterns observed in these two countries suggest a number of implications. Development promotion is strengthened when both state capacity to stimulate broad collective action, as found in Brazil, as well as embeddedness in strategic sectors, as found in India, are present. Yet, the political determinants of these capacities are quite different. The kinds of social coalitions that produce one kind of capacity differ from the social coalitions that produce other capacities.

In addition, both kinds of state capacity are extremely vulnerable to reversal, especially in developing countries. In Brazil, dependence on the cooperation of oligarchic elites left state capacity vulnerable, as evidenced by the rapid defection of oligarchic allies once commodity prices dropped. In India, dependence on the cooperation of elites atop strategic sectors left state capacity vulnerable in other ways, as they could turn even further away from excluded minorities at times of slowdown, as evidenced by the rise of the Hindu nationalist BJP. For late developers, state capacity including capacity to mobilize domestic resources through taxation is essential to catching up. Unfortunately, the political determinants of state capacity are subject to variation across context and vulnerable to shifts in domestic and international relations.

References

Abranches, Sérgio. 1988. Presidencialismo de Coalizão: O Dilema Institucional Brasileiro. *Dados* 31 (1): 5–33.

Afonso, José Roberto, Castro, K., and Soares, J. 2013. *Avaliação da estrutura e do desempenho do sistema tributário Brasileiro: Livro branco da tributação Brasileira*. IADB Working Paper No. 265. Washington, DC: Inter-American Development Bank.

Arora, Balveer, and K.K. Kailash. 2015. Strengthening Legislative Capabilities of Parliament: The National Advisory Council. In *The Indian Parliament*, ed. Sudha Pai and Avinash Kumar, 183–215. New Delhi: Orient Blackswan.

Avritzer, Leonardo, Adalmir Marquetti, and Zander Navarro. 2003. *A Inovação Democrática no Brasil: Orçamento Participativo*. Curitiba: Cortez Editora.

Baker, Andy. 2010. *The Market and the Masses in Latin America*. New York: Cambridge University Press.

Barbosa, Nelson. 2010. Counter-Cyclical Policies in Brazil. *Journal of Globalization and Development* 1 (1): 1–14.

Bardhan, Pranab. 1984. *Political Economy of Development in India*. Oxford: Oxford University Press.

Brass, Paul. 1984. The Politicization of the Peasantry in a North Indian State. *Journal of Political Studies* 8 (1): 3–36.

Bresser-Pereira, Luis Carlos. 2015. Brazil's 35 Years-Old Quasi-Stagnation: Facts and Theory. Working Paper No. 399, Sao Paolo School of Economics. Sao Paolo: Fundação Getulio Vargas and EESP.

Buchanan, James M. 1963. The Economics of Earmarked Taxes. *Journal of Political Economy* 71 (5): 457–469.

Castiñeira, B.R., L.C. Nunes, and P. Rungo. 2009. Impacto de los Programas de Transferência Condicionada de Renta sobre el Estado de Salud: el Programa Bolsa Familia de Brasil. *Revista Español de Salud Pública* 83: 85–97.

CBGA (Centre for Budget and Governance Accountability). 2013. *Tax Exemptions in India*. Policy Brief. New Delhi: CBGA.

CEPALSTAT (Economic Commission for Latin America and the Caribbean Statistics). 2015. Tax Revenue by Type of Taxes as a Percentage of GDP. Accessed June 2015. http://interwp.cepal.org/sisgen/ConsultaIntegrada.asp?idIndicador=821&idioma=i.

Corbridge, Stuart, and John Harriss. 2000. *Reinventing India: Liberalization, Hindu Nationalism and Popular Democracy*. Cambridge: Polity Press.

Dagnino, Evelina. 2007. Dimensions of Citizenship in Contemporary Brazil. *Fordham Law Review* 75: 24–69.

Datafolha. 2014. Public Opinion Surveys. Accessed 10 September 2014. http://datafolha.folha.uol.com.br/.

Desai, Sonalde, Prem Vashishtha, and Omkar Joshi. 2015. *Mahatma Gandhi National Rural Employment Guarantee Act: A Catalyst for Rural Transformation*. Working Paper No. 7259. New Delhi: National Council of Applied Economic Research.

DIEESE (Departamento Intersindical de Estatística e Estudos Socioeconômicos). 2009. *Salario Minimo no Brasil*. São Paulo: DIEESE.

Draibe, Sônia. 2003. A Política Social no Período FHC e o Sistema de Proteção Social. *Tempo Social*, November: 63-10.

Escobar, Arturo, and Sonia Alvarez. 1992. *The Making of Social Movements in Latin America*. Boulder: Westview Press.

Evans, Peter. 1995. *Embedded Autonomy*. New York: Cambridge University Press.

Fairfield, Tasha. 2015. *Private Wealth and Public Revenue in Latin America*. New York: Cambridge University Press.

Fenochietto, Ricardo, and Carola Pessino. 2010. *Understanding Countries' Tax Effort*. IMF Working Paper No. 13/244. Washington, DC: International Monetary Fund.

Fernandes, Leela, and Patrick Heller. 2006. Hegemonic Aspirations: New Middle-Class Politics and India's Democracy in Comparative Perspective. *Critical Asian Studies* 38 (4): 395–422.

Frankel, Francine. 2004. *India's Political Economy 1947–2004*. Oxford: Oxford University Press.

Goldfrank, Benjamin. 2011. *Deepening Democracy in Latin America*. University Park: Penn State University Press.

Gopalakrishnan, Shankar. 2006. Defining, Constructing, and Policing a New India: Relationship between Neoliberalism and Hindutva. *Economic and Political Weekly* 41 (26): 2803–2813.

Hagopian, Frances. 1996. *Traditional Politics and Regime Change in Brazil*. New York: Cambridge University Press.

Hagopian, Frances, Carlos Gervasoni, and Juan Andrés Moraes. 2009. From Patronage to Program: The Emergence of Party-Oriented Legislators in Brazil. *Comparative Political Studies* 42 (3): 360–391.

Hall, Anthony. 2006. From Fome Zero to Bolsa Familia: Social Policy and Poverty Alleviation under Lula. *Journal of Latin American Studies* 38 (4): 689–709.

Hasan, Zoya. 2012. *Congress after Indira*. Oxford: Oxford University Press.

Held, David. 1995. *Democracy and the Global Order*. Cambridge: Polity Press.

Holston, James. 2009. *Insurgent Citizenship*. Princeton: Princeton University Press.

Houtzager, Peter. 2000. Social Movements amidst Democratic Transitions: Lessons from the Brazilian Countryside. *Journal of Development Studies* 36 (5): 59–88.

Hunter, Wendy. 2010. *The Transformation of the Workers' Party in Brazil, 1989–2009*. New York: Cambridge University Press.

Huntington, Samuel. 1968. *Political Order in Changing Societies*. New Haven: Yale University Press.

IBOPE (Brazilian Institute of Public Opinion and Statistics). 2013. Public Opinion Survey: 1998 and 2002 Second Round Data. Accessed 18 August 2013. http://www.ibope.com.br/.

India Ministry of Commerce and Industry. 2015. *List of Exporting SEZ's*. Accessed 3 October 2015. http://www.sezindia.nic.in/writereaddata/pdf/ListofoperationalSEZs.pdf.

Indian Ministry of Finance. 2014–2015. *Statistical Appendix to India Statistical Yearbook*. Accessed May 2015. http://indiabudget.nic.in.

International Labour Organization (ILO). 2018. *Women and Men in the Informal Economy: A Statistical Picture*. Third Edition, Table B2. Accessed 8 February 2019. https://www.ilo.org/wcmsp5/groups/public/%2D%2D-dgreports/%2D%2D-dcomm/documents/publication/wcms_626831.pdf.

Jaffrelot, Christophe. 1996. *The Hindu Nationalist Movement in India*. Princeton: Princeton University Press.

———. 2003. *The Silent Revolution in India*. New York: Columbia University Press.

Jayal, Naraja. 2005. *Representing India*. New York: Palgrave Macmillan.

Jenkins, Rob. 2000. *Democratic Politics and Economic Reform in India*. New York: Cambridge University Press.

Jenkins, Rob, and Anne Marie Goetz. 2005. *Reinventing Accountability: Making Democracy Work for Human Development*. New York: Palgrave Macmillan.

Kaplinsky, Raphael. 2005. *Globalization, Poverty and Inequality*. London: Polity Press.

Kapur, Devesh. 2010. The Middle Class in India: A Social Formation or a Political Actor? In *Political Power and Social Theory*, ed. J. Go. Bingley, UK: Emerald Group.

Keck, Margaret. 1992. *The Workers' Party and Democratization in Brazil*. New Haven: Yale University Press.

Kinzo, Maria D'Alva. 2004. Partidos, Eleições, e Democracia no Brasil Pós-1985. *Revista Brasileira de Ciências Sociais* 19 (54): 23–40.

Kohli, Atul. 1987. *The State and Poverty in India*. New York: Cambridge University Press.

Kothari, Rajni. 1964. The Congress System in India. *Asian Survey* 4 (12): 1161–1173.

Kumar, Arun. 2017. *The Black Economy in India*. London: Penguin Books.

Kurtz, Marcus, and Andrew Schrank. 2005. Credit where Credit is Due: Open Economy Industrial Policy and Export Diversification in Latin America and the Caribbean. *Politics and Society* 33 (4): 671–702.

Lavalle, Adrian, Arnab Acharya, and Peter Houtzager. 2005. Beyond Comparative Anecdotalism: Lessons on Civil Society and Participation from São Paulo. *World Development* 33 (6): 951–964.

Lieberman, Evan. 2005. *Race and Regionalism in the Politics of Taxation in Brazil and South Africa*. New York: Cambridge University Press.

Lopez, Felix, and Roberto Pires. 2010. Instituições Participativas e Políticas Públicas no Brasil: Características e Evolução nas últimas Duas Décadas. In *Brasil em Desenvolvimento*. Brasília: Institute of Applied Economic Research.

Mahon, James. 2004. Causes of Tax Reform in Latin America, 1977–95. *Latin American Research Review* 39 (1): 3–30.

Mann, Michael. 1984. The Autonomous Power of the State: Its Origins, Mechanisms, and Results. *European Journal of Sociology* 25 (2): 185–213.

Mazzucato, Mariana. 2015. *The Entrepreneurial State*. New York: Public Affairs.

Melo, Marcus André. 2008. Unexpected Successes, Unanticipated Failures: Social Policy from Cardoso to Lula. In *Democratic Brazil Revisited*, ed. Peter R. Kingstone and Timothy Power, 161–184. University Park: Penn State University Press.

Meneguello, Raquel. 1998. *Partidos e Governos no Brasil Contemporâneo*. São Paulo: Paz e Terra.

Ministerio de Fazenda. 2012. *Brazilian Economic Outlook*. Brasilia: Ministry of Finance.

———. 2014. *Infrastrutura no Brasil: Projetos, Financiamento e Oportunidades*. Brasília: Ministry of Finance.

Ministry of Rural Development. 2012. *MGNREGA Sameeksha. An Anthology of Research Studies on the Mahatma Gandhi National Rural Employment Guarantee Act, 2005*. New Delhi: Orient Black Swan.

Money Control. 2018. Economic Survey 2018: More Women Than Men Take Benefit of MNREGA, Still Remain 'Most Disadvantaged'. Accessed 25 September 2019. https://www.moneycontrol.com/news/business/economy/economic-survey-2018-more-women-than-men-take-benefit-of-mnrega-still-remain-most-disadvantaged-2493781.html.

NIC (National Informatics Centre). 2019. Accessed 25 September 2019. http://mnregaweb4.nic.in/netnrega/all_lvl_details_dashboard_new.aspx.

Nobre, Marcos. 2010. O fim da polarização: A verdadeira força hegemônica da política brasleira é o pemedebismo. *Piauí* 51: 1–11.

Nylen, William R. 1997. Reconstructing the Workers' Party (PT): Lessons from North-Eastern Brazil. In *The New Politics of Inequality in Latin America: Rethinking Participation and Representation*, ed. Douglas Chalmers, Carlos Vilas, Katherine Hite, Scott B. Martin, Kerianne Piester, and Monique Segarra, 421–446. New York: Oxford University Press.

O'Donnell, Guillermo A. 1996. Illusions about Consolidation. *Journal of Democracy* 7 (2): 34–51.

Olson, Mancur. 1965. *The Logic of Collective Action*. Cambridge: Harvard University Press.

Putnam, Robert. 1994. *Making Democracy Work*. Princeton: Princeton University Press.

Reserve Bank of India. n.d. *Direct and Indirect Tax Revenues of Central and State Governments*. New Delhi: RBI.

Roberts, Ken. 1998. *Deepening Democracy? The Modern Left and Social Movements in Chile and Peru*. Palo Alto: Stanford University Press.

Roman, Andrei. 2012. *Brazilian New Deal? Accounting for the Emergence of the Class Cleavage in Brazilian Politics*. Presentation made at the XXX International Congress of the Latin American Studies Association, San Francisco, 23–26 May.

Rosenberg, Justin. 1996. Isaac Deutscher and the Lost History of International Relations. *New Left Review* 1 (215): 3–15.

Saez, Lawrence, and Gurharpal Singh. 2012. *New Dimensions of Politics in India: The United Progressive Alliance in Power*. London: Routledge Press.

Sanchez-Ancochea, Diego, and Juliana Martínez Franzoni. 2016. *The Quest for Universal Social Policy in the South*. New York: Cambridge University Press.

Schneider, Aaron. 2012. *State-Building and Tax Regimes in Central America*. New York: Cambridge University Press.

———. 2019. Federalism and Taxation: Periods of Brazilian International Insertion. In *Political Economy of Taxation in Latin America*, ed. Gustavo Macias-Flores, 114–143. New York: Cambridge University Press.

Secretaria de Receita Federal. n.d. *Dados Econômico-Tributários e Aduaneiros da Receita Federal*. Brasilia: Federal Revenue Office. Accessed September 2019. http://receita.economia.gov.br/dados.

Seidman, Gay W. 1994. *Manufacturing Militance: Workers' Movements in Brazil and South Africa, 1970–1985*. Berkeley: University of California Press.

Sinha, Aseema. 2005. *The Regional Roots of Developmental Politics in India: A Divided Leviathan*. Bloomington: Indiana University Press.

Sood, Atul, Paaritosh Nath, and Sangeeta Ghosh. 2014. Deregulating Capital, Regulating Labour: Dynamics in the Manufacturing Sector in India. *Economic and Political Weekly* 49 (26&27): 58–68.

Souza, Jessé. 2015. *A tolice da inteligência brasileira: ou como o país se deixa manipular pela elite*. São Paulo: LeYa.

Swamy, Arun. 2010. Cleavage and Strategy in Political Mobilization in India. In *The Oxford Companion to Politics in India*, ed. Niraja Jayal and Pratap Bhanu Mehta. Delhi: Oxford University Press.

Thachil, Tariq. 2011. Embedded Mobilization: Nonstate Service Provision as Electoral Strategy. *World Politics* 63 (3): 434–469.

Thorat, Sukhadeo. 2005. Reservation and Efficiency: Myth and Reality. *Economic and Political Weekly* 40 (9): 808–810.

Varshney, Ashutosh. 1998. Mass Politics or Elite Politics? India's Economic Reforms in Comparative Perspective. *Journal of Policy Reform* 2 (4): 301–335.

Wade, Robert. 1990. *Governing the Market: Economic Theory and the Role of Government in East Asian Industrialization*. Princeton: Princeton University Press.

Weber, Eugen. 1976. *Peasants into Frenchmen*. Palo Alto: Stanford University Press.

Weiner, Myron. 1967. *Party Building in a New Nation*. Chicago: University of Chicago Press.

Woolford, Wendy. 2010. *The Land Is Ours Now: Social Mobilization and the Meanings of Land in Brazil*. Durham: Duke University Press.

World Bank. n.d. *World Development Indicators*. Dataset. Washington, DC: The World Bank. Accessed 2 January 2014. http://databank.worldbank.org/.

Yadav, Yogendra, and Suhas Palshikar. 2006. Party System and Electoral Politics in the Indian States, 1952–2002: From Hegemony to Convergence. In *India's Political Parties*, ed. Peter R. de Souza and E. Sridharan, 73–115. New Delhi: Sage Publications.

Yashar, Deborah J. 2004. *Contesting Citizenship in Latin America*. Princeton: Princeton University Press.

Zockun, Maria Helena, Hélio Zylberstajn, Simão Silber, Juarez Rizzieri, André Portela Eli Pellin, and Luís Eduardo Afonso. 2007. *Simplificando o Brasil: Propostas de Reforma na Relação Econômica do Governo com o Setor Privado.* Fundação. Instituto de Pesquisas Econômicas (FIPE) Working Paper No. 3. Sao Paulo: FIPE.

7

Power and Politics: Taxation, Social and Labour Market Policies in Argentina and Chile, 1990–2010

Enrique Delamonica, Jamee K. Moudud, and Esteban Pérez Caldentey

Introduction

The goal of this chapter is to analyse recent attempts to construct social democratic[1] taxation, social and labour (TS&L) policies in the context of unequal power relations and struggles for social justice in Argentina and Chile. We argue that, as elsewhere, employers tend to oppose such policies using various formal and informal mechanisms to push back against them. We characterize the design and implementation of social

[1] In this chapter we use "social democratic", "egalitarian" and "progressive" interchangeably to refer to rights-based policies that attempt to create fairer, more inclusive, cohesive societies (ECLAC 2010; Kastning 2013).

E. Delamonica (✉)
UNICEF, New York, NY, USA
e-mail: edelamonica@unicef.org

J. K. Moudud
Sarah Lawrence College, Bronxville, NY, USA
e-mail: jmoudud@sarahlawrence.edu

K. Hujo (ed.), *The Politics of Domestic Resource Mobilization for Social Development*, Social Policy in a Development Context,
https://doi.org/10.1007/978-3-030-37595-9_7

democratic TS&L policies as a contested process since popular pressures for social justice have had to contend with business support for neoliberalism in the two countries after the fall of their respective dictatorships in the 1980s. We argue that the goals of profitability and productivity shape the types of pressures put on the state by organized business groups and also influence labour market outcomes (Schneider 2013). Further, power relations between state and business are shaped by the political cohesiveness of the latter, that is the ability of firms to act in concert to politically promote their own policy agendas.[2] At the same time, power struggles also include workers and social movements who exert pressures on the state for egalitarian policies.

The chapter is organized as follows: Section "Theoretical Framework: Fiscal Sociology, Power Relations and Institutional Variations" discusses the theoretical framework. Section "State-Business Relations and Taxation, Social and Labour Policies in Chile and Argentina" discusses the evolution of business-state relations in Argentina and Chile and the ways in which political and institutional factors have evolved in both countries to create opportunities and challenges for the implementation of progressive TS&L policies. Section "Comparison of Fiscal Policy in Argentina and Chile" analyses fiscal policy in Argentina and Chile as a way to gauge the success of business groups in influencing state policy. Section "Conclusion" summarizes key findings and discusses some policy challenges.

[2] More specifically, by political cohesiveness we mean the extent to which firms from within and across industrial sectors have been able to come together in what Schneider has called encompassing associations. We follow Schneider (2004) in defining business encompassing associations as cross-sectoral alliances between firms that may have little in common in terms of the nature of the market served or technology used. The degree of political cohesiveness will determine how effectively diverse firms and sectors can articulate their interests.

E. Pérez Caldentey
Economic Commission for Latin America and the Caribbean,
Vitacura Santiago, Chile
e-mail: esteban.perez@un.org

Theoretical Framework: Fiscal Sociology, Power Relations and Institutional Variations

The essence of our framework is the proposition that all policies, including TS&L ones, need to be analysed in the context of business power. Business will attempt to push back or mould those policies that are perceived as a threat to profitability. However, the political influence of business groups is shaped by their cohesiveness and inter-business rivalries over public policies. If, as stated earlier, cohesiveness reflects the extent to which businesses can articulate their demands "with one voice", their economic rivalries may make such cooperation difficult.

Business relations and strategies shift and evolve over time and are partially shaped by economic growth, distributive policies, market regulation, and so on. Policies may affect different sectors in different ways, given their respective economic needs. Since firms and their policy preferences are heterogeneous, the government may be able to increase its bargaining power via some sort of a "divide-and-rule" policy that promotes both social and economic rights as well as investor confidence. This particular policy combination, or policy and political mix (PPM), is profoundly shaped by power struggles, for example between the state and employers, employers and workers and so on. Further, a PPM is also influenced by taxation and, more broadly, public finance challenges, which are in turn shaped by existing monetary and fiscal rules and the influence of external actors such as the International Monetary Fund (IMF).

Fiscal Sociology: Power Struggles and Taxation

Power relations shape the PPM. In contrast to the macroeconomic literature,[3] and approaches related to human capabilities,[4] our framework deals explicitly with structural and instrumental power relations and the political contexts which shape them. As Gourevitch emphasizes:

---

[3] See for example Godley and Lavoie (2007), which has become well-established in non-neoclassical macroeconomics.

[4] See Sen (1999) and Nussbaum (2011) with their focus on human capabilities and a rights-based approach to policy.

> Policy requires politics. … Economic theory can tell us a lot about policy alternatives, *but unless our economics contains an understanding of power*, it will not tell us enough to understand the choices actually made.
>
> In prosperous times it is easy to forget the importance of power in the making of policy. … In difficult times this comfortable illusion disintegrates. (Gourevitch 1986:17, emphasis added)

For example, the taxes the state is able to impose are the consequence of a political process reflecting the power relations in society at a given historical moment, as observed by Nicholas Kaldor (1963). Kaldor's approach followed the tradition of Schumpeter who discussed the need for a fiscal sociology of taxation incorporating interlinked economic, political, sociological and historical factors to understand a society's tax structure and the role that power relations play in developing them. What Martin et al. (2009) call the new fiscal sociology "suggests that economic development does not inevitably lead to a particular form of taxation, but rather that institutional contexts, political conflicts and contingent events lead to a diversity of tax states in the modern world" (Martin et al. 2009:14). Put simply, the fiscal sociology perspective emphasizes that taxation is a deeply political issue and power struggles between the government and various segments of society over the level and composition of taxes is the centrepiece of the analysis.

Forms of Power and Their Evolution

In order to understand why some states have been more successful than others in raising taxes on the wealthy and corporations (see also Chap. 4 in this volume) we have to analyse how business power is exercised. Some recent literature on this question distinguishes between instrumental and structural power.[5] Structural power takes the form of reduced investment in domestic production and increased flows into speculative or external activities.[6] Instrumental power arises from planned political actions by

[5] Hacker and Pierson (2002); Fairfield (2010); Farnsworth (2004).

[6] From policymakers' standpoint it may, particularly in economically turbulent times, be difficult to gauge ex ante the policy mix that may or may not trigger a fall in business confidence. Hacker

business via different institutions, including business interest associations, government-business policy coordination, informal business networks, business lobbying and campaign contributions, business ties to political parties and so on (Fairfield 2010). The political and institutional contexts within which structural and institutional power are exercised are crucial to an understanding of variations of policies in different countries or within a given country over time (Hacker and Pierson 2002).

Business actors might oppose progressive TS&L policies, despite potential benefits arising from higher labour productivity as a result of social investments, if short-term profitability or business confidence are negatively affected (see also Keynes 1953).

Authors of the Power Resources Approach (PRA)[7] have observed that employers in the United States, Sweden and Germany accepted social reforms as a form of strategic accommodation when faced with massive political pressure (in particular from unions).[8] However, business also need positive incentives, otherwise such pressures could produce capital flight or disinvestment. One can therefore extend the PRA perspective by adding that business may accept egalitarian TS&L policies, if accompanied by a policy mix such as subsidies or protection from foreign competition. In short, there must be a political compromise.

Varieties of Capitalism

Our framework also builds on the varieties of capitalism (VoC) approach (Hall and Soskice 2001) which investigates institutional differences and similarities between developed countries, classifying them into liberal market economies (LME) and coordinated market economies (CME)

---

and Pierson (2002) emphasize the disinvestment that follows from capital flight as a prime way by which structural power is exercised. However, one could equally argue that a relative increase in speculative activity, as opposed to long-term production-oriented investment, can also have a deleterious impact on the economy.

[7] Paster (2012) was critical of the PRA with regard to his discussion on Bismarckian Germany. We have included Paster in the PRA because of his emphasis that left political pressure, rather than employer initiatives, is the primary impetus for social democratic (or egalitarian) reforms. See also Korpi (2006) and Paster (2013).

[8] This political mobilization took many forms such as strikes, leftist party organizing and so on.

according to the type of coordination mechanism chosen to manage key relations between firms and other actors.[9] At the heart of the VoC approach is the firm and its institutional embeddedness, looking into cross-sectoral interlinkages that shape and are shaped by business investment decisions (Hancké 2009). Against the neoliberal claim that globalization will (or should) lead to a policy convergence across nations, VoC authors have emphasized that countries, whether in the Organization for Economic Co-operation and Development (OECD) countries or Latin America, adapt to global integration in myriad ways (Schneider 2013, 2010).

State-Business Relations and Taxation, Social and Labour Policies in Chile and Argentina

This section describes state-business relationships and TS&L policies in Chile and Argentina and explores the impact of changing business cohesiveness in both countries. It discusses the activities of key business associations, the interests they represent and how effective they have been in shaping policies.

Chile

The Confederación de la Producción (CPC), Its Policy Influence and Legacy

The return to democracy in Chile in 1990 created increased political demands by labour for greater social and labour rights. On the other hand, business groups' central preoccupation was to maintain the privileged position they had attained during the military regime. Throughout the Pinochet dictatorship and beyond, the Confederación de la Producción (CPC—Production Confederation), a multi-sectoral

[9] See chapter 1 by Hall and Soskice in Hancké (2009).

business organization, played a central role in consolidating business hegemony (Silva 1997).

While Pinochet launched a radical neoliberal economic programme during the 1970s, his policies entered a more pragmatic phase after the Chilean economy collapsed in 1982 in the wake of massive financial speculation and crisis (Silva 1997).[10] Two features of this pragmatic neoliberalism phase are significant from the standpoint of business power. First, the newly empowered business groups, under the CPC umbrella, supported counter-cyclical deficit spending, including selective public investment policies benefitting certain sectors such as the building and construction sector. These were accompanied by steep cuts in social welfare expenditures; large-scale privatizations of pensions, health and education programmes; and sharp cuts in top marginal rates on personal income and corporate taxes (Schmidt-Hebbel 1999).[11] Such a policy mix accomplished two goals. To begin with, by downsizing the welfare state, workers' bargaining power fell. At the same time investors benefited from demand stimulation in the slump. Jointly, the policies raised profits relative to wages. Second, policy reforms lowered employers' contributions to social insurance and increased workers' contributions in a general context of lower employment security and increasing inequality (Illanes and Riesco 2007).

Democracy brought with it demands by workers for social justice, seen with unease by business. A key challenge for the new government was to calm investor fears and revive business confidence, while at the same time satisfying some of the demands from civil society. However, state-business networks continued to strengthen in democratic Chile. The military, given its control of the transition to civilian rule, managed to maintain a lopsided representation of conservative and pro-business members of parliament. This led to most policies being business-friendly, contributing to private investment growth and high profitability in the context of an economic boom in the 1990s (Schwab and Sala-i-Martin 2013).

[10] In 1982, GDP fell by 14 per cent and the unemployment rate shot up dramatically to above 30 per cent. Investment plummeted to 12.9 per cent in 1983 from 19.5 per cent of GDP in 1981. In 1980–1981, the industrial production index was 100 while it dropped precipitously to 85 in 1982 (Silva 1997).

[11] Sandbrook et al. (2007); Illanes and Riesco (2007); Silva (1997).

This economic strategy enhanced the instrumental power of business. On a range of issues including corporate taxation and labour policies, subsequent centre-left Chilean governments have had to counter considerable instrumental power wielded by well-organized business groups, in particular the CPC (Fairfield 2010). The power of such entities came from the particular set of political institutions crafted during the dictatorship. Essentially, such constitutional measures sought to sharply curtail the autonomy of elected representatives and marginalize leftists (Roberts 2011). Currently, business groups constitute the "core constituency" (Fairfield 2010) of the two main right-wing parties, Renovación Nacional (RN—National Renewal) and the Unión Democrática Independiente (UDI—Independent Democratic Union),[12] whose representatives have successfully blocked increases in tax rates on corporations (Fairfield 2010) and wealthy households (Solimano 2012). As a result, the alliance between business groups and the political Right increased the instrumental power of corporations considerably.

Taxation Policies

In general, Chilean business groups have opposed policies affecting profitability adversely. Looking at the period 1990–2009, the corporate tax rate was about 14 per cent from 1990 to 2001 and about 17 per cent from 2002 to 2009 (Fairfield 2010). Between 2009 and 2013 it was raised from 17 per cent to 20 per cent, with a brief dip to 18.5 per cent in 2012 (KPMG 2019).[13]

All in all, while in the early 2000s, the value-added tax (VAT) was raised by 1 per cent and royalty taxes on private mining companies were successfully imposed, aggregate tax rates remained low (Roberts 2011). During the first Bachelet government (2006–2010) aggregate tax rates declined from 22 per cent to 19.6 per cent of gross domestic product (GDP). Thereafter, during the first Piñera government (2010–2014) and

[12] There is some evidence to suggest that the UDI gets generous amounts of funding from powerful business groups (Fairfield 2010).

[13] The most recent tax reform increased corporate income taxes to 27 per cent in 2018; however, this figure is still below the Latin American average of around 30 per cent.

the second Bachelet government (2014–2018), aggregate taxes as a percentage of GDP remained anchored at roughly 20 per cent of GDP. For their part, income taxes which stood at 10 per cent of GDP in 2006 declined to 6.5 per cent and now stand at 7 per cent of GDP (OECD 2019b).

The performance of taxes has constrained funding for social programmes and limited the prospect for redistribution and for financing free education, which was one of the social goals of the Bachelet governments.[14] An analysis of the functional classification of government expenditure available for the period 2010–2018 shows that the increase registered in health and education expenditures (3.5 per cent and 4.7 per cent of GDP in 2010; 4.0 per cent and 5.1 per cent of GDP in 2018) was in part undertaken at the expense of social protection expenditure, declining from 6.7 per cent to 5.1 per cent of GDP for the same years.

Social and Labour Policies

Similarly, only limited success was achieved in the rolling back of Pinochet-era labour laws, which had weakened worker solidarity and their bargaining power. On the one hand, eliminating these laws has been a key demand of unions, but every government's attempt to satisfy these demands has been met with effective business opposition (Huber et al. 2010). On the other hand, since 1990, the democratic governments have been successful in more than doubling the minimum wage (Pribble and Huber 2011). Between 1990 and 2017, the minimum wage was increased by law every year.[15] There is an implicit quid pro quo: in return for increases in the minimum wage and monetary compensation to laid-off workers on the basis of the number of years worked (Huber et al. 2010), firms have successfully opposed efforts to roll back the flexible labour market policies dating from the Pinochet era.

[14] Starting in 2016, students belonging to the poorest segments of society could access public and private education gratuitously in educational institutions complying with certain government requirements. The funding for free education came from the government and from the educational institutions themselves.

[15] In 1990 and 2017 the monthly minimum wage was equivalent to Chilean peso (CLP) 116,818 and 274,271, respectively, expressed in 2018 pesos.

While informal employment represents roughly 40 per cent of total employment in Chile (El Mostrador 2019), a large proportion of formal sector employment is also precarious with high rates of turnover. Unionization and education levels of workers remain low. While Chile ranked second to Puerto Rico in Latin America and the Caribbean in the 2013 Global Competitiveness Index, a number of factors, including relatively low levels of education and negligible investment in research and development (Schneider 2013), have impeded transition to higher value-added production, reflecting "poor innovation capacity" on the part of private investment (Schwab and Sala-i-Martin 2013:37).

From a policy standpoint, the prevalence of low productivity firms and unstable labour markets has several implications.

First, as Schneider (2013) shows, measures of labour market regulation indicate that Latin American countries tend to rank as more regulated than what the VoC literature terms LME (such as the United States), and even CME (such as Germany) (Schneider 2013).[16] In contrast to developed economies, high levels of labour regulation tend to reduce median job tenure (Schneider 2013). Because severance pay proportional to the number of years of service is the norm and is also required to be paid by law,[17] low productivity firms with limited cash flow prefer to dismiss workers preventively before it might become costly to do so (Schneider 2013). This strategy is possible because of the limited capacity to monitor and implement regulations by state agencies—which is also the result of insufficient financing of the state due to low overall taxation.

Second, poverty reduction via the promotion of human capital,[18] recommended for example by neoclassical economists and the World Bank, is of limited effectiveness in such a context. While highly skilled workers will be demanded by high productivity firms, these constitute a relatively small share of the economy.

[16] See Hall and Soskice (2001). The neo-Marxist critique of the VoC literature sustain that the CME/LME distinction is irrelevant under neoliberal capitalism, see Coates (2005). The authors are thankful to an anonymous referee for pointing this out.

[17] See Código del Trabajo (2002).

[18] According to which providing health and education by the state is supposed to raise economic growth which will lead to employment, so monetary poverty will decline due to a "trickle-down" effect.

Third, such labour markets tend to deepen not only economic but also political inequalities by lowering the instrumental power of workers and of social movements. In Chile, the two main social democratic parties, the reconstituted Socialist Party (PS) and the Party for Democracy (PPD), have weak organizations because their monetary resource base is low, making "the Left parties dependent on large private donors for financing elections" (Huber et al. 2010:81–82).

This does not imply that the centre-left governments have not been able to push through important social policies. Rather than focusing on monetary poverty alleviation, successive governments in the 2000s have attempted to take seriously the notion of social citizenship by creating more universalistic and solidarity-based policies (Huber et al. 2010). Among the most important initiatives has been the creation of an accessible healthcare policy, the AUGE programme (Acceso Universal con Garantías Explícitas—Universal Access with Explicit Guarantees), by the Lagos government, as well as pension reform, and the gratuity of education under Bachelet, which have "constituted major departures from the neoliberal model of narrowly targeted and market-driven social policy" (Huber et al. 2010:95).

Beginning with the Lagos administration, the goal of health care reform was to make it more universal, affordable, and to include a greater number of illnesses in its benefit package. Yet its coverage leaves out informal sector workers and does not adequately deal with the inequities of the existing system (Huber et al. 2010). Finally, the AUGE programme was initially to be financed via a national solidarity fund, partly dependent on healthcare contributions. However, the private health insurance companies and the political Right opposed such a funding policy. Instead it is financed via a small increase in VAT and additional co-payments (Huber et al. 2010). Annual caps on co-payments by low-income beneficiaries exist to ease the financial burden on them and reduce regressivity (Pribble and Huber 2011).

Given the inequities of the Pinochet-era privatized pension system, there has been widespread support for a public one (Ewig and Kay 2011). A signal policy of the Bachelet government has thus been to "transform social security into an economic and social right" (Consejo Asesor Presidencial para la Reforma Previsional 2006, as cited in Ewig and Kay

2011:85). The state has been able to re-insert itself into pension insurance so as to incorporate universalistic and solidaristic features. Those too poor to contribute (the lower than 60 per cent income groups) are provided public pensions (the universalistic component) while those not wealthy enough to have accumulated sufficient savings are given supplementary benefits (the solidaristic component) (Huber et al. 2010).

By July 2011, the solidaristic component covered and still covers about 60 per cent of persons belonging to households in the three poorest income quintiles. The pension reform has also reduced gender disparities in several ways. First, the non-contributory component has benefited women because a great proportion of them works in the informal sector or is out of work for varying lengths of time. Second, each woman's pension is augmented per each additional live birth. Third, gender equality has been reached in terms of survivors' pension and disability insurance. Fourth, in the event that a couple divorces, pension savings accumulated during the time they were married must be split equally (Hujo and Rulli 2014).

The financing of the public component of pension policy is accomplished via the Pension Reserve Fund, funded via structural budget surpluses, and from general tax revenues (Huber et al. 2010). The key barrier to implementing a more radical pension policy was that the pension fund industry saw certain components as inimical to its interests, opposing for example the creation of a state-owned pension fund which would compete with private ones.

Both the private pension and healthcare (ISAPRES—Instituciones de Salud Previsional—private health insurance providers) industries wield significant structural and instrumental power, catering to some of the wealthiest Chileans (Ewig and Kay 2011). In terms of instrumental power, one-third of the Marcel Commission (Bachelet administration's Advisory Council for Pension Reform) consisted of individuals from pension funds (Ewig and Kay 2011). In the same vein, the ISAPRES had created a peak association closely linked to the government, legislators and the conservative Institute for Liberty and Development that provided the intellectual firepower needed to push the ISAPRES' policy agenda (Ewig and Kay 2011).

Argentina

Fragmented Business Associations and Neo-Developmentalism

The democratic government led by President Raúl Alfonsín that took power after the demise of military governments in 1983 provided an avenue for progressive reforms and increased social expenditures. Real social spending in the 1980s was around 30 per cent higher than in the 1970s, increasing as a proportion of total government spending, from 41.4 to 58.6 per cent between 1983 and 1990 (Beccaria and Carciofi 1995). However, increased social spending was not matched with higher fiscal revenues, creating financial imbalances in the social sector, with adverse effects for quality of service and employment conditions. A politically weakened government which had lost mid-term elections struggled to implement tax increases and enforce existing rules (Beccaria and Carciofi 1995).

Argentinian business groups had not coalesced into a politically powerful encompassing association such as the Chilean CPC, though individual businessmen continued to be appointed to senior government positions throughout the 1990s, in particular during the market-friendly Menem administration from 1989 to 1999 (Schneider 2004).[19] Historically fragmented, several business associations, both in the industrial and in agricultural sectors, were competing with each other, shaping the nature of state-business relations with regard to various types of policies.

The pursuit of austerity and privatization policies under the Menem government, following an economic crisis with hyperinflation in the late 1980s, was accompanied by some narrow social assistance programmes[20] which did little to alleviate the precarious nature of jobs or hardship

[19] Schneider argues that encompassing business associations were generally kept at arms' length by governments, even by the neoliberal Menem administration, and so they lacked the institutionalized access to state power that the CPC does have in Chile. However, the business-friendly Menem government distributed most ministries to conspicuous members of major corporations, corporate lawyers, business associations and leaders of business-financed think tanks.

[20] For example, the cash-for-work programme ("Plan Jefes y Jefas de Hogar", which means male and female heads of households).

(Barbeito and Goldberg 2007). Nevertheless, they constituted an attempt to garner political support for the Menem government and reduce opposition to shock therapy programmes. The neoliberal project, deeply rooted in the interests of business elites, received financial support from international financial institutions (IFI) to implement (and expand) policies similar to the ones under military rule, which the Alfonsín administration (1983–1989) had tried to revert. The neoliberal project of President Menem was supported by shifting alliances of both organized labour (which was greatly weakened) and organized business groups. The government secured support from business groups via its privatization policies (Weyland 2003) and from some union leaders who converted themselves into managers of the privatized firms, including private pension funds.

The collapse of the Argentinian economy in 2001, when the country had to declare bankruptcy, significantly altered the government's relationship with business.[21] The new economic model which followed the crisis reconfigured state-business relations under a new political leadership (after the election of Nestor Kirchner as president in 2002). Labelled the neo-developmentalist paradigm (Ban 2012; Féliz 2012), it involved an activist state that promoted private capital accumulation, productivity growth and export promotion, implementing industrial policies to promote capitalist development. Interestingly, this state-led model was profoundly integrated into the global economy. For example, foreign-owned enterprises that constituted 32 per cent of the biggest 500 firms in 1993, increased their share from 48 per cent in 1998 to 66 per cent in 2007 (Féliz 2012).

In addition to industrial policy, productivity growth and export promotion, the new Kirchner government was also committed to a range of policies favouring its core base of support among trade unions, social movements such as the organization of urban unemployed (piqueteros), and sizeable segments of the re-emerging middle class (Etchemendy and Garay 2011). While some policies targeted the improvement of material conditions, others were related to the prosecution of human rights

[21] See Cibils et al. (2002).

violators during the military dictatorship or the expansion of Lesbian, gay, bisexual, transgender and queer or questioning (LGBTQ) rights.[22]

Taxation Policies

The pro-business policy framework, which made Argentina a particularly attractive investment site in the 1990s (Fairfield 2010), limited increases of already high corporate tax rates (compared to the Latin American averages): tax policy changes in 1989–1991 had increased corporate tax rates from 20 to 35 per cent and have remained at that level until 2017.[23] This said, the taxation system generated insufficient revenues and remained regressive and pro-cyclical due to the dependence on consumption taxes (Cetrángolo and Gomez Sabaini 2007).

Export taxes were first reintroduced in 2002 (Richardson 2009), which had been discontinued under Menem in line with standard free trade theory (Bräutigam 2008). Growing political power of the state in the aftermath of the 2001 crisis enabled the new government to raise the tax rate on booming soy exports (Fairfield 2011) and other agricultural commodities (Richardson 2009). Similarly, the government did not hesitate to clamp down on other corporate tax privileges to raise revenue from this sector, despite significant business opposition (Fairfield 2010). Such measures were facilitated by further weakening of business structural and instrumental power as the nature of the economic model changed after the centre-left Kirchner administration assumed power in 2003 (Fairfield 2010; Féliz 2012).

Higher net exports significantly increased revenues enabling the state to engage in redistributive policies, using parts of export revenues to provide subsidies to a wide range of domestic business sectors including poultry, beef, dairy, wheat, flour, energy and transport and to increase the pensions and nominal wages of public sector workers (Richardson

[22] On 15 July 2010, Argentina became the first Latin American country to allow same-sex marriages with equal rights and provisions as heterosexual marriages (Law 26.618). On 9 May 2012, Law 26.743 recognized equal treatment based on gender identity.

[23] See Agosto (2017). In December 2017, the Macri government passed a law reducing the corporate tax rate from 35 per cent to 30 per cent with a view to reducing it further to 25 per cent in 2020.

2009). Moreover, the Kirchner government exploited the internal divisions between various business sectors. Many firms across different sectors benefitted from the export tax increases because they financed the subsidies they received. Thus major business associations such as the Asociación Empresaria Argentina (AEA—Argentinian Enterprise Association) and the Unión Industrial Argentina (UIA—Argentinian Industrial Union) supported this tax (Fairfield 2011) or did not oppose it.[24] Within the agricultural sector, divergent production structures resulted in different policy preferences, which precluded a unified front against the new government efforts (Richardson 2009). For example, the Sociedad Rural Argentina (SRA—Argentinian Rural Association) and the Confederaciones Rurales Argentinas (CRA—Argentinian Rural Confederations) consist of large agricultural farms while the Confederación Intercooperativa Agropecuaria (COINAGRO—Agricultural Intercooperative Confederation) represents smaller farmers organized as cooperatives and the Federación Agraria Argentina (FAA—Argentinian Agrarian Federation) represents the very small farmers. All the farming groups were opposed to having agricultural exports taxed, but the FAA were less hostile provided the taxes were connected to subsidies that benefited them (Fairfield 2011).

A conflict emerged however in 2008, when the Kirchner government proposed a new export tax reform, announcing to create an adjustable export tax rate that was to increase up to a maximum of 95 per cent if commodity prices, and thus profits, increased (and vice versa, decrease, if prices would fall) (Fairfield 2011). This tax reform law came on the heels of an increase in export tax rates on soy from 35 to 44 per cent, which hit small farmers particularly badly (Fairfield 2011). Led by a coalition of rural business association leaders, the government was confronted with widespread protests. Business opposition took the form of road blocks, demonstrations and commercial strikes (Fairfield 2011) suggesting that the agricultural sector's instrumental power was relatively weak (Richardson 2009; Fairfield 2011). The proposed tax policy was defeated

[24] They recognized the need for additional revenues and an export tax did not affect them directly. Moreover, successfully opposing this tax might have led the government to look for alternative sources of revenue which might have affected them.

in the senate by a tie-breaking vote by the vice-president (who belonged to a different party).

Social and Labour Policies

Compared to many other countries in the region, there is a high demand for skilled labour in Argentina given the presence of research and development sectors, high by Latin American standards (Schneider 2013:116). Compared to the Latin American median in the 2000s, while labour market regulation is low, union density and worker job tenure are high, while informal employment as a per cent of total non-agricultural employment was estimated at 48 per cent in 2018 (Schneider 2013:167; World Bank 2019). Thus, the labour market is less "flexible", giving formal sector workers, especially those with skills, greater political leverage. These facts partly explain the particular type of state-business relations that have come about under the neo-developmentalist paradigm.

Partly because of union pressure, the Argentinian government has pushed for corporatist arrangements involving workers in the formal sector. The government's wage policy has involved increases in the minimum wage as well as the inclusion of nominal wage increments in contract negotiations in all sectors. Active labour market policies (Weller 2009) have reduced labour market flexibility somewhat and increased the bargaining strength of national unions who have been involved in peak-level negotiations with employers' groups and the state around a range of job-related concerns (Etchemendy and Garay 2011).

Not only formal sector workers and unions have been the beneficiaries of the neo-developmentalist strategy. As Féliz (2012) notes, there was a qualitative change in the nature of the class composition supporting such a development strategy, reflected in the fact that unemployed and informal sector workers as well as community action groups engaged in various types of collective action to support the government's policies. Such groups were successful in forging alliances with certain unions (Garay 2007), resulting in social policies that have also benefited workers outside the formal sector.

First, the government continued with the Heads-of-Household Programme (Jefes y Jefas del Hogar), implemented initially by the

Duhalde administration (2002–2003), involving transfers to reduce poverty among informal sector workers and the unemployed. Several job programmes followed involving community projects and cash subsidies for microenterprise development. The community job projects involved the provision of social services (care for the elderly and children, healthcare, etc.) and consumer goods, as well as infrastructure projects (Etchemendy and Garay 2011; Kostzer 2008).

Second, because of political pressures from the unemployed in the post-2008 crisis period and in an effort to respond to policy initiatives proposed by the opposition (de facto taking it away from them and presenting it as a government initiative), the state initiated a major increase of family allowances targeting the informal sector (Etchemendy and Garay 2011). This programme, called the Universal Child Allowance (Asignación Universal por Hijo), has been characterized as "the most important social right created since the return of democracy in 1983" (Etchemendy and Garay 2011:296). The programme provides a cash transfer to families with children whose parents are unemployed or work in the informal sector (that is they are not eligible for formal sector allowances), with some of the cash provided as a grant and some of it, in contrast to the formal sector child benefits, being conditional on sending children to school and being immunized.

These measures have yielded very tangible social benefits since the early 2000s, including a decline in monetary poverty (Weisbrot et al. 2011), and complemented other social initiatives, especially with regard to adolescents, children and elderly persons. For example, important changes have occurred in the pension system. As part of the drive towards neoliberalism in the 1990s, the public sector pay-as-you-go pensions underwent privatization and were transformed into a mixed public-private system in 1994, with its institutional make up biased towards the accelerated development of the private component (Mesa-Lago 2009; Arza 2012). The private fully funded component was administered by Administradoras de Fondos de Jubilaciones y Pensiones (AFJP, Pensions and Retirement Account Managers). Privatization was beset with numerous problems.[25]

[25] Etchemendy and Garay (2011); Mesa-Lago (2009); Arza (2009, 2012); Hujo and Rulli (2014).

Given the poor performance of the private system and the global financial crisis of 2008, re-nationalization had the support of a large majority of the population (Arza 2012). This represented an important push back by the state against private stakeholders such as the pension fund industry which had been the beneficiaries of the earlier neoliberal reforms. Pension re-nationalization also contributed to the state's coffers in the post-2008 crisis context (Kay 2009): The re-nationalization absorbed the private pension system into the public National Social Security Administration (ANSES).

In terms of the impact of reverting pension privatization, between 2005 and 2010 the coverage of persons over 65 increased through several measures from 68.9 per cent to 90.7 per cent, with the main beneficiaries being women, elderly persons below age 70, and those with low income and little education. Both non- and semi-contributory (subsidized or topped-up contributions) benefits have increased social solidarity. Concerns were raised, however, with regard to the long-term financial sustainability of the system in a context of increasing shares of tax-financed benefits and macroeconomic instability (Hujo and Rulli 2014). Indeed, in a context of an accelerating economic crisis, the business-oriented Macri administration, which assumed power in late 2015, implemented a cut of 3 per cent and 8 per cent in retirement benefits for 2018 and 2019, respectively, and reduced the social security budget by approximately USD 4.1 billion for 2018.

In contrast to pensions, healthcare expenditures have been maintained with some small changes. In Argentina, between 2007 and 2018, healthcare expenditures averaged roughly 3.7 per cent of total government expenditures. From the point of view of state-business relations and business power maintaining health expenditures permits both the reproduction and working power of the labour force necessary for the production process.

The health sector is divided into a public programme (mainly financed through taxes); a contribution-financed social health insurance programme (Obras Sociales), which is mainly administered by unions and largely autonomous of the state; and the private sector (Cavagnero et al. 2006). In the 1990s, as part of the market-driven framework and the consolidation of business power, there was a major expansion of private health insurance (Lloyd-Sherlock 2005).

With regard to the public sector component, neoliberal restructuring in the 1990s included decentralization and reducing the role of the Ministry of Health. From the 1990s onwards, provincial and municipal governments have shouldered a greater burden of the public health cost and relied increasingly on regressive out-of-pocket expenses (Cavagnero et al. 2006). The federal government accounts for around 2 per cent of total expenditure. The decentralization was primarily motivated by the goal of reducing business payroll taxes (Lloyd-Sherlock 2004). This generated regional disparities between poorer and richer provinces in terms of the quality of healthcare provisioning (Lloyd-Sherlock 2004).

The Obras Sociales are financed by mandatory payroll taxes levied on employers and workers. Under the right-wing government in the 1990s, employers' contributions to social insurance fell from 6 to 5 per cent although the former was restored with the onset of the foreign debt crisis in 2001–2002 (Lloyd-Sherlock 2006). Still, state interventions have not improved the existing inequalities between different Obras Sociales because of differences in wages. Further, the benefits of the Obras Sociales have only accrued to formal sector workers and their dependents (Lloyd-Sherlock 2006).

Finally, starting with the beginning of the Kirchner government in 2003, major laws and reforms were implemented including on reproductive health, generic drugs, primary healthcare and tobacco consumption. However, private health insurance companies and hospitals and clinics now constitute a large share of the healthcare sector. Even the Obras Sociales make use of their services as well as wealthier Argentinians who can purchase services not affordable to the rest of the population (Cavagnero et al. 2006).

Comparison of Fiscal Policy in Argentina and Chile

A comparison between Argentina and Chile shows similarities in their approach to state-business relations. Both countries consolidated their neoliberal reform process starting in the early 1980s following systemic banking and debt crises in both countries.

In Chile the neoliberal reform process was completed throughout the 1990s under the Alwyn and Frei governments through four channels: the promotion of privatization and increased price flexibility including in social areas such as health, education and pension funds; the achievement of fiscal balance over the business cycle; the adoption of an independent monetary policy; and greater external commercial and financial integration.

Within this framework the role of government is recognized as being subsidiary to that of the market, and its interventions are limited to providing a minimal social safety net and correcting for market failures. This facilitated the growth of economic groups and thus strengthened the power of the entrepreneurial class.[26]

In the case of Argentina, the Alfonsín government carried out economic adjustment policies in the mid-1980s including the reduction of the public deficit and of investment and private consumption in order to generate foreign exchange to comply with external debt obligations. These policies led to declines in real wages, deterioration of social conditions and significant social conflicts. The Alfonsín government tried but failed to oppose corporate interests, while in the 1990s, the Menem government further strengthened business groups, weakened trade unions and continued to push for fiscal stabilization.

Thus in both cases fiscal policy, especially during neoliberal regimes, has pursued the objective of stability and promoting public and private savings materializing into regressive and pro-business fiscal regimes whose main pillars were established during the respective dictatorships, and which were not substantially modified following the restoration of democracy. The fiscal structure has three features: low income and corporate taxation, high consumption/VAT taxation and (as a result of the previous two) a regressive tax structure.

Available evidence for 1990, 1995 and 1999 shows that indirect taxes represented 8, 10.4 and 11.2 per cent for Argentina, and 11.2, 11.4 and 11.8 per cent for Chile. Direct taxes (mainly income taxes) account for a

[26] Available evidence by the Securities and Insurance Superintendency shows that the number of economic groups has increased significantly since the 1980s, recording 12, 86, 92 and 140 economic groups in 1988, 2002, 2004 and 2016.

much smaller share of GDP: in Argentina, 0.7, 3.9 and 2.3 per cent and in Chile 4.6, 3.3 and 3.6 per cent for the same period of time.[27]

The regressive nature of the tax systems in Argentina and Chile exacerbates income inequalities. The Gini coefficient in Argentina before taxes is 48.7 per cent and increases with the inclusion of income, VAT and payroll taxes to 55.9 per cent (Pessino and Fenochietto 2007). In Chile the imposition of taxes also increases the Gini coefficient albeit by a lower percentage than in Argentina: from 48.8 to 49.6 per cent (Engel et al. 1998). The more recent Gini computations for Chile place the current coefficient above 50 per cent (López Vega et al. 2013).

During this time, social expenditure (including pensions) in Argentina represented 63 per cent of total expenditure. Similarly, in the case of Chile, social expenditures accounted for 62 per cent of total expenditures during the period 1990–1994, increasing to 66 per cent in the period 1995–2000.

In the 2000s, both Argentina and Chile witnessed a move towards left-leaning governments. In both cases the tax/GDP ratio increased although the rise was much more pronounced in the case of Argentina compared to Chile (in Argentina 19.8 per cent, 29.1 per cent and 31.1 per cent; in Chile 18.8 per cent, 19.6 per cent and 19.1 per cent of GDP for 2000, 2010 and 2014 respectively). The significant increase in tax collection in the case of Argentina responds in part to the nationalization of pension funds, the rise in commodity prices which increased export tax collection, corporate taxes and to a lesser extent to indirect tax collection. Total consolidated government expenditure increased from 33.8 per cent to 45.0 per cent of GDP between 2000 and 2015. For the same years, education, health and pension expenditure rose from 5.0 per cent, 5.1 per cent and 8 per cent to 6.2 per cent, 6.5 per cent and 10.1 per cent of GDP respectively.

Throughout the 2000s, in spite of the increases in social expenditure, stability remained an important objective of economic policy and the secondary role of direct taxes, and heavy reliance on indirect and regressive taxation limited the states' capacity to finance social investments in a fairer way.

---

[27] See OECD (2019a).

In both countries the left-leaning governments were replaced with right-wing governments, Sebastián Piñera in Chile (2010–2014 and 2018–2022) and Mauricio Macri (2015–2019) in Argentina whose initial focus was to maintain fiscal discipline. In this sense, the increases in social expenditure since 2007 in both countries should be understood as a transitory change in the country's fiscal regime.

These expenditures are partly explained as a response to the 2008–2009 global financial crisis and its effects. More recently, the IMF has granted Argentina a USD 50 billion stand-by agreement to stabilize the currency and with stringent conditionalities, including a reduction in the primary sector deficit from 4.2 per cent of GDP in 2017 to 2.8 in 2018 and 1.3 in 2019 and a decline in primary government expenditure of 2 per cent of GDP between 2017 and 2019.

Mauricio Macri's presidency in Argentina (2015–2019) has returned to a pro-business-oriented development policy. The budget plan for 2018 points to important expenditure cuts by slashing subsidies while government revenue was expected to expand through privatization initiatives. Due to political and social pressures the Macri government planned to avoid cuts in social expenditure. However, the government was unable to live up to its promise. During the Macri administration most social and economic indicators deteriorated and his policies plunged the country into a crisis and deep recession.

In the case of Chile, the second government of Piñera favoured the entrepreneurial class and slashed public expenditures in order to reduce the budget deficit and provide the required confidence for private investors. However, these policies are being challenged by current low growth and greater social discontent.

Conclusion

This chapter analysed the attempts in Argentina and Chile (two countries that in the 1980s and 1990s respectively changed from a military dictatorship to a democracy) to construct social democratic TS&L policies in the context of business power and, more precisely, under situations of unequal power relations between labour and business. Business power is shaped by their cohesiveness and inter-rivalries over public policies. Business power is also shaped by a host of other factors including growth performance, distributive policies and market regulations.

Our chapter emphasizes the constraints that the state faces in implementing egalitarian TS&L policies and in increasing social investments. One constraint, common to both countries, pertains to the nature and levels of taxation with its excessive reliance on regressive taxes—key issues that relate directly to the structure of power relations in these two countries. With demands to reduce inequality and raise social protection, the political battle over the level and composition of taxes remains key in these countries' attempts to become developmental welfare states.

The chapter shows that the restoration of democracy in both countries was shaped by two conflicting tendencies. On the one hand, there were increased political and social demands and rights by labour. On the other hand, businesses were eager to maintain the privileged position attained during the dictatorship.

This tension shaped to a large extent government social and economic policies and expenditure and its composition, as well as the capacity to finance that government expenditure. In both cases, left- and right-leaning governments alternated power. The available evidence on the fiscal accounts shows that in both Argentina and Chile increases in social expenditure were oriented mainly towards health and education. At the same time, there was some retrenchment in pension and retirement-related expenditures. However, the business sector empowered by neoliberal regimes in both countries limited increased taxation and government intervention to fund higher public expenditure. During these periods, the focus was mainly placed on the reduction of government expenditures.

A key difference between Chile and Argentina is the high level of business cohesiveness in Chile. This has allowed business-encompassing associations such as the CPC to effectively influence the policy-making process, thereby limiting the creation and extension of egalitarian TS&L policies. On the other hand, the greater level of inter-business rivalries in Argentina, and concomitantly fluctuating instrumental power, has enabled the state to push through important social policies demanded by the population. Thus, the democratization process in Chile in the post-dictatorship era and the logic of capitalist investment in Argentina have produced distinctive PPMs in the two countries.

Concerted political pressure by unions and social movements is clearly necessary for democratic states to expand and sustain progressive TS&L policies. But in order to be successful these initiatives should be part of a pro-growth PPM. Lacklustre economic growth in Chile during the second Bachelet government was one of the main reasons that explains the return of the right-wing Piñera government to power. Similarly, the failure of the Macri government is in part explained by the dismal growth performance of the Argentinian economy, which slipped into a recession in 2018 and 2019.

Economic growth is key for the increase in public revenue and the expansion of the tax base which would allow for a more redistributive fiscal policy. Economic growth can also be used as a means to build consensus on the benefits of progressive TS&L policies. Economic growth can be promoted and sustained through more active government investment policies. There is ample space in both Argentina and Chile for increasing public investment, which stands below 3 per cent of GDP in both economies. Public investment is not only a source of demand expansion but also a means to crowd-in private investment. In addition, a growth strategy in favour of progressive TS&L policies should consider more active industrial policies which are certainly most needed in both Argentina and Chile. Argentina has an underexploited manufacturing and export base while Chile's economics performance is, to a great extent, anchored in natural resources.

References

Agosto, Walter. 2017. *El ABC del sistema tributario argentino*. Document of Public Policies No. 188. Buenos Aires: Centro Interdisciplinario para el Estudio de Politicas Públicas.

Arza, Camila. 2009. *Back to the State: Pension Fund Nationalization in Argentina*. Working Paper No. 73. Buenos Aires: Centro Interdisciplinario para el Estudio de Politicas Públicas.

———. 2012. The Politics of Counter-Reform in the Argentine Pension System: Actors, Political Discourse, and Policy Performance. *International Journal of Social Welfare* 21 (1): 46–S60.

Ban, Cornel. 2012. Brazil's Liberal Neo-Developmentalism: New Paradigm or Edited Orthodox. *Review of International Political Economy* 20 (2): 298–331.

Barbeito, Alberto, and Laura Goldberg. 2007. Social Policy and Economic Regime in Argentina: Crisis and Retrenchment of Social Protection. In *Latin America: A New Developmental Welfare State Model in the Making?* ed. Manuel Riesco, 187–216. Hampshire; New York: Palgrave Macmillan and United Nations Research Institute for Social Development.

Beccaria, Luis, and Ricardo Carciofi. 1995. Argentina: Social Policy and Adjustment during the 1980s. In *Coping with Austerity: Poverty and Inequality in Latin America*, ed. Nora Lustig, 187–236. Washington, DC: The Brookings Institution Press.

Bräutigam, Deborah. 2008. Contingent Capacity: Export Taxation and State Building in Mauritius. In *Taxation and State-Building in Developing Countries: Capacity and Consent*, ed. Deborah Bräutigam, Odd-Helge Fjelstad, and Mick Moore, 135–159. Cambridge: Cambridge University Press.

Cavagnero, Eleonora, Guy Carrin, Ke Xu, and Ana Mylena Aguilar-Rivera. 2006. Health Financing in Argentina: An Empirical Study of Health Care Expenditure and Utilization. In *Innovations in Health Financing*, ed. Felicia Marie Knaul, M. Stefano Bertozzi, and Héctor Arreola-Ornelas, 1–32. Fundación Mexicana Para La Salud/A. C. Instituto Nacional De Salud Pública.

Cetrángolo, O., and J.C. Gomez Sabaini. 2007. *Política Tributaria en Argentina. Entre la Slovenia y la Emergencia*, Serie Estudios y Perspectivas No. 38. Buenos Aires: United Nations Economic Commission for Latin America and the Caribbean (ECLAC).

Cibils, A., M. Weisbrot, and D. Kar. 2002. *Argentina Since Default: The IMF and the Depression.* CEPR Briefing Paper. Washington, DC: Center for Economic and Policy Research.

Coates, David. 2005. *Varieties of Capitalism, Varieties of Approaches*. London: Palgrave Macmillan UK.

Consejo Asesor Presidencial para la Reforma Previsional. 2006. *El Derecho a una Vida Digna en la Vejez: Bacia un Contrato Social con la Previsión en Chile.* Santiago de Chile: Presidencia De La República De Chile.

Código del Trabajo. 2002. Dirección Del Trabajo. Santiago de Chile.

ECLAC (United Nations Economic Commission for Latin America and the Caribbean). 2010. *Time for Equality: Closing Gaps, Opening Trails*. Santiago de Chile: ECLAC.

El Mostrador. 2019. *Informalidad laboral en Chile llega al 40% y la mala calidad del trabajo se transforma en epidemia en Latinoamérica*. 27th February.

Engel, Eduardo M.R.A., Alexander Galetovic, and Claudio E. Raddatz. 1998. *Taxes and Income Distribution in Chile: Some Unpleasant Redistributive Arithmetic*. Working Paper No. 6828. Cambridge, MA: National Bureau of Economic Research.

Etchemendy, Sebastián, and Candelaria Garay. 2011. Argentina: Left Populism in Comparative Perspective, 2003–2009. In *The Resurgence of the Latin American Left*, ed. Steven Levitsky and Kenneth M. Roberts, 283–305. Baltimore, MD: The Johns Hopkins University Press.

Ewig, Christina, and Stephen J. Kay. 2011. Postretrenchment Politics: Policy Feedback in Chile's Health and Pension Reforms. *Latin American Politics and Society* 53 (4): 67–99.

Fairfield, Tasha. 2010. Business Power and Tax Reform: Taxing Income and Profits in Chile and Argentina. *Latin American Politics and Society* 52 (2): 37–71.

———. 2011. Business Power and Protest: Argentina's Agricultural Producers Protest in Comparative Context. *Studies in Comparative International Development* 46: 424–453.

Farnsworth, Kevin. 2004. *Corporate Power and Social Policy in a Global Economy: British Welfare Under the Influence*. Bristol: The Policy Press.

Féliz, Mariano. 2012. Neo-developmentalism: Beyond Neoliberalism? Capitalist Crisis and Argentina's Development since the 1990s. *Historical Materialism* 20 (2): 105–123.

Garay, Candelaria. 2007. Social Policy and Collective Action: Unemployed Workers, Community Associations, and Protest in Argentina. *Politics and Society* 35 (2): 301–328.

Godley, Wynne, and M. Lavoie. 2007. *Monetary Economics: An Integrated Approach to Credit, Money, Income, Production and Wealth*. New York: Palgrave Macmillan.

Gourevitch, Peter. 1986. *Politics in Hard Times: Comparative Responses to International Economic Crises*. Ithaca: Cornell University Press.

Hacker, Jacob S., and Paul Pierson. 2002. Business Power and Social Policy: Employers and the Formation of the American Welfare State. *Politics & Society* 30 (2): 277–325.

Hall, Peter A., and D. Soskice, eds. 2001. *Varieties of Capitalism: The Institutional Foundations of Comparative Advantage*. Oxford: Oxford University Press.

Hancké, Bob, ed. 2009. *Debating Varieties of Capitalism: A Reader*. Oxford; New York: Oxford University Press.

Huber, Evelyne, Jennifer Pribble, and John D. Stephens. 2010. The Chilean Left in Power: Achievements, Failures, and Omissions. In *Leftist Governments in*

Latin America: Successes and Shortcomings, ed. Kurt Weyland, Raúl Madrid, and Wendy Hunter, 77–97. New York: Cambridge University Press.

Hujo, Katja, and Mariana Rulli. 2014. *The Political Economy of Pension re-Reform in Chile and Argentina*. Research Paper No. 2014-1. Geneva: United Nations Research Institute for Social Development.

Illanes, María Angélica, and Manuel Riesco. 2007. Developmentalism and Social Change in Chile. In *Latin America: A New Developmental Welfare State in the Making?* ed. Manuel Riesco, 378–424. Basingstoke; New York: Palgrave Macmillan and United Nations Research Institute for Social Development.

Kaldor, Nicholas. 1963. Will Underdeveloped Countries Learn to Tax? *Foreign Affairs* 41: 410–419.

Kastning, Thomas. 2013. *Basics on Social Democracy*. Ghana: Friedrich Ebert Stiftung.

Kay, Stephen J. 2009. Political Risk and Pension Privatization: The Case of Argentina (1994–2008). *International Social Security Review* 62 (3): 1–21.

Keynes, John Maynard. 1953. *The General Theory of Employment, Interest, and Money*. San Diego; New York: Harcourt Brace Jovanovich Publishers.

Korpi, Walter. 2006. Power Resources and Employer-Centered Approaches in Explanations of Welfare States and Varieties of Capitalism: Protagonists, Consenters, and Antagonists. *World Politics* 58 (2): 167–206.

Kostzer, Daniel. 2008. *Argentina – A Case Study on the Plan Jefes y Jefas de Hogar Desocupados, or the Employment Road to Economic Recovery*. Economics Working Paper No. 534. New York: Levy Economics Institute.

KPMG (Klynveld Peat Marwick Goerdeler). 2019. Corporate Tax Rates Table. Accessed 30 September 2019. www.home.kpmg.

Lloyd-Sherlock, Peter. 2004. Ambitious Plans, Modest Outcomes: The Politics of Health Care Reform in Argentina. In *Crucial Needs, Weak Incentives: Social Sector Reform, Democratization, and Globalization in Latin America*, ed. Robert R. Kaufman and Joan M. Nelson, 93–123. Washington, DC; Baltimore; London: Woodrow Wilson Center Press and The Johns Hopkins University Press.

———. 2005. Health Sector Reform in Argentina: A Cautionary Tale. *Social Science & Medicine* 60: 1893–1903.

———. 2006. When Social Health Insurance Goes Wrong: Lessons from Argentina and Mexico. *Social Policy & Administration* 40 (4): 353–368.

López Vega, Ramón, Eugenio Figueroa Benavides, and Pablo Gutierrez. 2013. *La Parte del León: Nuevas Estimaciones de la participación de los Súper Ricos en el Ingreso en Chile*. Working Papers Series No. 379. Santiago de Chile: Universidad de Chile.

Martin, Isaac M., Ajay K. Mehrotra, and Monica Prasad, eds. 2009. *The New Fiscal Sociology: Taxation in Comparative and Historical Perspective*. New York: Cambridge University Press.

Mesa-Lago, Carmelo. 2009. Re-Reform of Latin American Private Pensions Systems: Argentinian and Chilean Models and Lessons. *The Geneva Papers* 34: 602–617.

Nussbaum, M.C. 2011. *Creating Capabilities: The Human Development Approach*. Cambridge, MA; London: The Belknap Press of Harvard University Press.

OECD. 2019a. Global Tax Data Base. Accessed 7 September 2019. http://www.oecd.org/tax/tax-policy/base-de-datos-global-de-estadisticas-tributarias.htm.

———. 2019b. *Revenue Statistics*. OECD Comparative Tables. Accessed 7 September 2019. https://stats.oecd.org/index.aspx?DataSetCode=REV.

Paster, Thomas. 2012. *The Role of Business in the Development of the Welfare State and Labor Markets in Germany: Containing Social Reforms*. London; New York: Routledge.

———. 2013. Business and Welfare State Development: Why Did Employers Accept Social Reforms? *World Politics* 65 (3): 416–451.

Pessino, Carola, and Ricardo Fenochietto. 2007. *Efficiency and Equity of the Tax Structure in Argentina, Brazil, and Chile: Analysis and Policy Consider-ations*. Working Paper. Washington, DC: Center for Global Development and Inter-American Dialogue.

Pribble, Jennifer, and Evelyne Huber. 2011. Social Policy and Redistribution: Chile and Uruguay. In *The Resurgence of the Latin American Left*, ed. Steven Levitsky and Kenneth M. Roberts, 117–138. Baltimore, MD: Johns Hopkins University Press.

Richardson, Neal P. 2009. Export-Oriented Populism: Commodities and Coalitions in Argentina. *Studies in Comparative International Development* 44 (3): 288–255.

Roberts, Kenneth. 2011. Chile: The Left after Neoliberalism. In *The Resurgence of the Latin American Left*, ed. Steven Levitsky and Kenneth M. Roberts, 325–347. Baltimore, MD: The Johns Hopkins University Press.

Sandbrook, R., M. Edelman, P. Heller, and J. Teichman. 2007. *Social Democracy in the Global Periphery: Origins, Challenges, Prospects*. Cambridge: Cambridge University Press.

Schmidt-Hebbel, Klaus. 1999. Chile's Takeoff: Facts, Challenges, Lessons. In *Chile: Recent Policy Lessons and Emerging Challenges*, ed. Guillermo Perry and Danny M. Leipziger, 63–108. Washington, DC: The World Bank.

Schneider, Ben Ross. 2004. *Business Politics and the State in Twentieth-Century Latin America*. Cambridge; New York: Cambridge University Press.

———. 2010. Business Politics in Latin America: Patterns of Fragmentation and Centralization. In *The Handbook of Business and Government*, ed. David Coen, Wyn Grant, and Graham Wilson, 307–329. Oxford: Oxford University Press.

———. 2013. *Hierarchical Capitalism in Latin America: Business; Labor, and the Challenges of Equitable Development*. New York: Cambridge University Press.

Schwab, Klaus, and Xavier Sala-i-Martin. 2013. *The Global Competitiveness Report 2013–14*. Geneva: World Economic Forum.

Sen, Amartya. 1999. *Development as Freedom*. New York: Alfred Knopf.

Silva, Eduardo. 1997. Business Elites and the State in Chile. In *Business and the State in Developing Countries*, ed. Sylvia Maxfield and Ben Ross Schneider, 152–188. Ithaca; London: Cornell University Press.

Solimano, Andrés. 2012. *Capitalismo a la Chilena*. Santiago de Chile: Catalonia.

Weisbrot, Mark, Rebecca Ray, Juan A. Montecino, and Sara Kozameh. 2011. *The Argentine Success Story and its Implications*. Washington, DC: Center for Economic Policy Research.

Weller, Jurgen, ed. 2009. *Regulation, Worker Protection, and Active Labour-Market Policies in Latin America*. Santiago de Chile: United Nations Publications.

Weyland, Kurt. 2003. Neopopulism and Neoliberalism in Latin America: How Much Affinity? *Third World Quarterly* 24 (6): 1095–1115.

World Bank. 2019. *Informal Employment (% of Total Non-Agricultural Employment)*. Accessed 30 September 2019. https://data.worldbank.org/indicator/SL.ISV.IFRM.ZS.

8

Sharing the Wealth: The Politics of Subnational Distribution of Natural Resource Revenues

Javier Arellano-Yanguas and Andrés Mejía-Acosta

Introduction

The recent price and investment boom in the mining and hydrocarbon sectors has triggered widespread expectations for greater economic and social development, especially among developing countries. The potential success of a development strategy based on the extraction of non-renewable resources is largely dependent on the share of revenue captured by the state from the extractive sector, and the methods that governments adopt to use and distribute that revenue (Bebbington 2012; Hujo 2012). This study acknowledges existing dilemmas around the mobilization of revenue—through taxes and royalties—and focuses on the criteria used

J. Arellano-Yanguas (✉)
University of Deusto, Bilbao, Spain
e-mail: javier.arellano@deusto.es

A. Mejía-Acosta
King's College London, London, UK
e-mail: andres.mejia@kcl.ac.uk

K. Hujo (ed.), *The Politics of Domestic Resource Mobilization for Social Development*, Social Policy in a Development Context,
https://doi.org/10.1007/978-3-030-37595-9_8

to allocate revenue from extractive industries (EI) to different levels of government.

Mobilizing domestic revenues has been correctly identified by the United Nations Research Institute for Social Development (UNRISD) as a precondition to meet the Sustainable Development Goals (SDGs) and potentially trigger broader transformative change (UNRISD 2016). The formation of progressive coalitions, however, where wealthier sectors of the economy contribute relatively more than less privileged groups, requires a more detailed understanding of how countries will design their own financing strategies according to their economic and political structures and specific needs (UNRISD 2016). The specific architecture, composition and nature of the fiscal contract will vary in each country.

The abundance of natural resource revenues poses an opportunity and a challenge to the nature of fiscal contracts. Between 2003 and 2010, several Latin American countries including Argentina, Brazil, Bolivia, Chile, Colombia, Ecuador, Peru, Uruguay and Venezuela benefited from a booming natural resource sector and rising international prices for agricultural, mining and fuel products (UNRISD 2016). In Bolivia, for example, public revenues had stagnated at approximately 31 per cent of gross domestic product (GDP) between 1990 and 2005, but with the advent of the commodities boom and associated economic growth, government revenues increased to 39 per cent in 2006 and peaked at 48.4 per cent of GDP in 2008. This substantial increase was key to financing a new social development strategy in a context of declining aid receipts and increased policy-making autonomy of the Bolivian government more generally (UNRISD 2016).

The actual choice of fiscal mechanisms to distribute natural resource revenues, however, varies tremendously across countries and reflects internal political tensions. The distribution of natural resource revenues has different features than those used to distribute central government transfers. Firstly, minerals, oil and gas are frequently concentrated in specific territories; the people living there are likely to demand a share of the proceeds from the extraction to compensate for the use of their resources and the negative externalities associated with extraction. Secondly, minerals and hydrocarbons are non-renewable, which puts additional pressure on replacing the extracted resources with some investment in durable assets, giving tangible (e.g. physical infrastructure) or intangible (e.g. education) benefits. These features have led to greater decentralization of EI-related revenue in recent years, but the methods and mechanisms adopted vary widely across countries. We find that distributive mechanisms do not necessarily follow existing lines of administrative or fiscal decentralization, but, rather, are the object of a permanent negotiation across existing political stakeholders, especially between national and subnational political elites. As we argue towards the end of this chapter, local governments that were able to mobilize active constituencies and/or offer significant political support to the central government gained greater bargaining power to influence decision-making at the central level.

Using comparative data for selected cases, this chapter explores three questions[1]:

- How do central governments allocate and distribute the revenues accrued from EI to different levels of subnational government?
- When subnational governments benefit from direct EI transfers, how are those revenues distributed across similar jurisdictions, some of which host extractive activities while others do not?
- How do political and institutional factors determine the degree of decentralization and the modality of distribution of EI revenues?

In this chapter we contend that variations in the *vertical* and *horizontal* distribution of revenues depend not only on technical considerations for optimal distribution but also on the political motivations and coalitions to distribute EI revenues. We highlight the relative importance of the timing of reforms to the EI sector, the importance of having federal versus unitary states, and the relative bargaining power and alignment of subnational actors vis-à-vis the central government. We discuss some preliminary explanations and draw some policy implications.

The chapter proceeds as follows: The section "Methods for the Distribution of Resource Revenue" reviews the main features of existing methods,

[1] This chapter is based on research conducted by the authors for the Politics of Domestic Resource Mobilization project (Arellano-Yanguas and Mejía-Acosta 2014b). A preliminary, shorter version of this chapter was published as Arellano-Yanguas and Mejía-Acosta (2014a). We are grateful to Maria Aguado for her brilliant research assistance; all errors remain our own.

rules and practices for allocating resource revenues at the subnational level. The section "Subnational Transfers in Comparative Perspective" shows the variation in ten countries worldwide for which we have identified reliable and comparable data on the distribution of natural resource revenues. The section "Political Dynamics and the Underlying Factors of Revenue Sharing" discusses some underlying political factors that influence the adoption of different revenue allocation policies. Finally, the section "Final Remarks" summarizes the key arguments made in this chapter and identifies knowledge gaps that would need to be closed to better understand the linkage between allocation formulas and development outcomes at the local level.

Methods for the Distribution of Resource Revenue

Revenues accrued from the extractives sector can adopt the form of direct taxes to production, royalties on profits and production income, and value-added taxes from the extractive activity. For governments, the first-order question is whether accrued revenues are merged with general revenues and therefore treated as central government finances, or whether they are independently transferred to subnational governments according to pre-determined distribution formulas. This is a significant distinction because it determines whether the central government can manage and administer these revenues with a fair degree of discretion or whether it devolves spending autonomy to subnational jurisdictions. While central governments may (correctly) argue that certain discretion is necessary to ensure a balanced management of public finances, the abundance and volatility of revenues can also increase the temptation for rent seeking, misallocation of funds or arbitrary government cuts. This chapter focuses on the adoption of formal rules to transfer natural resource revenues to subnational allocations. Such rules create legal entitlements that cannot be arbitrarily changed and they reduce the scope for discretionary fiscal allocations.

When central governments agree to transfer EI revenues to subnational jurisdictions, they often create allocation rules to maximize the long-term impact of transfers while—ideally—protecting these transfers from volatile fluctuations in commodity prices. Many countries such as Peru, Ecuador, Bolivia, Mexico, Brazil and Ghana seek to spend a high proportion of EI transfers in capital investment. The logic is to replace the natural capital that is extracted by other types of capital in order to avoid the loss of productivity after the exhaustion of the mineral resource (Auty 2004). Capital investment is also prioritized, as opposed to current spending, as a way to protect investments from the volatility in the price of commodities in international markets (Ahmad and Singh 2003). Nevertheless, these recommendations must be adapted to the situation of each country. When EI are the main source of revenues, governments will always face the temptation to use such revenues to finance current expenses, particularly during boom times. Using non-permanent revenues to finance current spending could create major fiscal imbalances at the end of bonanza periods.

Despite that last caveat, it could be argued that promoting investment in physical infrastructure is a good mechanism to maximize the use of transfers, provided that associated costs in the form of maintenance, current salary costs or human capital formation are properly budgeted as well. Any investment in physical infrastructure may prove to be counterproductive if the recurring or rising costs in terms of human resources and staff costs are not sustainable in the long run. It is therefore recommended that the investment in capital or physical infrastructure is accompanied by a sustainable government effort to strengthen human capital by allocating a percentage of the amount transferred to specific sectors such as health or education, as it is for example done in Brazil or Bolivia. Other countries, such as Colombia, have tried to simultaneously advance flexibility and efficiency in public spending by formulating a set of goals for the improvement of social indicators and by mandating subnational governments to invest in those sectors until they reach such goals. However, more effort is needed to collect the necessary fiscal transfer and social indicator data to allow for a proper monitoring of social indicators at the local level in order to assess compliance with the stated goals.

Following this general discussion on the use of transfers, the next section presents an overview of common criteria used to distribute EI-related revenue from central to subnational governments (vertical distribution), as well as commonly used methods to determine the distribution across subnational governments (horizontal distribution).

Vertical Distribution of EI Revenues

The vertical distribution refers to the share of EI revenues that central governments "devolve" to subnational jurisdictions, whether these are regional, state and/or local governments vis-à-vis the share of revenues that central governments keep in their coffers. Similar to fiscal decentralization debates, revenue sharing poses some inherent redistributive dilemmas. On the one hand, central governments would prefer to centralize the control of most revenues in order to ensure more targeted, egalitarian and balanced fiscal management. Central government planners believe they will be in a better position to prioritize investment in key areas while minimizing the financial liabilities caused by volatile revenues or subnational debt. Subnational entities, on the other hand, would advocate for a more effective and generous allocation of EI revenues, particularly if subnational governments claim to have greater electoral legitimacy, a direct political mandate and better information about the key investment areas and needs of the population. In all cases, the availability and redistribution of natural resource revenues exacerbate political tensions across territories.

There are three common criteria taken into consideration when deciding the distribution of EI revenues (Ahmad and Singh 2003): (1) whether allocated fiscal transfers match administrative responsibilities; (2) whether revenue sharing ensures a political equilibrium between the centre and the periphery; and (3) whether there are mechanisms in place to manage revenue volatility and/or minimize debt liabilities.

Matching Responsibilities

The first allocation criteria is that the share of transfers and other income (including EI-related transfers, other fiscal transfers and locally raised taxes) should match the revenue needed by subnational governments to fund the public services they are responsible for (Schoeder and Smoke 2002). Evaluating the actual or "appropriate" level of administrative responsibilities for the delivery of public services, as well as the "matching revenue" needed to fund them, is in practice a difficult task. Central governments may claim that some of the public services are delivered through their ministerial offices anyway, and that local governments lack the technical or administrative capacity to handle larger shares of fiscal transfers. In addition, there are many de facto accounting and procurement rules that can be set in place by finance ministers to limit the access to funding to subnational governments. Thus, the actual and effective fiscal transfers remain subject to political interpretation and intense bargaining.

Political Equilibrium Between Centre and Subnational Governments

The debate about the allocation of EI-related fiscal transfers has taken place in the context of decentralization reforms. Subnational governments have claimed their "entitlement" to participate in the distribution of EI-related wealth, and in some cases, this right has been enshrined in the constitutions of the countries (Ahmad and Mottu 2003; Ross 2007). In practice, however, central governments face the decision of whether to empower local governments with revenue sharing rights and thus raise their political profile vis-à-vis the centre or rather maintain centralized control and possibly face discontent from local actors and potential voters. In the end, and fairly consistent with the logic of fiscal decentralization, central governments are likely to give in to fiscal decentralization demands when they are able to ensure political control and electoral victories at the subnational level or when they confront strong opposition parties and subnational actors who demand greater decentralization reforms (Falleti 2010). In an ideal sequence, central governments are likely to grant and test a gradual administrative decentralization before conceding greater fiscal and political autonomy to subnational governments.

Managing Volatile Revenues

Given the relatively unpredictable nature of commodity prices, revenue from EI has the potential to induce fiscal volatility in national and subnational public finances (Ahmad and Singh 2003). To minimize the impact of revenue volatility, some have advocated a centralized management of EI revenue through a savings or stabilization fund (Ahmad and Mottu 2003). This is done partly to accumulate savings at the central level but also to protect subnational entities from the problems arising from handling revenue windfalls. If fiscal centralization is neither technically feasible nor politically desirable, it is recommended to devolve more "stable" revenue that is independent from international prices—such as royalties (when these are calculated based on gross production), licences and other fees (Davis et al. 2003). The main challenge with creating and sustaining sovereign wealth or stabilization funds has been to create the institutional safeguards and the political credibility to make them work. While more work is needed to explore subnational stabilization funds, it has been documented that national funds tend to be more successful when they operate in a context of balance of powers and/or organized civil society has an active and vested interest in monitoring for its success (Bagattini 2011).

In summary, this section has briefly illustrated that, while the adoption of (vertical) revenue sharing formulas is generally informed by technical allocation formulas, their effective success depends more on political economy considerations to embed them in pre-existing decentralization arrangements and ensure they are safeguarded by patterns of democratic competition and overseen and monitored by an active role from civil society organizations. The next section discusses so-called horizontal allocation criteria for distributing rents across producing and non-producing districts.

Horizontal Distribution of Revenue from EI

The second question concerning distribution of EI revenues is whether central governments should share EI revenues with producing districts only or whether transfers should be allocated more broadly to include non-producing districts as well. The argument in favour of straightforward devolution (to producing districts only) builds on the entitlements to wealth discussed previously. However, non-producing districts can also make a claim to these EI revenues if they suffer from negative externalities of production, contribute to the transport or shipping of minerals or hydrocarbons, or have equal or greater socioeconomic needs compared to producing districts.

Yet, the adoption of a formula to enable horizontal distribution of EI revenues would have to choose the criteria along which non-producing districts will be compensated. Would central governments adopt a principle of subsidiarity to compensate producing and non-producing districts along their socioeconomic needs, deprivation levels or poverty lines? Or would they encourage good fiscal effort by rewarding with greater transfers or tax concessions those districts that display good macroeconomic management? Alongside the distributive question, central governments face the question of how the allocation of transfers would help the formation of subnational coalitions supporting the national executive or not (González 2012).

The existing literature has identified three types of mechanisms: (1) devolution, (2) direct allocation from the central government and (3) formula-based participation. In practice, countries combine two or more criteria when adopting redistribution formulas.

Devolution

Devolution involves the transfer of revenue, or a proportion of it, to the jurisdiction where the income has been generated.[2] In the case of revenue from EI, devolution makes the producing regions, and sometimes those

[2] This mechanism is also known as "derivation" according to Ahmad et al. (2003), but we refer to it as "devolution" in this chapter.

that host some infrastructure for exploitation (mainly ports), the only recipients of transfers. This mechanism aims to compensate producing regions for negative externalities linked to extraction, and directs funds to adjust infrastructure and public services to the presence of mining and oil operations (Brosio 2003). However, the concentration of transfers in producing regions could generate three types of problems: (1) inequality between producing and non-producing regions; (2) problems of revenue volatility in producing regions; and (3) discouraged collection of local taxes and distortion of resource allocation at the local level. The inequality between regions is an especially acute political problem in periods of high prices in countries that transfer a high proportion of their natural resource revenues through this mechanism (Bauer et al. 2016:48).

The implementation of devolution mechanisms requires identification of the jurisdictions that should be prioritized. The following two criteria are the most frequently used: (1) the geographical origin of the revenue and (2) territories affected by negative externalities linked to extraction.[3] The criterion of origin tries to compensate for the loss of natural capital (the mineral) by financial transfers to the governments of the territories where the extraction takes place. Such transfers should in principle help to develop other types of capital (human, physical, etc.) to enhance the developmental potential of those territories. Frequently, the strict application of this criterion leaves out neighbouring jurisdictions that are also affected by extraction. The criterion of negative externalities tries to solve this limitation. It takes into account environmental damage but also the need to improve physical infrastructure (roads, the electrical grid, etc.) and to scale up public services in order to respond to the likely increase in population due to immigration from other regions of the country.

Allocation from the Central Government

In this scenario, central governments seek to centralize the macroeconomic management of revenue to minimize the risk of uncontrolled subnational expenditure. Government finance is usually transferred on an

[3] These territories are usually identified with hosting infrastructure needed for the exploitation or transportation of minerals.

annual basis for specific projects and development or regional investment funds. Governments could also distribute available revenue through competitive investment grants aimed at supporting specific types of projects. In principle, the adoption of competitive grant mechanisms by the central government has the potential to reinforce pre-existing economic inequalities and power asymmetries between subnational governments. Some territories with solid public finances may have greater expenditure capabilities or possess the technical ability to formulate and obtain additional resources through competitive grant schemes. In any case, these mechanisms of competitive allocation offer more transparent alternatives than allocating valuable resources through protracted or clandestine or discretionary political negotiations which may intensify existing political divides.

Formula-Based Participation

Through this mechanism, subnational governments receive a predetermined share of the revenue raised nationally. A formula set by law determines both the amount to be allocated and the obligation of the central government to transfer those resources to both producing and non-producing territories. The different needs and characteristics of each jurisdiction can be factored into the formula to compensate for pre-existing inequalities, the size of the population and, in some cases, the tax gap. The allocation formula can also reflect different variables for measuring government performance, such as the fiscal effort of each territorial unit. In countries like Bolivia, Brazil, Colombia and Peru, the central government earmarks revenue transfers to specific line items by law, as a way to limit the discretion of subnational governments in planning how such revenues might be spent (Bauer et al. 2016).

While formulas can become more complex to reflect different dynamics, the ultimate challenge for policy makers is to ensure fairness and efficiency. Excessive complexity can trigger conflicts regarding interpretation of the formula, counteracting any marginal gain in terms of equity and efficiency. However, formula-based participation, even if well designed, can also have some drawbacks. It reduces the flexibility of the central government to manage the macroeconomic challenges associated with EI and does not take into consideration the geographical source of tax revenue.

This section discussed the extent to which political or technical criteria largely informs the distribution of EI revenues. The next section looks at comparative data from a set of ten resource-rich countries to determine, for example, whether countries with greater fiscal and administrative decentralization are in fact more likely to distribute a larger share of EI revenues to subnational governments than formal unitary countries.

Subnational Transfers in Comparative Perspective

A brief review of the comparative evidence available (see Table 8.1) shows that existing methods for distributing EI revenues between central and subnational governments (vertical distribution), and across producing and non-producing regions (horizontal distribution), vary widely. The data, collected for ten resource-rich countries (oil and mining) where reliable and comparable information was located (Bolivia, Brazil, Colombia, Ecuador, Ghana, Indonesia, Mexico, Nigeria, Papua New Guinea and Peru), shows that allocations do not reflect the "pure types" identified in the literature. Table 8.1 summarizes the distribution of EI revenues between central, regional, state and local government levels according to the last reform in each country. As noted in the previous section, the reported data reflects formal EI revenue entitlements that central governments transfer to subnational entities. The data does not report other forms of non-EI government transfers, or other types of EI revenues such as margins of profit from state-owned oil and mining companies that are managed by the national government and may be allocated in the form of discretional transfers. This section highlights some patterns and regularities found in the distribution.

Table 8.1 Models of decentralization of EI revenues in selected countries[a]

			Bolivia (oil and gas)	Brazil[b] (oil and gas)	Peru (mining and gas)	Nigeria (oil)	Colombia (oil since 2011)	Mexico (oil)	Indonesia (oil)	Ecuador (oil)	Ghana (mining)	Papua New Guinea (oil and gas)
Type of revenue transferred			Royalties and IDH	Royalties	Royalties and income taxes	Total oil revenue	Royalties	Total oil revenue	Total oil revenue	Total oil revenue	Royalties	Royalties
Date of the last reform			2007	2012	2004	1999	2011	1978	2004	2010	1992–1999	1998
Degree of decentralization			High	High	Medium	Medium	Medium	Low	Low	Low	Low	Low
Vertical distribution		National government and centralized funds	37%	15%	45%	46%	52%	83%	85%	98%	91%	93%
		Regional/state governments	37%	45%	12%	36%	48%	17%	3%	1%	5%	3%
		Local governments	26%	40%	43%	18%		–	12%	1%	2%	2%
		Private landlords	–	–	–	–	–	–	–	–	2%	2%
Horizontal distribution	Devolution	Producing region/state	28%	20%	12%	13%	10%	–	3%	1%	5%	3%
		Producing localities	13%	15%	5%	–		–	6%	1%	2%	2%
		Localities in producing regions	–	–	38%	–	–	–	6%	–	–	–
		Total devolution	41%	35%	55%	13%	10%	–	15%	2%	7%	5%
	Formula-based	Region/state	9%	25%	–	23%	38%	17%	–	–	–	–
		Localities	13%	25%	–	18%		–	–	–	–	–
		Total formula-based	22%	50%	–	41%	38%	17%	–	–	–	–

Sources: Author elaboration based on data from Agustina et al. (2012), Banful (2011), Departamento Nacional de Planeación-Colombia (2012), Energy Sector Management Assistance Programme (2005), Iledare and Suberu (2012), Morgandi (2008), and Viale (2015)

[a]Some data on percentages reflects quantities for specific years. The degree of decentralization has been assessed according to the following criteria: High (decentralization > 60 per cent), Medium (decentralization between 60 per cent and 30 per cent) and Low (decentralization < 30 per cent)

[b]In 2012, Brazil introduced new rules for the distribution of oil royalties. The distribution varies according to the type of agreement with the companies (shared production or concession) and the geographic location (inland or offshore). This table includes the criteria for inland share-production agreements

Vertical Distribution

Table 8.1 reports countries according to their degree of decentralization of EI revenues. Decentralization is (1) *low* if all subnational governments receive less than 20 per cent of state EI revenue (Ecuador, Ghana, Papua New Guinea, Indonesia and Mexico); (2) *medium* if subnational governments receive between 20 per cent and 60 per cent of the EI revenue (Colombia, Peru and Nigeria); and (3) *high* if subnational governments receive more than 60 per cent of the EI revenue accrued to the central government (Bolivia, Brazil). The table also provides information on the share of total EI revenue that is formally allocated to each tier of government.

The first striking feature is that decentralization of EI revenue is directly related neither to the formal territorial structure nor to the general level of decentralization of the country. While there are federal countries like Brazil and Nigeria that effectively share a medium or high proportion of EI revenues with regions, other federal countries share less, for example Mexico,

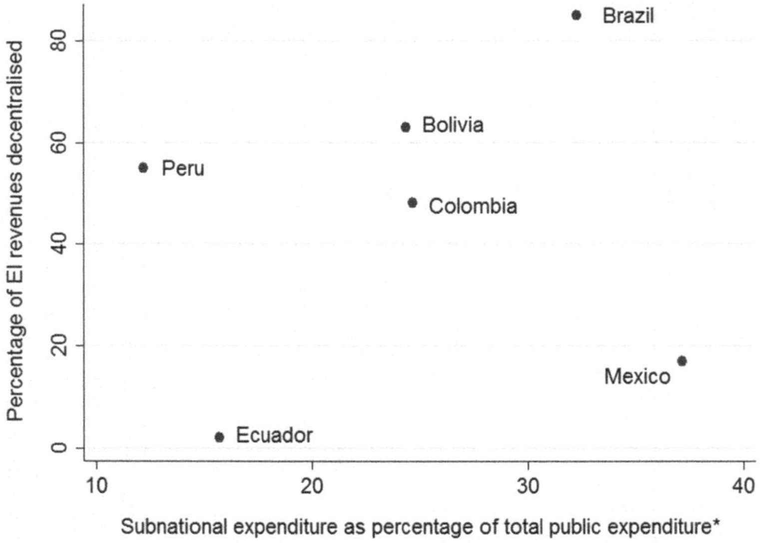

Fig. 8.1 Relation between fiscal decentralization and decentralization of EI revenues. (Source: Author elaboration based on data from el Ruiz Duran (2011:50). Note: *Average for years 2000–2007)

which has traditionally transferred less than 20 per cent of EI revenue. Conversely, some formally unitary (non-federal) countries such as Bolivia and Peru redistribute up to 60 per cent of their EI revenue to subnational units. There is no clear association between the allocation of EI revenues and the share of fiscal decentralization in each country either. Figure 8.1 shows that subnational public expenditure as a share of total public expenditure is not associated with the decentralization of EI revenues in six Latin American countries. Even though Peru and Ecuador have relatively low levels of fiscal decentralization, the Peruvian state is highly decentralized when it comes to allocating EI revenues. Similarly, a comparison between two federal and decentralized countries Brazil and Mexico shows that the latter tends to favour centralization of EI revenues.

A second feature of vertical distribution is that subnational beneficiaries (regional, state and local level governments) vary widely as well. In federal states like Brazil, Nigeria and even Mexico, most of the allocated transfers go to state-level governments, probably because the central government spending is channelled through the existing fiscal decentralization structure. By contrast, in non-federal (or unitary) systems like Peru and Indonesia where decentralization had recently been adopted, local-level governments receive more than three times the share of EI revenues than state-level counterparts (43 per cent for municipalities compared to 12 per cent for regions in Peru, and 12 per cent compared to 3 per cent in Indonesia). Bolivia initially had a more equitable distribution across the three tiers of government (37 per cent to the national government, 37 per cent to the regional governments and 26 per cent to municipalities). After 2012, President Morales increased fiscal transfers in favour of local governments (in the form of cash transfer schemes managed by the central government) while reducing transfers to regions (prefecturas), most of which were governed by opposition parties. These changes confirm the political nature of decentralizing EI revenues: "if confronted with the opportunity or need to decentralize, the national executive prefers to do it toward the local level, since mayors pose less of an electoral and financial threat than governors" (Falleti 2010: 47).

The presence of central government transfers can be essential for the fiscal sustainability of the local government, but it can also create negative dependencies. In Peru, for example, it is estimated that central government transfers can represent more than 80 per cent of local governments' budgets (Bauer et al. 2016). By the same token, not all municipal governments have the capacity to spend revenues. The Peruvian Ministry of Economy reported significant underspending rates of natural resource transfers to municipal governments between 2004 and 2011 (Bauer et al. 2016), and similar problems are observed in Bolivia (Jiménez Pozo 2017). In other cases, it is unclear that the abundance of resources necessarily led to improved provision of public services; in Brazil it is reported that access to piped water, trash collection and connection to sewage networks actually deteriorated as more oil revenues flowed into municipal coffers (Bauer et al. 2016). A possible explanation is that oil wealth creates greater rent seeking and corruption incentives as it increases the amount of revenues available while reducing fiscal transparency. It remains an empirical question to explore the ways in which subnational governments can invest resource revenues to effectively improve local growth, education and health indicators for their own populations (Bauer et al. 2016).

Horizontal Distribution

Table 8.1 also shows significant variation in the existing methods for distributing EI revenue, ranging from distributing only to producing districts versus favouring a more equitable distribution across all territories including non-producing areas (horizontal distribution). Once again, the degree of decentralization of EI revenues is not related to the type of beneficiaries. At high levels of decentralization, countries like Bolivia prioritize transfers to producing departments and districts. Royalties constitute the main source of oil and gas income for the four producing departments (Santa Cruz, Tarija, Cochabamba and Chuquisaca) but revenues are also distributed across non-producing departments (Bauer et al. 2016).[4] Conversely, in Nigeria, the government has adopted formula-based participation to benefit all subnational governments and restrict the funds directed to producing states only (Kâ Diongue et al. 2011).

[4] Although there is clear and available information about the distribution of royalties, it is harder to determine how the regional governments allocate transfers across municipalities.

In contrast, Peru has preferred formulas that devolve revenue back to the producing region and localities in producing regions. Until 2012, Brazil also transferred most EI revenues to the producing states, reinforcing some pre-existing economic inequalities. For example, the revenue sharing regime disproportionately benefited oil-rich Rio de Janeiro state, the nation's third wealthiest in terms of GDP per capita, given that Rio is one of the country's largest off-shore oil producers (Bauer et al. 2016). In 2012, the Brazilian government adopted new legislation that balances the situation by distributing a percentage of EI revenues to non-producing states and localities.[5] Other reforms also sought to compensate non-producing regions by investing in essential infrastructure (ports, roads, pipelines and railways) to support extractive activities.

In countries with a medium level of decentralization of EI revenue, revenue tends to be distributed through a combination of devolution- and formula-based mechanisms. Colombia has moved in a similar direction as Brazil, from a system that concentrated transfers of royalties to the producing regions, to a more equitable system where a significant proportion of the royalties are distributed between all subnational jurisdictions. It is reported that 90 per cent of natural resource royalties from EI in Colombia go to five funds: (1) a Territorial Pension Fund; (2) a subnational Savings and Stabilization Fund; (3) a Regional Development Fund; (4) a Regional Compensation Fund; and (5) a Science, Technology and Innovation Fund. The remaining 10 per cent of royalties are allocated directly to producing regions, down from 80 per cent previously (Bauer et al. 2016). The Regional Compensation and Development Funds that jointly account for almost 40 per cent of the total amount of all the royalties are distributed to all municipalities and regions in proportion to their population and poverty indicators.

In Indonesia, oil-related transfers go exclusively to the producing areas (provinces and districts), but 50 per cent of the value of these transfers is discounted from the ordinary transfers that these provinces and districts should receive from the national government (Morgandi 2008). More recently, a percentage of the EI revenue has been given to jurisdictions adjacent to the producing ones to compensate negative externalities

[5] Law 12734, articles 48 and 49.

linked to extraction. However, these criteria frequently generate grievances because negative externalities do not coincide with the boundaries of official jurisdictions. This opens the way for continuous demands from populations that feel excluded from fiscal distribution. Mexico is the only country reported to distribute EI revenues proportionally across the entire country through an allocation formula.

In countries with low levels of EI decentralization (Ecuador, Ghana and Papua New Guinea), most EI transfers tend to favour producing regions only. In Ecuador, subnational governments (provinces and municipalities) have benefited from fiscal decentralization since the mid-1990s, but this devolution did not include the specific transfer of EI revenues. With the advent of the commodities boom after 2004, the government further centralized the allocation of EI revenues. The government levies USD 1 per barrel of oil produced in the Amazon region, with the purpose of financing "environmental restoration, health, road works, building and equipping of schools and rural community facilities, and tourism projects, including the necessary costs to perform studies" (Bauer et al. 2016:62).

The overview of the different criteria followed by the selected countries gives us some preliminary evidence about diverse distribution patterns. The overall tendency is that fiscal decentralization informs but does not determine the patterns of subnational redistribution of revenues. In general, we observe that countries with higher levels of fiscal decentralization (Brazil) tend to prioritize a type of redistribution that benefits both producing and non-producing regions across the country, whereas unitary countries with weak fiscal decentralization (Peru and Ecuador) tend to concentrate the transfers in producing jurisdictions. Countries with moderate to low levels of fiscal decentralization (Colombia and Mexico) tend to combine devolution to the producing regions with formula-based distribution to all the territories. More detailed research is needed to uncover the actual allocation and spending dynamics between the central government and subnational governments as well as across and within subnational governments. The next section explores some of the underlying factors determining the political choice of different distribution formulas.

Political Dynamics and the Underlying Factors of Revenue Sharing

The empirical overview of allocation formulas suggests that technical criteria are often insufficient to explain the adoption of different revenue sharing formulas and ensure "optimal" distribution mechanisms. In this section, we outline some of the political institutions, incentives and cooperation dynamics that shape the form of revenue allocation, with reference to a selected group of cases. In a previous publication, we have discussed in greater length how these political dynamics have played out in a smaller range of Andean cases (Arellano-Yanguas and Mejía-Acosta 2014b). Here, the general question is to explore when and why central governments are more likely to be responsive to subnational demands for revenue sharing. We identify and develop some key contributing factors.

Relative Strength of Subnational Governments Vis-À-Vis Central Governments

We have observed that in countries with more generous patterns of revenue sharing, such as Brazil, Bolivia and Peru, subnational governments obtained a greater share of EI revenues based on the specific nature of their political processes and historical circumstances. In Bolivia, for example, the strength of the opposition in gas-producing regions and the need of the new Movimiento al Socialismo (MAS) government to build a broad coalition of municipalities against those opposition regions created additional pressure to increase redistribution to the municipal level, which was reflected in the 2005 reforms (Eaton 2014). Similarly, in Peru, a long tradition of mining conflicts and the active lobbying of the extractives sector help to explain why the central government accepted a generous distribution of revenues through the Canon Minero (Arellano-Yanguas 2012). In both countries, subnational governments used local mobilizations to gain leverage in the negotiation with the central government on the distribution of EI revenues. Conversely, in Colombia and Ecuador, governments were able to recentralize the management of EI revenues. In

Colombia, subnational governments of producing regions did not offer the same degree of political mobilization as their Peruvian or Bolivian counterparts; instead, some of their representatives in the national parliament covertly agreed to negotiate a new redistribution of revenues across producing and non-producing regions that, in fact, represented a centralization of the management of those resources (Rudas Lleras and Espitia Zamora 2013). In Ecuador, conflicts and demands for greater redistribution were concentrated in a few remote oil-producing districts of the Amazon region and could not provoke greater devolution on the part of the central government.

Nevertheless, there seems to be considerable variation in the way EI revenues are distributed to local governments. Most, but not all, federal states tend to privilege allocations to state or regional governments (Brazil and Nigeria) whereas unitary states tend to benefit local or municipal governments. A potential explanation is that central governments in unitary states prefer to target resources directly to municipal governments because they can wield greater fiscal influence and political leverage over relatively weaker local governments (as in the case of Indonesia and Peru). By contrast, central governments in federal countries are legally mandated to devolve fiscal and administrative resources and therefore are less able to influence the policy preferences of subnational governments and recentralize fiscal—particularly EI—revenues.

Partisan Alignment

We argue that central governments are more likely to favour more generous and equitable distribution of EI revenues when subnational governments also take part (directly or indirectly) in the national governing coalition. As noted, fiscal devolution comes with political devolution and central governments are unlikely to share the wealth if that helps to strengthen the role of a subnational opposition. Conversely, if local elites have strong connections with central governments, they may be able to gain access to fiscal resources, projects, discretionary transfers and policy influence. One example comes from Bolivia, where President Evo Morales would have preferred to recentralize revenues after the 2005 reforms but had to compromise a greater distribution of revenues with mayors across the country in order to counteract the opposition of governors in the main hydrocarbon-rich regions (Eaton 2014).

Party congruence across the territories however is not necessarily a condition for effective cooperation, since it can also create greater subnational dependency on the executive and reduced autonomy to pursue the regions' own development strategies.

Fiscal Decentralization

Much of the debate around the allocation of EI revenues fails to take into account the relative weight of the extractives sector in the overall fiscal decentralization and budgetary management. A preliminary comparison suggests that there is no apparent proportionality between the share of government revenues (as percentage of GDP) transferred from central to subnational governments (fiscal decentralization) and the share of EI revenues. In countries like Ecuador and Mexico, the share of fiscal transfers tends to be greater than the share of EI transfers, whereas in Bolivia, Peru, Brazil and Colombia, the opposite is true, there being greater decentralization of EI revenues.

We find that a federal structure facilitates but does not guarantee greater availability of EI revenues at the subnational level. Certainly, federal countries are legally mandated and administratively more organized to facilitate the transfer of EI revenues to state governments in a more efficient and accountable manner (Ahmad and Mottu 2003). By contrast, subnational (local) governments in a unitary state generally have less fiscal and administrative autonomy to extract and manage their own revenues. Central governments in such countries have greater power to centralize revenue transfers and to exert greater discretion when deciding which regions and local governments benefit from—or have limited access to—such revenues.

Sequencing

The design and adoption of revenue sharing formulas tend to follow path-dependent trajectories: once a structure of intergovernmental transfers has been adopted, it is fairly difficult to change or revert it without upsetting existing political balances or broader institutional arrangements. Revenue sharing formulas, forms of fiscal decentralization, are closely tied to the specific timing of political processes in two ways. First, they are affected by the overall sequence of decentralization reforms, so that fiscal transfers are more likely to succeed when they are preceded by political and administrative devolution of powers. In other words, if sub-national entities have experienced greater devolution of administrative responsibilities over time and have elected their own political authorities, they are more likely to obtain and effectively administer fiscal transfers (Falleti 2010). Conversely, in a context of restrictive political competition or the absence of free and fair elections, the adoption of revenue sharing formulas is less likely to take place.

Second, the overall state of commodity markets affects the success of adopted revenue sharing reforms. The presence of a commodities bonanza or the anticipation of new discoveries is likely to trigger demands from local actors who, in turn, may be able to mobilize against the government or even threaten to disrupt the workings of extractive activities in order to demand greater attention from the centre (Crabtree and Chaplin 2013; Arellano-Yanguas 2012). The adoption of the IDH tax (Impuesto Directo a los Hidrocarburos—Direct Tax on Hydrocarbons) in Bolivia in 2005 comes both in the process of growing commodity prices and a highly politicized movement which eventually elected Evo Morales into office. Conversely, in Ecuador, the local and political actors who pushed for greater fiscal decentralization in the late 1990s, at a time of record low oil prices, did not take into consideration the distribution of oil revenues as part of intergovernmental transfers. Once the most recent oil boom was underway, local actors could not organize to revert the centralization of oil revenues established a decade earlier. The relevance of sequencing should come as a warning for policy makers: the adoption of revenue sharing reforms cannot be conceived as a quick fix for appeasing local tensions against extraction, as temporary solutions could lead to increased conflicts and negative developmental results in the future (Arellano-Yanguas 2011).

Final Remarks

The growing importance of the extractive sector in the developmental strategy of many poor and middle-income countries raises the question of the distribution of EI revenues among levels of government and across different jurisdictions at a given level. Theory provides clear guidance for designing such redistributive policies. Regarding vertical distribution, theory suggests that each government tier should receive a proportion of government transfers according to their functional responsibilities and warns that subnational governments should not overly rely on volatile revenues for their financial management. Regarding horizontal distribution, technical criteria highlight the importance of compensating the producing jurisdictions for negative externalities linked to extraction without generating territorial unbalances or grievances due to an extremely unequal distribution of revenues.

Our review of redistributive policies in ten resource-rich countries shows that institutional considerations are not sufficient to determine actual revenue sharing. The variety of criteria for the distribution of EI revenues points to political factors as the main drivers of those policies. In this chapter, we have attempted a first cut at understanding what those political factors might be. The data suggests that the level of fiscal decentralization or the federal or unitary nature of the state alone does not determine the proportion of EI revenues transferred to subnational governments. Rather, it appears that the historical context in which EI-related transfers are negotiated and the relative strength of the subnational governments vis-à-vis the central government seem to have greater influence on revenue sharing formulas. We also find that the way in which the decentralized revenues are distributed between producing and non-producing territories varies greatly in our sample countries. Here, the level of fiscal decentralization does seem to matter. Higher levels of fiscal decentralization in the country are correlated with a more equal distribution across all the regions of the country. This suggests that when all subnational governments have been equally strengthened by previous fiscal decentralization, they are better able to demand a more equal distribution.

Our conclusions call for better understandings of the nature of such bargaining power, the actual management of revenue transfers and their consequences. In the following paragraphs, we outline some issues of policy relevance that emerge from our analysis.

The Link Between Central and Subnational Governments

A Colombian presidential candidate once stated, "The government has used the debate over the distribution of royalties to avoid the debate over the remaining 95 percent of the fiscal revenues".[6] The discussion around the adoption and implementation of distribution formulas for EI transfers must take place within broader fiscal decentralization debates. More work is needed to understand the evolution of cooperation between central and subnational governments, including political and administrative interactions, and the responsibilities and capacities to effectively manage public finance flows; secondly, the relative capacity of subnational governments to raise non-extractive revenues and how this fiscal effort reflects their capacity to govern effectively[7]; and finally, the borrowing capacity of subnational governments and how central governments cope with such liabilities.

Earmarked Versus Discretional Allocations

While this chapter shows that there is no unique or optimal allocation mechanism, the cases presented illustrate the need to combine some type of fixed devolution to producing districts with some equalizing criteria according to subnational needs (poverty levels, local extractive capacity

[6] Interview COL-09, 16-05-2013.

[7] An important contribution for the case of Bolivia is Jiménez Pozo (2017).

and basic infrastructure) in order to promote sustainable development objectives. Furthermore, expenditure rules could combine some specific spending priorities on specific sectors (such as capital over current spending or nutrition, health or education benchmarks) with a degree of flexibility so that local authorities can prioritize spending according to local objectives. The challenge, however, is to empirically determine how budget discretion actually works, under what conditions greater flexibility does not lead to unbridled discretion and how to promote the adoption of effective and transparent accountability mechanisms so that local government officials remain responsible for the use and investment of revenues vis-à-vis their electorate and the central government (González Espinosa 2013). Bolivia is an interesting case because a significant degree of flexibility in the allocation of resources worked for a while in regions in which the competition between opposition governors and the MAS reinforced de facto checks and balances for the use of royalty transfers. However, once the MAS became the dominant party in those regions and the central government had no incentives for controlling the regional government's use of the revenues, transparency reduced and rent seeking increased (Humphreys Bebbington and Grisi Huber 2017).

Subnational Stabilization Funds

It is well known that given the variation in commodity prices and production costs, EI-related revenues are too volatile to make long-term spending commitments or develop long-term investments. Moreover, sudden revenue windfalls can exceed the spending capacity of small subnational districts (as was the case in some Bolivian, Colombian and Peruvian regions), thus opening the door to clientelistic or wasteful spending. Yet, the case studies show that the option to (re)introduce stabilization funds at the national and local level is at its best an emerging policy discussion (Bauer 2013). The introduction of subnational stabilization mechanisms would also require medium-term expenditure frameworks to make these instruments compatible with national budgeting priorities and such changes may require further legal and constitutional reforms. Nevertheless, it is necessary to reinvigorate discussions about the adoption and implementation of revenue smoothing formulas and the employment of political safeguards to ensure that such funds are invested and used in a responsible manner.

Fiscal and EI Transparency

The existing lack of reliable sources of data obstructs the objective assessment of the magnitude of the problem, blocks the evaluation of existing policies and allows room for discretionary decisionmaking. Despite the importance and intensity of debates around EI revenues, the availability and quality of subnational data has stalled or worsened in the past decade in many resource-rich countries (Open Budget Partnership 2018). In some cases, this has induced weaknesses, as unreliable or incomplete data affects the nature of political bargaining across government units and the nature of spending. Therefore, the survey, collection and compatibility of existing sources of subnational revenue, socioeconomic indicators and production data produced by governments and extractive companies must be improved.

It remains an empirical question to which extent greater recentralization of EI revenues in the hands of the executive may offer greater opportunities for discretionary use of EI revenues in the form of off-budgetary expenditures, for example. As a direct policy implication, it is relevant to reinvigorate budget transparency debates for the management of EI revenues to ensure that citizens, parliaments and independent audit institutions are able to monitor and oversee the transparent execution of these resources.

Development Impacts

More research is needed to define and measure the impact of different types of investments (capital, human, infrastructure) on achieving long-term development goals. As a first step, greater precision is needed to distinguish the political implications of adopting local and selective investments that do not turn into clientelistic or personalistic spending or favouring flexible/discretionary spending versus rigid or earmarked spending patterns. Greater effort is also needed to define an underlying model of change that explains how a greater devolution of EI revenues may in fact produce—or undermine—meaningful changes in development outcomes (Mejía-Acosta 2013). Such review should explicitly address the ways in which EI, donors, governments and civil society groups can enhance good governance in the management of EI revenues. Further work is needed to systematically define and measure the ways in which subnational governments have successfully managed EI revenues to promote development outcomes for the benefit of all or not.

The most recent commodities boom has revitalized policy debates and scholarly attention to the role that subnational governments can play to advance development objectives such as the Sustainable Development Goals. Subnational governments have the potential to fulfil decentralization promises and provide effective and accountable public services, but they can also obstruct service provision and reproduce rent seeking networks at the local level.

This chapter has explained the sources and types of existing revenue sharing formulas, but more importantly, it has sought to explain the role of political actors, motivations and rules behind the adoption of such formulas. This is a necessary first step to understand why and when an effective mobilization of domestic revenues can help improve the well-being of the population, particularly the least privileged.

References

Agustina, Cut Dian, Ehtisham Ahmad, Dhanie Nugroho, and Herbert Siagian. 2012. *Political Economy of Natural Resources Revenue Sharing in Indonesia*. London: London School of Economics and Political Science.

Ahmad, Ehtisham, and Eric Mottu. 2003. Oil Revenue Assignments: Country Experiences and Issues. In *Fiscal Policy Formulation and Implementation in Oil-Producing Countries*, ed. Jeffrey Davis, Rolando Ossowski, and Annalisa Fedelino, 216–241. Washington, DC: International Monetary Fund.

Ahmad, Ehtisham, and Raju Singh. 2003. *Political Economy of Oil-Revenue Sharing in a Developing Country: Illustrations from Nigeria*. Washington, DC: International Monetary Fund.

Arellano-Yanguas, Javier. 2011. Aggravating the Resource Curse: Decentralisation, Mining and Conflict in Peru. *Journal of Development Studies* 47 (4): 617–638.

———. 2012. Mining and Conflict in Peru: Sowing the Minerals, Reaping a Hail of Stones. In *Social Conflict, Economic Development and the Extractive Industry: Evidence from South America*, ed. Anthony Bebbington, 89–111. London: Routledge.

Arellano-Yanguas, Javier, and Andrés Mejía-Acosta. 2014a. Distributing the Wealth from the Earth. *IDS Bulletin* 45 (5): 58–68.

———. 2014b. *Extractive Industries, Revenue Allocation and Local Politics*. PDRM Working Paper No. 2014-4. Geneva: United Nations Research Institute for Social Development.

Auty, Richard. 2004. *Resource Abundance and Economic Development*. Oxford: Oxford University Press.

Bagattini, Gustavo. 2011. *The Political Economy of Stabilisation Funds: Measuring Their Success in Resource-Dependent Countries*. IDS Working Paper 356. Brighton: Institute of Development Studies.

Banful, Afua Branoah. 2011. Do Formula-Based Intergovernmental Transfer Mechanisms Eliminate Politically Motivated Targeting? Evidence from Ghana. *Journal of Development Economics* 96 (2): 380–390.

Bauer, Andrew. 2013. *Subnational Oil, Gas and Mineral Revenue Management*. New York: Revenue Watch Institute.

Bauer, Andrew, Uyanga Gankhuyag, Sofi Halling, David Manley, and Varsha Venugopal. 2016. *Natural Resource Revenue Sharing*. New York: Natural Resource Governance Institute/United Nations Development Programme.

Bebbington, Anthony. 2012. Extractive Industries, Socio-environmental Conflicts and Political Economic Transformations in Andean America. In *Social Conflict, Economic Development and Extractive Industry: Evidence from South America*, ed. Anthony Bebbington, 1–26. Abingdon: Routledge.

Brosio, Giorgio. 2003. Oil Revenue and Fiscal Federalism. In *Fiscal Policy Formulation and Implementation in Oil-Producing Countries*, ed. Jeffrey Davis, Rolando Ossowski, and Annalisa Fedelino, 243–314. Washington, DC: International Monetary Fund.

Crabtree, John, and Ann Chaplin. 2013. *Bolivia: Processes of Change*. London: Zed Books.

Davis, Jeffrey, Rolando Ossowski, James Daniel, and Steven Barnett. 2003. Stabilization and Saving Funds for Non-Renewable Resources: Experience and Fiscal Policy Implications. In *Fiscal Policy Formulation and Implementation in Oil-producing Countries*, ed. Jeffrey Davis, Rolando Ossowski, and Annalisa Fedelino, 273–314. Washington, DC: International Monetary Fund.

Departamento Nacional de Planeación-Colombia. 2012. *Sistema General de Regalías*. Bogotá: Departamento Nacional de Planeación.

Eaton, Kent. 2014. Recentralization and the Left Turn in Latin America: Diverging Outcomes in Bolivia, Ecuador, and Venezuela. *Comparative Political Studies* 47 (8): 1130–1157.

Energy Sector Management Assistance Programme. 2005. *Comparative Study on the Distribution of Oil Rents in Bolivia, Colombia, Ecuador, and Peru*. Washington, DC: United Nations Development Programme/World Bank.

Falleti, Tulia. 2010. *Decentralization and Subnational Politics in Latin America*. Cambridge: Cambridge University Press.

González, Lucas. 2012. The Redistributive Effects of Centralization and Decentralization across Subnational Units. *Latin American Research Review* 47 (3): 109–133.

González Espinosa, Ana Carolina. 2013. ¿La Sociedad Civil como 'Conjuro' a la Maldición de los Recursos Naturales? Vigilancia Ciudadana a la Renta Extractiva en Colombia y Perú. In *Los Retos de la Gobernanza Minero-Energética*, ed. Ana Carolina González Espinosa, 105–145. Bogotá: Universidad Externado de Colombia.

Hujo, Katja, ed. 2012. *Mineral Rents and the Financing of Social Policy: Opportunities and Challenges*. Basingstoke: Palgrave MacMillan and United Nations Research Institute for Social Development.

Humphreys Bebbington, Denise, and Celina Grisi Huber. 2017. *Political Settlements, Natural Resource Extraction, and Inclusion in Bolivia*. ESID Working Paper No. 77. Manchester: The University of Manchester.

Iledare, Wumi, and Rotimi Suberu. 2012. Nigeria. In *Oil and Gas in Federal Systems*, ed. George Anderson, 227–256. Ontario: Oxford University Press.

Jiménez Pozo, Wilson. 2017. *Movilización de Recursos Domésticos, Desarrollo Social y Cambio Institucional: Descentralización y Autonomías Municipales en Bolivia*. PDRM Working Paper No. 2017-1. Geneva: United Nations Research Institute for Social Development.

Kâ Diongue, Abdou, Gaël Giraud, and Cécile Renouard. 2011. *Measuring the Contribution of Extractive Industries to Local Development: The Case of Oil Companies in Nigeria*. Paris: Cergy-Pontoise ESSEC.

Mejía-Acosta, Andrés. 2013. The Governance of Natural Resources: Review of Impact and Effectiveness of Accountability and Transparency Initiatives. *Development Policy Review* 31 (Suppl s1): 89–105.

Morgandi, Matteo. 2008. *Extractive Industries Revenues Distribution at the Subnational Level: The Experience in Seven Resource-Rich Countries*. New York: Revenue Watch Institute.

Open Budget Partnership. 2018. *Open Budget Survey 2017*. Washington, DC: Open Budget Partnership. Accessed 19 August 2019. https://www.internationalbudget.org/wp-content/uploads/open-budget-survey-2017-report-english.pdf.

Ross, Michael. 2007. How Can Mineral Rich States Reduce Inequality? In *Escaping the Resource Curse*, ed. Jeffrey Sachs, Joseph E. Stiglitz, and Macartan Humphreys, 237–255. New York: Columbia University Press.

Rudas Lleras, Guillermo, and Jorge Enrique Espitia Zamora. 2013. Participación del Estado y la Sociedad en la Renta Minera. In *Minería en Colombia: Fundamentos para Superar el Modelo Extractivista*, ed. Luis Jorge Garay Salamanca, 125–172. Bogota: Contraloría General de la República.

Ruiz Duran, Clemente. 2011. *Financiación y Fiscalidad Locales en América Latina. Colección de Estudios sobre Políticas Públicas Locales y Regionales de Cohesión Social*. Barcelona: Programa URB-ALIII.

Schoeder, Larry, and Paul Smoke. 2002. Intergovernmental Transfers in Developing Countries: Concepts, International Practices and Policy Issues. In *Intergovernmental Transfers in Asia: Current Practice and Challenges for the Future*, ed. Paul Smoke and Yun-Hwan Kim, 20–59. Manila: Asian Development Bank.

UNRISD (United Nations Research Institute for Social Development). 2016. Mobilizing Domestic Resources for Sustainable Development: Toward a Progressive Fiscal Contract. In *Policy Innovations for Transformative Change. Implementing the 2030 Agenda for Sustainable Development*, 167–195. Geneva: UNRISD.

Viale, Claudia. 2015. *Distribución de la Renta de las Industrias Extractivas a los Gobiernos Subnacionales en América Latina: Análisis Comparativo y de Tendencias*. Lima: Instituto de Ciencias de la Naturaleza, Territorio y Energias Renovables.

Part II

The Politics of Domestic Resource Mobilization: Case Studies

9

Domestic Resource Mobilization for Social Development in Bolivia (1985–2014): Protests, Hydrocarbons and a New State Project

Verónica Paz Arauco

Introduction

In recent years Bolivia has mobilized domestic resources for social development at a level unprecedented in the country's history. This process began with the election of Evo Morales, the first indigenous president in the country's history, in 2005. The expansion of public revenue recorded since 2006, girded by the nationalization of the hydrocarbon sector and an increase in international energy prices, was also reflected in a continuous rise in tax revenue, reaching 21.6 per cent of the gross domestic product (GDP) in 2014 (Ministerio de Economía y Finanzas Públicas 2015).

Contributions made by Santiago Daroca Oller and Wilson Jiménez Pozo are gratefully acknowledged.

V. Paz Arauco (✉)
Oxfam, La Paz, Bolivia

K. Hujo (ed.), *The Politics of Domestic Resource Mobilization for Social Development*, Social Policy in a Development Context,
https://doi.org/10.1007/978-3-030-37595-9_9

During the same period, the level of social expenditure in relation to GDP increased by almost six percentage points, reaching 22 per cent in 2014 (UDAPE 2015). As a result of this trend, by the end of the first decade of the new millennium, both indicators—tax revenue and social expenditure—exceeded the regional average.[1] This mobilization of resources for social development took place within a context of sustained economic growth: the Bolivian GDP grew in those years at an average rate of 5 per cent and the country maintained a positive global fiscal balance for eight consecutive years. Furthermore, Bolivia recorded one of the highest rates of extreme and medium poverty reduction, as well as one of the most significant decreases in income inequality, both from a historical national perspective and compared to regional averages (UDAPE 2015).

This chapter analyses the linkages between domestic resource mobilization (DRM) and the impressive social development outcomes described earlier, studying processes and the mechanisms that connect DRM policies (taxes, hydrocarbon revenues or mining royalties) with demands for the delivery of basic services (water, sanitation and electricity), social policies (education, health) and social protection programmes for the period 1985–2014. The main argument for carrying out an integrated analysis of revenue and expenditure policies is that sustainable social policy requires a sustainable fiscal basis; similarly, the study is premised on the idea that the generation of fiscal revenues is essential for implementing public policies (see Chap. 1 in this volume). Social development is promoted when financing and expenditure policies are progressive and fair, catering for the needs of the population, especially the most vulnerable groups.

The chapter focuses on three axes of analysis: processes of contestation and social mobilization related to fiscal policy and DRM; changes in key relationships such as state-donor and state-civil society relations; and institutional changes associated with DRM and social policy. The analysis is guided by the following questions: What were the key milestones in the mobilization of resources in Bolivia during the 1985–2014 period? What

[1] For comparative figures on tax collections in the region, see OECD et al. (2017). For social expenditure, consult database and statistical publications from the Economic Commission for Latin America and the Caribbean (ECLAC), available at: https://estadisticas.cepal.org/cepalstat/Portada.html.

economic, social and political conditions were drivers of DRM? Which institutional changes and reforms occurred that contributed to greater equality and better living conditions of the population?

The analysis is based on four reports that address the process of DRM in Bolivia between 1985 and 2014 from different perspectives.[2] It draws on quantitative and qualitative data; secondary sources such as national statistical databases (household surveys, demographic and housing censuses, opinion and perception surveys), reports, institutional memoirs and statistical dossiers, in particular from the National Statistics Institute (INE), the Social and Economic Policy Analysis Unit (UDAPE), the Public Service of Autonomies (SEA), the Ministry of the Economy and Public Finance (MEFP) and the Vice Ministry for Public Investment and External Financing. The analysis also drew on 16 semi-structured interviews with former and current officials from the international aid sector, the public sector, policy makers and experts.

The chapter is divided into six sections. The first section presents the analytical framework. The second section summarizes the historical background. The third section analyses the mobilization of resources for social development in the 1985–2000 period. The fourth section analyses the changes in the relationship between state and civil society and the role of social mobilization and contestation during the crisis years 2000–2003. The fifth section analyses the new state project and related DRM strategies during the Morales government, including institutional and governance changes and their impact on social development at the local level. The sixth section provides conclusions and an outlook into the future.

Analytical Framework

The literature on DRM tends to emphasize the importance of taxation.[3] Taxes are considered a key measure of power and legitimacy of states; they are part of the social contract between the state and its citizens (Di John 2010), and they can contribute to positive state-society relations if they are based on transparent, fair and consensual resource bargains, if

[2] Daroca Oller 2016; Paz Arauco 2016; Jiménez Pozo 2017; Paz Arauco and Daroca Oller 2014.

[3] UNCTAD 2007; United Nations 2003, 2015; Moore 2013.

the state has credibility, and if beneficiaries of resource allocation are clear (Daroca Oller 2016; UNRISD 2012a). In the case of Bolivia, however, revenues from mineral resources and their contribution to development finance take centre stage, for two main reasons: firstly, the country is historically dependent on mineral rents for financing public expenditures and, secondly, attempts to implement a tax on salaries in 2003 to increase the contribution of direct taxes in the funding of the fiscal budget failed, producing widespread and immediate social protests and violent conflict. As a result of the failed tax reform, development financing through mineral rents became once more the most feasible policy option for DRM, especially as aid levels started to decline and Bolivia aimed to gain more sovereignty over resource mobilization and allocation during the Movement for Socialism (MAS) government.

Academic debates on the development impact of natural resource wealth are, however, controversial (Hujo 2012). The so-called resource curse literature emphasizes negative development impacts of mineral-dependent development related to volatile international prices and the enclave nature of mining, as well as a potential expansion of the state including corruption, rent-seeking, inefficiencies and market distortions. On the other hand, those that reject the resource curse thesis hold that good management of natural resource wealth determines developmental results rather than the existence of mineral wealth per se (UNRISD 2012b). The present study follows the second approach, focusing on both challenges and opportunities associated with mineral wealth.

In this chapter, we depart from the fact that natural resource wealth, particularly minerals and hydrocarbons, constitute a fundamental characteristic of Bolivia's economic structure determining DRM throughout its history. In addition to this long-term structural driver, recent DRM strategies were shaped by the social, economic and political crisis the country faced at the end of the 1990s and beginning of the 2000s (Paz Arauco and Daroca Oller 2014).

At the beginning of 2000, 15 years after adopting and enacting the recommendations of the so-called Washington Consensus in Bolivia (Machicado Saravia 2010), leading to structural reforms of the pension and education system, privatization of public enterprises, liberalization, deregulation and decentralization reforms, poverty and inequality remained basically unchanged recording the highest levels in the region.

This situation provoked a general social discontent that manifested in social protests and demonstrations, challenging in particular the unsuccessful negotiation results between the government and foreign enterprises regarding their fiscal contributions and demanding the reversal of the privatizations of public enterprises (Daroca Oller 2016). In addition to the economic and social crisis, Bolivia was affected by a deep political crisis. After more than 20 years of a democratic representative system that put an end to almost two decades of military dictatorships (1964–1982), the political party system seemed incapable of genuinely representing the majority of the population and responding to their most urgent needs, failing to promote inclusive social development.

Figure 9.1 presents a simple analytical framework that guides the analysis in this chapter. It shows that a combination of structural and historical drivers combines with conjunctural crisis factors resulting in social contestation and protest at the beginning of the millennium, paving the way for a change in government and a profound redefinition of the development model and the role of the state, reflected in four key institutional reforms: a new law on hydrocarbons, nationalization of hydrocarbons, a new constitution and a new decentralization law (autonomies). These factors lead to changes in key relationships and new DRM strategies, which in turn impact on social development outcomes.

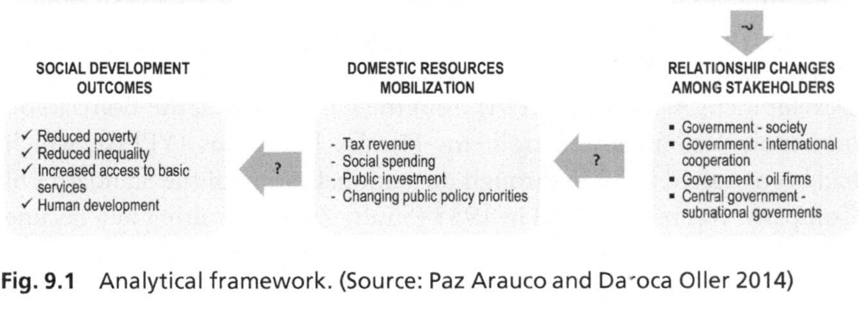

Fig. 9.1 Analytical framework. (Source: Paz Arauco and Daroca Oller 2014)

Historical Background: Natural Resource Dependence and Foreign Debt (1910–1980)

Throughout Bolivia's history, the exploitation of natural resources has been the engine of growth and the main domestic revenue source for the public sector (see Table 9.1). However, since the beginning of the twentieth century, the Bolivian state struggled to cover its expenditures, having to resort to loans from local banks to honour foreign debt service and rising budget deficits (UNDP 2007; Peres Cajías 2014).

In a context of scarce domestic resources, the Bolivian population frequently mobilized around claims for regaining ownership of mining and hydrocarbon resources, which were in the hands of foreign companies. Indeed, in some cases exploration and production concessions presented excessively favourable conditions for these firms, resulting in significant losses for the Bolivian state (Shultz 2008). From the early to mid-twentieth century, mining rents were captured by the so-called tin barons, a mining elite dominated by three major companies, which exported up to 79 per cent of tin. While disputes between the state and foreign companies about exploitation of minerals had existed in the past, it was not until the mid-1950s that mineral resources acquired more importance for the national economy.

The National Revolution of 1952 which brought the Nationalist Revolutionary Movement (MNR) into power triggered substantive social transformations in Bolivia, among which feature the Agrarian Reform of 1953 (Law 3464), universal suffrage which increased the number of voters fivefold and the nationalization of the three biggest tin mines, Patiño, Hochschild and Aramayo, creating a state monopoly for export and sale of all minerals, administered by the state-owned Mining Bank of Bolivia and run by the Bolivian Mining Corporation (COMIBOL). On the other hand, and in response to substantial increases of Official Development Assistance (ODA) from the United States, the Bolivian oil monopoly Yacimientos Petrolíferos Fiscales Bolivianos (YPFB), which had been created in 1936 through the nationalization of the Standard Oil Company, was re-privatized in 1955 (Shultz 2008), resulting in a decline in state revenue from the sector and subsequent renationalization in

Table 9.1 Natural resources, foreign debt and financing the non-financial public sector

Characterization of the period	1913–1930 The tin era and the nationalization of hydrocarbons	1936–1952 The boom of tin and era of consolidation for the mining elites	1952–1964 Nationalization of mining and state capitalism	1964–1982 The beginning of the military cycle and the era of indebtedness	1983–2003 Crisis period wrought by neoliberal policies
Ownership of minerals and hydrocarbons	**1921:** Sale of the Bolivian state oil company to US standard oil company.		**1952:** Mines are nationalized and COMIBOL established. **1955:** Hydrocarbons back to foreign ownership.	**1969**: Nationalization of the Gulf oil company.	**1994**: YPFB is privatized.
Growth, fiscal deficit and indebtedness	Between 1913 and 1920, Bolivia's foreign debt quadruples.	In January 1931 debt moratorium imposed due to fall of international tin prices. Bolivia defaults on its external debt in 1948.	US aid flows increase.		1997: Bolivia is granted debt relief within the framework of the HIPC initiative.

(*continued*)

Table 9.1 (continued)

Characterization of the period	1913–1930 The tin era and the nationalization of hydrocarbons	1936–1952 The boom of tin and era of consolidation for the mining elites	1952–1964 Nationalization of mining and state capitalism	1964–1982 The beginning of the military cycle and the era of indebtedness	1983–2003 Crisis period wrought by neoliberal policies
Public revenue and expenditure	The central government only generates revenue equivalent to 4.5 per cent of GDP. The foreign indebtedness cycle begins.	The power consolidated by mining elites impedes the collection of taxes. Mining exports represent 70 per cent of total exports in 1970.	Until 1959, the state's domestic revenues do not exceed 4.5 per cent of GDP. Oil companies only contribute 20 per cent of their income in taxes to the state.	During the 1960s, the central government generates revenues that account for 10 per cent of GDP. At the end of the decade, growing fiscal imbalances experienced, as expenditure amounts to twice that of revenues collected.	YPFB is the main source of revenue for the state between 1985 and 1995, generating 50 per cent of total revenue.

Source: Paz Arauco and Daroca Oller (2014)

Note: COMIBOL: Mining Corporation of Bolivia; YPFB: Yacimientos Petrolíferos Fiscales Bolivianos (Bolivian National Hydrocarbons Company)

1969. Regarding the nationalized mining companies, their fiscal contribution fell short of expectations, with increasingly unsustainable levels of indebtedness in the early 1960s.

While the 1970s was a politically unstable period of consecutive military coup d'états and dictatorships, it was also one of high fiscal revenues resulting from increasing international tin and oil prices, allowing Bolivia to achieve trade surpluses. Generous availability of foreign credit supported economic growth but resulted in unprecedented levels of external debt. The state-led development model Bolivia had adopted since the 1950s was finally challenged when the country entered a deep economic crisis in the early 1980s.[4]

Domestic Resource Mobilization, Social Policies and Social Outcomes (1985–2000)

With the fall of tin prices at the beginning of the 1980s, revenues from mining companies declined and the public oil company YPFB became the main source of revenue for the Bolivian state, generating almost 50 per cent of the total revenue through the expansion of foreign markets into Chile and Argentina. Against the backdrop of neoliberal stabilization and adjustment policies (SAP), poverty and inequality remained at high levels and public investment was increasingly funded through external resources, including with funds made available through the Heavily Indebted Poor Countries (HIPC) initiative (Paz Arauco 2016).

Economic and social policies during the period were shaped by the crisis context and increasing donor influence. After a long period of gradually increasing public social investments during the state-led development model, public expenditures contracted sharply between 1980 and 1989, decreasing from 7.2 per cent of GDP to 4.6 per cent (UNDP 2007). The focus of social policies shifted from expansion of national education and health provision in the previous period towards poverty

[4] In 1982 GDP declined by 3.9 per cent. Between 1980 and 1985 regular revenues from the state fell from 40.1 to 27.1 per cent of GDP. However, during the same period, the interest payments on external debt increased from 3 to 7.2 per cent of GDP (Humérez Quiroz and Mariscal Ayaviri 2005). Hyperinflation reached 27.000 per cent during the first semester of 1985 (Echazú 2002).

relief programmes such as the Social Emergency Fund (FSE), implemented in 1987 to mitigate adverse social effects of the economic crisis and of SAP programmes. A second fund called Social Investment Fund (FIS), supported by the World Bank and later developing into one of the flagship projects of the Bank, was established as part of a more extensive social investment strategy towards the end of the decade. However, weak institutional capacity and the compensatory character of the programmes and institutions that were created during this period led to insufficient results, as social expenditures remained too low to address the huge challenge of social exclusion the country's majority population was facing (see Table 9.2) (Paz Arauco 2016).

During the 1990s, a wave of new social reforms was implemented, such as a new Education Law (No. 1565) in 1994; a Mother-Child Healthcare Insurance programme; and the first non-contributive pension for elderly persons, called Bonosol, funded by profits from the privatization of public enterprises that took place during that period. Fiscal decentralization was regulated through the Law on Popular Participation and Administrative Decentralization (1994), which played an important role in the institutionalization of financial transfers towards local government levels. Local governments became responsible for social infrastructure in their jurisdictions receiving in turn financial resources from the co-participation (20 per cent) in several national taxes such as value-added tax (VAT), customs tax, inheritance tax or presumed corporate income tax (Paz Arauco and Daroca Oller 2014; Jiménez Pozo 2017).

The HIPC debt relief process started in 1996, led by the World Bank and the Inter-American Development Bank (IADB).[5] Despite the fact that financial resources freed up through the initiative had to be spent on poverty reduction and social services and were mainly channelled to the municipal level to be spent on education, health and productive and social infrastructure, funds were once again insufficient to address inequality and poverty in the country at that time. At the turn of the new millennium, persistent poverty and the deepening of social and economic inequalities reflected the failure of poverty reduction strategies, as well as the financing of social development through external resources. Poverty

[5] See Table 9.2 and Paz Arauco (2016).

Table 9.2 Institutions and resources for social policy (1985–2014)

	1985–1992	1993–1997	1998–2001	2002–2005	2006–2014
Institutions and social policies, policies for poverty reduction.	**1987:** Social emergency fund (FSE). **1989:** Fund for peasant development. **1991:** Bolivian social strategy and social investment fund.	Creation of the human development ministry. **1994:** Education reform law; law of popular participation and administrative decentralization; pension law; Bonosol	Relief programmes through the HIPC initiative and national dialogues.		**2006**: Nationalization of hydrocarbons. *Bono Juancito Pinto* (cash transfer school attendance). **2008**: *Renta Dignidad* (social pension). **2009**: *Bono Juana Azurduy* (cash transfer mother-infant health). **2010:** Educational law *Avelino Siñani y Elizardo Pérez.* **2010:** Autonomies law and annual increase of the minimum salary and wages.

(*continued*)

Table 9.2 (continued)

	1985–1992	1993–1997	1998–2001	2002–2005	2006–2014
Expenditure and social investment	Between 1987 and 1991, social expenditure was maintained at 5 per cent of GDP.	Social expenditure expands from 24 to 49 per cent. Education earned the highest proportion of these resources during that period.	It was estimated that in 1999 the budget saved through the HIPC initiative reached 0.8 per cent of the GDP, which was to be spent on poverty reduction policies.		Social expenditure/GDP increases from 16.2 to 20 per cent.
Origin of the mobilization of resources: Foreign debt, debt relief, taxes	High indebtedness and low tax collection	**1996**: First debt relief programme under HIPC.	**2001:** Reprogramming of the HIPC initiative.	ODA reaches its peak of 11 per cent of GDP in 2003. Taxes/GDP equivalent to 12 per cent. **2003**: 63 per cent of public investment funded with foreign resources.	Between 2006 and 2013, the ODA/GDP ratio decreases from 7.4 to 2.3 per cent. Tax/GDP ratio increases to 19 per cent. **2013**: 18 per cent of public investment funded by foreign resources, 82 per cent with domestic resources.

Source: Paz Arauco and Daroca Oller (2014)

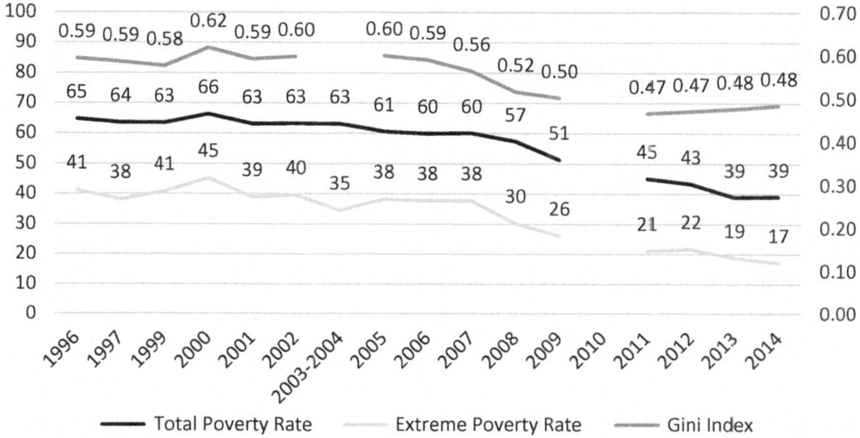

Fig. 9.2 Tendencies of poverty and inequality reduction (1996–2014). (Source: Author elaboration based on data from UDAPE (2016). Note: No information available for the year 2010 as no household survey was conducted)

remained high at 60 per cent of the population, with extreme poverty increasing between 1997 and 2000 from 38 to 45 per cent, and the Gini coefficient reaching 0.62 in 2000 (Fig. 9.2). In addition, horizontal inequalities were enormous, for example between men and women, the indigenous and non-indigenous populations and between geographical departments. Taking a more long-term view, some development progress was achieved between 1980 and 2000: the Human Development Index increased from 0.546 to 0.653, an improvement that was driven by major advances in education and health indicators, while per capita income growth showed less improvement (UNDP 2005).

With regard to resource mobilization, a tax reform in 1986 (Law 843) which increased direct taxes while broadening the base of indirect taxes such as VAT resulted in growing tax collection, which was accompanied by increasing public expenditure. However, as the latter grew more than the additional revenue created, the fiscal deficit increased steadily reaching 8.8 per cent of GDP in 2002.

Crisis, Protest and Changes in Key Relationships

State-civil society relations in Bolivia at the start of the new millennium were marked by several long-standing unresolved issues regarding ownership of the country's natural resource wealth, the multicultural nature of society, and the relationship between the central state and subnational governance levels (Crabtree et al. 2009; UNDP 2007). Tensions manifested in large-scale social mobilizations, resulting in several "wars", as the conflicts around natural resource governance were labelled. The first large-scale protest, the so-called Cochabamba Water War of 2000, was initiated by the inhabitants of the city of Cochabamba in response to the privatization of the city's municipal water supply and sewerage company SEMAPA (Servicio Municipal de Agua Potable y Alcantarillado—Municipal Water and Sewage Service) as part of loan conditionality of the World Bank for investment support in the sector. One of the key issues of concern, next to discontent about a rise in consumer prices, was that the government had approved a law transferring the irrigation channels built by farmers to the transnational investor consortium that would deliver drinking water on a commercial basis (Shultz 2008).

The Water War of April 2000 did not only challenge an economic model based on market-oriented reforms, in particular privatization, and external financing but also questioned the system of political representation which has been labelled a political pact democracy, given that governments since 1985 were constituted by political coalitions binding together diverse interests to stay in power. The divide between social movements and the government stance was reflected in the broad-based support water privatization received from all formal political institutions, from the executive to the legislative branch to local level institutions (prefecture and municipality), including organized interest groups such as business associations in the so-called Civic Committee.[6] Groups which did not feel represented through these structures, such as labour unions,

---

[6] Civic Committees represent regional interests to the state. They include organizations such as chambers of commerce and industry, professional boards, business people or neighbourhood associations.

urban workers, small farmers and producers, neighbourhood associations and environmental groups, staged their protests by creating a new association to defend communal water resources, the Water Coordination Body (Coordinadora del Agua). The protests eventually led to the reconversion of SEMAPA into a state-owned municipal enterprise (Paz Arauco and Daroca Oller 2014).

During 2003, two additional important conflicts emerged around issues related to DRM, showing that DRM strategies in Bolivia are highly contentious political issues (Daroca Oller 2016). The first, known as the impuestazo, a term which can be circumscribed as a substantial increase of a specific tax, occurred in February. Protests broke out in response to an attempt by the national government to implement a tax reform as part of negotiations with the International Monetary Fund (IMF) that sought to reduce the fiscal deficit through, among other measures, introduction of a tax on salaries.[7] The reform was perceived as unfair as it targeted the relatively small formal wage sector (30 per cent of the economically active population) and started from a relatively low threshold of two minimum wages, despite increasing at a progressive scale. Concrete benefits of the reform, apart from closing the fiscal deficit, remained unclear and lack of time for consultations to consider alternative resource mobilization strategies raised criticism. Widespread protests, staged by the political opposition, business actors and workers, as well as violent threats from the military police, which was one of the affected groups, led to a quick withdrawal of the tax reform proposal to restore public security (Daroca Oller 2016).

The second conflict, which took place in October of the same year, called the Gas War, centred on the claim to recover property rights over hydrocarbon resources, which, at the time, were in the hands of foreign corporations. These conflicts not only resulted in the highest levels of violence and repression registered in over 30 years of continuous democracy and the resignation of former President Sánchez de Lozada but,

[7] This measure was highly unpopular; 94 per cent of Bolivians expressed their inconformity with the impuestazo, leading to a decrease of the government's approval rate from 49 to 15 per cent (Daroca Oller 2016).

more importantly, paved the way for a new political leadership and profound changes in the Bolivian development model.[8]

In addition to the three social conflicts, which served as important triggers of following reform processes, the following changes in key relationships, between state and society, between different state levels, and between state actors and corporations, were crucial for subsequent DRM strategies Bolivian policy makers pursued from 2003 to 2008 (Table 9.3).

Firstly, an implicit agreement on the future governance of hydrocarbon resources emerged between the state and civil society in response to the protests, which put state-society relations on a new footing.[9] In response to the Gas War, a referendum on Bolivia's gas reserves was held by Vice-President Carlos Mesa, where Bolivians voted for the abrogation of the former hydrocarbon law; the recovery in terms of national ownership of all hydrocarbon resources at the well head; the re-founding of the national oil and gas company YPFB; the use of natural gas for Bolivia's strategy to achieve sovereign access to the ocean; and the earmarking of public revenues from hydrocarbon exploitation to fund education, health, road infrastructure and employment.

Secondly, and related to the gas referendum, was a process of bargaining and contestation between the central government and subnational governments regarding fiscal decentralization, mineral rent capture and allocation towards social programmes. In the referendum on hydrocarbons, voters formally mandated the state to allocate mineral rents to social expenditures. However, the institutional structures and mechanisms for revenue sharing were not established yet. In this context, two subnational departments—Santa Cruz and Tarija[10]—started demanding greater political and administrative decentralization through a project of

[8] The various protests and conflicts further spurred the loss of credibility of the political system for large parts of the population and a growing distrust of the country's leadership (Daroca Oller 2016). This was reflected in several opinion surveys that were carried out at the time showing the population's diminishing faith in the capacity of the state to address people's needs: the ratio of respondents with a negative perspective on state capacity doubled between the years 1998 and 2003, according to the Latinobarómetro (2002–2011).

[9] Implicit in the sense that it was not the result of formal negotiation processes (Daroca Oller 2016).

[10] Bolivia is politically and administratively structured in nine departments: La Paz, Oruro, Potosí, Cochabamba, Chuquisaca, Tarija, Santa Cruz, Beni and Pando. These nine departments represent a total of 339 municipalities.

Table 9.3 Synthesis of bargaining and contestation around DRM in Bolivia (2003–2008)

Process of mobilization of resources	Background	Construction of implicit agreements between the state and civil society		Negotiation between levels of government Phase 1	Negotiation state—oil companies		Negotiation between levels of government Phase 2
Milestone	**Impuestazo**	**Gas war**	**Referendum on gas**	**Law 3058—hydrocarbons**	**Supreme Decree 28701 of nationalization**	**Negotiation of new contracts**	**Supreme Decree 29322 new distribution of IDH**
Date	February 2003	October 2003	July 18, 2004	Between July and May 2005	May 1, 2006	Between May and October 2006	Between October 2007 and October 2008
Description	Violent protests against the fiscal initiative to tax salaries.	Violent protests against the government initiative of exporting hydrocarbons to the USA via Chilean ports.	Binding referendum which results in the return to state ownership of hydrocarbons and defined a new hydrocarbons' policy.	Debate and approval of a new hydrocarbons' law that incorporates the mandates of the Gas Referendum.	Nationalization without expropriation, redefinition of production value distribution. Re-founding of YPFB.	Period of 180 days in which new contracts between the state and 12 oil companies are to be negotiated.	IDH is allocated to fund Renta Dignidad (social pension).
Actors	• Executive power • Social organizations • Police • Military	• Executive power • FEJUVE El alto • Social organizations	• Executive power • Civil society	• Executive power • Presidencies of both congressional houses • Representatives from MAS	• Executive power	• YPFB • 12 oil companies	• Executive power • Departments

(continued)

Table 9.3 (continued)

Process of mobilization of resources				Negotiation between levels of government Phase 1	Negotiation state—oil companies		Negotiation between levels of government Phase 2
	Background	Construction of implicit agreements between the state and civil society					
Consequence	• Tax reform fails, governance deteriorates. • Restriction of the state's fiscal space.	• Resignation of President Lozada and executive branch. • October agenda (recovery of hydrocarbons constituent assembly, etc.).	• The state receives the popular mandate to re-appropriate hydrocarbons and tax companies up to 50 per cent of their production value and allocate those resources towards increasing education, health, road infrastructure and employment.	• Fulfilment of the October agenda • State captures up to 50 per cent of production value of oil companies through royalties and IDH • Redistribution of the IDH has positive impact on departmental levels • Resources are used for education, health, road infrastructure and employment.	• Creation of a legal obligation of negotiating and signing new contracts between the state and corporations • Companies failing to sign new contracts within 180 days not allowed to continue operating in Bolivia.	• 44 new contracts are negotiated with 12 oil companies. • Increased state participation in the distribution of production value of hydrocarbons.	• Redistribution implies an increase in the resources available for the national and sub-national levels of government (municipal and departmental).

departmental autonomy. These powerful subnational departments, which are also the main mineral and gas-producing regions, dominated negotiations with a weakened interim president, leading to a favourable distribution of mineral rents for departments and, in particular, hydrocarbon-producing ones.[11]

Thirdly, and again related to the outcome of the gas referendum, which eventually led to the nationalization of the hydrocarbon sector under the Morales government in May 2006, was a process of bargaining between the state and private oil companies (the largest being Petrobras, Repsol-YPF, Total and British Gas) in order to modify the existing contracts and adjust them to the new legal framework the newly elected President Morales established in 2006, re-establishing national ownership and the payment of 50 per cent of production value to the state. The government was able to negotiate successfully due to a favourable social and economic context; the legal design of the Nationalization Decree, which obliged companies to renegotiate contracts within six months if they did not want to risk being forced to cease operations; and the deployment of a carrot-stick bargaining strategy which combined confrontational tactics (traditionally used by the Bolivian trade unions) with technical information, positive incentives and compensations (especially for small companies) that allowed for reaching a mutually beneficial agreement (Daroca Oller 2016).[12]

Regarding state-society relations, the mobilization of resources from minerals under the new government and related public investment led to profound changes (Daroca Oller 2016). Popular demands expressed through the referendum on hydrocarbons were materialized by the enactment of a new Hydrocarbons' Law in 2005 (Law 3058). This Law established the Direct Hydrocarbon Tax (IDH), and it determined its distribution and sectoral allocation, mainly towards social services. As a result, perceptions of the population on government's problem-solving capacity, credibility and performance improved considerably, as shown in Fig. 9.3.

[11] Producing regions obtain 11 per cent of royalties; almost 60 per cent of IDH revenues are distributed to the departmental level (Jiménez Pozo 2017; Daroca Oller 2016).

[12] For an overview of how renegotiated contracts based on Law 3058 and Decree 28701 compare with the previous law 1689 (Daroca Oller 2016): table 2. Key differences are related to risk distribution, hydrocarbon ownership, distribution of rents, asset ownership and location of arbitration courts.

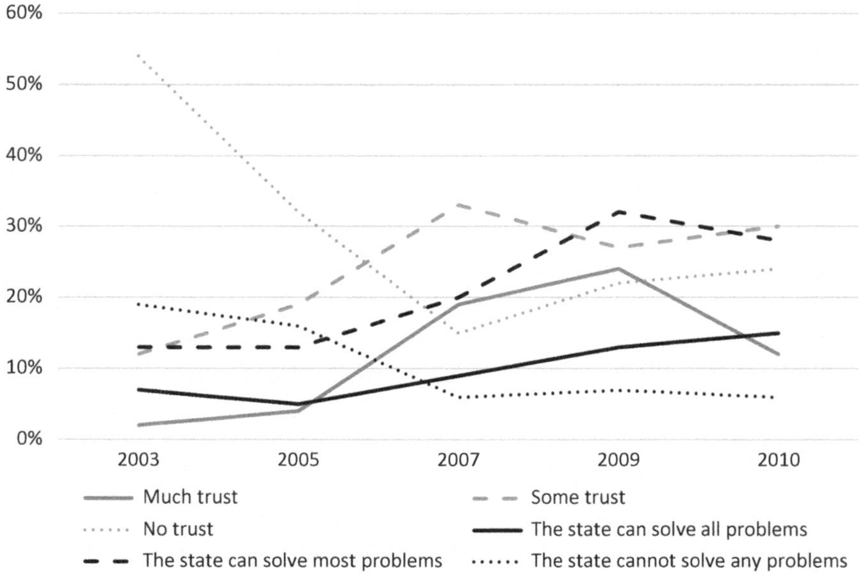

Fig. 9.3 Trust in the government and the state's capacity to solve problems. (Source: Daroca Oller 2016)

Domestic Resource Mobilization Under a New State Project: 2006–2014

The cycle of mobilizations and protests against the shortcomings of the neoliberal economic model and the elite-driven political party system that began in the early 2000s in Bolivia resulted in the consecutive resignation of two presidents: Sánchez de Lozada in 2003 and his former vice-president, Carlos D. Mesa, in 2005. The victory of Evo Morales in the presidential elections of 2005, back then an indigenous leader of coca leaf producers and head of the MAS party, prompted a profound transformation of the Bolivian state. This transformation was guided by two political agendas that had emerged from the various processes of contestation and bargaining analysed in the previous section: The so-called October Agenda of 2003 called for the convocation of a constituent assembly and the nationalization of the hydrocarbon industry, and the

January Agenda of 2005 articulated the demand for decentralization and departmental autonomy (Daroca Oller 2016).

During the first years of the Morales government, these agendas were implemented, creating the political, social, institutional and legal pillars of the new state project. The new constitution of the plurinational state was proclaimed in 2010, recognizing the multiple dimensions of the Bolivian reality which is based on a combination of liberal, communitarian, regional and cultural values; the diversity of its population; and the common history of social struggle. The political base of Evo Morales's new government, rooted in social organizations and alliances and pacts between different social stakeholders, substantially modified the political arena and power relations between the state and societal actors (UNDP 2011).

This new state model and associated legal frameworks were furthermore reflected in the 2006 National Development Plan based on the Buen Vivir—Living Well paradigm—a holistic and culturally inspired development vision promoting harmonious relationships between humans and nature and a balance between satisfaction of material basic needs and immaterial needs such as recognition and affection (Ministerio de Planificación del Desarrollo 2006). The objective of the development plan was to reorient public policies towards building a society based on values of equality, solidarity, reciprocity and respect for difference, promoting social inclusion through redistribution, recognition and participation.

An enabling economic and political context supported the scope and depth of institutional changes the MAS government enacted between 2005 and 2010, in particular the Hydrocarbons' Law (2005) and the creation of the Direct Hydrocarbon Tax, the Law of Nationalization of Hydrocarbons (2006), the approval of the new constitution (2009) and the Framework Law for Autonomies and Decentralization (2010) (Fig. 9.1). Strategy documents such as the National Development Plan (2006) and a new economic model labelled Social Communitarian Productive Economic Model complemented the legal changes.[13]

[13] The Social Communitarian Productive Economic Model is based on the existence and interaction between two economic sectors: strategic sectors generating a surplus and sectors generating

Institutional and policy change redefined the rules of the game for the mobilization and allocation of fiscal resources in the country, changing key relations and resulting in unprecedented social development outcomes, as the next section shows.

Boom of Hydrocarbons, Nationalization, Financing and Social Development

In 2006, in a context of favourable international mineral prices, the country emerged from the economic crisis entering a period of sustained growth, where the new government was able to finance public expenditure with recurrent fiscal income. Social expenditure increased gradually from 16 to 22 per cent of GDP and the country recorded the highest decrease of poverty and inequality in its history. The increasing availability of domestic resources for financing public policies was also due to growth-induced increases in tax revenue, as well as more effective tax collection procedures. Central government tax revenues, which include all direct and indirect taxes except from gas production, increased more than 5 per cent between 2006 and 2014 (Paz Arauco 2016).

The major trend in this period was a reversal in the financing structure of public investment, shifting from foreign resources to domestic resources. While external funding of public investment decreased from 63 to 15 per cent of GDP between 2005 and 2014 (Paz Arauco 2016), domestic finance increased from 37 to 85 per cent in the same period (Fig. 9.4). This occurred when public investment more than doubled, representing 14 per cent of GDP in 2014 (Fig. 9.4).[14]

The substitution of foreign resources with domestic revenue was possible thanks to the successful generation of additional public tax and non-tax revenues. Between 2006 and 2013, these revenues reached 19.2 per cent of GDP, while ODA decreased from 7.4 to 2.3 per cent of GDP

revenue and employment. The strategic sectors are hydrocarbons, mining, electricity and natural resources; the sectors that generate employment and revenues are manufacturing, agriculture, services, trade and others. The role of the state under this new model consists in the redistribution of surpluses from strategic sectors towards sectors that generate employment and revenues (Ministerio de Economía y Finanzas Públicas 2011).

[14] Between 2014 and 2017, public investment in relation to GDP remained above 12 per cent.

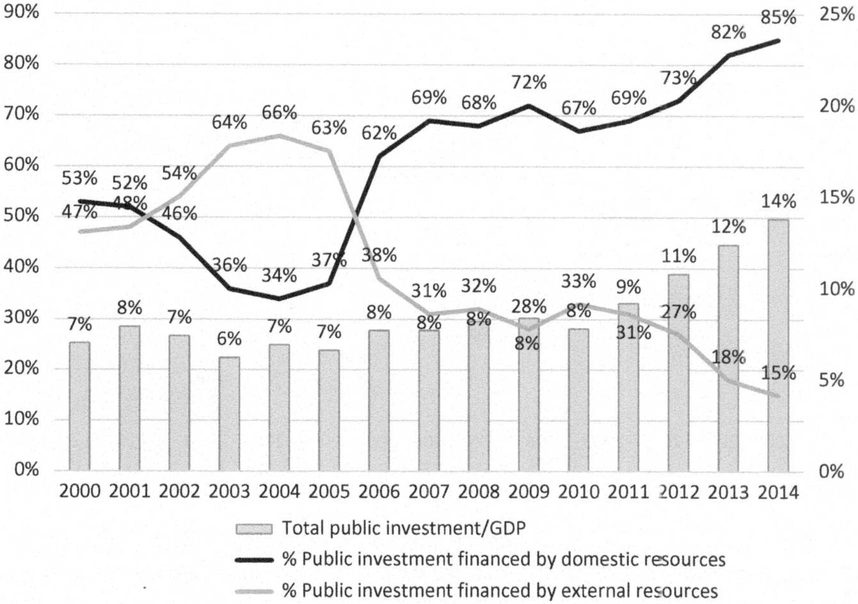

Fig. 9.4 Evolution of public investment as percentage of GDP and source of financing (2000–2014). (Source: Author elaboration based on data from Ministerio de Economía y Finanzas Públicas (2014) and UDAPE (2018). Note: External resources (loans and grants) include resources from the HIPC II in the corresponding item for grants)

(Fig. 9.5). The substitution of external funding with increased DRM led to a change in relations between the Bolivian government and external donors in a context where ODA started shifting towards poorer world regions and Bolivia graduated towards middle-income status.

Due to the leadership exercised by Evo Morales's government with regard to resource allocation and public policy design, as well as his general strategy to regain full sovereignty in decision-making concerning the Bolivian development strategy, policy space of the Bolivian government increased. International aid actors aligned their credit portfolio and interventions increasingly with national planning instruments instead of implementing an agenda of their own, a process that was supported by new international aid agendas such as the Paris Declaration and the Buzan Conference (Paz Arauco 2016). In general, foreign funding became

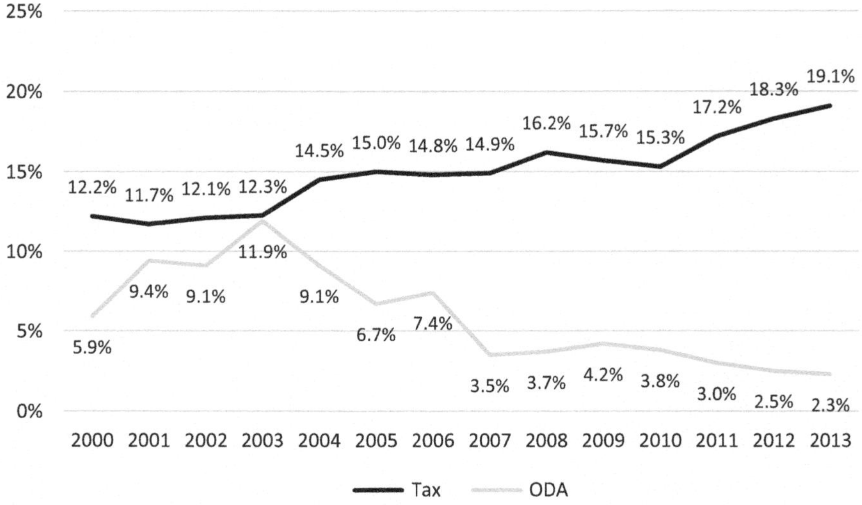

Fig. 9.5 ODA and direct and indirect taxes as percentage of GDP (2000–2013). (Source: Paz Arauco 2016. Author elaboration based on data from the Ministerio de Economía y Finanzas Públicas (2014), for the ratio between tax revenues and the GDP, and World Bank (2015), for the ratio between ODA and GDP. Note: Tax revenues do not include tax collection and/or royalties from the extractive sector (mining and hydrocarbons) or revenues from customs duties)

more commercial and less concessional, funding concrete investment and infrastructure projects rather than the strengthening of institutions or budgetary support (Paz Arauco 2016). In addition to traditional donors, new donor countries such as Argentina, China and Venezuela started to establish credit relations with the new Bolivian government, with China constituting the most important bilateral donor in 2012.

While foreign resources would mainly finance infrastructure projects, government funded a large proportion of the social contract, such as social services (health and education) and the new social protection policies implemented since the year 2006, redistributing the surplus from the hydrocarbon sector with the aim to reduce school desertion and improve nutrition levels of beneficiaries (Paz Arauco 2014). Key social protection programmes implemented were the cash transfer Bono Juancito Pinto which benefits children and youth from 6 to 19 years of age, promoting school attendance; the cash transfer Bono Juana Azurduy[15] promoting access to healthcare services for pregnant women and infants up to two years of age; and, Renta Dignidad, a non-contributory pension for elderly persons over 60 years of age with the objective of guaranteeing a minimum universal retirement pension. While having a limited impact on income redistribution (Paz Arauco 2014), these cash transfers together with the progressive universalization of access to education and health services were seen as key steps to guarantee the individual and collective rights established in the new constitution.[16]

In 2014, almost ten years after the nationalization of hydrocarbons and the reorientation towards a greater role of the state in the economy, Bolivia recorded the highest reduction in poverty and inequality since its registration and made significant progress with regard to the Millennium Development Goals (MDGs).[17] According to the World Bank, the country led the global ranking on "shared prosperity" during the period, with a higher growth of revenues of 40 per cent of the poorest population, in relation to the average income of the population (World Bank 2014).

This success is explained by the positive leadership of the president and a favourable evolution of the labour component of household income in addition to the expansion of social benefits (Fundación Aru 2015; UNDP 2015). The prudent economic management during the boom period of high hydrocarbon prices allowed the government to expand public investment and social expenditure, moving towards universalization of public services and introducing, through cash transfer programmes, new incentives for beneficiary households that currently demand public services, as well as stimulating internal demand.

Nevertheless, since 2011, the pace of growth with redistribution and social transformation has slowed down, with reduction rates of poverty and inequality decreasing (Fig. 9.2). Questions arise therefore on the

[15] Contrary to the Bono Juancito Pinto and the Renta Dignidad, which have been funded by revenues generated by public enterprises, Bono Juana Azurduy has been funded with foreign resources.

[16] For a detailed description of social policies that have been implemented since 2006 see UDAPE (2016).

[17] With regard to the MDGs, Bolivia has been able to reach several of the objectives that had been established until the year 2015, among them MDG 1 (Eradicate Poverty and Hunger), 3 (Promote Gender Equality and Empower Women), 6 (Combat HIV/AIDS, Malaria and other Diseases) and 7 (Ensure Environmental Sustainability) (UDAPE 2015).

future relationship between resource mobilization and social achievements, the objective being to maintain progress and avoid regression. Today, these challenges remain important. Even though between the years 2014 and 2017 total poverty was reduced by almost 3 per cent, extreme poverty remained unchanged.[18] Regarding tax collection, since the year 2014 a steep decrease in the collection from the IDH was recorded, the result of decreasing international hydrocarbon prices, while tax collection excluding IDH increased.[19]

Institutional Changes, Fiscal Decentralization and Limits to Social Development at the Local Level

The institutional changes that took place since the first quinquennium of the twenty-first century, among them the enactment of the Hydrocarbon's Law (2005) and the creation of the Direct Hydrocarbon Tax, the Law of Nationalization of Hydrocarbons (2006), the approval of the New Political Constitution of the State (2009), the Framework Law for Autonomies and Decentralization (2010) and finally the implementation of the new Social Communitarian Productive Economic Model, provided new conditions for resource mobilization, distribution and allocation, between sectors and different governance levels.

Starting in the 1990s, hydrocarbons turned into the main income source for the central government. In the beginning, royalties constituted the largest source of revenue, with income from the Impuesto Especial a los Hidrocarburos y sus Derivados (IEHD—Special Tax on Hydrocarbons and their By-products) picking up after 1995 (Fig. 9.6).[20] Finally, since 2004 and in the context of the international oil boom and the new Hydrocarbon's Law and the creation of the IDH, the contributions from the hydrocarbon sector through taxes and royalties came to represent a third of total revenues of the central government. These resources had to

[18] Data for the year 2017 are available from Ministerio de Economía y Finanzas Públicas (2015).

[19] Between 2014 and 2017, tax revenues from the hydrocarbon tax decreased from BOB (Bolivian bolivianos) 15.602 million to 6.313 million. See Ministerio de Economía y Finanzas Públicas (2015).

[20] This tax was created with the objective of taxing internal and external commercialization of hydrocarbons.

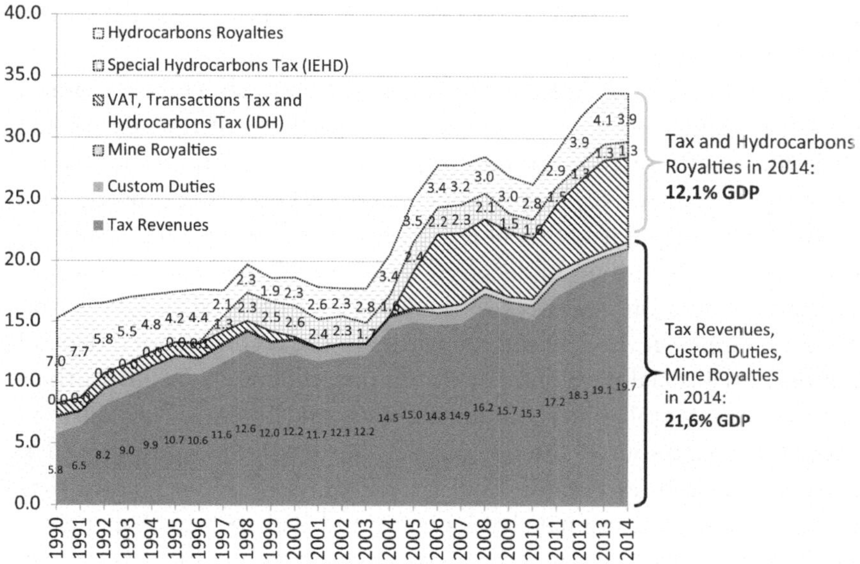

Fig. 9.6 Revenue structure of the government as percentage of GDP (1990–2014). (Source: Author elaboration based on Paz Arauco (2014))

be distributed among the regions, the departments, municipalities, universities, indigenous communities, the armed forces, the police force and, the national treasury, according to the rules established by law.

Rules for intergovernmental transfers and competencies of different government levels were redefined through the new Law of Autonomies and Decentralization (2010). As a result of new rules of co-participation of the IDH tax, and due to the price boom from 2010 to 2014, economic resources transferred from central government to local governments increased substantially, (Jiménez Pozo 2017; Chap. 8 in this volume). Transfers from the central government towards the autonomous municipal governments practically doubled, increasing from BOB (Bolivian bolivianos) 7 billion to 14 billion. IDH's contribution to these transfers represented almost 50 per cent of the total amount of transfers received by municipal governments in 2013, the year in which the highest revenue from this tax was registered in the period of analysis (Jiménez Pozo 2017). Resources from the co-participation tax allocated to subnational levels grew 4.5 times, while IDH transfers destined to municipal governments increased 27 times.

Aside from the new rules for financing subnational levels, the autonomy law granted local governments the possibility of directly electing their local authorities, of administering their economic resources and exercising legislative, regulatory, supervisory and executive powers.

The high availability of fiscal resources created new pressures on local state capacity, including budgetary execution. Furthermore, the impact of channelling more resources to the local level on local social development outcomes in the 339 municipalities in the country varied depending on initial social development conditions, differences in institutional capacities and availability of income sources (Jiménez Pozo 2017).[21] More financial resources did not translate automatically into better management capabilities because local governments were not able to overcome the low institutional development and had to face challenges in implementing budgets, as well as challenges in launching projects and decreasing the existing gaps in well-being indicators (Jiménez Pozo 2017). Availability of total financial resources per capita differed greatly between municipalities, ranging from BOB 200 (approximately USD 30) per person per year to BOB 8000 (approximately USD 1180) in 2013. Information derived from two population and housing census (2001 and 2012) showed that more than two decades after municipal decentralization, living conditions of local populations, measured using (1) an index of household assets and appliances[22] and (2) availability of basic social services at the local level, varied greatly among municipalities, displaying a high degree of social inequalities at the spatial level (Jiménez Pozo 2017).

Census data showed further a positive relation between wealth, measured by the household asset index in a municipality, and the coverage of certain basic services provided by the municipality. Figure 9.7 shows the relation between the Bolivian household asset index at the municipal level and the coverage with services such as electricity, coated floors in

[21] These resources include municipal revenues and central government transfers.

[22] This asset index takes into account two components: (1) household property of communication appliances, such as television and radio as well as appliances for access to information such as access to Internet, computers, landline phones or mobile phones and (2) goods that are used as means of transportation, such as cars, motorcycles or others.

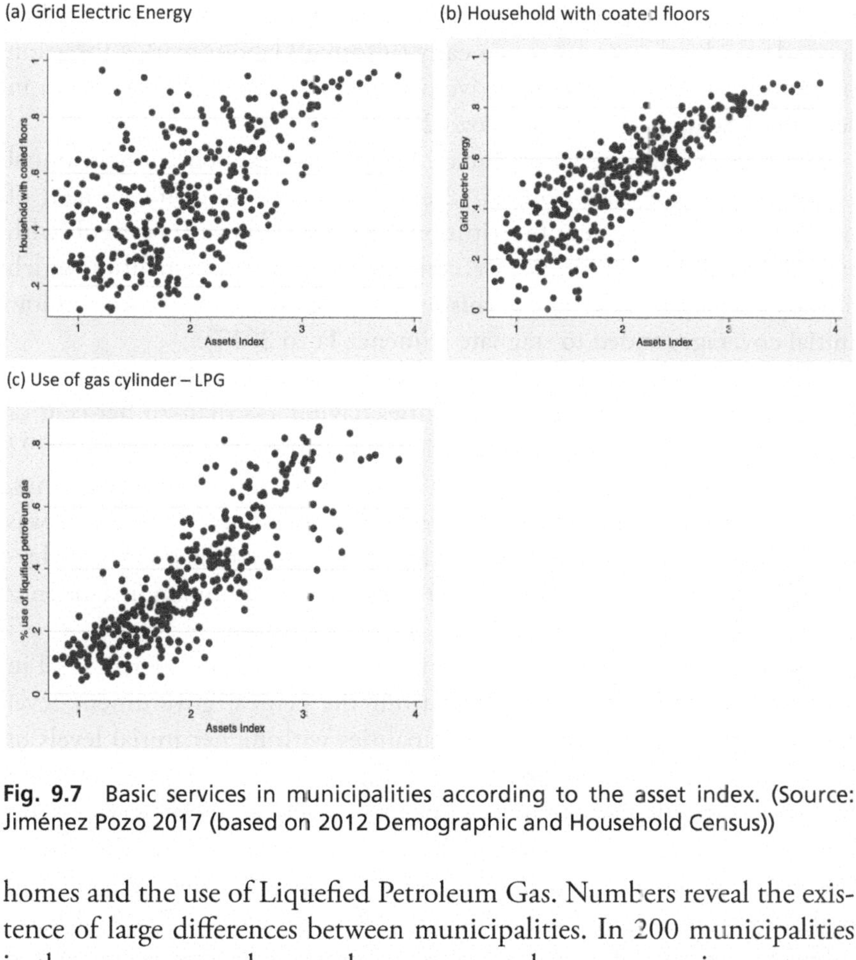

Fig. 9.7 Basic services in municipalities according to the asset index. (Source: Jiménez Pozo 2017 (based on 2012 Demographic and Household Census))

homes and the use of Liquefied Petroleum Gas. Numbers reveal the existence of large differences between municipalities. In 200 municipalities in the country, people owned on average only one or two items among those selected for the index (Fig. 9.7), and they also showed high disparities with regard to access to basic services (electricity, gas, water and sanitation) as well as access to and coverage of education and health services for their respective populations.

Disparities in access to education were particularly significant at the secondary level, and despite increasing incentives provided through new cash transfer programmes, with school attendance for grades 7–12 as low as 50 per cent in some municipalities, while attendance at the primary level exceeding 90 per cent in most municipalities. One reason for low secondary school attendance was early (informal) labour market insertion of youth, calling for more effective programmes to increase retention in secondary schooling (Jiménez Pozo 2017).

In terms of coverage with primary health services such as institutional childbirth, census data from 2012 showed that around 40 per cent of municipalities have rates of institutional delivery below 50 per cent, with improvements of this indicator concentrated in municipalities which already had higher coverage of this service in 2002, while those with low initial coverage tended to stagnate (Jiménez Pozo 2017).

Finally, coverage of water services has increased considerably over two decades, with the share of municipalities having less than 20 per cent of households covered with water services presenting 45 per cent in 1992 and decreasing to 6 per cent in 2012. Access to sanitation services has, however, improved more slowly, especially in locations where access was already low. In 2012, 70 per cent of municipalities still had coverage levels of basic sanitation below 20 per cent of their population (Jiménez Pozo 2017).

The analysis of social development outcomes at the municipal level in a context of rising fiscal transfers from the central government level reveals persisting disparities. Municipalities with higher initial levels of living standards, greater capacity to mobilize own revenues in addition to fiscal co-participation, higher coverage levels of social services and higher household asset ownership have improved social conditions over the past two decades, whereas poorer municipalities have struggled to make progress despite higher fiscal transfers. A legacy of lack of basic infrastructure, insufficient state capacity, in terms of both financial and human resources, as well as fragmentation of projects with few economies of scale, and lack of incentive to mobilize more financial resources at the municipal level are challenges that need to be overcome to equalize local development outcomes and to fully comply with the tasks assigned to municipalities by the new constitution and autonomous framework (Jiménez Pozo 2017).

Conclusions and Implications

This chapter presented key findings from a case study on the politics of domestic resource mobilization for social development in Bolivia in the 1985–2014 period. The country's historical dependence on mineral resources was identified as a key conditioning factor in the analysis, defining to a large extent the growth trajectory of the country, its fiscal capacity and the use of resources for different development models: one elite-driven with benefits accruing to the few and one aiming for shared benefits for the entire population.

The period under study was marked by a profound transformation of state-society relations against the backdrop of protest movements and large-scale social mobilizations reclaiming state ownership of natural resources, indigenous and regional empowerment and an economic alternative to neoliberalism. In the early 2000s, in a context of economic and political crisis and social conflicts, protests opened the way to successfully claim and negotiate public revenue mobilization from mineral resources, resulting in different bargaining processes between state and societal actors, mining companies and subnational state actors. The election of the first indigenous president in the country's history in the year 2005 paved the road to the transformation of the previous system of political representation, opening spaces for decision-making and direct representation of those sectors that were hitherto excluded.

In this scenario of profound political changes, the nationalization of the hydrocarbon sector led to positive economic and distributional outcomes, allowing simultaneously to achieve sustainable growth and the reduction of poverty and inequality. On the fiscal side, for the first time in the history of Bolivian public finances, the country stopped depending on foreign resources for funding its social contract and managed to run fiscal surpluses for several years. As a consequence, the country became more independent politically and economically from ODA and the international aid community, launching a new cycle of relations with donors and reprioritizing allocation of ODA in line with domestic development agendas.

The set of public policies implemented by the state also recorded important changes: the transition from universal to more targeted programmes, the implementation of a universal non-contributory pension Renta Dignidad, a more integrated social policy combining free universal services provision and demand incentive schemes as the cash transfers providing incentives to education and health access, and the minimum wage policy that increased annually as a means to reduce social and economic exclusion.

Today, with over ten years of having adopted landmark institutional reforms, the mobilization of domestic resources for social development faces new challenges that threaten its sustainability. Challenges exist for example with regard to development planning and coordination between different state levels, also in view of diverging levels of state capacity especially at the municipal level; with regard to maintaining growth with equity and redistribution; and with regard to sustaining effectiveness and progressiveness of social expenditure. Social policies implemented during the past decade have partly exhausted their transformative potential, after having made huge strides into poverty and inequality. What is needed now is to define a new social question and corresponding policies which can guarantee inclusive social development in the middle to long run.

References

Crabtree, John, George Gray Molina, and Laurence Whitehead, eds. 2009. *Bolivia, Pasado y Presente*. La Paz: Plural.

Daroca Oller, Santiago. 2016. *Protesta Social y Movilización de Recursos para el Desarrollo social en Bolivia*. PDRM Working Paper No. 2016-3. Geneva: United Nations Research Institute for Social Development.

Di John, Jonathan. 2010. *The Political Economy of Taxation and State Resilience in Zambia Since 1990*. Working Paper No. 78, Crisis States Working Papers Series No. 2. London: Crisis States Research Centre at LSE.

Echazú, Luis Alberto. 2002. Historia de la Deuda Externa Boliviana (primera parte). *Red Voltaire*, 1 October. Accessed 28 December 2013. http://www.voltairenet.org/article120336.html.

Fundación Aru. 2015. *Explicando Cambios en Bienestar, Distribución del Ingreso y Pobreza en Bolivia durante los Años 2000*. La Paz: Fundación Aru.

Hujo, Katja, ed. 2012. *Mineral Rents and the Financing of Social Policy: Opportunities and Challenges*. Basingstoke: Palgrave Macmillan and United Nations Research Institute for Social Development.

Humérez Quiroz, Julio, and Mirna Mariscal Ayaviri. 2005. Sostenibilidad y Gestión de la Deuda Pública Externa. *Análisis Económico Volúmen 20*. Unidad de Análisis de Políticas Sociales y Económicas. La Paz: Government of Bolivia.

Jiménez Pozo, Wilson. 2017. *Movilización de Recursos Domésticos, Desarrollo Social y Cambio Institucional: Descentralización y Autonomías Municipales en Bolivia*. PDRM Working Paper 2017–1. Geneva: United Nations Research Institute for Social Development.

Latinobarómetro. 2002–2011. Anual, Corporación Latinobarómetro. *Online Data Bank*. Accessed 27 September 2019. http://www.latinobarometro.org.

Machicado Saravia, Flavio. 2010. *Historia Económica de la República de Bolivia (1952–2009)*. La Paz: Creativa.

Ministerio de Economía y Finanzas Públicas. 2011. *El Nuevo Modelo Económico, Social, Comunitario y Productivo*. Economía Plural. Monthly Publication of the Ministerio de Economía y Finanzas Públicas No. 1. La Paz: Ministerio de Economía y Finanzas Públicas.

———. 2014. *Memoria de le Economía Boliviana 2013*. Report. La Paz: Ministerio de Economía y Finanzas Públicas.

———. 2015. *Memoria de le Economía Boliviana 2014*. Report. La Paz: Ministerio de Economía y Finanzas Públicas.

Ministerio de Planificación del Desarrollo. 2006. *Plan Nacional de Desarrollo*. La Paz: Ministerio de Planificación del Desarrollo.

Moore, Mick. 2013. *Obstacles to Increasing Tax Revenues in Low Income Countries*. ICTD Working Paper No. 15. Brighton: International Centre for Tax and Development/United Nations Research Institute for Social Development/Swiss Agency for Development and Cooperation.

OECD (Organisation for Economic Co-operation and Development), ECLAC (Economic Commission for Latin America and The Caribbean), CIAT (Inter-American Center of Tax Administrations) and IDB (Inter-American Development Bank). 2017. *Revenue Statistics in Latin America and the Caribbean 2017*. Paris: OECD.

Paz Arauco, Verónica. 2014. *Nuevos Caminos de la Política Social en Bolivia. El rol de las Transferencias en Efectivo*. La Paz: United Nations Development Programme.

———. 2016. *El Financiamiento del Desarrollo en Bolivia: Cambios y Continuidades en la Relación Estado-Cooperación Internacional (2006–2013).* PDRM Working Paper 2016-15. Geneva: United Nations Research Institute for Social Development.

Paz Arauco, Verónica, and Santiago Daroca Oller. 2014. *La Movilización de Recursos Domésticos para el Desarrollo Social en Bolivia (1985–2012).* Mimeo. Geneva: United Nations Research Institute for Social Development.

Peres Cajías, José. 2014. Bolivian Public Finances 1882–2010. The Challenge to Make Social Spending Sustainable. *Revista de Historia Economica - Journal of Iberian and Latin American Economic History* 32 (1): 77–117.

Shultz, Jim. 2008. La Guerra del Agua en Cochabamaba y sus Secuelas. In *Desafiando a la Globalización: Historias de la Experiencia Boliviana*, ed. Jim Shultz and Melissa Crane Draper, 17–51. La Paz: El Centro para la Democracia.

UDAPE (Unidad de Análisis de la Política Económica). 2015. *Dossier de Estadísticas Sociales y Económicas.* La Paz: UDAPE. Accessed 13 July 2015. www.udape.gob.bo.

———. 2016. *La Política Social en Bolivia.* La Paz: UDAPE. Accessed September 2019. http://www.udape.gob.bo/.

———. 2018. *Dossier de Estadísticas Sociales y Económicas.* Dataset. Accessed August 2018. www.udape.gob.bo.

UN (United Nations). 2003. *Monterrey Consensus of the International Conference on Financing for Development.* New York: United Nations.

———. 2015. *Addis Ababa Action Agenda of the Third International Conference on Financing for Development.* New York: United Nations.

UNCTAD (United Nations Conference on Trade and Development). 2007. *Reclaiming Policy Space: Domestic Resource Mobilization and Developmental States.* Geneva: UNCTAD.

UNDP (United Nations Development Programme). 2005. *Informe Temático sobre Desarrollo Humano en Bolivia: La economía más allá del gas.* La Paz: UNDP.

———. 2007. *Informe Nacional sobre Desarrollo Humano: El Estado del Estado en Bolivia.* La Paz: UNDP.

———. 2011. *Claves de la Transición del Poder.* Cuaderno de Futuro No. 26. La Paz: UNDP.

———. 2015. *Informe Regional sobre Desarrollo Humano en América Latina y el Caribe.* UNDP Report. La Paz: UNDP.

UNRISD (United Nations Research Institute for Social Development). 2012a. *Politics of Domestic Resource Mobilization*. Project Proposal. Geneva: UNRISD.

———. 2012b. *Mineral Rents and the Financing of Social Policy: Options and Constraints*. Research and Policy Brief No. 15. Geneva: UNRISD.

World Bank. 2014. *A Measured Approach to Ending Poverty and Boosting Shared Prosperity: Concepts, Data and Twin Goals*. Policy Research Report. Washington, DC: The World Bank.

———. 2015. *World Bank Open Data*. Washington, DC: The World Bank. Accessed 14 December 2015. http://data.worldbank.org/.

10

The Political Economy of Domestic Resource Mobilization in Nicaragua: Changing State-Citizen Relations and Social Development

Gloria Carrión

Introduction

Nicaragua has gone through profound political, economic and social transitions in recent decades. Following a turbulent history of dictatorship (Somoza 1936–1979), the Sandinista revolution (1979–1989) and neoliberal adjustment (1990–2006), it remains one of the poorest countries in Latin America, second only to Haiti. Periods of high social tension and violence were followed by relative peace and democratic transitions. Social conflicts and contradictions, however, have continued to emerge. These dynamics have circumscribed strategies for domestic resource mobilization (DRM) for social development.

G. Carrión (✉)
Fundación Nicaraguense para el Desarrollo Económico y Social (FUNIDES), Managua, Nicaragua

K. Hujo (ed.), *The Politics of Domestic Resource Mobilization for Social Development*, Social Policy in a Development Context,
https://doi.org/10.1007/978-3-030-37595-9_10

This chapter aims to offer an explanation for the failure (or relative success) of revenue mobilization to translate into substantive social benefits and better institutions.

The Nicaragua case study[1] shows that when strong state-society relations are fostered, effective bargaining and inclusive participation of civil society in social policy making and spending occurs, the state secures mechanisms to prevent elite capture of resources, civil society successfully mobilizes and negotiates with the state regarding the distribution of revenues from extractive industries and democratization and institution-building processes are strengthened, social policy spending tends to increase and expand. In Nicaragua, distinct political periods are associated with different strategies and outcomes regarding both social spending and mobilization of fiscal revenues. The extent to which these strategies have positively impacted social development show important links with the quality of state-society relations.

In Nicaragua, weak state-society relations have taken the form of limited spaces for citizen participation, failure of the state to respond to citizen demands, lack of transparency and accountability, and the influence of external actors in policy making. And, even as spaces for contestation and bargaining have materialized in moments of political opening, fragile institutions and unequal power relations have greatly truncated the potential for this to lead to substantive social development benefits.

After the US-backed Somoza family's rule ended in 1979, the Sandinista revolution introduced land redistribution and considerable expansion of health and education services. Civil society and social movements flourished during this period, which opened up bargaining and participatory spaces, elevating the role of social policy and social spending. In 1990, the Sandinistas were defeated at the ballot box following a bloody civil war. With the new centre-right governments came some economic recovery, reflected in resuming growth and declining inflation but also privatization, trade liberalization and a sharp contraction of the public sector,

[1] This chapter presents findings from four research papers on the politics of domestic resource mobilization in Nicaragua: (a) on the political economy of tax reforms and social spending, (b) on bargaining and contestation in the mining sector, (c) on state-society and state-donor relations and (d) on institutional change related to health financing.

which all fuelled unemployment. There was also considerable dismantling of the social policy architecture of the 1980s, and a counter-agrarian reform that negatively affected many small agricultural producers and cooperatives. In 2007, the Sandinistas (Sandinista National Liberation Front—FSLN) returned to power, continuing the economic liberalization policies of former neoliberal governments and thereby inverting the policy stance the FSLN had pursued in the 1980s. While President Ortega achieved some successes as a result of the implementation of several social and economic empowerment and food security programmes, a number of crucial challenges remain, as will be discussed in this chapter.

Regarding resource mobilization, recent history shows mixed outcomes. Efforts to increase tax revenues over past decades have generated limited results, and consequently Nicaragua remains a low-tax country. Despite frequent tax reforms, measures to attract foreign direct investment (FDI) and increasing mining revenues, the Nicaraguan government has not managed to provide a stable domestic resource base to underpin a social contract.[2] Historically aid-dependent and a beneficiary of the Heavily Indebted Poor Countries (HIPC) initiative, Nicaragua has recently received less official development assistance (ODA) as the reconfiguration of aid governance at the global level, donor fatigue and the global economic crisis in 2008 have prompted a decrease in traditional ODA levels. Nicaragua has therefore sought new partnerships with the governments of Venezuela and China. However, these alliances have to be considered as relatively fragile since they depend on partner governments' political priorities and economic situation, as will be shown in this chapter.

The structure of the chapter is as follows: Section "The Background: DRM and Social Spending in Nicaragua from a Historical Perspective" explains the historical background of DRM and social development in Nicaragua; Section "PDRM in Nicaragua: Four Case Studies" presents key findings from four case studies on taxation, state–citizen and state-donor relations, mining, and health sector financing; and Section "Main Conclusions and Policy Recommendations" develops the main conclusions and policy recommendations.

[2] In effect, private financial flows are crucial. Remittances constitute an important source of household and national income, currently 9.7 per cent of GDP (World Bank 2014).

The Background: DRM and Social Spending in Nicaragua from a Historical Perspective

This section explores the history of DRM in Nicaragua in the context of the stark political transitions the country has experienced in the last half century. It focuses on four key historical periods: the late period of the Somoza dictatorship (1972–1979), the Sandinista revolution and government (1979–1989), the neoliberal period (1990–2006) and the latest Ortega administration (2007–present).

Anastacio Somoza's Late Period (1972–1979)

Anastacio Somoza García installed a 45-year dictatorship in Nicaragua, supported by the United States. During the strong hand rule of Somoza, social organization was permitted, though true bargaining and contestation were very limited as a result of his highly repressive apparatus (Borchgrevink 2006). Further, social spending levels were very low, with fiscal policies favouring large businesses and elites rather than broader social development for the entire population. These factors had deep implications for state-society relations during this period, culminating in the overthrowing of the regime through a leftist insurrection.

Table 10.1 Sectoral distribution of central government expenditure as percentage of GDP (1970–1992)

Sector	1970–1975	1985	1990	1992
Social services	5.2	13.1	14.7	8.4
Education	2.4	5.5	7.1	3.7
Health	1.6	4.9	6.6	4.5
Infrastructure & Production	4	9.8	4.7	5.6
Defense & police	1.6	15.9	18.9	4.2
Foreign debt service	0.7	2.7	0.59	2.8
Other	3.3	13.1	8.5	7
Total	**18.8**	**65**	**60.5**	**36.2**
GDP per capita in USD	1052	670	485	457

Source: Author elaboration based on Arana et al. (1999)
Note: Data based on constant USD 1980

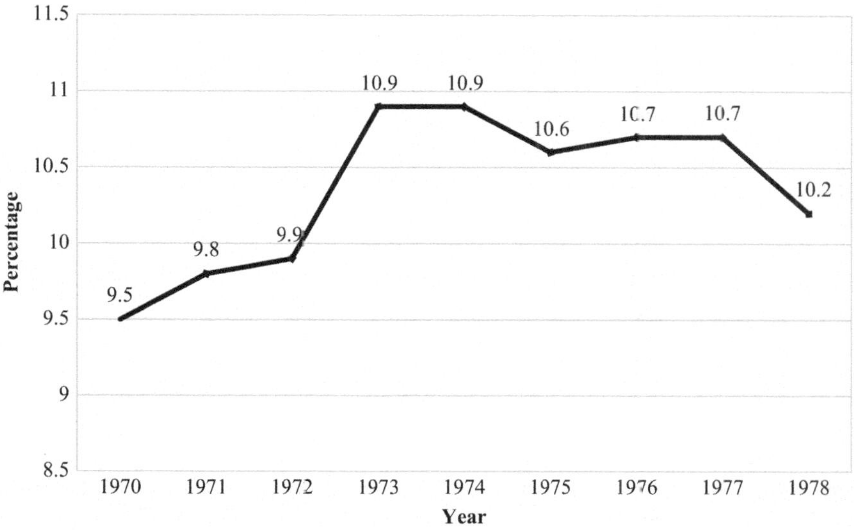

Fig. 10.1 Tax revenue as a percentage of GDP, current prices (1970–1978). (Source: Molina (2017), based on data from Acevedo (2011b))

While the late Somoza period was marked by economic growth, little of these benefits were seen by the majority of the population. With the government's support of large capitalist producers, export production capacity increased markedly in the 1970s (Curtis 1998; Torres-Rivas 2011). Financing technical assistance programmes, infrastructure, agro-industry development and loans, the Somozas promoted their own businesses and those of a few select elite groups, including the Grupo Banco de Nicaragua, Grupo Banco de América and Grupo Somoza (Zaremba 1992:20), major players in the finance, construction, agricultural, machinery and car industries (Mayorga 2007).

The Somoza regime also favoured businesses and elites in its tax structure. Despite several weak attempts at income and property tax reform, indirect taxation based on foreign trade and internal consumption provided most of the revenue (Fig. 10.2).[3] Figure 10.1 shows the tax revenue as a percentage of gross domestic product (GDP) between 1970 and 1978.

[3]Taxes as a share of GDP did not exceed 10 per cent.

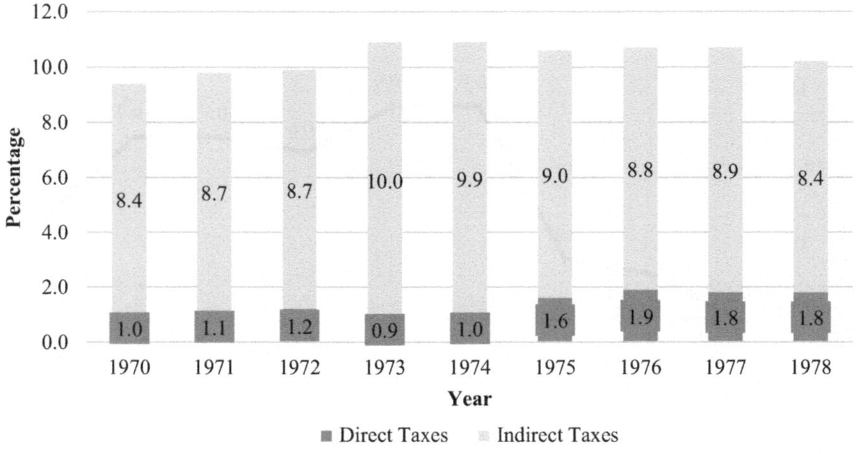

Fig. 10.2 Direct and indirect taxes as percentage of GDP, current prices (1970–1978). (Source: Molina (2017), based on data from Acevedo (2011b))

Figure 10.2 shows direct and indirect taxes as a percentage of GDP between 1970 and 1978.

Due to the government's unwillingness to tax wealth and income, Nicaragua financed only a small portion of public investment from domestic resources (Biderman 1983). Instead, until 1977, the government was able to finance the fiscal deficit and a large part of social spending with aid (Carrión 2017). In total, for the period between 1973 and 1979, health received USD 29.7 million in aid, including both loans and donations (Arana et al. 1999), while education obtained USD 30.3 million (Arana et al. 1999). However, overall social spending levels were very low in the 1970s under Somoza, limiting access to social services for the majority of the population. Table 10.2 shows that education spending represented only 2.4 per cent of GDP and health 1.6 per cent for the period 1970–1975. Before 1979, only 28 per cent of Nicaraguans had access to modern health provision.

Despite this, some gains were made by civil society, including the inclusion of the right to free public education in the 1974 Constitution (D'Castilla 1999). However, these gains were overshadowed by the lack of democracy, economic inequalities, rampant corruption and military repression (Merril 1993). The resulting deterioration of state-citizen relations was the main cause of the popular insurrection, led by the FSLN, a leftist guerrilla movement, which defeated Somoza on July 19, 1979.

The Sandinista Revolution Period (1979–1989)

The revolutionary period was characterized by an opening up of space for civic engagement and increased DRM through taxation, translating into increased social spending, but also deep social and political tensions. The Sandinistas sought to establish a mixed economy and social benefit networks for the poor by instituting large-scale agrarian reform through expropriation of former Somoza properties, and starting ambitious social programmes based on grassroots volunteerism (Walker and Wade 2011). By 1988, land in the hands of big business was reduced to 6 per cent of the total, while 40 per cent was occupied by small and medium enterprises (Mayorga 2007). Further, new participatory spaces opened up for subaltern groups (workers, women, peasants and indigenous people) to be linked directly to the state and gain more citizenship rights through mass organizations, including the Sandinista Federation of Health Workers (FETSALUD), the Rural Workers' Association (ATC), the National Teacher's Association (ANDEN) and the FSLN Women's Association Luisa Amanda Espinoza (AMLAE), among others (Borchgrevink 2006).

Swinging cuts in public sector salaries helped finance government expenditures aimed at raising the income of the poorest Nicaraguans, subsidizing basic necessities such as food and energy, and expanding health, education and housing (Carrión 2017). Similarly, selective excise taxes (alcohol, gasoline) were instituted in the context of fiscal reform aimed at raising tax revenue between 1982 and 1987. During those years, two additional new taxes were created to increase progressivity through wealth redistribution and revenue collection: the property tax and the capital gains tax (Molina 2017). Between 1980 and 1984, tax collection increased (see Fig. 10.3).

Revenue from direct taxes as a percentage of GDP increased and reached the highest point in 1984 with 10.3 per cent of GDP, although

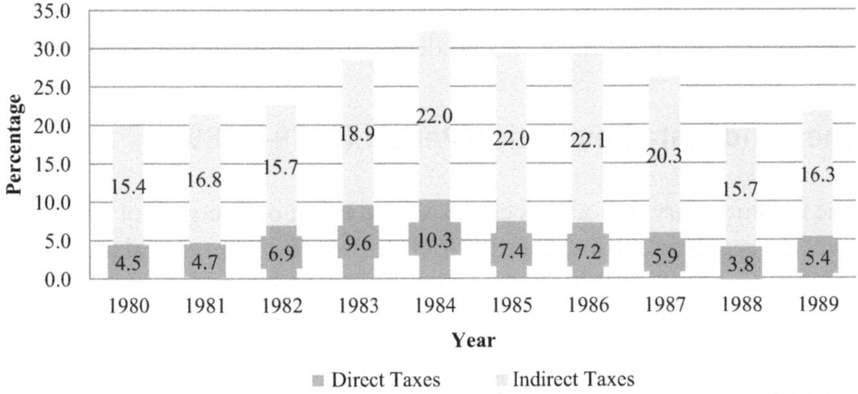

Fig. 10.3 Direct and indirect taxes as a percentage of GDP, current prices (1980–1989). (Source: Molina (2017), based on data from Acevedo (2011b))

the overall system remained regressive, with indirect taxes reaching 22 per cent of GDP. Total tax take stood at 32.4 per cent of GDP in 1984 compared to around 20 per cent in 1980, which reflected an impressive increase compared to the previous administration (see Fig. 10.4) (Molina 2017).

Under Sandinista rule, overall public spending more than tripled from 18.8 per cent during the Somoza period to 65 per cent of GDP in 1985 (see Table 10.1). Table 10.2 shows social spending levels between 1982 and 1989. Health and education spending as a percentage of total spending were slightly higher in 1982 compared to health and education spending under Somoza between 1970 and 1975 (see Table 10.1 for data under Somoza).

However, the gains in social development during the revolutionary period were limited by the extent of opposition that arose, both nationally and abroad. Animosities emerged between the revolutionary government and economic elites as economic power was transferred from big business to workers and peasants, through land reforms, state expropriation and new tax policies.

As part of a large-scale effort to stem the tide of socialism in the Western Hemisphere, the United States imposed an economic embargo in 1985 and also trained and funded counter-revolutionary groups,

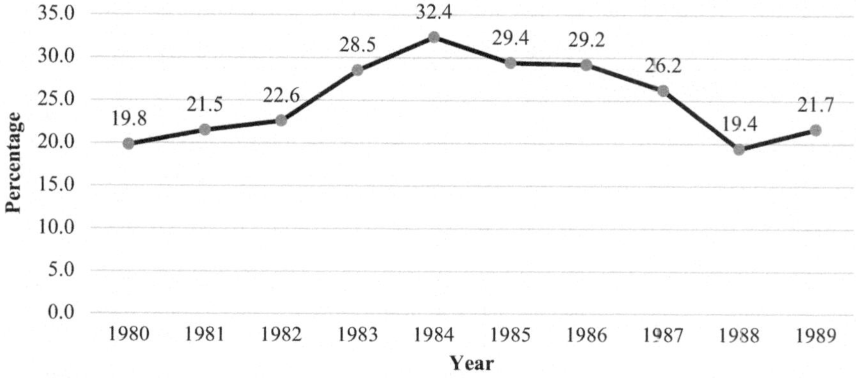

Fig. 10.4 Tax revenue as a percentage of GDP, current prices (1980–1989). (Source: Molina (2017), based on data from Acevedo (2011b))

known as the Contras, spurring more than a decade of conflict marked by deep repression and violence on all sides. In the midst of violence and political strife, the progressive resource mobilization and social spending policies of the revolutionary government began to lose their teeth. For one, political and economic instability and the government's financing of the monetary deficit by issuing money led to an increase in inflation rates (Acevedo 2011a), which also eroded tax collection in the second half of the decade (see Fig. 10.4). Also, as the 1980s progressed and the relations with the US government further soured, social spending decreased, while military spending increased (see Table 10.2).

By the end of the 1980s, the situation was unsustainable: the death toll of the civil war had reached 50,000 people and the country experienced economic recession and hyperinflation in 1989.[4] Eventually a ceasefire and peace agreement was signed. General amnesty was granted, and national elections were scheduled for early 1990.

[4]Additionally, the national GDP growth rate (at constant 2005 USD) went from 4.6 per cent in 1980 to −0.8 per cent in 1982. In 1984, it declined by 1.6 per cent (World Bank 2015).

Table 10.2 Social spending (percentage/USD millions) in Nicaragua (1982–1989)

Sector	1982	1983	1984	1985	1986	1987	1988	1989
% of social expenditure								
Total	23.87	22.25	19.23	19.27	20.66	21.18	18.2	24.6
Education	10.91	12.55	7.53	8.74	9.11	10.38	7.47	9.11
Health	10.71	7.53	7.44	8.81	10.58	9.63	9.15	13.16
Housing	2.25	2.17	4.26	1.72	0.97	1.17	0	2.29
Other	–	–	–	–	–	–	1.58	2.29
Millions of 1996 USD								
Total	213.36	316.2	279.2	276	279.4	234.4	158	132.7
Education	97.56	178.4	109.3	125.2	123.2	114.8	64.8	49.1
Health	95.7	107	108	126.2	143.1	106.6	79.4	71
Housing	20.1	30.8	61.9	24.6	13.1	13	–	0.2
Other	–	–	–	–	–	–	13.8	12.4
Social spending as % of GDP	10	14	13	13	13	11	9	7

Source: Author elaboration based on Arana et al. (1999)
Notes: 1996 Córdobas (NIO) and US dollars (USD)

The Chamorro, Alemán and Bolaños Administrations (1990–2006)

On February 25, 1990, the Sandinistas were defeated in national elections by Violeta Barrios de Chamorro of the National Opposition Union (Unión Nacional Opositora, UNO), a 14-party alliance across the political spectrum. While this period was characterized by neoliberal reforms, DRM strategies varied. President Violeta Barrios' administration (1990–1996) focused on macroeconomic stabilization, privatization and other structural adjustment reforms, while the subsequent President Arnoldo Aleman (1996–2001) deepened privatization and promoted trade liberalization. President Enrique Bolaños (2001–2006) designed a national development plan based on small and medium as well as large business clusters, and public investment according to poverty maps and donors' Poverty Reduction Strategy Papers (PRSPs). Under Bolaños, the state-business nexus, in particular with large companies, deepened. The role of bilateral and multilateral donors was also strengthened, granting these actors considerable influence regarding public spending and policy-making processes.

The governments of the 1990s onwards engaged with the IMF and the World Bank to implement stabilization programmes, which focused on balancing budgets and debt repayment at the cost of social programmes. This austerity turn impacted poor Nicaraguans negatively. Privatization caused massive unemployment going up from 20.9 per cent in 1985 to more than 60 per cent in 1993 (Curtis 1998). Health spending was cut from USD 58 per person per year in 1988 to USD 17 per person per year in 1991 (Curtis 1998). Social expenditure as a percentage of GDP (see Fig. 10.5) reached its lowest level in 1998, 6 per cent of GDP). Since 2002, public social expenditure began to show a small, though steady, increase, with a positive effect on inequality: the Gini Index decreased from 0.58 in 2001 to 0.47 in 2011 (BTI 2014).

Tax reforms under the Alemán's administration reduced the tax burden of workers. However, it did not revert the system's regressive nature, with the majority of taxes continuing to be indirect (Arana et al. 1999). As a consequence, the burden of the tax system remained centred on the poor and more vulnerable sectors of society. In 2002, taxes on consumption, including customs revenues, contributed around 80 per cent of the government's resources (Gasparini and Artana 2003). The Tax Equity Law, passed in 2003 during the Bolaños administration, aimed at increasing government revenues to bridge the fiscal gap, reduce distortions, and

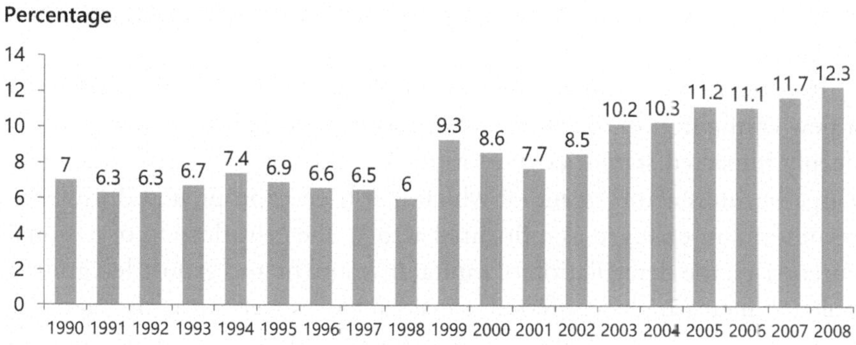

Fig. 10.5 Public social expenditure as a percentage of GDP (1990–2008). (Source: Author elaboration based on data from CEPAL (2009). Notes: Chamorro administration (1990–1996); Alemán administration (1997–2001); Bolaños administration (2002–2006))

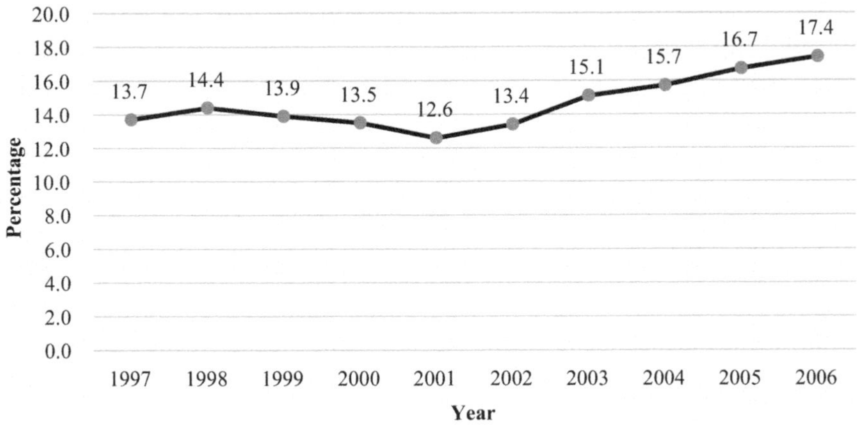

Fig. 10.6 Tax revenue as a percentage of GDP, current prices (1997–2006). (Source: Molina (2017), based on data from Acevedo (2011b))

improve accountability and equity. Indeed, the law did lead to increased tax revenue (Molina 2017) and reduced some distortions (see Fig. 10.6), mainly due to a more progressive legislation: no new indirect taxes were created, and three additional direct taxes were introduced, including taxes on luxury goods, bank deposits and business assets (Molina 2017).

However, the exonerations and tax breaks granted to big businesses were largely maintained, which watered down its potential effect on the reduction of inequalities in the fiscal regime (Gasparini and Artana 2003; Molina 2017).

In general, the neoliberal reforms implemented in the 1990s reflected a new configuration of actors and economic and political power, which deeply impacted state-society relations in post-revolutionary Nicaragua. Large business actors, some of which had been expropriated during the revolution, re-emerged as influential actors. The privatization of national enterprises, the deregulation of capital investment and export-led growth policies increasingly conferred considerable power to actors like the Supreme Council of Private Enterprise (COSEP), a confederation of mainly large business groups.

The policy turn triggered social tensions, including national strikes such as the one in 1990 that mobilized 80,000 state, industrial and rural workers against these policies (Pallais 1990). Such resistance signalled the newly elected government that its reform course needed to be implemented gradually. In response, the country experienced "cycles of stand-off, negotiation, and compromise alternated with peaceful and violent strikes, demonstrations and clashes" (Robinson 1995:1). Nicaraguan civil society became a highly diversified and fragmented player. In this period, mass organizations and grassroots movements were weakened, though they also gained autonomy from the FSLN (Borchgrevink 2006), while NGOs rapidly gained influence.

International aid complemented DRM strategies. Between 1990 and 2002, aid amounted to a total of USD 7500 million, out of which 56 per cent were donations and 44 per cent loans (Gobierno de Nicaragua 2003). From 1990 to 2001, health received USD 250 million in aid and education USD 189.7 million (Gobierno de Nicaragua 2003). International aid peaked in 1992 to account for 40 per cent of Nicaragua's GDP (see Fig. 10.7). In the following years, however, aid levels decreased. The year 1999 is the only exception as aid increased due to the international response prompted by the devastating effects of Hurricane Mitch, which, in 1997, destroyed most of the country's infrastructure, killing thousands of people.

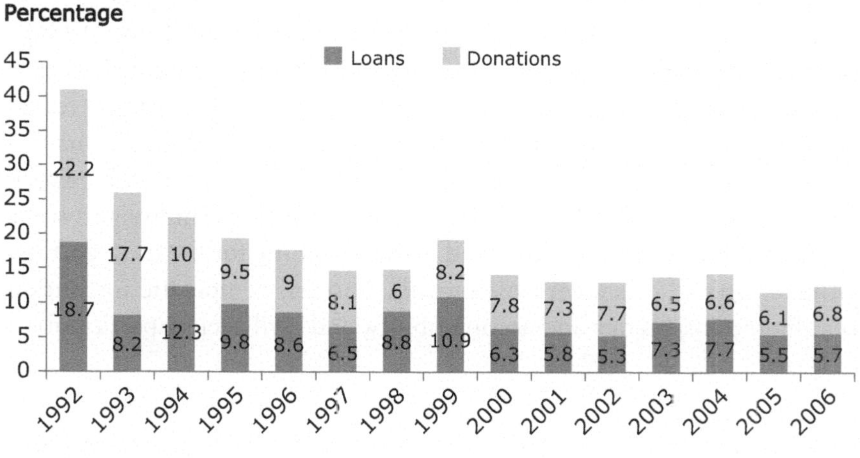

Fig. 10.7 Evolution of foreign aid as a percentage of GDP (1992–2006). (Source: Carrión (2017), based on data from Acevedo (2011a))

In 2005, Nicaragua signed the Joint Financing Agreement (Acuerdo Conjunto de Financiamiento) with the Budget Support Group comprising bilateral and multilateral donors who provided budget support for the government in the form of loans and donations.[5]

In 2000, Nicaragua was included in the HIPC debt relief initiative; however, the expected results of the initiative's financial relief did not fully materialize, as Nicaragua's internal debt previously acquired with commercial banks became the main burden (Portocarrero 2004). Instead of increasing social spending, the state used the freed-up resources to service this debt. Out of the approximately USD 200 million external debt relief, only USD 7 million were spent on social programmes in 2004 (Acevedo 2005). This, along with a highly regressive fiscal system, the privatization of state property and the strengthening of political and economic power of big business vis-à-vis workers and social movements, had negative effects on social indicators,[6] deepening the inequalities that persist today.

The Ortega Administration (2007–Present)

In 2007, Daniel Ortega was elected President of Nicaragua and was re-elected in 2016, in violation of the constitution, which prohibits re-election. Since the 1990 electoral defeat of the Sandinistas, Daniel Ortega has been the leader of the FSLN party and its recurrent presidential candidate. During his administration, resource availability has increased (despite declines in traditional aid) through emerging non-traditional aid schemes and substantial increases in tax and mining revenues. However, while some of this has been channelled to social programmes and some key social indicators have improved, social spending for the most part has either stagnated or shown little growth. Further, democratic institution building, transparency and accountability, and civil society participation

[5] Including the World Bank, the European Union, the Inter-American Development Bank (IADB), Sweden, Norway, Finland, the United Kingdom, Germany, the Netherlands and Switzerland.

[6] In 2005, for example, only 40 per cent of the population had access to essential drugs. Families, and not the state, assumed two-thirds of pharmaceutical spending (Acevedo 2005).

and bargaining have declined, while the state-business nexus has deepened.

In 2008, the Budget Support Group ceased operations due to emerging tensions between traditional donors and the newly elected government,[7] as well as changes in the international aid paradigm. Ortega's government rhetoric reasserted the state's role in development vis-à-vis donors. As part of this strategy, the government aimed to develop new partnerships with the Global South, and in 2007 Nicaragua joined the Bolivarian Alternative for the Americas (ALBA), a left-wing counterproposal to the US-led Free Trade Area of the Americas (FTAA).

Traditional bilateral donors, such as the aid agencies from the United Kingdom, Germany and Finland, left Nicaragua in 2009.[8] Multilateral aid disbursements, however, increased from USD 491.8 million in 2007 to USD 532.9 million in 2013 (IADB 2015), in tandem with the emergence of new donors such as Russia whose aid went from USD 5 million in 2007 to USD 35.1 million in 2013 (IADB 2015) and Venezuela, which increased its aid flows from USD 139.2 million in 2007 to USD 559.1 million in 2013 (IADB 2015).

Despite high levels of resource mobilization through ALBA, partner countries and emerging donors, along with higher revenues from taxation and mining, both of which began to increase in 2007 (see Fig. 10.8 and Table 10.3), health and education spending as a percentage of GDP remained relatively constant with some increases, particularly between 2004 (9.1 per cent) and 2009 (12.4 per cent), as Table 10.4 shows.

State-society relations under Ortega have remained fraught. For one, shrinking ODA and the departure of traditional donors have deeply impacted Nicaraguan civil society. Given the high dependency on aid, many NGOs and associations that advocated for social development have

---

[7] President Ortega stated that Europeans were like "flies that step on dirt. … What they provide is not aid, but bread crumbs, small payments for the enormous unpayable debt they have with the people of the Americas" (*Noticias24* 2008). The conflict reached a critical point, when political opposition parties accused the Sandinista National Liberation Front (FSLN) of committing fraud during municipal elections in 2008 and violating the national constitution, which prohibits re-election.

[8] As aid resources were shrinking, many donors prioritized their funds and development efforts in Africa. Additionally, Nicaragua's GDP surpassed the middle-income country threshold in 2014, leading to further aid declines.

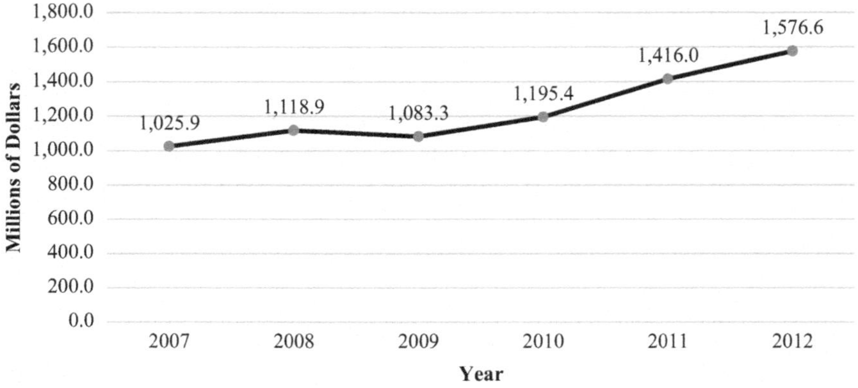

Fig. 10.8 Total tax revenue trend (2007–2012) (USD millions). (Source: Molina (2017), based on DGP (2007–2012)

Table 10.3 Revenues to the Nicaraguan Treasury from tax and royalties on mining (USD millions)

Concept	2007	2012	2013
State's total tax revenue from the mining sector	1115.8	1729.7	1781.4
Internal taxes	7.1	30.7	42.1
Mining surface rights (land use tax)	1.6	2.9	2.9
Mining extraction rights	1.8	12.1	12.1
Fines for surface rights and right of extraction	0.01	0.01	0.02
Total mining royalties and taxes	10.6	45.7	57.1
As percentage of state tax revenue	0.95	2.64	3.21

Source: Gutiérrez (2015) using data from the Ministerio de Hacienda y Crédito Público (Ministry of Finance)

Note: Deductible from income tax

disappeared due to lack of funding. Tensions between the state and society also encompass other disputed topics, such as opposition from peasant and indigenous communities to state-led development projects and outcry from women's movements in response to the government's policies on reproductive rights and violence against women. Ortega administration's top-down approach to governing has left little room for civil society participation, as it favours a hierarchical model of state-citizen relations, with little space for autonomous civil society actors, who have been presented by government as "public enemies".

Table 10.4 Social spending in Nicaragua as a percentage of GDP (2003–2014)

Year	Total social spending	Education spending	Health spending	Housing spending	Social services (bonus, scholarships)	Recreational services (parks, improvements)
2003	9.2	4.8	3.5	0.9	–	–
2004	9.1	4.5	3.2	1.4	–	–
2005	10.2	4.9	3.5	1.8	–	–
2006	10.4	5	3.4	2	–	–
2007	10.6	5.2	3.7	1.7	–	–
2008	11.3	5.5	3.7	2.1	–	–
2009	12.4	6.1	4.1	2.2	–	–
2010	9.4	4.1	2.8	1.8	0.6	0.1
2011	9.8	4.1	2.9	2	0.7	0.1
2012	9.8	3.9	3	2.1	0.7	0.1
2013	9.8	3.9	3	2.1	0.6	0.2
2014	10.5	4.2	3.4	2.1	0.6	0.2

Source: Author elaboration based on CEPAL (2015) and BCN (2016)

While state-society relations have suffered, state-business relations have improved. According to José Adán Aguerri, President of COSEP, since 2008, the association has managed to bargain with the current government on an unprecedented number of 91 laws and 42 implementing frameworks regarding the economy. Additionally, COSEP has appointed 41 representatives in the executive boards of key public institutions where economic and social policy decisions are made.

State-society relations deteriorated further in 2018, when peaceful protests in response to a new social security reform, which increased workers' and employers' contributions and reduced retiree pensions by 5 per cent (IACHR 2018), were met with violent opposition by national police forces and parapolice groups.

As the protests grew larger and spread throughout the country, the state violence escalated, resulting in at least 212 deaths, 1337 persons wounded as of June 19, 2018, and 507 persons deprived of liberty as of June 6, 2018 (IACHR 2018). This generated a political, social, economic and human rights crisis that persists today. Despite its ties to the revolutionary period, Ortega's government has failed to open up significant spaces for popular participation, and he has further entrenched his power and the power of large businesses and elites.

The Politics of Domestic Resource Mobilization in Nicaragua: Four Case Studies

This section presents four case studies related to the mobilization of fiscal revenues in Nicaragua, exploring why recent resource mobilization policies have failed to result in significant improvements in social development outcomes in Nicaragua. The case studies include the tax concertation law implemented by the Ortega government in 2012, the new aid alliances forged in the context of ALBA, popular contestation around a mining project in the municipality of Rancho Grande and the linkages between resource mobilization and institution building in the health sector.

The Tax Concertation Law: A Stalled Attempt to Create a More Equitable Tax System

The Tax Concertation Law was passed in 2012 with the objective of modernizing the fiscal system and mobilizing public resources for social development (GEE 2006).[9] While the process was originally designed to be participatory and involve various actors, it has been highly contested by tax experts and civil society organizations (CSOs), mainly due to power differentials during the negotiating process, which favoured large businesses over social actors.

The Tax Concertation Law aimed to correct distortions within the tax system, provide order to the existing system and stimulate higher participation of tax revenue in the financing of public expenditures. As previous tax laws attempted in the past, the law aimed to expand the tax base and reduce tax evasion by introducing changes in income tax, sales tax, selective consumption taxes, tax benefits and the tax administration (GEE 2006: 83). A further increase in tax revenue collection was also expected from the law, mostly through the elimination of different tax

[9] This case study draws on the report prepared by Molina (2017) for the PDRM project, unless other literature cited.

exonerations and exemptions, to be implemented gradually over a five-year period starting in 2015.

The law's reach, however, fell short, mainly due to asymmetrical power dynamics. During Tax Concertation Law negotiations, the business confederation COSEP used its structural and instrumental power to prevent the reform from achieving the changes it originally intended and managed to "water-down" the proposal. The result was a partial reform of the Tax Equity Law approved in 2003 in order to generate higher revenues without having to create major changes to the fiscal system, undermining possible redistributive benefits of the Tax Concertation Law, in particular due to continued exonerations.

Actors at the negotiating table included the government, COSEP, the National Workers Front (FNT) and the Ministry of Finance. However, as said, they did not participate on equal terms. COSEP had special access to state representatives and key technical information, which strengthened its position, while actors such as the FNT did not have the resources to hire tax specialists and consultants to develop technically sound proposals. Issues of representation also arose as COSEP is not representative of all enterprises, neither the FNT representative of all workers. In fact, the majority of workers in the country affiliated with micro and small businesses are not involved in unions (Potosme 2013).

CSOs were not included in the negotiations. Instead, they formed the Nicaraguan Alliance for Fiscal Justice,[10] which drafted a joint agenda and a technical proposal for the government. The Alliance engaged the media and developed an ambitious lobby strategy to influence the negotiations (Molina 2017); however, none of the Alliance's proposals were captured in the law's final draft, due in part to the fact that the government sped up the process, reaching an agreement with COSEP only five months after the negotiations began.

[10] These organizations included cooperatives' federations, rural women's and youth organizations, NGOs like OXFAM and Christian Aid, research centres working on tax issues, academics and civil society actors like the Coordinadora Civil comprising both Nicaraguan NGOs and social movements (Molina 2017).

ALBA: Challenges and Opportunities of Venezuelan Aid

The Bolivarian Alliance for the Peoples of Our America, or ALBA, is a consortium of Latin American nations that aims to promote social, political and economic prosperity in the region through trade, knowledge-sharing and intergovernmental cooperation.[11] It proposes a shift from the neoliberal paradigm of integration and economic growth to a model centred on cooperation, poverty eradication and social inclusion. ALBA funds and resources contributed to social development in Nicaragua, providing necessary resources for various social programmes. However, problems stemming from intransparency, clientelism and poor state-society relations limited its ability to create transformative change.

One of ALBA's key pillars is an energy cooperation agreement known as Petrocaribe, launched by Venezuela in 2005, that aims to contribute to energy sustainability and security in its 17-member countries by accessing Venezuelan crude oil at concessionary prices (Carrión 2017). Once refined, oil derivatives, like gas, are commercialized in Nicaragua by ALBANISA (ALBA de Nicaragua Sociedad Anónima—ALBA of Nigaragua S.A.), a public enterprise of Nicaraguan and Venezuelan joint ownership, consisting of national energy generators and a network of gas stations. ALBANISA sets the prices for oil and its derivatives and finances itself by selling them on the internal market (Acevedo 2012). Issues of transparency and accountability have arisen regarding the implementation and allocation of ALBA funds as ALBANISA created a number of private enterprises in diverse economic sectors with public resources. Furthermore, the ownership of these companies has been linked to party members and the president's family, including the Distribuidora Nicaragüense de Petróleo (DNP—Nicaraguan Oil Distributor), which has a network of 50 gas stations and oil storage capacity of up to 60,000 barrels.[12]

[11] This section draws on the report by Carrión (2017) prepared for the PDRM project.

[12] Galeano 2009; Martínez 2009; Central America Data 2009; *El Nuevo Diario* 2009; *El Heraldo* 2010; Salinas 2011a, b, c; Córdoba 2012; Martínez and Enríquez 2012; Enríquez 2014, 2015a, b; Olivares 2016a, b.

Under Petrocaribe, the state has actively implemented policies such as the current modern barter system used to honour payments for oil quotas instead of using foreign currency, positively impacting foreign exchange availability. Half of the oil quota Nicaragua receives under ALBA can be paid with agricultural exports, including sugar, beef, beans, coffee and dairy products (Carrión 2012). ALBANISA sets the price and buys the products from Nicaraguan producers, and then sells to Venezuela at beneficial (higher) prices. ALBANISA's profit under ALBA from agricultural products' sales, increased the levels and availability of public financial resources. In 2009, ALBANISA's assets were estimated at USD 290 million and annual sales at approximately USD 400 million (Chamorro and Salinas 2012). According to Olivares (2016a), ALBANISA has managed a total of USD 3500 million since its creation. However, not all of these funds have been used to finance social spending. Only 38 per cent of ALBA funds finance the government's social and productive programmes (Chamorro and Utting 2015).

These programmes comprise financing for social housing (Casas para el Pueblo); health services in low-income neighbourhoods, such as Operación Milagro (Miracle Operation) and Operación Sonrisa (Smile Operation); credit for urban entrepreneurs, particularly women, like Usura Cero (Zero Usury); the construction and maintenance of roads and streets such as Calles para el Pueblo (Streets for the People); a productive and food security bonus—Hambre Cero (Zero Hunger) of up to USD 1500 for women with small plots of land that includes a cow, hens and pigs; Plan Techo (Roof Plan), which provides zinc sheets for rooftops in disadvantaged neighbourhoods; and the Programa Cristiano Socialista y Solidario (CRISSOL) (Christian, Socialist and Solidarity Programme), promoting productivity improvements and price bargaining capacity of small producers of basic grains, including rice, beans, maize and sorghum by providing low-interest credit.

Bilateral and multilateral donors have also supported the implementation of social programmes. More recently, though, falling oil prices and Venezuela's ongoing humanitarian and political crisis have significantly reduced Venezuelan cooperation funds to Nicaragua (from USD 461.1 million in 2008 to USD 193.3 million in 2015) (Carrión 2017). As a result, most social programmes are currently financed through the national budget (La Voz del Sandinismo 2016; Navas and López 2014). In 2018, ALBA funds went down by 85.5 per cent compared to 2017. ALBA funds in 2018 amounted to USD 9.2 million compared to USD 63.5 million in 2017 (Efe 2018). They were used for energy subsidies (USD 2.5 million), fair trade development (USD 2.2 million) and housing infrastructure (USD 1.5 million) (Efe 2018).

The various programmes advanced some key development indicators. For instance, the Programa Hambre Cero had an overall positive impact on food production, consumption and certain elements of women's empowerment.[13] However, Hambre Cero's political bias in the selection of beneficiaries, lack of government information regarding the programme's design and implementation, lack of accountability of programme officials and limited or no access to government data on the programme's impact evaluation and monitoring are major challenges.[14] ALBA funds are not accounted for in the national budget, and information about their availability, monitoring and implementation is unavailable. This makes in-depth and independent evaluation and state accountability processes difficult tasks.

In sum, the lack of accountability and state-society dialogue around ALBA funds are crucial obstacles to realizing the transformative potential that non-traditional aid schemes could have on Nicaragua's social development.

Contested Mining: The Case of Rancho Grande

Mining revenues increased substantively from 0.95 per cent of total state revenues in 2007 to 3.21 per cent in 2013.[15] Social mobilization against a mining concession granted in the municipality of Rancho Grande in 2004 shows how mining relates to contestation and bargaining processes, impacting state-society, state-state and state-investor relations. It illustrates how power asymmetries and institutional weaknesses have negatively impacted ecological and broader social interests related to mining.

[13] IEEPP 2011; Kester 2010; Grupo Venancias 2014.

[14] Kester 2010; IEEPP 2011; Grupo Venancias 2014.

[15] This section draws on the report prepared by Gutiérrez (2015) for the PDRM project.

Rancho Grande's economy has been primarily based on small-scale agricultural production. In 2004, the government granted a concession to the Canadian mining company MINESA (Sociedad Minera de Santander—Santander Mining Society) without prior community consultation or approval. However, the law mandates that the state solicits and takes into account the views of local governments prior to the approval of contracts for the exploitation of natural resources.[16] The mayor at that time, however, did not conduct a public consultation on the grounds that it was an election year and though his successor, Alfredo Zamora, tried to revoke the mining permit for exploration, he was unsuccessful. This launched a dispute between the municipality of Rancho Grande and the government.

In 2010, the transnational corporation B2Gold bought MINESA's mining concession and began its exploration project, called "El Pavón". The community mobilized against the project, creating a coalition led by the Catholic Church and a group called Guardians of Yaoska with diverse community actors. Each community had a local directive made up of leaders from the Catholic Church. Guardians of Yaoska mobilized thousands of people against mining in Rancho Grande. They sought to counteract the close relationship between the government and the mining company, which allowed the latter to have more leverage with the state than the community. Guardians of Yaoska collected 7000 signatures against mining and presented them at the president's office in Managua and the mayor's office in Rancho Grande, but obtained no answer. At that point, Rancho Grande witnessed a struggle for the collection of signatures in support of or against the mining company. Guardians of Yaoska and other community members accused the state of organizing non-mining-related events in order to collect signatures in support of the mining project without the consent of participants.

While the case of Rancho Grande had an unexpected happy ending, as President Ortega finally made the ad hoc decision to declare the mineral exploitation in the municipality as inviable for ecological reasons in

[16] Special Law on Exploration and Mining (Law 387), Chapter IV. Mining Concessions, Article 36–38.

October 2015,[17] it also shows that resource mobilization based on extractive industries relies on powerful alliances between state and industry actors, promoting profit and revenue interests which frequently collide with social and environmental objectives, threatening to destroy traditional livelihoods, sustaining local populations in more sustainable ways. The original granting of the mining concession involved a top-down approach, which denied the community's right to participate in the decision-making process, leading to social conflict and increasing alienation between community and state actors. Big business actors, however, had direct access to and influence on the state, and were able to secure their interests over those of the community. This was evidenced by the militarization of the area protecting the mining campsite, the collection of signatures in support of the mining project by the municipality, and police and military interventions to stop the community's social mobilization against mining. However, the example also shows that the organized and visible protest, the direct links of the Catholic Church with the presidential office (through the person of provincial bishop Alvarez) and the scientific validation of the protest movements' claims through ecological impact studies conducted by the Ministry for Environment and Natural Resources (MARENA) eventually resulted in the victory of the movement.

Health Sector Financing and Institution Building

Studying health sector financing reveals the connection between resource mobilization strategies, social spending and institutional reform, which is at the heart of the PDRM project.[18] The health system in Nicaragua has transformed significantly over time, moving from a fragmented and stratified system, favouring mostly the rich (1970s), to a system with strong community participation and a preventive health focus (1980s), to a decentralized system with the emergence of new for-profit actors (1990–2006).

[17] See various press articles, for example Aburto (2015).

[18] This section draws on the report prepared by Delmelle and Mendoza (2017) for the PDRM project, unless other literature is cited.

The health sector's institutional structure during the 1970s was fragmented. Health services were concentrated in wealthy urban areas serving a small minority, while rural areas were undersupplied. Health services and financing transformed during the revolution; they were free-of-charge and widely provided. The system became institutionalized and the structure set up then continues today. The approach was both preventive and curative, and relied on mass volunteerism.

International aid was fundamental to the expansion of the health system in the 1980s. Resources were provided, both financial and in-kind, such as from Cuba, whose government sent medical brigades and medicine. Internally, tensions between the Ministry of Health and the Ministry of Finance emerged as the Contra War intensified, prompting the redirection of most public resources to defence. This had a negative impact on the Ministry of Health's resource availability.

The structural adjustment and privatization policies of the 1990s impacted on the health sector's institutional structure. The health system was largely decentralized, divided into for-profit services run by private clinics and hospitals and state-run services for the poor, partly financed by NGOs and aid actors.

In 2005, donors and the government agreed on Agenda PROSALUD, a platform to channel aid funds to health, which granted donors important influence over health policy. The Ministry of Finance gained more power vis-à-vis the Ministry of Health due to the relevance placed on macroeconomic stability above other public matters. Although the free nature of health services was maintained at a discursive level, the quality of services at public hospitals and clinics deteriorated. Access and availability of medicines in public health entities also declined, and less emphasis was placed on prevention.

Institution strengthening in the health sector has not seen major advancements under the current Ortega administration. It has largely maintained the institutional structure that was constituted in the 1980s, while reintroducing a stronger emphasis on prevention as compared to the neoliberal era. Links have been reinstituted with volunteers while the state's and the FSLN's role and influence have increased in provisional local clinics and medicine imports. NGOs have decreased in number as a result of ODA's decline (Carrión 2017), while health coverage by the state has increased. Additionally, lack of access to public health data has limited social mobilization and independent assessments around health issues.

Generally, health services have improved under the current administration. However, the health sector is still highly dependent on external resources, which currently make up about 22 per cent of the total health budget (Delmelle and Mendonza 2017). This dependence renders the sector particularly vulnerable to changes in aid flows from both traditional and non-traditional sources. One major challenge of the Nicaraguan health system is ensuring the sustainability of financing schemes in the face of declining ODA levels and ALBA funds.

More stable domestic revenues would help to make free health care a reality. Stable DRM sources would reduce out-of-pocket expenditure and weaken the power and influence of large businesses in health as the state could provide reliable public health services. Finally, securing sustainable domestic resources could also improve fragmentation in the health sector by strengthening institution building and state-society dialogue.

Main Conclusions and Policy Recommendations

Nicaragua has undergone significant political, economic and social transformations in a few decades. This has shaped the scope and continuity of DRM policies. Since the 1970s, Nicaragua has relied heavily on international aid, traditional and non-traditional, to finance social development. Fiscal revenues have shown an upward trend due to reforms and episodes of economic growth. However, the overall tax system is still regressive due to the dominance of indirect taxes, though less so than in the past. Although efforts have been made to limit tax exemptions to the wealthy, these still prevail.

State-society relations have fluctuated since the 1970s, shifting from "less to more conducive" and then back to less conducive relations for social development. Social mobilization flourished in the 1980s. However, in the 1990s, privatization and structural adjustment policies weakened and fragmented Nicaraguan civil society, while large business actors enhanced their power. Democratization and institution building have also fluctuated since the 1970s, from dictatorship with little contestation and bargaining processes, to democracy where contestation and bargaining processes emerged and flourished, and back to autocratic power and state repression (GIEI 2018). In effect, the state's current top-down governance approach is eroding democratic spaces and compromising institution building and human rights advancements, undermining state-society relations in the short and long term in Nicaragua.

Today, Ortega's administration (2007–present) pursues a model of traditional economic growth with social programme provisioning. The current government's social model has discursively reasserted the role of the state in social provisioning and restored the free-of-charge nature of health care and education. However, the model has shortcomings. Social policy is still largely segmented. Efforts have been made in order to expand coverage; however, its financial sustainability in the context of decreasing levels of Venezuelan aid flows and the largely urban coverage of social programmes (for instance, Usura Cero, Operación Milagro) are challenges for long-term social policy making. Despite economic growth, several social indicators lag behind, and social services are not being upgraded. Social policy effort is uneven. While there have been significant advances in literacy, social security and aspects of food security, per capita expenditure on conventional health and education services remains very low. Big challenges are also reflected in the fragmentation of services, limited cooperation with parts of civil society and insufficient state capacity to implement social and economic programmes, including those aimed at empowering poor rural and urban women. The current political crisis has deeply impacted the economy. The United States passed the Nica Act Law, which includes individual sanctions against high government officials and the conditioning of loans from international financial institutions such as the IMF, World Bank, and Inter-American Development Bank—IADB (Miranda 2018). If implemented, the Nica Act Law could affect public financing and social policy.

To secure stable and sustainable DRM sources, Nicaragua's fiscal regime must be restructured to mobilize resources from the economy's strongest sectors and close existing loopholes like tax exonerations, exemptions and evasion, which reduces revenue collection from the Corporate Income Tax. Improving the tax administration would ensure greater control and capacity to follow up on the universe of contributors. The state has the responsibility of providing transparency to reach a level of legitimacy and accountability, and maintain the trust of its contributors, which will in turn help reduce tax evasion. Progressivity of the tax system must also improve. Even though there has been a small trend towards higher progressivity, additional weight should be given to direct taxes over indirect ones.

Social services also need to improve in terms of access, coverage and quality. Access to health and education data and indicators could play a crucial role by increasing, optimizing and prioritizing social spending in both sectors and engaging civil society actors. Moreover, enhancing the health sector's structure through strong institution building could address problems and provide spaces for state-society dialogue. It is necessary to link DRM strategies to social policy, aiming at crucial and transformative issues such as poverty eradication, enhanced social spending, higher quality of education and health, and the effective empowerment of subaltern groups.

The current top-down approach to governance needs to change and the implementation of social programmes be de-politicized. Social programmes should be granted according to specific socioeconomic needs and inclusive development criteria. Both official and non-official monitoring and evaluation of these programmes should be allowed in order to improve, expand and deepen their impacts. The government should provide a thorough process for state-society negotiations regarding tax reforms, aid allocation and natural resource extraction such as mining. Strong community organizing, coalition building and information sharing by social actors are needed to pressure the government to be inclusive and just in the context of DRM.

In conclusion, the analysis of DRM for social development in Nicaragua reveals that there must be spaces for citizen engagement in determining both the processes of resource mobilization and the distribution of revenues. Further, states must prevent elite's capture of resources and policy influence. States need to be responsive to citizen demands and rights, and ensure that private interests do not impinge on the public interest, placing state-citizen relations above donor-recipient and state-investor ones. For such processes to engender substantive and equitable social development, strong institutional capacity is necessary. In the context of the current political and human rights crisis, justice and compensation of victims by the state will be crucial in order to promote real and meaningful reconciliation. Finally, a negotiated solution between the opposition and the government needs to yield structural transformations to attain real and effective democratization in Nicaragua.

References

Aburto, Wilfredo Miranda. 2015. Gobierno se Retracta: Minería no va en Rancho Grande. *Confidencial*, 12 October. Accessed 7 November 2017. https://confidencial.com.ni/gobierno-se-retracta-mineria-no-va-en-rancho-grande/.

Acevedo, Adolfo. 2005. Nicaragua: Debemos Reclamar, Con Todas Las Voces, la Reestructuración de la Deuda Interna. *Envío* No. 275. Accessed 9 March 2015. http://www.envio.org.ni/articulo/2814.

———. 2011a. *Evolución de la Cooperación Externa 1992–2012*. Mimeo.

———. 2011b. *Hacia un Sistema Tributario con Justicia y Equidad. Análisis del Sistema Tributario y Propuesta para su Transformación*. Report. Accessed 3 September 2014. https://www.ieepp.org/media/files/publicacion-6-142.pdf.

———. 2012. *Sobre la Cooperación de Venezuela y los Programas Sociales del Gobierno*. Mimeo.

Arana, Mario, Juan Sebastián Chamorro, Silvio De Franco, Raul Rivera, and Manuel Rodríguez. 1999. Nicaragua. In *Gasto Público en Servicios Sociales Básicos en América Latina y el Caribe. Análisis desde la Perspectiva de la Iniciativa 20/20*, ed. Enrique Ganuza, Arturo León, and Pablo Sauma, 585–632. Santiago de Chile: United Nations Development Programme/ United Nations Economic Commission for Latin America and the Caribbean/ United Nations Children's Fund.

BCN (Banco Central de Nicaragua). 2016. *Producto Interno Bruto*. Managua: BCN. Accessed 26 February 2016. http://www.bcn.gob.ni/estadisticas/sector_real/produccion/1-1.htm.

Biderman, Jaime. 1983. The Development of Capitalism in Nicaragua: A Political Economic History. *Latin American Perspectives* 10 (1): 7–32.

Borchgrevink, Axel. 2006. *A Study of Civil Society in Nicaragua: A Report Commissioned by Norad.* Norwegian Institute of International Affairs (NUPI) Working Paper No. 699. Oslo: NUPI.

BTI (Bertelsmann Transformation Index). 2014. Nicaragua. Accessed 7 February 2016. http://www.bti-project.org/en/home/.

Carrión, Gloria. 2012. *El Acuerdo de Asociación con la Unión Europea y el ALBA: Dinámicas Político-económicas en Nicaragua.* Cuaderno de Investigación No. 44. Managua: Nitlapan-UCA.

———. 2017. *State-Society and Donor Relations. The Political Economy of Domestic Resource Mobilization in Nicaragua.* PDRM Working Paper No. 2-2017. Geneva: United Nations Research Institute for Social Development.

Central America Data. 2009. Grupo ALBA Compra Gasolineras en Nicaragua. Accessed August 2014. http://www.centralamericadata.com/es/article/home/Grupo_Alba_compra_gasolineras_en_Nicaragua.

CEPAL (Comisión Económica para América Latina y el Caribe). 2009. Dinámica del Gasto Social, las Transferencias Monetarias, y los Programas de Transferencias Condicionadas. *Panorama Social de América Latina.* Accessed 5 March 2015. http://www.cepal.org/es/publicaciones/1232-panorama-social-de-america-latina-2009.

———. 2015. *Bases de Datos y Publicaciones Estadísticas.* CEPALSTAT-CEPAL. Accessed 1 March 2016. http://interwp.cepal.org/cepalstat/WEB_CEPALSTAT/estadisticasIndicadores.asp?idioma=e.

Chamorro, Carlos F., and Carlos Salinas. 2012. Las Cuentas Secretas de Albanisa. *Confidencial.* Accessed 29 September 2015. http://www.confidencial.com.ni/archivos/articulo/7100/las-cuentas-secretas-de-albanisa.

Chamorro, Amalia, and Peter Utting. 2015. *Políticas Públicas para la Economía Social Solidaria: Hacia un Entorno Favorable: El Caso de Nicaragua.* Turin: ILO International Training Centre/International Labour Organisation.

Córdoba, M. 2012. Petrocaribe Saca las Uñas. *El Nuevo Diario.* Accessed 8 April 2014 http://www.elnuevodiario.com.ni/nacionales/248466-petrocaribe-saca/.

Curtis, Emma. 1998. Child Health and the International Monetary Fund: The Nicaraguan Experience. *Lancet* 352 (9140): 1622–1624.

D'Castilla, M. 1999. La Constitución de 1974 (Pacto Somoza-Agüero). *El Nuevo Diario*. Mimeo.

Delmelle, Guy, and René Mendoza. 2017. *Reformas Estatales, Fortalecimiento Institucional y Políticas de Movilización de Recursos en Nicaragua: El Caso del Sector de la Salud.* PDRM Working Paper No. 2017-9. Geneva: United Nations Research Institute for Social Development.

Efe. 2018. Cooperación Venezolana Cae un 85.5% en Primer Semestre de 2018. *Confidencial*, 18 October. Accessed 14 May 2019. https://confidencial.com.ni/cooperacion-venezolana-cae-un-85-5-en-primer-semestre-de-2018/.

El Heraldo. 2010. Venezuela es Dueña de Canal 8 de Nicaragua. Accessed 3 November 2014. http://archivo.elheraldo.hn/Ediciones/2010/01/30/Noticias/Venezuela-es-duena-de-Canal-8-de-Nicaragua.

El Nuevo Diario. 2009. Corrupción en Tiempos del ALBA: Radiografía de un País Recurrentemente Malversado. 22 November. Accessed 1 October 2015. http://www.elnuevodiario.com.ni/nacionales/62395-corrupcion-tiempos-alba/.

Enríquez, Octavio. 2014. El Ordeño de ALBANISA: El Desvío de la Cooperación Venezolana Hacia Negocios Privados. *Confidencial*. Accessed 1 October 2015. http://confidencial.com.ni/archivos/articulo/16446/el039-ordeno-039-de-albanisa.

———. 2015a. El Botín de los Petrodólares: Desvío de Más de 3,000 Millones de Dólares de la Cooperación Venezolana a las Arcas de Ortega. *Confidencial*. Accessed 1 October 2015. http://www.confidencial.com.ni/archivos/articulo/21937/el-quot-botin-quot-de-los-petrodolares.

———. 2015b. La Operación Retorno de DNP: La segunda Red de Gasolineras del País Ahora Forma Parte de Empresas de Familia Presidencial. *Confidencial*. Accessed 1 October 2015. http://www.confidencial.com.ni/archivos/articulo/22083/la-quot-operacion-retorno-quot-de-dnp.

Galeano, Luis. 2009. Intento por Legitimar Operación Petronic. *El Nuevo Diario*. Accessed 20 June 2015. http://archivo.elnuevodiario.com.ni/nacional/270390-intento-legitimar-operacion-petronic/.

Gasparini, Leonardo, and Daniel Artana. 2003. *The Distributional Impact of the Nicaraguan Fiscal Equity Law*. Washington, DC: World Bank. Mimeo.

GEE (Gerencia de Estudios Económicos). 2006. Informe Anual 2005. Banco Central de Nicaragua (BCN). Accessed 15 November 2014. http://www.bcn.gob.ni/publicaciones/periodicidad/anual/informe_anual/2005/informe_anual_2005.pdf.

GIEI (Grupo interdisciplinario de expertos independientes). 2018. *Nicaragua: Informe sobre los Hechos de Violencia Ocurridos entre el 18 de Abril y el 30 de Mayo de 2018*. Report. https://gieinicaragua.org/.

Gobierno de Nicaragua. 2003. *Enfoque Sectorial para la Coordinación Internacional. Documento*. Mimeo.

Grupo Venancias. 2014. *Hambre Cero y el Empoderamiento de las Mujeres: Los Casos de Matiguás, Muy Muy, Río Blanco*. Documento. Mimeo.

Gutiérrez, Hilda. 2015. *Mining and Resource Mobilization: The Case of Nicaragua*. PDRM Working Paper 2015-9. Geneva: United Nations Research Institute for Social Development.

IACHR (Inter-American Commission on Human Rights). 2018. *Gross Human Rights Violations in the Context of Social Protests in Nicaragua*. Organization of American States. Accessed 14 May 2019. https://www.oas.org/en/iachr/reports/pdfs/Nicaragua2018-en.pdf.

IADB (Inter-American Development Bank). 2015. *Cooperación al Desarrollo: Bilaterales*. Washington, DC: IADB. Mimeo.

IEEPP (Instituto de Estudios Estratégicos y Políticas Públicas). 2011. *Hambre Cero: Avances y Desafíos*. Accessed 17 October 2015. http://enlaceacademico.ucr.ac.cr/node/753.

Kester, Paul. 2010. Hambre Cero: ¿Desarrollo o Gotas de Lluvia? *Envío*, 334. Accessed 11 October 2015. http://www.envio.org.ni/articulo/4121.

La Voz del Sandinismo. 2016. Bono Solidario se Incluirá en el Presupuesto a partir del 2014. Accessed 20 April 2016. http://www.lavozdelsandinismo.com/nicaragua/2013-09-12/bono-solidario-se-incluira-en-el-presupuesto-a-partir-del-2014/.

Martínez, Moisés. 2009. USD 50 Millones Pagó el Grupo ALBA por la DNP. *La Prensa*. Accessed 5 May 2014. http://archivo.laprensa.com.ni/archivo/2009/septiembre/07/noticias/nacionales/347927.shtml.

Martínez, Moisés, and Octavio Enríquez. 2012. Impacto Alba Solo en la Fortuna de Ortega. *La Prensa*, 18 October. Accessed 14 March 2015. http://www.laprensa.com.ni/2012/01/18/nacionales/87497-impacto-alba-solo-en-la-fortuna-de-ortega.

Mayorga, Francisco. 2007. *Megacapitales de Nicaragua*. Managua: Ediciones Albertus.

Merril, Tim. 1993. Nicaragua: A Country Study. End of the Anastasio Somoza Debayle Era. Accessed 14 November 2014. http://countrystudies.us/nicaragua/13.htm.

Miranda, Wilfredo. 2018. Congreso Bipartidista Apruebla la Nica Act. *Confidencial*, 11 December. Accessed 14 May 2019. https://confidencial.com.ni/congreso-bipartidista-aprueba-la-nica-act/.

Molina, Roberto. 2017. *The Political Economy of Tax Reforms and the Implications for Social Development in Nicaragua*. PDRM Working Paper No. 7-2017. Geneva: United Nations Research Institute for Social Development.

Navas, Lucía, and Yohany López. 2014. Menos Presupuesto a Programas Sociales. *La Prensa*, 30 October. Accessed 25 April 2016. http://www.laprensa.com.

ni/2014/10/30/nacionales/216424-menos-presupuestoa-programas-sociales-menos-presupuestoa-programas-sociales.

Noticias24. 2008. América Latina: Compara a los Europeos con Moscas que se Paran en la Inmundicia. 22 June. Accessed 21 March 2015. www.noticias24.com/actualidad/noticia/15427/compara-a-los-europeos-con-moscas-que-se-paran-en-la-inmundicia/.

Olivares, Iván. 2016a. Gestión Fraudulenta de Cooperación Venezolana. *Confidencial*. Accessed 20 April 2016. http://confidencial.com.ni/gestion-fraudulenta-cooperacion-venezolana/.

———. 2016b. La alcancía de ALBANISA. *Confidencial*. Accessed 11 April 2016. http://confidencial.com.ni/la-alcancia-de-albanisa/.

Pallais, M. Lourdes. 1990. La Huelga de Nicaragua se Radicaliza con Enfrentamientos Civiles. *El País*, 10 July. Accessed 24 February 2016. http://elpais.com/diario/1990/07/10/internacional/647560818_850215.html.

Portocarrero, Ana Victoria. 2004. ¿A Dónde Van los Fondos HIPC?: Una Cuestión de Prioridades. *El Observador Económico*. Accessed 20 March 2015. http://www.elobservadoreconomico.com/archivo_anterior/152/principal.php.

Potosme, Ramón. 2013. Ejecutivo Legisla. Accessed 1 February 2017. http://www.laprensa.com.ni/2013/02/04/politica/133298-ejecutivo-legisla.

Robinson, William. 1995. Sandinistas Face the Future. *CrossRoads Magazine*. Accessed 24 February 2015. http://www.hartford-hwp.com/archives/47/026.html.

Salinas, Carlos. 2011a. El Destape de las Cuentas de Albanisa. *Confidencial*, 27 December. Accessed 19 November 2014. http://confidencial.com.ni/archivos/articulo/5634/el-destape-de-las-cuentas-de-albanisa.

———. 2011b. Las Empresas del Grupo ALBA. *Confidencial*, 5 March. Accessed 15 February 2015. http://confidencial.com.ni/archivos/articulo/3395/las-empresas-del-grupo-alba.

———. 2011c. Los Negocios Privados de ALBANISA. *Confidencial*, 5 March. Accessed 2 February 2015. http://confidencial.com.ni/archivos/articulo/3394/los-negocios-privados-de-albanisa.

Torres-Rivas, Edelberto. 2011. *Revoluciones sin Cambios Revolucionarios: Ensayos sobre la Crisis en Centroamérica*. Guatemala City: F&G Editores.

Walker, Thomas, and Christine Wade. 2011. *Nicaragua: Living in the Shadow of the Eagle*. Boulder: Westview Press.

World Bank. 2014. *World Development Indicators - Nicaragua*. Washington, DC: World Bank. Accessed 20 October 2017. https://data.worldbank.org/products/wdi

———. 2015. Data: GDP Growth (Annual %). Washington, DC: World Bank. Accessed October 2015. http://data.worldbank.org/indicator/NY.GDP.MKTP.KD.ZG?page=6.

Zaremba, Laura M. 1992. *Nicaragua: Before and After the Revolution*. Honour Thesis. Paper No. 21. Carbondale: Southern Illinois University.

11

The Political Economy of Resource Mobilization for Social Development in Uganda

Anne Mette Kjær and Marianne S. Ulriksen

Introduction[1]

Domestic resource mobilization (DRM) is increasingly regarded as a central element in financing social development as well as broader development goals in the Global South, and for good reasons. As an alternative and complement to aid, the mobilization of domestic resources can bridge critical funding gaps, enhance national ownership, and strengthen citizen influence on the spending priorities of governments, all factors that have the potential of improving social development. As DRM

[1] The authors would like to acknowledge Arlind Grajcevci for excellent research assistance.

A. M. Kjær (✉)
University of Aarhus, Aarhus, Denmark
e-mail: mkjaer@ps.au.dk

M. S. Ulriksen
University of Southern Denmark, Odense, Denmark
e-mail: mu@sam.sdu.dk

K. Hujo (ed.), *The Politics of Domestic Resource Mobilization for Social Development*, Social Policy in a Development Context,
https://doi.org/10.1007/978-3-030-37595-9_11

attracts attention, there is increasing focus on how political dynamics affect taxation and other income generation to the state and how this in turn influences social development. The growing body of literature focuses on revenue bargaining in developing countries and whether a fiscal contract is being established between the states and their citizens (Moore 2008; Prichard 2015).

We establish a broad framework inspired by fiscal contract theory and political settlement theory which helps us point to political economy factors that constitute constraints and opportunities for policy making.[2] A political settlement approach focuses on the balances of power of different groups and interests and thereby brings us closer to the political realities within which revenue bargains are both formal and informal in nature. Based on this theoretical framework, we explore three instances of revenue bargains in Uganda: legislative tax reform, the institutional performance of the Uganda Revenue Authority (URA), and policy making in the field of social policy. The first two instances affect the actual mobilization of resources, whereas the third focuses on bargains over spending priorities within a given revenue base.

In the first case, we analyse how different actors write their voices into legislation through a politicized process of tax reform and tax bargaining. We find that this process results in a taxation system which is not characterized by a strong fiscal contract between state and society. The second case of revenue bargaining illustrates that building institutional capacity to mobilize domestic revenue is difficult due to economic and political constraints. These first two instances of revenue bargaining show that DRM is still a major challenge in Uganda, and that the Ugandan citizens in general have limited influence on policy in their position as taxpayers. In the final part of our analysis, we explore spending priorities and find that decreasing dependence on traditional donors may have increased policy space and thereby allowed the Ugandan government to focus more on promoting its original development vision of industrialization and economic transformation.

[2] Khan 2010, 2012; Mirza and Prichard 2013; Hickey and Gulooba-Mutebi 2013; Kjær 2015.

The Political Economy of Domestic Resource Mobilization in Low-Income Countries

Two strands of literature inform our framework applied to the study of DRM and social spending in Uganda. The first is the literature on political settlements. It argues that socioeconomic structures shape the distribution of power and constitute the conditions under which political factions must gain and maintain power.[3] This distribution of power and the institutions that sustain it define political settlements (Khan 2010). Central to a political settlement is the ruling coalition, which consists of specific groups that either have government power or support and sustain the ruling elite (Whitfield et al. 2015). Such ruling coalitions are maintained through the allocation of resources. Low-income countries are characterized as low-productivity economies with large informal sectors of low-technology agriculture or micro-enterprises (Whitfield et al. 2015). Raising revenues to finance public spending in these settings is challenging, as taxing informal sectors requires extensive administrative capacity and is costly because it requires that each small firm or farm is registered and assessed. Low-income economies also have small national budgets. Political stability in such settings is often maintained by giving political access to the most powerful groups (North et al. 2009) and through rents and patronage.

The second body of literature used in our analytical framework is fiscal contract theory, which points to the importance of bargaining between governments and taxpayers (see Chap. 1 in this volume). The central argument is that when citizens pay tax, they raise demands to get a return for their tax monies.[4] One can therefore speak of revenue bargaining where the government and contributors to revenue negotiate over "returns" for contributions. A "revenue bargain" is not uniformly defined in this literature, but here we use it broadly along the lines of Moore (2008:37–38) to refer to a "wide range of types of (political) exchange, ranging from explicit haggling ('If you do this, I will do that') to indirect, strategic, anticipatory interaction ('Let us announce more public

[3] North et al. 2009; Khan 2010, 2012.

[4] Levi 1988; Ali et al. 2014; Prichard 2015.

spending on health now, in the hope that Parliament will be ready to accept an increase in VAT [value added tax] rates next year')". In other words, a revenue bargain is an explicit or implicit agreement reached between the contributors of government revenue (taxes, fees, royalties, grants) and the government about what to contribute and what to get in return. Revenue bargains can take place in different contexts. Potential contributors may influence the ruling coalition during the legislative process where tax reforms are decided upon, just as they may push public policy spending priorities in directions that favour their own interests and needs. Within the ruling coalition itself, bargains can also affect the institutional performance of tax revenue agencies in their ability to mobilize resources. Hence, bargains are political in nature—different actors seek to further their own interests through negotiations, haggling, and manipulation by various means and in different contexts.

A political settlement approach in combination with fiscal contract theory brings our attention to the political costs of a potential revenue-raising policy. Any initiative that would impinge on an important group's or individual's privileges would invite resistance and could be destabilizing. Those making and implementing policy must consider how an initiative to raise more tax will affect the interests of important supporters of the ruling coalition, and key supporters are likely to want something in return for their (increased) contributions. An important implication of a small budget is that it limits expenditures, so not everyone can have access to social services, infrastructure or other types of public goods and resources. Bargains over revenue and spending policy may therefore involve other forms of allocation, such as positions in government, access to land or the granting of tax exemptions. The outcomes of revenue bargains may cause the government to provide social services or infrastructure from the incomes raised, but bargains may also lead to tax exemptions or the abolition of taxes, whereby governments forgo revenue and therefore have less revenue available for social development or other national development priorities (Hujo 2012).

The scope for mobilizing resources in low-income countries with a small national budget is further circumscribed by the landscape of external actors, who become important partners in providing grants and loans to development projects (Therkildsen 2002; Morrissey 2014). Although international donors weigh recipient countries' national priorities, they also have their own policy priority areas. Thus, international aid agencies are stakeholders in revenue bargaining processes in which they will seek to influence how resources are spent. Ultimately, external actors influence the nature of the political settlements, at least indirectly.

Finally, the introduction of competitive elections has a bearing on the nature of established political settlements and the way ruling elites enter into revenue bargains. Elections are an avenue for ordinary citizens to influence policy as it is assumed that ruling elites will seek to meet voters' demands, such as by providing essential social services (Stasavage 2005; Kjær and Therkildsen 2013). However, elections also open the political space for lower factions in the political settlement, for example, when ruling party members at the local level become important agents in winning votes. This in turn makes elections more costly for the ruling elite as they need to maintain the support of lower-level political factions (Whitfield et al. 2015).

As we shall see in the rest of the chapter, the largely informal structure of Uganda's economy means that raising taxes can be difficult and costly. The ruling coalition in Uganda has become more fragmented as competition among factions has increased. At the same time, the inner circle of the ruling elite has narrowed and the costs of staying in power have increased.[5] It is within this structural, political and economic context that we analyse three different instances of revenue bargains that together affect DRM and the extent to which social development is prioritized in spending decisions. In all three cases we focus on the political aspects of revenue bargains, that is, how different groups within or of importance to the ruling coalition seek to promote their position and/or interests. The first case—the politics of tax reform—analyses the legislative outcomes of revenue bargains between the ruling coalition and potential taxpayers over legislation intended to mobilize domestic resources. The second case—politics of the Uganda Revenue Authority (URA)—focuses on how political bargaining can affect the institutional capacity of Uganda's primary revenue agency to raise domestic resources. The last case—politics of spending—explores how the composition of revenue and the

[5] Barkan 2011; Kjær 2015; Golooba-Mutebi and Hickey 2016.

role of different contributors to revenue affect spending priorities. However, to give sufficient background to the cases, we first describe Uganda's political economy in more detail.

The Ugandan Political Economy as It Affects DRM

The ruling elite in Uganda operates in an economic environment of low domestic revenue and relatively enduring support over time from international aid agencies. The structure of the economy has been transforming slowly, with a growing service sector, while agriculture has declined as proportion of gross domestic product (GDP), as can be seen from Fig. 11.1.

However, the majority of Ugandans are still employed in low-technology agriculture or in small-scale enterprises in the informal sector. As Fig. 11.2 demonstrates, agriculture still makes up 70 per cent of total employment. Services constitute slightly over 20 per cent, while the share

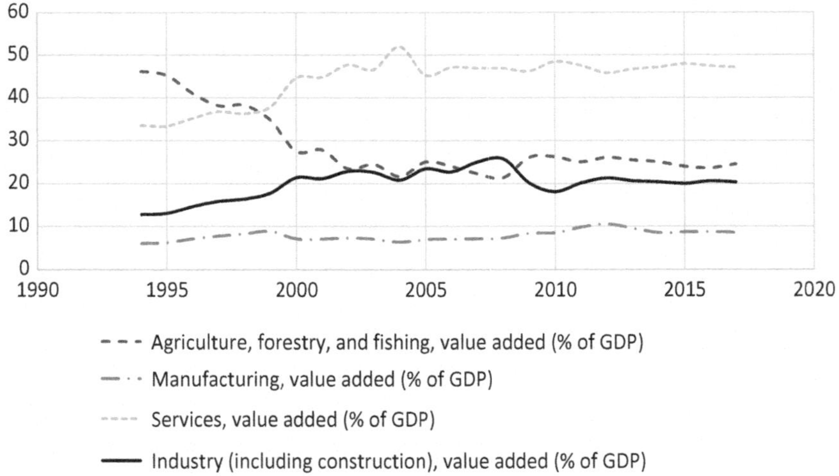

Fig. 11.1 Sectoral composition of GDP (1994–2017). (Source: Author elaboration based on World Bank (2019))

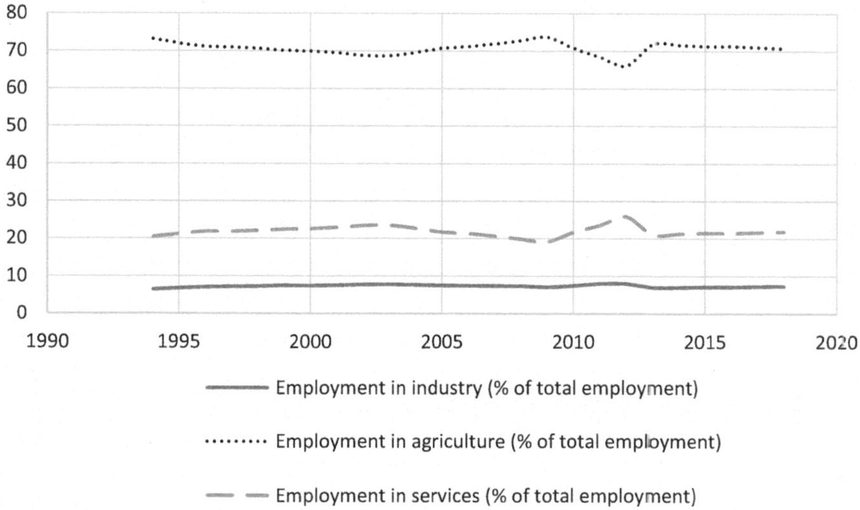

Fig. 11.2 Sectoral composition of employment (1994–2018). (Source: Author elaboration based on World Bank (2019). Note: Modeled ILO estimate)

employed in industry has remained at about 7.3 per cent over the last two decades. This composition of employment naturally reflects the fact that Uganda has a large informal sector, estimated at over 40 per cent of the economy.[6]

This means that the tax base is narrow. Although domestic tax revenues have risen slightly in recent years, to 13.3 per cent of GDP, domestic revenue collection has remained low compared to neighbouring countries (Fig. 11.3).

The nature of Uganda's economy has both direct and indirect implications for DRM. *Directly*, many economic activities are difficult to tax, which is evident from the fact that a relatively large share of revenues comes from international trade taxes (although this has declined) (World Bank 2018). It also means that raising revenue through income taxes, the taxes that historically have helped states and citizens enter into fiscal contracts, is harder. Personal Income Tax makes up 18 per cent of total tax

[6] Some even estimate the informal sector at 48 per cent of GDP (Global Financial Integrity 2018).

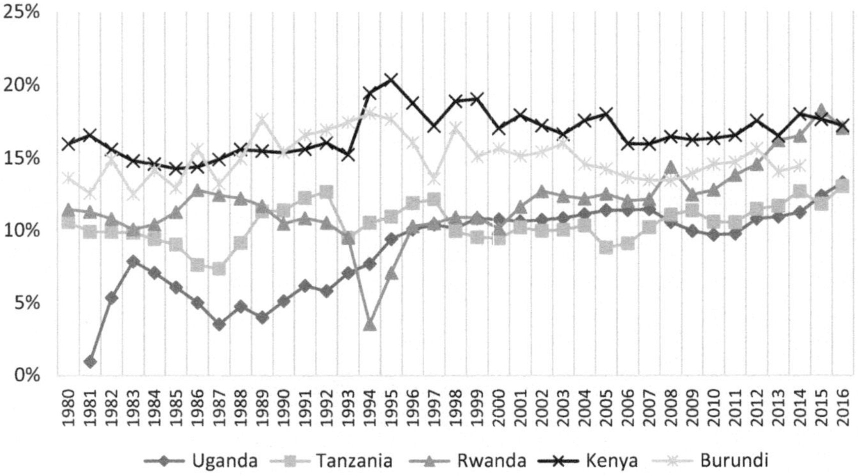

Fig. 11.3 Tax revenue as a percentage of GDP, excluding grants and social contributions, Uganda compared (1980–2016). (Source: Author elaboration based on ICTD (2019))

revenues, which is the lowest proportion in East Africa (World Bank 2018:38).

Indirectly, a poor economy with a large informal sector and a small tax base also has a relatively small budget which is at the same time under a lot of spending pressure. It is not easy to keep promises of better public services under severe budget constraints. Politically, the country is riven by ethno-regional, religious and social cleavages which may often have a greater bearing on political tensions and resource allocations than do economic divisions. These cleavages have made it difficult for post-independence leaders to build stable coalitions because they have had to accommodate a variety of competing factions. The Buganda kingdom, for example, has been one strong faction with which all post-independence leaders have had to deal. The current National Resistance Movement (NRM) regime originally built upon an alliance between key actors from President Museveni's home region of south-western Ankole and key elites of the south-central Buganda region (established before winning the civil war in 1986).

This original alliance ensured the NRM ruling coalition the most stable political settlement in Uganda since independence in 1962. However, the alliance has gradually fallen apart due to deep-seated disagreements over land issues, the status of the kingdom, and the issue of federalism (Lindemann 2011; Goodfellow and Lindemann 2012). Factions from the south-west that used to belong to the NRM have also broken away over the years, including some important military officers. As a result, a number of relatively powerful political factions have been excluded from the ruling coalition, narrowing its base. Thus, although formal political opposition parties are weak, fragmented, and underresourced, the ruling elite is more vulnerable than prior to the breaking away of important factions. Competition among factions *within* the coalition has also increased its vulnerability. There is, today, more resistance against President Museveni and the group around him from within the NRM party, particularly from younger party members who were not part of the National Resistance Army's guerrilla war in the early 1980s. This is perhaps the reason why the regime has become more repressive and on occasion relies on the direct or indirect show of its capacity for coercion. Hickey and Golooba-Mutebi (2013 and Golooba-Mutebi and Hickey 2016) thus call Uganda's political settlement "weak dominant" because of the fact that NRM still dominates but at the same time is fragmented, and there is a lot of internal and external factionalism.

With the introduction of regular elections since 1996 under the movement system and 2006 under a multiparty system, lower-level factions in the ruling coalition have grown stronger because they are necessary to mobilize votes (Kjær and Therkildsen 2013). Local council chairmen at the district and subcounty level who mainly belong to the NRM play especially important roles before elections, and they are able to block or affect the implementation of policies at the local level. At the same time, as the ruling coalition has become more fragmented and to some extent vulnerable, it depends more on its top leadership and the president's ability to control the military and persuade the most powerful factions to remain within the coalition. Winning elections with a considerable margin is important to the ruling government, too, because the regime needs to demonstrate that the opposition does not offer a viable alternative (Kjær and Therkildsen 2013). Juggling factions and election campaigns is costly, and hence, the cost of staying in power has been increasing (Barkan 2011; Kjær and Katusiimeh 2012). This has led to extra-budgetary allocations in terms of both having the parliament pass bills on additional expenses and by way of using funds originally approved for purposes other than election campaigns. The International Monetary Fund (IMF) and the World Bank have expressed concern about fiscal discipline.[7] The 2016 election campaigns were said to be the most costly ever, and the NRM and the president were said to be openly handing out cash, livestock, and vehicles in the campaign (*Africa Confidential* 2016).

Tax Reform Bargains: The Role of Business and Civil Society[8]

In the following, we explore how bargains around tax reform unfold, and we focus the analysis on the role of actual or potential revenue providers—the corporate sector and citizens more broadly. Of course, other actors may influence tax reforms, but their role is not as contributors to government revenue. Members of parliament (MPs) play a role in legal reform as they confirm bills tabled before them. However, although there are examples of MPs critically debating bills and pushing through amendments, the MPs are generally perceived to have limited impact on tax reforms: some amendments to tax laws are not contained in bills discussed in parliament, and MPs may be compromised due to their willingness to receive favours (Kangave and Katusiimeh 2015). The international financial institutions (IFIs) have been key advisors on tax reforms in Uganda, with the IMF providing high-quality technical assistance and know-how in addition to loans. The IMF has been the primary driver of tax reforms on a global scale, and in Africa it has focused on eliminating tariffs and introducing value-added tax (VAT), as well as administrative reforms such as supporting the establishment of semi-autonomous revenue authorities (Fjeldstad and Rakner 2003; Fjeldstad and Moore 2007). Civil society organizations (CSOs) have started to engage with tax issues

[7] Makuma and Akello 2011; Busuulwa 2010; Oketch 2015.

[8] This section is based primarily on the case study report by Kangave and Katusiimeh (2015).

through awareness campaigns and the facilitation of dialogue between government and local community actors. Thus, these actors have some influence on tax reforms. As we are interested in the politics of revenue mobilization, we concentrate on two groups of actors—corporate and civil society—and explore how the business sector and citizens try to influence tax reform processes with the purpose of limiting their own contributions.

The Business Community

Due to the narrow tax base, "the only group visibly affected by the central government tax reforms are the formal business corporations" (Rakner and Gloppen 2003:13). The business community is generally characterized by a few strong "big players" who in negotiations with government pursue objectives that favour the business sector, such as tax exemptions and investments in infrastructure, resulting in lower production costs. As shown in the following (and as further elaborated in Kangave and Katusiimeh 2015), the business sector is able to formally push for tax exemptions, or at least more favourable tax terms, because it is well institutionalized and resourceful. In Uganda, it represents a narrow sector with a common profit motive, which has organized itself in different institutions that can lobby for certain policy reforms or changes. The business sector has the resources to hire tax professionals who understand and navigate the complex laws, and due to the financial or social status of some key members of its group, it can gain audience with the Ministry of Finance Planning and Economic Development (MOFPED) or influence change through the court system.

The business sector has been able to lobby for tax exemptions and reductions of the levels of income tax liability through institutional affiliations or umbrella organizations such as the Private Sector Foundation (PSF), the Uganda Manufacturers Association (UMA), and the National Chamber of Commerce (NCC). For instance, the PSF was able to push for changes in the individual income tax threshold and the elimination of initial allowances under the Income Tax Act (Private Sector Foundation 2009; Government of Uganda 2014).

Many big businesses also pay tax advisors who lobby the MOFPED directly by putting forward proposals that benefit their clients and the sector in general. They convene business forums bringing together their clients, MOFPED, the URA and other interest groups to discuss the concerns of the business sector, and the tax advisors compile reports that they present to the MOFPED for consideration in legal amendments. Around the time of the annual budget speech, tax advisors write articles on tax issues in the business columns of the main newspapers, communicating some of the policy changes that they would advise (Kangave and Katusiimeh 2015:12). However, tax bargains concerning the corporate sector are not one-sided. Sometimes investors and their advisors are approached directly by the MOFPED. For example, before the annual amendments to tax statutes, the MOFPED invites stakeholders such as UMA, PSF, NCC, and accounting firms to provide proposals on the changes that they would like to see in tax laws.

Investors do not only work collectively through their organizations but also engage in individual tax bargains, usually with the aim of receiving tax exemptions. According to Tangri and Mwenda (2013), for example, the VAT exemption on hotels was intended to benefit hotel owners with close political ties to the president, and various local businesses have obtained concessions in the form of tax waivers and exemptions in exchange for financing elections. The auditor general has in a recent report noted how it is possible for the Ministry of Finance to grant unplanned tax exemptions:

> Ministry introduced a policy of paying taxes to URA on behalf of companies in specific sectors such as the steel sector. In addition, the ministry also agreed to settle electricity bills for some firms in the textile industry. However, due to lack of a proper policy, it was observed that incentives are given without accompanying budget provisions and as such, this has always led to creation of domestic arrears under the Ministry. As such, by the close of the 2017/2018 fiscal year, domestic arrears attributable to these incentives had grown to UGX 153 billion[9] up from UGX 83 billion in the previous year, an 83 percent increase. (Government of Uganda 2018b:57)

[9] Equivalent to USD 41 million in 2018.

The URA tries to identify wealthy individuals who either evade taxes or do not pay enough taxes, in order to increase the share of revenue from individual income taxes (Kangave and Katusiimeh 2015). When such individuals have political connections, they may be able to continue evading taxes (such as the hotel owners mentioned above). The URA estimates that out of a sample of 71 government officials who also own businesses, only one was paying income tax (Kangave et al. 2018:12).

In addition to the above formal means of influencing legal change, resistance has also been employed—to a limited extent—by the business community to shift the law. Perhaps the most notable act of contestation was the one-week strike organized through the Uganda Import and Export and Traders Association (UGIETA) against the introduction of VAT in 1996 (Rakner and Gloppen 2003). Partly as a result of the strike, the VAT threshold was increased from UGX 20 million (USD 7734) to UGX 50 million (USD 19,335) (Kangave and Katusiimeh 2015).

The Citizenry[10]

In Uganda, taxation is a policy area where citizens have had very limited direct influence. Most citizens are engaged in informal economic activities, and while there may be a lot of bargaining around various informal payments in that sector, the citizenry has not engaged in direct revenue bargaining with the government. However, they have influenced tax reform in their capacity as voters. Reform and eventual abolition in 2005 of the Graduated Personal Tax is perhaps the best example of how, during election time, local governments are used as sites for political contestation, using local taxes as bait (Fjeldstad and Rakner 2003; Kjær and Therkildsen 2013). The Graduated Personal Tax was the only tax targeting the informal sector, levied on all able-bodied men and women with an income and constituting an important source of revenue for local governments. In 1984, however, citizens rebelled against the Obote II government (1980–1985) because of a tenfold increase in the tax (Mamdani 2008). Later, in the early 1990s, citizens in the eastern part of the country

[10] This section is based on Kangave and Katusiimeh (2015).

staged protests against the tax (Kjær and Therkildsen 2013). In the 2001 election campaign, the incumbent, President Yoweri Museveni, promised to reduce the minimum tax payable from UGX 11,000 (USD 4.3) to UGX 3000 (USD 1.2) per year, a promise which he honoured after the elections. In 2005, as the 2006 elections drew closer, he abolished the tax (Therkildsen 2002).

With the exception of graduated tax, there is little evidence that citizen action has been able to influence on tax reform.[11] The limited engagement with tax issues can be explained by a number of factors. First, taxation is too frequently perceived as a technical issue, which should be handled by experts. Second, taxpayers are often unaware of the magnitude of taxes they pay. Especially in rural areas, many assume that their tax obligations ended with the abolition of graduated tax. Third, there is a tendency for the public to be unsettled more by socio-cultural issues (which are perceived as central to core values) than with tax issues. Fourth, the lack of taxpayer associations and other forms of institutionalization has limited the extent to which ordinary citizens can mobilize around tax issues. As with any amorphous group, non-institutionalized actors are often restricted by an inability to act collectively (Olson 1971; Garay 2007).

While citizens have had limited active engagement with tax issues, we may see a change in their role in the foreseeable future. CSOs working on local government issues are engaging community members in calling for a reintroduction of the graduated tax, as they see it as a positive obligation for the population to increase their productivity and work supply and to demand accountability from governments in return (Kangave and Katusiimeh 2015). They base this on an argument that having to pay this personal tax forces individuals to take a paid job. Women's organizations have made this argument because they believe the abolishment of graduated tax made some men less active in the labour market. Finally, widespread scepticism towards taxes and how they are used may lead citizens to feel that attempts at influence may be futile. The 2017–2018 Afrobarometer survey indicated that 86 per cent of respondents think

[11] However, they may affect the amount of tax collected by trying to avoid paying taxes, such as through informal trading.

rich people can get away with not paying taxes. In addition, 86 per cent (up from 75 per cent in 2014) thinks the government is handling the job of fighting corruption badly or very badly (Afrobarometer 2015, 2018).

In sum, DRM in Uganda has been low but relatively stable for the last two decades, and the country has had some success with the introduction of VAT where contestation has not been strong. Nevertheless, it has been politically difficult to introduce and/or expand taxes. The business sector is well-organized and resourceful, and uses a range of different avenues to lower its tax obligations. Organized citizens may pressure political leaders to abolish unpopular taxes in exchange for votes.

The Uganda Revenue Authority[12]

The central national tax collection institution in Uganda—the URA—has been instrumental in increasing domestic revenues, especially in the early 1990s.

The URA was established in 1991 as a semi-autonomous agency charged with responsibilities of tax administration, including the assessment, collection and accounting for various forms of tax revenue. The operational autonomy for day-to-day affairs was expected to reduce the scope for political interference and allow the URA to collect taxes in accordance with the targets set by the Ministry of Finance. Its semi-autonomous status meant that it was exempted from civil service rules concerning recruitment, retention, pay, and other working conditions, allowing it to recruit internationally at competitive market rates (Robinson 2007; Kangave 2005). The URA also has autonomy in setting all financial policies, with the exception of procurement.

The URA's tax collection ability was impressive initially, with tax revenues growing from 7 per cent of GDP in 1992 to 11 per cent in 1997. Since then, the tax-to-GDP ratio has remained around 11–13 per cent (see Fig. 11.3). The lack of progress from the mid-1990s onwards led to widespread accusations of corruption that resulted in a restructuring of the URA in 2004 (Kagina 2012), reducing the number of departments in

[12] This section builds upon Katusiimeh and Kangave (2015).

order to lower administrative costs and improve efficiency and the quality of services (Kangave 2005). In 2006, the URA developed a modernization plan (2006–2010) to improve its revenue collection. The plan aimed at adopting modern, efficient and effective processes and systems to collect tax and customs revenues, and at achieving a high level of voluntary compliance from taxpayers (Kagina 2012). Subsequently, other reforms were made to URA's operations such as the introduction of an electronic tax administration platform for domestic taxes.

The Difficult Balance Between Autonomy and Political Intervention

Overall, the reforms made within the URA have produced mixed results in terms of the organization's capacity to mobilize revenues. This is because the autonomy and capacity of the URA were also affected by the political priority given to strengthening the institution and its top management. The initial ability of the URA to mobilize domestic resources and revenues was attributable to the general post-war recovery and, more importantly, to the ruling elites' political prioritization of the URA, whereby the institution was given resources and autonomy to improve its organizational operations.

At the time that the URA was established, salaries were radically increased to provide an incentive regime that would be conducive to enhancing productivity and curbing corruption (Therkildsen 2002; Robinson 2007). In 1993, URA staff salaries were higher than for other civil servants. The salary increases arguably improved institutional capacity and employee performance. In contrast, by 2000 the salary scales of URA employees were not much higher than those of other civil service employees, whereas other, more recently established authorities such as the Petroleum Authority, were known to have better paid staff.[13] Specialized skills and institutional knowledge were lost as staff left the URA.

[13] Personal interview by the authors with former URA staff, June 2019.

Staffing of the URA faces a number of shortcomings. The recruitment of staff has not been free from political interference. According to one interview respondent who worked in the URA in the 1990s, "shortly after its establishment, we received lists from the State House about whom to employ".[14] The URA is also considerably understaffed. In a recent study of 15 tax authorities carried out by the African Tax Administration Forum, URA was ranked as the second most understaffed authority (after the Burundi Revenue Authority), with the population to tax administrator ratio being over 6000:1 (Kangave et al. 2018). The technical capacity of staff also faces challenges. The frequent transfer of officials from one office to another means that despite investment in training or capacity building, staff may be transferred just as they are beginning to understand their new roles. In some cases, resources have been spent on external training of an official or a specific role, and the training is not directly applicable to their new role.

The URA also faces political pressure on tax policy implementation. A recent World Bank analysis on domestic revenue mobilization observes that the URA is told to implement a number of tax exemptions (World Bank 2018:xii). Consequently, on the one hand, the URA is given politically set revenue targets (currently of 15 per cent), while on the other hand, the URA is not given optimal conditions under which to reach those targets. The policy discretion to grant exemptions (also noted by the auditor general as mentioned above) also affects the ability of the URA to reach targets. The World Bank report estimates that revenue forgone under the current tax system across all tax sources due to exemptions to be in the range of 4.5–5.0 per cent of GDP in 2016–2017 (World Bank 2018; see also SEATINI 2019).

The ability to balance political pressures depends largely on the top management of the time. Annebrit Aslund, the third Commissioner General of the URA, only served for three years. As one former URA employee explained, "her contract could not be renewed because she wanted to stick to the standards and not listen to the big taxpayers who didn't want to pay tax but instead reported her to President Museveni for killing their businesses" (Katusiimeh and Kangave 2015:6). Allen Kagina,

[14] Personal interview by the authors with former URA staff, January 2019.

who served for ten years as commissioner general (2004–2014), was more successful at accessing the top political leadership to negotiate better conditions for staff and at the same time increase the operational autonomy of the URA. Kagina was able, for example, to ensure better financing of salary increments and thereby enhance the human resource capacity of the URA. The present commissioner general, now in her second term, is reportedly finding it difficult to navigate the many cross-pressures.[15]

To sum up, the case study of the URA shows that even if it is possible to establish institutions to improve tax collection, the functioning of those institutions cannot be seen as separate from a country's political economy. The cross-pressures described above remain, and with the upcoming 2021 elections, political pressure on the revenue authority is not likely to diminish.

Spending Priorities

In a low-income country like Uganda where the pace of structural transformation of the economy is slow, the large majority of the population is taxed only indirectly through consumption taxes such as VAT. Citizens are rarely involved in tax bargains with the government. However, regular elections imply that the ruling party wants to appeal to voters, and especially rural constituencies, for two reasons: the majority live in the rural areas, and the opposition is stronger in the cities which makes it more worthwhile trying to win votes in the rural areas. Foreign aid also plays a significant role, funding a large part of the national budget. In the following, we examine how the government's shifting relationship with aid donors and its reliance on electoral support from citizens are related to changing government spending, focusing specifically on social development spending.[16]

Figures 11.4 and 11.5 illustrate budget allocations to the education and health sectors as indicators of the government's commitment to address social development. Although increasing in absolute terms,

[15] Personal interview by the authors with former URA staff, June 2019.

[16] This section builds partly on Ulriksen and Katusiimeh (2014) and Kjær and Ulriksen (2014).

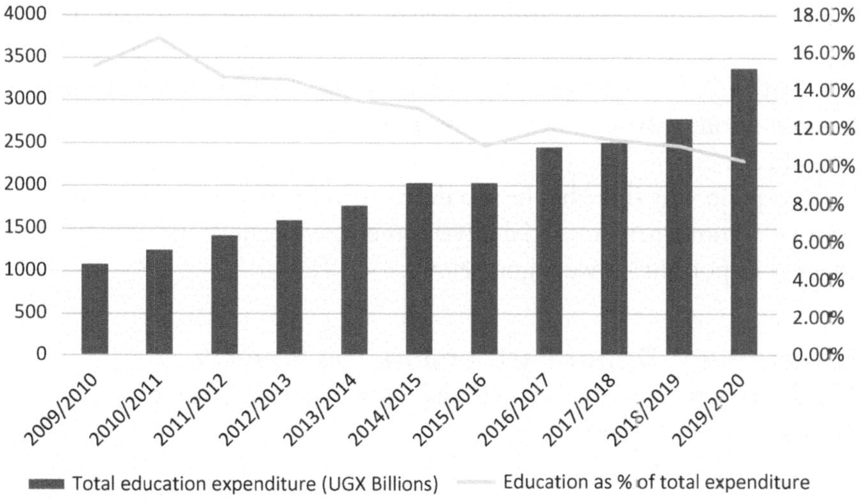

Fig. 11.4 Budget allocation to education (2009/2010–2019/2020). (Source: Author elaboration based on Government of Uganda (2009, 2010a, 2011a, 2012, 2013, 2014, 2015, 2016, 2017, 2018a). Notes: Data for 2019/2020 are an estimate)

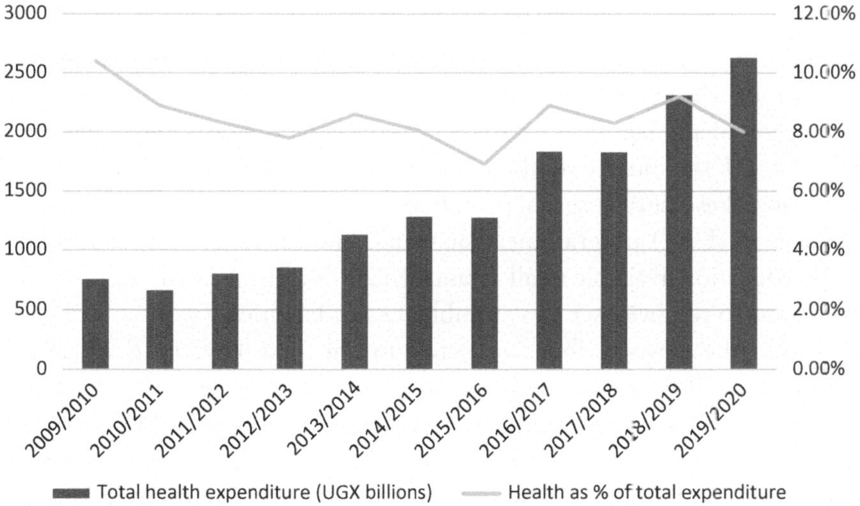

Fig. 11.5 Budget allocation to health (2009/2010–2019/2020). (Source: Author elaboration based on Government of Uganda (2009, 2010a, 2011a, 2012, 2013, 2014, 2015, 2016, 2017, 2018a). Notes: Data for 2019/2020 are an estimate)

budget allocation for education as a share of the total government budget has steadily decreased from 20 per cent in 1999–2000 (DI 2012) to 15 per cent in 2011–2012 and 10 per cent in 2018–2019. Similarly, health has gone from a share of the total budget of 11–12 per cent to 8 per cent (Fig. 11.5).

To explain why there has been a decrease in the Ugandan government's relative commitment to social development, we believe increased policy space is important, as we argue below.

Government-Donor Partnership, the Poverty Eradication Action Plan (PEAP) and Subsequent Development Plans[17]

The 1996 elections significantly shifted the government's focus towards poverty eradication and social programmes. The government's explicit priority until then had been infrastructure and industrialization (Museveni 1992; Kjær and Muhumuza 2009). Several observers noted that the president's campaign tours prior to the elections alerted him that poverty was widespread (Stasavage 2004). The dominance of user fees to access even basic health services and primary education was deeply resented by the population (Mugaju 1996), and the Museveni government realized that expansion of and better access to social services would be popular and help win votes (Kjær and Therkildsen 2013). Thus, in the hotly contested 1996 elections, President Museveni promised to implement a Universal Primary Education (UPE) programme that would abolish school fees and make basic education available to all (Stasavage 2005). In the 2001 elections, he promised to remove user fees at public health facilities.

While the poverty focus reflected in the first Poverty Eradication Action Plan (PEAP) was largely a result of the elite's perception of the popularity of social programmes, donor pressure also played a role (Kjær and Muhumuza 2009). The PEAP contained several priorities, with social spending and generally pro-poor spending being high on the list (Oxford Policy Management 2008:12). The Poverty Action Fund (PAF)

[17] This section is based primarily upon Kjær and Ulriksen (2014).

was set up to protect funding for pro-poor purposes by ring-fencing budget allocations for sectors such as health, education, as well as rural water and sanitation services.

The increasing expenditure required under PEAP was financed by foreign aid as well as debt relief through the Heavily Indebted Poor Countries (HIPC) initiative for which Uganda became eligible in 1998. Although the original purpose of the PAF was to create a transparent mechanism for ensuring that all resources saved from the HIPC initiative were channelled to poverty eradication programmes, the PAF also "attracted additional donor funding for poverty programmes over and above the regular donor programmes" (Kutesa et al. 2006:11). Most notable among the PEAP programmes were the above-mentioned provision of and access to basic social services, such as the Universal Primary Education programme of 1996–1997 and the reforms in basic health care in 2001 (Kjær and Ulriksen 2014).

Reflecting the political elite's priority of social spending, government expenditures (excluding aid) increased for all PEAP priority areas, and the education and health sectors were the larger programmes in terms of budget allocation. Donors were important partners in financing social development although the government's own commitments also increased in this period: domestic allocations to the UPE went from 57 per cent of the education budget to 68 per cent (from 1997–1998 to 2005–2006), and to primary health care the government allocation went from 8 per cent to 85 per cent of the health budget (Hedger et al. 2010).

Greater Governmental Policy Space and Shifting Priorities

In the new millennium, we observe an increased autonomy on the part of the Ugandan government vis-à-vis traditional donors. This is due to several developments, the most important being the emergence of other sources of income, less dependence on Organisation for Economic Co-operation and Development's Development Assistance Committee (OECD DAC) aid, and less amicable relations with the Western donors. As Fig. 11.6 shows, the proportion of aid grants to total revenue declined

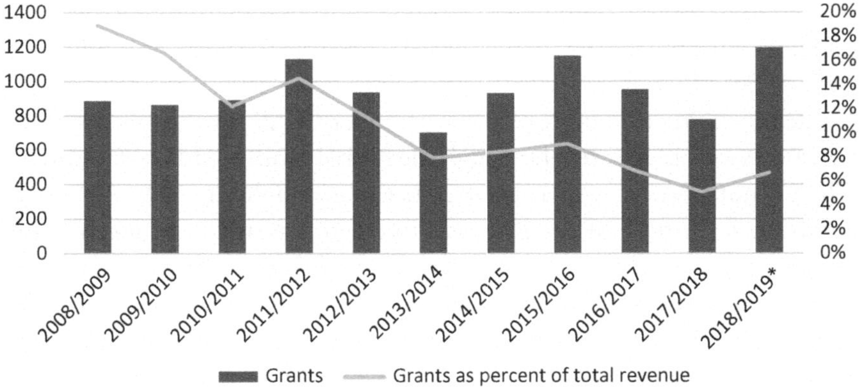

Fig. 11.6 Grants to Uganda (current UGX billions) and as proportion of total revenue (2008/2009–2018/2019). (Source: Author elaboration based on Government of Uganda (2009, 2010a, 2011a, 2012, 2013, 2014, 2015, 2016, 2017, 2018a). Notes: *Data for 2019 are an estimate)

in the decade from 2008 to 2018. During this period, oil was discovered, and preparations are currently under way to extract it. A pipeline is planned through Tanzania, and a refinery is under construction in the Hoima region of Uganda. Even though oil has not yet been pumped, some revenues from the sector in the form of stamp duties and other fees have been raised. The promise of future oil revenues may be behind higher government borrowing as well, which has led to rising public debt (World Bank 2018).

During the mid-2000s, the government's relationship with Western donors worsened somewhat. This was partly due to some big corruption cases, including one in the prime minister's office and another involving a Global Fund for Health allocation (Tangri and Mwenda 2013). Yet the security imperative, and the fact that Uganda is considered an ally in the fight against terrorism, have arguably given the Ugandan government increased policy space, as Western donors have moderated their responses to bad governance (Fisher 2012). Finally, Uganda also receives loans and investments from non-Western donors, most significantly from China, which does not necessarily seek to promote social spending via its financial investments (Guloba et al. 2010).

The changing revenue-policy space that the ruling elite operates in has allowed it to re-prioritize other spending categories apart from social spending, a return to its previous developmental agenda targeted at a structural transformation of the economy as a pre-condition for greater social investments (Kjær and Muhumuza, 2009). In breaking with the past focus on poverty eradication, the government's current overall development framework is Vision 2040, through which the government aims to develop "a transformed Ugandan society from a peasant to a modern and prosperous country within thirty years" (Government of Uganda 2011b:3), reaching annual per capita income of USD 9500 by 2040.

In order to reach the aims of Vision 2040, five-year development plans are made, and the first National Development Plan (NDP) was presented in 2010 (Government of Uganda 2010b).[18] In the plan, a strategy was laid out to address key constraints to transform the economy. A mixed economy approach is adopted, and key priority areas are infrastructure development, human resource development, promotion of science, technology and innovation, and facilitating availability and access to critical production inputs. The strategy also mentions targeted initiatives to promote industry and the development of technological capabilities in Uganda. "The plan is to maximize future revenues from the oil industry and utilize them for high return public investments in the longer term" (Government of Uganda 2010b:54). The focus on structural transformation of the economy is also underlined in the second development plan (Government of Uganda 2015), titled *Strengthening Uganda's Competitiveness for Sustainable Wealth Creation, Employment, and Inclusive Growth*. The transformation agenda contrasts with the focus on services and poverty reduction in the PEAP years. For example, the title of the 2000–2001 Background to the Budget document was *Increasing Efficiency in Poverty Reduction Service Delivery* (Government of Uganda 2000).

The high priority given to economic transformation is also visible in budget allocations. Between 2008–2009 and 2016–2017, the "road and works" sector's share of total government expenditure increased from 13.7 per cent to 15.6 per cent, and the sector now receives larger relative

[18] While the Vision 2040 document was published in 2011 (Government of Uganda 2011b), some of its key ideas already formed part of the NDP presented in 2010.

Table 11.1 Consolidated expenditures for selected sectors, excluding donor projects, as percentage of total government budget (2008–2009, 2010–2011, 2012–2013, 2014–2015, and 2017–2018)

	2008–2009	2010–2011	2012–2013	2014–2015	2017–2018
Education	17.1	14.1	17.0	15.4	13.4
Health	8.5	7.3	7.8	6.6	6.4
Social development	0.5	0.3	0.4	0.7	1.0
Agriculture	3.9	3.6	3.3	3.4	4.0
Roads and works	13.7	9.5	15.1	16.8	15.6
Public administration	14.4	15.7	14.4	13.4	11.4
Parliament	2.7	2.0	2.9	2.9	3.7
Security	12.9	20.9	9.5	9.8	9.8
Energy and minerals	2.8	4.7	1.5	2.0	2.7

Source: Author elaboration based on Government of Uganda (2008, 2010a, 2012, 2014, 2017)

shares than education. Spending on education and health have both dropped somewhat and although there is a slight increase in social protection[19] spending, this sector is still at a very low level of 1 per cent of total government spending (Table 11.1).

This change in policy priorities towards industrial policy, infrastructure and energy sectors is very much in line with the initial focus of the NRM government on industrialization and structural change of the economy. It is also in line with a change that is observable in other African countries and which has shaped debates on the 2030 Agenda for Sustainable Development (Abugre and Ndomo 2014). It is probable that the policy change has been possible because the NRM government has been able to act more independently from the donor community. Thus, starting already with the 2006 elections, the government gradually moved away from the PEAPs and instead, with limited external inputs, developed the National Development Plan to reflect the new policy directions.

The declining priority of education and health services may be the reason why Ugandan citizens, according to the Afrobarometer survey, perceive services as having deteriorated. In 1999, 25 per cent of citizens

[19] Termed social development in the budget.

said the government was handling the improvement of health services very badly or fairly badly, which grew to 55 per cent in 2017. In terms of addressing educational needs, this opinion grew from 11 per cent to 46 per cent (Afrobarometer 2015, 2018).

Conclusion

In this chapter, we set out to examine how political economy factors affect revenue raising and spending priorities in Uganda. We established a broad theoretical framework, inspired by the fiscal contract literature and political settlement theory, within which we explored different instances of revenue bargaining. Within a fragmented political settlement, it is a challenge to increase domestic revenue collection. There are further constraints such as a large informal sector and political pressure to introduce exemptions and lower tax rates at election time. The URA has built up some institutional capacity and is making efforts to expand the tax base. To the extent that it enjoys formal autonomy from political intervention, the URA has been able to take some initiatives in that direction, but as the analysis has shown, URA operates at cross-pressure and whether it manages to navigate in this terrain depends to a large extent on the serving commissioner general at the time.

Domestic civil society actors influence tax policy decisions to a limited extent, even if there are signs that tax associations are being formed and are increasingly vocal. It is also a challenge to increase social spending with a limited national budget where the spending pressures are high. Within this context, changes have, however, taken place. The Ugandan government has become gradually less dependent on aid, and the promise of oil revenues, however delayed they may be, in addition to increased loans and grants from Chinese partners, appear to have affected government priorities. The government is less accommodating to the traditional Western-based donors. One of the implications seems to be that the Ugandan government returned to its original focus on transforming the economy, and less on the social sectors. While this is a legitimate priority based on a vision of structural transformation prior to social development, it does not help to promote a fiscal contract where there is a sense of quid pro quo. Ugandans' perception of the government's ability to provide services has thus declined, according to the Afrobarometer (2015, 2018). These political economy features on the revenue and spending sides make for a very weak fiscal contract in the sense where taxes are paid and reciprocity exists in terms of a return to the citizens.

The increasing attention to DRM in low-income, aid-dependent countries is a promising agenda for sustainable development. However, to fully appreciate the opportunities and challenges in raising revenue for social spending, it is critical to understand the political structures and bargains that take place in resource-constrained electoral democracies. Domestic policy makers may objectively agree that improving the tax system to raise revenue is a worthwhile pursuit, but their attention to policy is marked by their need to remain in power. Hence, revenue raising is strongly linked to government spending priorities, which may favour sectoral or individual interests rather than the broader population through social spending. A political economy analysis, based on the political settlement theory, thus allows us to discern the dynamics behind domestic policy making with respect to both social spending and resource mobilization, which in turn provides the opportunity to consider options for policy reform that take into account the varied political interests of key domestic stakeholders.

Our findings suggest that given Uganda's current political economy, it is not straightforward to increase financing for social spending. The URA has taken interesting initiatives to increase DRM in recent years, for example by attempting to identify and tax high net worth individuals (Kangave et al. 2018). It is still to be seen whether such attempts will lead to increased revenue mobilization. It also remains to be seen whether increased revenues will then translate into increased social expenditure, given the many pressures on the budget in general and the current policy prioritization of infrastructural improvements. In the long run, however, a gradual structural transformation of the economy would lead to an expanded revenue base. Combined with electoral pressures for public goods, this could lead to more public debate and higher prioritization of social spending.

References

Abugre, Charles, and Atieno Ndomo. 2014. *Financing Africa's Post-2015 Development Agenda*. Nairobi: UN Regional Office. Accessed 25 April 2016. http://africainequalities.org/wp-content/uploads/2014/03/AF_Financing-Africas-Post2015.pdf.

Africa Confidential. 2016. Uganda. How the Next Election Will Be Won. *Africa Confidential* 57: 3.

Afrobarometer. 2015. Round 6 Data. Accessed 30 September 2019. http://afrobarometer.org/data/uganda-round-6-data-2015.

———. 2018. Round 7 Data. Accessed 30 September 2019. http://afrobarometer.org/data/uganda-round-7-data.

Ali, Merima, Odd-Helge Fjeldstad, and Ingrid H. Sjursen. 2014. To Pay or Not to Pay? Citizens' Attitudes Towards Taxation in Kenya, Tanzania, Uganda and South Africa. *World Development* 64: 828–842.

Barkan, Joel D. 2011. *Uganda: Assessing Risks to Stability. CSIS Report*. Washington, DC: Center for Strategic and International Studies.

Busuulwa, Bernard. 2010. IMF Warns Uganda of Fallout from EU Debt Crisis. *The East African*, 21 June. Accessed 25 April 2016. http://www.theeastafrican.co.ke/news/IMF-warns-Uganda-of-fallout-from-EU-debt-crisis/-/2558/942384/-/item/0/-/lvmiep/-/index.html.

DI (Development Initiatives). 2012. *Uganda: Resources for Poverty Eradication: A Background Paper*. Bristol: DI.

Fisher, Jonathan. 2012. Managing Donor Perceptions: Conceptualizing Uganda's 2007 Intervention in Somalia. *African Affairs* 111 (444): 404–423.

Fjeldstad, Odd-Helge, and Mick Moore. 2007. *Taxation and State Building: Poor Countries in a Globalised World*. CMI Working Paper No. 11. Bergen: Chr. Michelsen Institute.

Fjeldstad, Odd-Helge, and Lise Rakner. 2003. *Taxation and Tax Reforms in Developing Countries: Illustrations from Sub-Saharan Africa*. CMI Report No. 2006-6. Bergen: Chr. Michelsen Institute.

Garay, Candelaria. 2007. Social Policy and Collective Action: Unemployed Workers, Community Associations, and Protest in Argentina. *Politics & Society* 35 (2): 301–328.

Global Financial Integrity. 2018. A Scoping Study of Illicit Financial Flows Impacting Uganda. Accessed 30 September 2019. https://gfintegrity.org/report/a-scoping-study-of-illicit-financial-flows-impacting-uganda/.

Golooba-Mutebi, Frederick, and Sam Hickey. 2016. The Master of Institutional Multiplicity? The Shifting Politics of Regime Survival, State-Building and Democratization in Museveni's Uganda. *Journal of Eastern African Studies* 10 (4): 601–618.

Goodfellow, Tom, and Stefan Lindemann. 2012. The Clash of Institutions: Traditional Authority, Conflict and the Failure of Hybridity in Buganda. *Commonwealth and Comparative Politics* 51 (1): 3–26.

Government of Uganda. 2000. *Background to the Budget, 2000/01*. Kampala: Ministry of Finance, Planning and Economic Development.

———. 2008. *Background to the Budget: 2008/2009 Fiscal Year*. Kampala: Ministry of Finance, Planning, and Economic Development.

———. 2009. *Background to the Budget: 2009/2010 Fiscal Year*. Kampala: Ministry of Finance, Planning, and Economic Development.

———. 2010a. *Background to the Budget: 2010/2011 Fiscal Year*. Kampala: Ministry of Finance, Planning, and Economic Development.

———. 2010b. *National Development Plan*. Kampala.

———. 2011a. *Background to the Budget: 2011/2012 Fiscal Year*. Kampala: Ministry of Finance, Planning, and Economic Development.

———. 2011b. *Vision 2040*. Kampala: Government of Uganda.

———. 2012. *Background to the Budget: 2012/2013 Fiscal Year*. Kampala: Ministry of Finance, Planning, and Economic Development.

———. 2013. *Background to the Budget: 2013/2014 Fiscal Year*. Kampala: Ministry of Finance, Planning, and Economic Development.

———. 2014. *Background to the Budget 2014/15*. Kampala: Ministry of Finance, Planning, and Economic Development.

———. 2015. Second National Development Plan (NDPII).

———. 2016. *Background to the Budget: Fiscal Year 2016/17*. Kampala: Ministry of Finance, Planning, and Economic Development.

———. 2017. *Background to the Budget: Fiscal Year 2017/18*. Kampala: Ministry of Finance, Planning, and Economic Development.

———. 2018a. *Background to the Budget: Fiscal Year 2018/19*. Kampala: Ministry of Finance, Planning, and Economic Development.

———. 2018b. *Report of the Auditor General for the Financial Year Ending 2018*. Kampala: Office of the Auditor General.

Guloba, Madina, Nicholas Kilimani, and Winnie Nabiddo. 2010. *Impact of China-Africa Aid Relations: A Case Study of Uganda*. Final Report submitted to the African Economic Research Consortium (AERC). Kampala: Economic Policy Research Centre.

Hedger, Edward, Tim Williamson, Tom Muzoora, and Justina Stroh. 2010. *Sector Budget Support in Practice, Case Study, Education Sector in Uganda*. Case Study Report. London/Oxford: Overseas Development Institute/Mokoro.

Hickey, Sam, and Frederick Gulooba-Mutebi. 2013. *Investigating the Links between Political Settlements and Inclusive Development in Uganda: Towards a Research Agenda*. Working Paper No. 20. Manchester: Effective States and Inclusive Development Research Centre.

Hujo, Katja, ed. 2012. *Mineral Rents and the Financing of Social Policy: Opportunities and Challenges*. Basingstoke: Palgrave Macmillan and United Nations Research Institute for Social Development.

ICTD (International Centre for Tax and Development). 2019. ICTD Government Revenue Dataset 2019. Accessed September 2019. www.ictd.ac/en/node/436/#Dataset.

Kagina, Allen. 2012. *Aid as a Catalyst to Increase Domestic Revenue Mobilization in Sub-Saharan Africa*. Background Study for the 2012 DCF-Aid as a Catalyst. New York: United Nations Economic and Social Council.

Kangave, Jalia. 2005. Improving Tax Administration: A Case Study of the Uganda Revenue Authority. *Journal of African Law* 49 (2): 145–176.

Kangave, Jalia, and Mesharch Katusiimeh. 2015. *Tax Bargains: Understanding the Role Played by Public and Private Actors in Influencing Tax Policy Reform in Uganda*. PDRM Working Paper No. 2015-2. Geneva: United Nations Research Institute for Social Development.

Kangave, Jalia, Susan Nakato, Ronald Waiswa, Milly Naklukwago, and Patrick Lumala Zzimbe, 2018. *What Can We Learn from the Uganda Revenue Authority's Approach to Taxing High Net Worth Individuals?* ICTD Working Paper No. 72. Brighton: International Centre for Tax and Development.

Katusiimeh, Mescharch, and Jalia Kangave. 2015. *Politics and Organizational Capacities of Selected Key Fiscal and Social Institutions in Uganda*. PDRM Working Paper No. 2015-12. Geneva: United Nations Research Institute for Social Development.

Khan, Mushtaq H. 2010. *Political Settlements and the Governance of Growth-enhancing Institutions*. SOAS Working Paper. London: School of Oriental and African Studies, London University.

———. 2012. Governance and Growth: History, Ideology, and Methods of Proof. In *Good Growth and Governance in Africa: Rethinking Development Strategies*, ed. Agbar Noman, Kwesi Botchwey, Howard Stein, and Joseph Stiglitz, 51–80. Oxford: Oxford University Press.

Kjær, Anne Mette. 2015. Political Settlements and Productive Sector Policies: Understanding Sector Differences in Uganda. *World Development* 68: s. 230–241. https://doi.org/10.1016/j.worlddev.2014.12.004.

Kjær, Anne Mette, and Mesharch Katusiimeh. 2012. *Political Settlements, Growth, and the Lack of Structural Transformation in Uganda*. DIIS Working Paper. Copenhagen: Danish Institute for International Studies.

Kjær, Anne Mette, and Fred Muhumuza. 2009. *The New Poverty Agenda in Uganda*. DIIS Working Paper. Copenhagen: Danish Institute for International Studies.

Kjær, Anne Mette, and Ole Therkildsen. 2013. Elections and Landmark Policies in Uganda and Tanzania. *Democratization* 40 (4): 592–614.

Kjær, Anne Mette, and Marianne S. Ulriksen. 2014. *From Consensus to Contention: Changing Revenue and Policy Dynamics in Uganda*. PDRM Working Paper No. 2014-21. Geneva: United Nations Research Institute for Social Development.

Kutesa, Florence, Ishmael Magona, Maris Wanyera, and James Wokadala. 2006. Uganda: A Decade of Budget Reform and Poverty Reduction. *OECD Journal of Budgeting* 6 (2): 1–25.

Levi, Margaret. 1988. *Of Rule and Revenue*. Berkeley: University of California Press.

Lindemann, Stefan. 2011. Just Another Change of Guard? Broad-based Politics and Civil War in Museveni's Uganda. *African Affairs* 110 (440): 387–416.

Makuma, Rukiya, and Joan Akello. 2011. Post-Election Economic Woes. *The Independent*, 18 March. Accessed 25 April 2016. http://allafrica.com/stories/201103190112.html.

Mamdani, Mahmood. 2008. A Response to Critics. *Development and Change* 22 (2): 351–366.

Mirza, Hassan, and Wilson Prichard. 2013. *The Political Economy of Tax Reform in Bangladesh: Political Settlements, Informal Institutions and the Negotiation of Reform*. ICTD Working Paper No. 14. Brighton: International Centre for Tax and Development.

Moore, Mick. 2008. Between Coercion and Contract: Competing Narratives on Taxation and Governance. In *Taxation and State-Building in Developing Countries. Capacity and Consent*, ed. D. Brautigam, O.H. Fjeldstad, and M. Moore, 34–63. Cambridge: Cambridge University Press.

Morrissey, Oliver. 2014. Aid and Government Fiscal Behavior: Assessing Recent Evidence. *World Development* 69: 98–105.

Mugaju, Justus B., ed. 1996. *An Analytical Review of Uganda's Decade of Reforms, 1986–1996*. Kampala: Fountain Publishers.

Museveni, Yoweri. 1992. *What Is Africa's Problem?* Kampala: NRM Publications.

North, Douglass C., J.J. Wallis, and B.R. Weingast. 2009. *Violence and Social Orders: A Conceptual Framework for Interpreting Human History*. Cambridge: Cambridge University Press.

Oketch, Martin Luther. 2015. IMF Warns on Elections Cash. *The Monitor*, 13 July. Accessed 25 April 2016. http://www.monitor.co.ug/Business/IMF-warns-elections-cash/-/688322/2786824/-/wthb2xz/-/index.html.

Olson, Mancur. 1971. *The Logic of Collective Action: Public Goods and the Theory of Groups*. Cambridge: Harvard University Press.

Oxford Policy Management. 2008. *Independent Evaluation of Uganda's Poverty Eradication Action Plan (PEAP)*. Oxford: Oxford Policy Management.

Prichard, Wilson. 2015. *Taxation, Responsiveness and Accountability in Sub-Saharan Africa*. Cambridge: Cambridge University Press.

Private Sector Foundation Uganda. 2009. *Widening Uganda's Tax Base and Improving Tax Administration: Final Report*. Kampala: Private Sector Foundation Uganda.

Rakner, Lise, and Siri Gloppen. 2003. Tax Reform and Democratic Accountability in Sub-Saharan Africa. Accessed 14 July 2013. http://www2.ids.ac.uk/gdr/cfs/pdfs/Rakner-Gloppen.pdf.

Robinson, Mark. 2007. The Political Economy of Governance Reforms in Uganda. *Commonwealth & Comparative Politics* 45 (4): 452–474.

SEATINI (Southern and Eastern Africa Trade Information and Negotiations Institute). 2019. *Impact of Harmful Tax Incentives and Exemptions in Uganda*. Report. Kampala: SEATINI/Democratic Governance Facility.

Stasavage, David. 2004. The Role of Democracy in Uganda's Move to Universal Primary Education. *Journal of Modern African Studies* 43 (1): 53–73.

———. 2005. Democracy and Educational Spending in Africa. *American Journal of Political Science* 49 (2): 343–358.

Tangri, Roger, and Andrew M. Mwenda. 2013. *The Politics of Elite Corruption in Africa*. London: Routledge.

Therkildsen, Ole. 2002. Keeping the State Accountable: Is Aid No Better than Oil? *IDS Bulletin* 33 (3): 41–50.

Ulriksen, Marianne, and Mesharch Katusiimeh. 2014. *The History of Resource Mobilization and Social Spending in Uganda*. PDRM Working Paper No. 2014-6. Geneva: United Nations Research Institute for Social Development.

Whitfield, Laurence, Therkildsen Ole, L. Buur, and Anne Mette Kjær. 2015. *The Politics of African Industrial Policy*. Cambridge: Cambridge University Press.

World Bank. 2018. *Financing Growth and Development. Options for Raising More Domestic Revenues*. Uganda Economic Update No. 11. Washington, DC: World Bank.

———. 2019. *World Development Indicators*. Washington, DC: World Bank. Accessed August 2019. http://data.worldbank.org/data-catalog/world-development-indicators.

12

The Politics of Resource Bargaining, Social Relations and Institutional Development in Zimbabwe Since Independence

Richard Saunders

Introduction

If successful models of domestic resource mobilization (DRM) in the Global South rest on the pillars of stable economic growth, state capacity for collecting and distributing revenues, and mechanisms enabling effective and inclusive participation of citizens in shaping the priorities of social investment, then Zimbabwe appeared well-placed in 1980 to succeed as a newly independent African country.[1] Having commenced

[1] This chapter draws on the findings of three United Nations Research Institute for Social Development (UNRISD) working papers and unpublished research commissioned for the Zimbabwe study; see Saunders (2017, 2018) and Mate (2018). Key research sources included

R. Saunders (✉)
York University, Toronto, ON, Canada

Department of Anthropology and Development Studies,
University of Johannesburg, Johannesburg, South Africa
e-mail: rsaunder@yorku.ca

K. Hujo (ed.), *The Politics of Domestic Resource Mobilization for Social Development*,
Social Policy in a Development Context,
https://doi.org/10.1007/978-3-030-37595-9_12

independence with a diversified formal economy, strong state institutions and a government backed by a broad consensus around the need for expansive and sustainable social investment, the prospects for a domestically driven, large-scale pro-poor development programme seemed bright. Nearly 40 years later, however, the reality of Zimbabwe's overall *anti*-developmental trajectory is more readily visible, punctuated by the withering of state institutions, the dramatic contraction of the formal economy, and the increasing fragility of both social investment and the livelihoods of most Zimbabweans. The contradictory nature of the country's development path is especially reflected in the experiences of the 2000s. The site of several innovative and enduring experiments in revenue generation in the midst of economic crisis, Zimbabwe simultaneously witnessed excessive elite rent-seeking, spiralling debt dependence and severe decay in social services. This toxic mix of circumstances was the culmination of successive failed DRM strategies since the 1980s.

This chapter argues that understanding the obstacles and opportunities for Zimbabwe's current political, social and economic recovery requires an appreciation of the uneven and contradictory interests, powers and objectives bound up in DRM frameworks since independence. Such dynamics extend beyond the realm of "elite interests," "political settlements" and "market imperatives," to include questions of institutional autonomy and integrity, elite coherence and inequities of participation among social stakeholders. The paradoxes at the heart of Zimbabwe's recent development dilemmas—a capacitated state wracked by low policy autonomy and fragmented coherence; a highly organized society whose engagements with government have often been instrumentalized by the latter—demand a careful consideration of both the dynamics, trajectories and constraints of resource bargaining, and the politics of DRM more broadly.

In recent years, DRM has attracted increasing attention as a source of finance for social and development spending by governments in the Global South. In a period of unsteady and unpredictable aid flows, rising

official policy, budget and report documents issued by government departments and statutory institutions. Reports and research produced by business, civil society, donor institutions, media and academic researchers are also cited. Interviews for the working papers by the UNRISD Zimbabwe project team were conducted in 2013–2016 with government officials, business representatives, civil society actors and key informants for case studies.

national demands for fiscal accountability and greater policy ownership and direction in the social sector, DRM has been seen by researchers and policy makers as an important alternative and complement to donor-derived development finance (Chap. 2 in this volume). But while DRM's political and developmental benefits have been suggested by researchers, evidence concerning the dynamics, opportunities and limitations of DRM in practice remains weak. Further investigation of the modalities of DRM initiatives are needed; these include the translation of bargaining processes into enduring practices, the mechanisms developed for ensuring the effective inclusion of disparate social constituencies, and the innovations undertaken to strengthen institutional capacity for managing and adapting DRM frameworks (Prichard 2015; Moore 2013).

The Zimbabwean case raises critical questions about the relative impact of institutional integrity, bargaining relationships among key actors, and national politics in the shaping of DRM strategies and outcomes. In this sense, the study expands the scope of inquiry beyond questions of elite-focused "political settlements."[2] It recognises the important contributions of significant other interests active in Zimbabwean public debates, such as business associations, labour movement organizations and civil society groups, and donors, among others, and acknowledges the impact of institutional fragmentation, economic shocks and instability stemming from elite interventions. The findings underscore the negative repercussions of state capture and weakened bureaucratic policy autonomy for resource bargaining, sustained revenue mobilization and social spending outcomes. At the same time, in contrast, the study identifies the benefits accruing from more transparent and inclusive forms of revenue mobilization, involving a wide array of social and economic actors. Evidence of the complex relationship between politics and DRM suggests the need to assess DRM strategies from the perspective of fragmented and contradictory institutions and elites, unevenly empowered stakeholders, and differently scaled focal points of revenue mobilization and spending.

The discussion proceeds by first establishing the political and economic context of DRM in Zimbabwe by means of an account of the early post-independence period and its social and economic reforms. The study

[2] For example, Bebbington et al. (2018), Whitfield et al. (2015) and Khan (2010).

then examines the impact of neoliberal restructuring on state-society relations and government's DRM strategy. The primary focus of the discussion is the period of political and economic crisis in the 2000s, during which a variety of DRM innovations emerged in response to diverse fiscal, political and social challenges. Three case studies from this more recent phase of policy making illuminate the multiple and competing factors which shaped the elaboration and implementation of various DRM approaches, and allow an assessment of the evolving nature of institutional, resource bargaining and state-citizen relations in a period of crisis. The conclusion draws on the lessons from four decades of DRM experimentation to recommend research and policy priorities moving forward.

The Political and Economic Context of DRM in Zimbabwe

At independence in 1980, the new Zimbabwe African National Union (Patriotic Front) (ZANU-PF) government led by then-Prime Minister Robert Mugabe was faced with the daunting task of mobilizing resources to fund extensive post-war recovery and development. The 1966–1979 liberation struggle against Rhodesian colonialism had prioritized Africans' demands for access to land, education, health and economic participation, and these goals were placed at the heart of the government's development agenda. The revenue requirements implied by the resulting investments were met by a variety of means, under conditions constrained by the priorities of international donors, the fragile foundations of the post-war Zimbabwean economy and the capacity of the state to raise and administer new revenue. The resulting clash of development objectives and resource mobilization realities produced mixed outcomes that were increasingly (albeit unevenly) shaped by the influence of donors and business. As economic growth became increasingly volatile, buffeted by occasional severe droughts, slumps in international commodity markets and domestic production bottlenecks, capital shortages and weak markets, the state's exposure to the demands of international lenders and the private sector grew. At the same time, the influence of the national labour

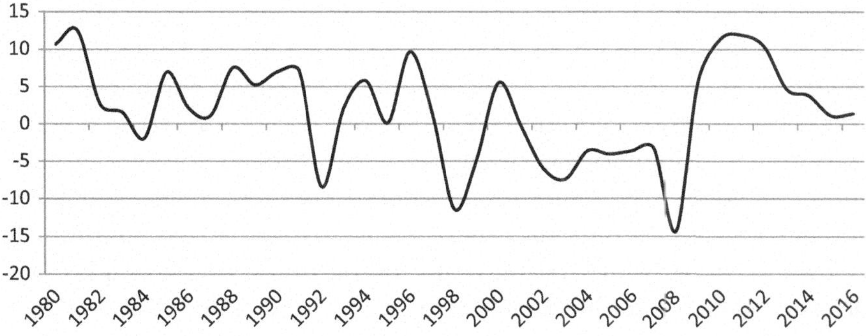

Fig. 12.1 Real GDP growth rate (1980–2016). (Source: ZIMSTAT (various years))

movement and other important social constituencies allied to the ruling party waned. In successive periods, deeper and more extended cycles of economic contraction exacerbated an entrenched pattern of crisis, fiscal vulnerability and policy shifts (see Fig. 12.1).

Donors initially played a central role in the provision of development resources. In 1980 Zimbabwe joined the International Monetary Fund (IMF) and World Bank to qualify for balance of payment support and concessionary loans for financing development programmes. Substantial foreign support was sought via a 1981 donor conference, the Zimbabwe Conference on Reconstruction and Development (ZIMCORD), which saw 31 countries and 26 international organizations pledge USD 2.2 billion (approximately 59.7 per cent of identified requirements), to be disbursed over three years (World Bank 1985). However, ZIMCORD funds were slow to materialize and fell far short of the 1981 pledges. The impact of these shortfalls was exacerbated by a severe drought in 1981–1983 that led to a sharp downturn in growth (Kanyenze 2014). Under pressure from donors, government tightened capital controls, moved to contain social spending and raised short-term taxes to fund its drought relief efforts (Mate 2018).

This early episode of fiscal constraints leading to policy recalibration under conditions of donor and business pressure foreshadowed a recurring pattern of DRM dynamics. The bulk of DRM and development funding in the 1980s relied on formal sector growth, and this proved to be an unstable foundation. Capital and skills shortages, infrastructure gaps and volatile international markets dampened opportunities for growth, while pressing social demands for redistribution limited government's room for manoeuvre. In a fragile business climate and under threat of business crashes, government chose to forego short-term revenue expansion and support the productive sector through a variety of measures, including export incentives, reduced tax rates, grants, soft loans and other means. At the same time, the state maintained its commitment to debt servicing while resisting calls for expansion of real wages. This delicate balancing act in raising revenue to match rising social spending needs and expectations was increasingly destabilized by resource shortfalls, and concerns emerged around the quality, impact and sustainability of social investments (Mate 2018).

By the mid-1980s recurrent expenditure was increasingly funded by borrowing, and government explored options for improving sustainability, equity, revenue growth and tax compliance (Government of Zimbabwe, Commission of Inquiry into Taxation 1986). Under the influence of leading business organizations and donors, a strategy emerged for the widening of the tax base, including the lowering of tax rates on the formal sector, the reduction of pro-poor consumer subsidies and tax exemptions, and stronger efforts to mobilize domestic savings. While these recommendations were strongly resisted by the national labour movement, which had distanced itself from the ruling party by the late 1980s, they served as the basis of tax policy reforms and DRM strategies into the next decade. In 1991 these proposals were consolidated and formalized with government's adoption of the Economic Structural Adjustment Programme (ESAP), a neoliberal development framework which had the strong backing of local business and international donors (Government of Zimbabwe 1991).

ESAP underscored the shift in the centre of gravity of government policy making and marked a profound rupture in the consensus around post-independence social redistribution. Donors and businesses came to exert greater influence, and social policies were increasingly tailored to the needs of the market, particularly foreign interests. New local business players included "indigenous" empowerment associations, which lobbied for government support. With strong connections to

ZANU-PF, indigenous businesspeople became prominent supporters of the party's neoliberal turn. Conversely, labour came under attack from the state, and popular social constituencies previously allied with the ruling party distanced themselves (Bond and Saunders 2005). The labour movement led criticisms of ESAP, driven by a wave of labour militancy, leading to the establishment in 1998 of the Tripartite Negotiating Forum (TNF) as a structure for engaging around social contract issues (Dansereau 1997; Kanyenze 2017). More broadly, civil society witnessed a rapid growth in non-governmental organizations, grassroots initiatives and networks focused on issues of socio-economic rights and public sector accountability (Saunders 2000). With the labour movement, these emerged as effective critics of government's neoliberal turn.

Rising social conflict and growing economic instability under ESAP eroded the impact of DRM initiatives in the 1990s. Tax cuts and concessions for new investors helped to restrict opportunities for revenue expansion. Meanwhile, an economic slump, and the weakening of the state's monitoring and collection capacities, compounded revenue challenges. The stagnant formal sector undermined the DRM potential of the National Social Security Authority, the national pension scheme established in 1993. At the same time, DRM opportunities arising from the liberalization of domestic finance markets and the rapid expansion of branch banks, networks and special finance vehicles were blunted by government's policy reversals and domestic borrowing. When government made large politically driven payments to protesting war veterans in 1997, the resulting explosion in the budget deficit sealed the fate of ESAP and its associated DRM strategies. The ballooning deficit sent the economy into a sharp decline and government's emergency attempts to fund the shortfall through new taxes failed in the face of nationwide demonstrations. The political culmination of this growing crisis instigated by ESAP's implosion was the emergence of a new opposition political party, the Movement for Democratic Change (MDC), which was formed in 1999 under the leadership of labour movement and civil society representatives. This constituted the first serious national political challenge to ZANU-PF since the 1980s and found popular resonance in its appeals for a return to a redistributive, pro-poor development framework.

DRM Transitions and the Legacy of Crisis in the 2000s

The collapse of the neoliberal consensus in the late 1990s and establishment of the MDC set the foundations for new governing arrangements characterized by escalated political tensions, economic decline and state restructuring. After its defeat in a 2000 Constitutional Referendum, ZANU-PF adopted increasingly aggressive tactics for confronting its critics. It facilitated the mobilization of "war veterans," landless people and party loyalists in the Fast Track Land Reform (FTLR) programme, which decimated the commercial agricultural sector and had severe consequences for local industry.[3] The party's new strategy depended on the militarization of key state structures, the effective abrogation of established administrative processes and the waging of violence against civil society and business actors.

A devastating economic downturn ensued. Amid foreign currency shortages and rising production costs, GDP declined by more than 7 per cent, initiating eight consecutive years of worsening macroeconomic indicators. The consequences for the social sector were unprecedented: more than a fifth of the population fell into extreme poverty and social services all but collapsed.[4] Health and education indicators dropped precipitously, reversing key gains since independence (Mate 2018). By 2008 the economy had nearly halved in size, culminating in a ruinous period of hyperinflation in 2007–2008 as government addressed rampant inflation by an erratic combination of price controls, massive expansions of money supply and successive currency revaluations.[5] Facing a donor boycott, collapsing revenues and rising social protests, ZANU-PF was forced

[3] See Hammar et al. (2003), Moyo (2011), Scoones et al. (2010), and Rutherford (2012).

[4] More than 70 per cent of the population was classified as poor and Zimbabwe's Human Development Index slid to 173 out of 187 countries by 2011 (World Bank 2018).

[5] Inflation rose close to 600 per cent by the end of 2005 before exploding in late 2007, reaching approximately 230 million per cent before official calculations were suspended (RBZ 2008).

to accept a political solution after controversial national elections in 2008 saw it lose its majority to the MDC. An internationally brokered Government of National Unity (GNU) brought the MDC into government with ZANU-PF in a power-sharing arrangement for five years. This resulted in government's immediate re-engagement with donors, development partners, business and civil society actors. There was rapid economic stabilization as Zimbabwe abandoned its hyperinflated currency and moved to a multi-currency regime based on the US dollar.

DRM Under Duress

The extended crisis beginning in the early 2000s reconfigured the context of DRM in essential ways. The dramatic decline of commercial agriculture and important components of industry, mining and commerce decimated export earnings and severely eroded state revenues. In the absence of official development assistance (ODA) and new foreign direct investment (FDI), state revenues dwindled to crisis levels, forcing the government to explore new funding options. At the same time, "state capture" by the ruling elite degraded the autonomy and capacity of key state structures, exacerbating the impact of neoliberal austerity in the 1990s. Elite factional differences replicated in state institutions contributed further to the fragmentation of state coordination, policy coherence and engagement with stakeholders. In this context, state legitimacy eroded rapidly. While the overall conditions for state-society engagement improved markedly after 2009, the legacy of economic crisis and compromised institutional autonomy heavily influenced the shaping of DRM into the 2010s. In new efforts to raise revenues, the government struggled to manage contradictory fiscal needs, political interests, institutional constraints and stakeholder resistance. The result was an evolving, uneven and sometimes unpredictable set of experiments in resource mobilization, reflecting elements of both elite political expediency and popular inclusion.

Critical institutional reforms in this period led to contradictory outcomes. One key innovation was the Zimbabwe Revenue Authority (ZIMRA), established in 2001 as a successor organization to the

Department of Taxes and Department of Customs and Excise. ZIMRA was tasked with centralizing and coordinating key income, indirect and trade-related taxes, and oversaw the switch from a sales tax to a valued-added tax (VAT) system of indirect taxation. Enabling legislation gave the Authority expansive jurisdiction in tax collection, monitoring and enforcement, and investment in recruitment and training supported these moves. A second institutional innovation pertained to the decentralization of taxation involving levies, licenses and other taxes collected by statutory authorities or government departments. As fiscal shortfalls and inefficiencies in central government transfers to state agencies worsened in the 2000s, pressure grew for the local retention and spending of indirect taxes. In 2009 the Public Finance Management Act facilitated extensive decentralization of these revenues. This situation presented opportunities for efficiencies in the collection and direct funding of services, but also created openings for reduced transparency, corruption, duplication of services and aggressive tax enforcement practices, motivated by agency self-funding. Moreover, the overlapping reach of collection agencies provoked tax resistance as the viability of vulnerable businesses and households was threatened.

The intensification of indirect taxation contributed importantly to the reshaping of state-society relations in the 2000s. While tax consolidation under ZIMRA was accepted, the rapid expansion of tax instruments in the midst of continuing economic crisis fuelled friction between the state, businesses, labour and civil society. Businesses criticized the complexity, cost and unpredictability of tax instruments; labour sought to link taxation to income, pricing and investment in employment; and civil society criticized taxation's anti-poor, pro-business bias. Business demands for tax relief resulted in the scaling back of corporate income tax (from 35 per cent in 2001 to 25 per cent by 2010), but overall, private sector taxation likely rose due to the proliferation of fees, licenses and other fiscal costs. Consequently, when growth fell sharply in 2005–2008, tax arrears, defaults and avoidance came to feature prominently in business-state relations.

In this context, corporate tax revenues and export earnings depended increasingly on large established companies, particularly in the mining sector. Paradoxically, this gave such enterprises increased leverage with the state at a time when it sought to extract further tax and developmental concessions—most notably following the enactment of the Indigenization and Economic Empowerment Act (IEE) in 2008. Confronted by the economic bargaining power and political adroitness of leading corporates, government often made concessions around tax bargaining. Smaller enterprises and informal operators were less successful in this regard. The latter increasingly faced the overlapping burdens of multiple taxation, declining markets and low access to finance. The 2005 introduction of a "presumptive tax" for the informal sector following little consultation of stakeholders met with strong resistance and disappointing revenue outcomes, and underscored the state's increasingly antagonistic relationship with small businesses (Dube 2014; ZEPARU 2015).

VAT, the leading contributor to state revenue after 2009, became a key focal point of complaint. The labour movement and civil society tax justice groups cited VAT's regressive character and pointed to an underlying corporate bias in government's tax strategy (ZIMCODD 2014, 2018). Civil society welcomed new taxes earmarked for social spending and government's modest subsidies for low-income households. But critics also disparaged the state's rewarding of companies and foreign investors with tax breaks while it punished the poor by expanding taxes on consumable services like cell phone use and electronic commerce. Businesses complained about the complexity and administrative costs of VAT accounting and payment, and pointed to the state's poor revenue accountability and the low level of discernible benefits for the private sector. In response to business resistance, ZIMRA initiated in 2010 the "fiscalization" of taxable sales by requiring companies to use digital devices that linked payment transactions directly to ZIMRA, thereby strengthening the Authority's supervisory capacity.[6]

[6] "Fiscalization" refers to the recording of VAT transactions using electronic devices linked directly to ZIMRA (ZEPARU 2015).

Re-engagement During the GNU

The state's re-engagement with business, civil society and donors during the GNU opened pathways for constructive dialogue on economic recovery and DRM. With the support of donors, progress was made in discussions around ease of doing business, improving fiscal discipline and the inclusion of developmental strategies in government's economic recovery framework, notably in the mining sector. The TNF, dormant since the early 2000s, was revived as space for stakeholder engagement. A new Constitution, developed under the GNU and inaugurated in 2013, reflected civil society and business inputs by enshrining principles of public finance transparency and equity, acknowledging community's rights to participate in and benefit from resource governance. These and other forms of state-society engagement emerged against the backdrop of economic stabilization and helped to consolidate government's fiscal stability, beginning in 2009. Nevertheless, the impact and effectiveness of these engagements were sharply limited by the commitment of the political leadership and, particularly after 2013, when ZANU-PF was returned to unilateral power in national elections and GNU power-sharing with the MDC ended. It became clear that while the state strongly supported various tax innovations of the 2000s supporting social spending, the leadership was less amenable to reforms that diminished its opportunities for patronage and rent-seeking. Discussion around this contradiction was a focal point of high-level dialogue between government, local stakeholders and donors after 2013, and underscored both the leadership's willingness to engage and its hesitancy to act. A key stumbling block was the ruling party's refusal to address high wage and employment costs in the public sector, which were both a critical contributor to the state's spiralling deficit and a vital source of ZANU-PF patronage. The budget needs implied by these costs catalysed the state's drive towards regressive taxation that exacerbated tax inequities and increasingly antagonized poorer Zimbabweans.

The sudden ouster of President Mugabe by military intervention in November 2017 appeared to open the opportunity for new paths forward for government in its engagements with stakeholders. The administration of President Mnangagwa announced a shift in government's development framework. Claiming to adopt a market-friendly approach and declaring that Zimbabwe was "open for business," the president committed government to clamping down on corruption, appointed a technocrat with international finance experience to run the finance ministry and called for the deepening of engagement with local business and civil society (Ndimande and Moyo 2018; Dzirutwe 2018). While initially welcomed by a wide range of actors, the new regime soon raised doubts about the extent of real change under the repackaged ZANU-PF government. The new administration's liberal economic policy shift provoked hostile responses from labour and civil society groups, which questioned the state's privileging of business' investment and profit priorities over those of labour and social protection (Mahove 2018; Githahu 2018). There were also broader indications of the attenuation of the improved state-society relations seen after 2009: despite promises of meaningful dialogue, government did not formally participate in the TNF for two years starting in 2016 (*Newsday* 2018). In a period of heightened political competition and debate catalysed by national elections in 2018 which returned President Mnangagwa and ZANU-PF to power, the foundations of a new DRM framework were slow to emerge.

Case Studies

Taxation Innovations

Overall, Zimbabwe compares favourably to sub-Saharan African countries in terms of its relative revenue outcomes, diversification of tax instruments and tax effort.[7] Its performance reflects successive innovations in taxation since 1980. In the first years of independence, the rapid expansion of expenditure in the context of large reconstruction and development needs and new social spending was partly covered by new

---

[7] Tax effort is a measure of tax collection efficiency. The ratio is derived by dividing the actual tax share by an estimate of how much revenue could be collected, given the structural characteristics of an economy.

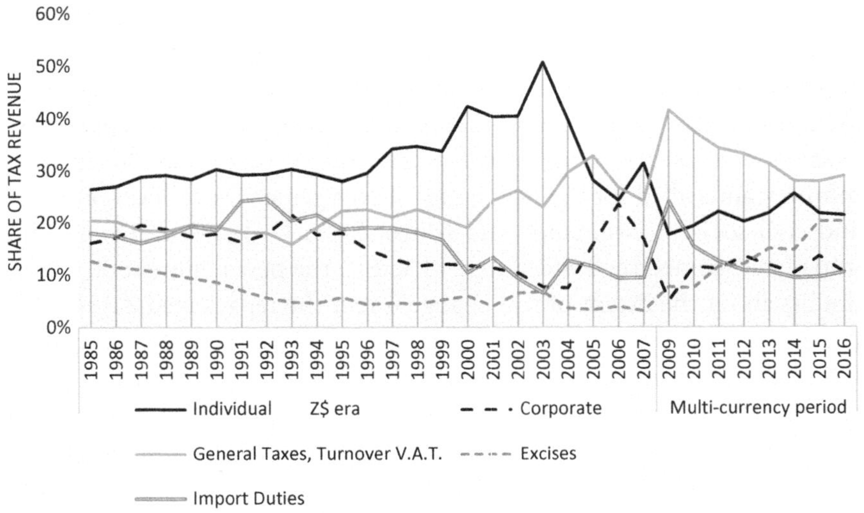

Fig. 12.2 Performance and contribution of revenue heads (1985–2016). (Source: Author elaboration based on Government of Zimbabwe, Ministry of Finance and Economic Development (data for years indicated))

tax efforts. Higher tax rates and wider coverage, and greater dependence on import tariffs saw revenues surge from 25 per cent of GDP in 1979–1980 to average 29 per cent for the 1980s.[8] But as multiple constraints imposed themselves on tax base expansion, and tax rate hikes and new tax instruments were constrained by neoliberal policies in the 1990s, the proportional contribution of income taxes to revenue trended downward (see Fig. 12.2).

In the first years of the 2000s, revenues declined further amid the rising political and economic crisis, punctuated by the collapse of commercial agriculture and contraction of the formal sector. Policy uncertainty and reversals, state capture and the militarization of political contestation, and heightened fiscal indiscipline linked to state patronage, combined to constrict access to capital. FDI crashed, a donor boycott saw the

[8] Zimbabwe's Revenue/GDP ratio was significantly higher than the 21.2 per cent average for sub-Saharan Africa over the period 1997–2002 (UNDP 2008). As Kanyenze (2014) noted, Zimbabwe also enjoyed a similarly high ratio of tax/GDP at 22.7 per cent, compared to the sub-Saharan Africa's average of 16.5 per cent.

Table 12.1 Summary: Revenues and expenditures as a percentage of GDP (1980–2013)

	1980–1989	1990–1999	2000–2008	2009–2013
Revenues/GDP	29	27.5	19.7	23.2
Expenditures/GDP	40.8	33.3	27.3	24.9

Source: Kanyenze 2014, calculated from unpublished ZIMSTAT and Ministry of Finance and Economic Development data

suspension of ODA and domestic savings fell off sharply. With formal sector revenues in sharp decline and demands for expenditure rising, fiscal imbalances exploded. In 2000–2008 the ratio of Revenue/GDP fell to 19.7 per cent from 27.5 per cent in the previous decade and expenditure's share of GDP shot to 27.3 per cent (Kanyenze 2014) (see Table 12.1).

The ensuing fiscal crisis prompted a series of innovations in the 2000s. One critical change, first proposed in the late 1990s, involved the strengthening of tax efficiency. This resulted in 2001 in the establishment of a unified tax authority, the Zimbabwe Revenue Authority (ZIMRA), and the switch from sales tax to VAT. In the 2000s, ZIMRA and VAT emerged as the mainstays of the state's intensification and widening of taxation. VAT became the leading contributor to revenues by 2009, and ZIMRA was the focal point of state investment for the centralization, supervision and enforcement of tax collection. A second innovation aimed at the expansion of taxation through the decentralization of revenue collection and distribution. There was a rapid growth in new revenue vehicles as the state's fiscal needs mounted, and legislative provisions enacted in 2009 enabling decentralized collection and retention of revenues led to a diverse array of indirect taxes.[9] New levies, licenses and other fees were designed to directly fund specific services such as health care and education, and capital investments in rural electrification, water development and transportation (among other sectors). In several instances statutory institutions were established to manage earmarked tax proceeds; more broadly, Local Authorities, state-owned enterprises and government departments and service providers were given powers to

[9] The Public Finance Management Act (2009) introduced specific provisions (Section 18) for the collection and retention of levies, licenses, user fees and other revenues by diverse public institutions.

Table 12.2 Summary of contributions to total revenue by direct and indirect taxation (1980–2013)

	1980–1989	1990–1999	2000–2008	2009–2013
Direct taxation	41.6	42.1	51.8	28.6
Indirect taxation	42.5	40.6	35.5	56.8

Source: Kanyenze 2014, calculated from unpublished Zimstat and Ministry of Finance and Economic Development data

collect and retain fees and levies. Incentives for local collection and retention intensified amid waning transfers from central government in the period of severe economic crisis. By 2011, the central government accounted for less than 50 per cent of revenue collection, with Local Authorities and state enterprises making up the bulk. By 2016, at least 24 government departments and agencies were collecting and retaining indirect taxes, comprising 12 per cent of state budget resources, and at least 64 statutory and retention funds were in operation (Government of Zimbabwe and World Bank 2017; *Financial Gazette* 2017). Whereas in the 1980s and 1990s direct and indirect taxation had been roughly equivalent with each providing 40–42 per cent of revenue, by 2009–2013, direct taxation made up just 28.6 per cent of state revenue, and indirect taxation soared to 56.8 per cent (Kanyenze 2014) (see Table 12.2).

These shifts critically altered the state's relations with business and citizens. After two decades of relatively consistent and predictable business taxation, companies faced a growing array of tax costs due to ZIMRA's intensification of enforcement (e.g. through the fiscalization of VAT collection) and the proliferation of taxes and fees charged by different government structures. By 2014, a typical company faced an average of 49 separate tax payments per year, a burden beyond the means of many medium and small businesses (World Bank 2014). Government also sought to expand revenue by taxing the growing informal sector via a widely unpopular "presumptive tax." Such measures overwhelmed the limited corporate tax relief enacted by the government during the worst crisis years and blunted the impact of partial exemptions and subsidies for poorer Zimbabweans put in place in response to criticism over VAT's tax equity impacts. Among registered businesses and informal operators, state efforts at revenue growth fuelled tax resistance and a rising "culture of non-compliance." Both complained of overlapping and complicated taxation, unduly high rates and tight payment schedules, and the lack of identifiable direct benefits for their operations. Meanwhile, the proliferation of collection agencies made it difficult to coordinate effective stakeholder dialogue with the state.

High levels of tax default, amounting to more than USD 4 billion in arrears owed to ZIMRA by 2018, reflected the weakening capacity—and willingness—of businesses and citizens to pay. In response, government increasingly sought to boost revenues through new indirect taxes that were more difficult to avoid. These included levies and fees related to the use of mobile phones, including controversial taxes introduced in 2018 on electronic financial transactions, the main form of commerce in the "cashless" Zimbabwean economy.[10] These taxes disproportionately affected low-income Zimbabweans and led to further popular outcries about tax fairness and equity. But they were also a stark representation of the deeply contradictory interests at stake: for the government, the electronic transactional tax enabled higher, wide-reaching tax efficiencies; for most Zimbabweans, it was a symbol of a regressive, inescapable and unwanted tax burden. More broadly, aggressive tax collection by state institutions incentivized by local revenue retention fuelled popular criticism and micro-tax revolts.[11]

However, while the cycle of tax innovation in the 2000s was uneven in its revenue and social outcomes, it also contained notable examples of initiatives which strengthened revenue, improved transparency, supported social investments and won public confidence and compliance. The success of the AIDS Levy in funding HIV/AIDS medicines and related interventions, and of road tolls managed by the Zimbabwe National Roads Authority (ZINARA) in supporting the rehabilitation of the national road network, underscored the potential of earmarked taxes. A key sustaining factor was the degree of stakeholder participation in the

[10] In the 2010s electronic payments for goods and services using mobile telephones and domestic cash cards became the dominant form of financial transaction for most Zimbabweans in the absence of ready access to paper currency.

[11] For example, intense enforcement of traffic fines by the police was widely disparaged as motivated by the desire to finance salaries, not protect road safety, and taxpayer boycotts of rising electricity tariffs and municipal property taxes in protest at poor delivery of services became commonplace.

formation and governance of institutions overseeing decentralized revenue streams. High levels of stakeholder inclusion and mechanisms aimed at ensuring accountability and transparency—as seen, for example, with the AIDS Levy—resulted in greater public trust and engagement with the trajectory of revenue collection and social spending. In contrast, in instances where decentralization of revenue collection was not accompanied by enforced standards of accountability, as with ZINARA, there were opportunities for abuse and corruption involving funds: efficiency of collection was not matched with effective expenditure management. Tellingly, data on locally collected revenues and expenditures were not systematically tracked or reported by the central government until 2015, when controls on expenditure were tightened with the encouragement of donors (Government of Zimbabwe and World Bank 2017). By 2016 there were calls within government to rethink the administration of tax decentralization (PBO 2016).

In 2018 President Mnangagwa campaigned for election on the theme of Zimbabwe being open for business. Since his return to power, dialogue with domestic and international business actors has ensued, continuing a process hesitantly pursued after 2013 by his predecessor President Mugabe. A litmus test of this process will involve the extent to which the lessons of constructive taxation initiatives from the 2000s are identified, emulated and extended more widely. This will require further institutional innovation, greater stakeholder participation and the intensification of both revenue collection and accountability surrounding state expenditure.

Power and Vulnerability in Resource Bargaining: The Mining Sector

Zimbabwe's mining sector, a modest contributor to production and export earnings since independence, took on wider economic importance in the 2000s as commercial agriculture and industry contracted.[12] Booming commodities markets in 2001–2010 helped mining to become

[12] This case study is based on two UNRISD Politics of Domestic Resource Mobilization Working Papers on the Zimbabwe minerals sector: Saunders (2017, 2018).

the leading GDP and export contributor, and a focal point for government's revenue-boosting efforts. Government's DRM strategy involved reform of the mining fiscal regime, initiatives to promote "indigenization and empowerment," and the state's direct participation in extraction and mineral trading. Contestation around these issues in the 2000s underscored the harmful impacts of state capture and weak institutional capacity and revealed the power of mining capital to resist efforts to intensify taxation and restructure ownership of the sector. Together, these dynamics inflected the course of DRM bargaining in the 2000s, limiting the state's capacity to expand revenue from this key sector, and narrowing the space for state-citizen bargaining around minerals in ways that empowered large-scale players and elites and blunted opportunities for more inclusive participation of citizens in the governance of mining revenues.

Until the 2000s there had been few significant and lasting changes to the mining fiscal regime inherited from colonial Rhodesia. The most important of these reforms were associated with ESAP in the 1990s and involved taxation concessions to attract large-scale foreign investors in the fledgling platinum sector.[13] In the early 2000s, however, state-industry engagements turned sharply towards confrontation as the state's fiscal crisis deepened. Scrambling to raise revenue, the government significantly increased royalties, other taxes and fees, and sought to renegotiate concessionary agreements. Challenged by these pressures and skyrocketing costs, production was suspended in much of the gold sector, and new platinum projects were secured only by government's agreement to maintain fiscal concessions. These conflicts in the early 2000s set the stage for subsequent bargaining over the mining fiscal regime.

This contestation illuminated the contradiction at the core of the state's DRM strategy for mining: on the one hand, the sector was a critical source of revenue and foreign exchange; on the other hand, it offered important developmental benefits such as forward/backward industrial linkages, improved value added (beneficiation) and greater local participation. The discordance between these fiscal and developmental goals

[13] These included Special Mining Leases, which reduced corporate taxation from 25 per cent to 15 per cent on projects of USD 100 million and exempted them from several other taxes (Government of Zimbabwe 2019).

increasingly shaped bargaining as state-stakeholder engagements expanded during the GNU. An intense state-business dialogue focused on a "developmental" strategy for the sector was supported by donors and drew heavily on external policy frameworks like the African Mining Vision.[14] Yet the strategic goals and principles, spelt out in draft policy documents and agreed to by business and donors, rarely came to fruition. While miners insisted that fiscal reforms recognize the sector's sensitivity to taxation, regulatory signals and investment protection, government repeatedly sought fiscal quick fixes by rate hikes and "windfall" taxes, new tax instruments and ad hoc threats (Hawkins 2014; Mupamhadzi, et al. 2014). These had the effect of chilling foreign investment, while placing disproportionate tax burdens on smaller local firms, and undercutting the prospects of a developmental strategy supported by coordinated fiscal incentives. Significantly, larger miners retained key fiscal concessions, as medium- and small-scale gold operators complained of unpredictable fiscal burdens. By 2015 mining's absolute and relative contribution to revenues had declined.[15] In contrast, the small-scale gold sector illustrated the benefits of sensitive fiscal reform: a short-term boom in small-scale gold deliveries in the 2010s was the result of miner-friendly fiscal terms introduced to boost export earnings and consolidate rural support in advance of elections in 2018.[16]

Government's contradictory approach to mining DRM was also reflected in its indigenization and empowerment policies. Under the IEE of 2008, the state required the transfer of at least 51 per cent of foreign firms' equity to indigenous Zimbabweans. Regulations setting the terms for the mining sector followed in 2011 (Government of Zimbabwe 2011). The IEE brought to an abrupt conclusion long-standing discussions between the state, business and donors over a phased programme of mining empowerment (Saunders 2017). For some observers, the IEE was

[14] The African Mining Vision is a regulatory framework adopted in 2009 by 54 member states of the African Union and endorsed by international business and donor institutions (African Union 2009). Key studies funded by donors include Government of Zimbabwe (2013). McMahon et al. (2012), Hawkins (2009), Jourdan et al. (2012), Kanyenze et al. (2011) and ZELA (2012).

[15] Mining tax revenue fell to USD 75.7 million (2.2 per cent of all revenue) in 2016, from USD 245.8 million (7 per cent) in 2012; see Government of Zimbabwe (2017).

[16] Reforms included increases in the gold purchase price, payment in foreign exchange, purchasing from unlicensed producers and loans to small producers to enable investment.

borne of urgent political expediency, its timing and content explained by the erosion of ZANU-PF's political legitimacy ahead of closely fought national elections in 2008 (Matyszak 2011).

For government, mining indigenization would redress problems of foreign domination of the sector, including transfer pricing, illicit trading and profit repatriation. Restructuring would unlock local investment, inject liquidity into the national economy and ensure that the benefits of growth were distributed more equitably. However, government's implementation of indigenization belied this official strategy. In reality, IEE institutions were underfunded, accorded ambiguous powers and beset by inter-institutional conflict. Political threats from ministers and declining investment, rather than coherent developmental strategies and equitable redistribution, became IEE's hallmarks in mining.

Paradoxically, this situation created opportunities for mining companies endowed with strong technical and economic capacity to negotiate favourable indigenization deals. These deals conveyed the impression of substantial shifts in control without delivering significant material change. Both government and miners saw gains: government claimed the localization of majority shareholdings, while miners retained effective control and a preferential tax regime. In some cases, the IEE likely enabled companies to reduce local "development" costs like corporate social responsibility (Mawowa 2013; Moyo and Hwenga 2010). Some argued that mining tax receipts could drop due to the financial re-engineering of "indigenized" companies (Hawkins 2014). In this context, business embraced a mining-friendly version of restructuring which followed the letter, if not the spirit, of the IEE law (BCZ 2011). Still, the IEE unquestionably dampened mining FDI, growth and revenue. Recognizing the opportunity cost of retaining IEE rhetoric without a matching DRM strategy, the new government of President Mnangagwa effectively abandoned indigenization in 2018, but was slow to propose a DRM strategy to replace it.

In 2006, the discovery of world-class deposits of alluvial diamonds in Marange District in eastern Zimbabwe offered important new opportunities for revenue mobilization in a period of severe economic crisis. The Marange strike, which ranked the country among the world's leading producers (Global Witness 2017), became the focus of intense contestation among state actors, miners, mining communities, civil society and donors. As the state moved to assert its control of the diamond fields, it secretively manipulated the process of mine contracting and displayed hostility towards local business, civil society and community critics, souring state-society relations and effectively removing diamond revenues from public scrutiny and social bargaining. These conflicts deepened divisions around resource governance and revealed the vulnerabilities of DRM bargaining in the context of weak state capacity, a rent-seeking elite, poor information flow and the complicity of the international diamond trade.

State capture weakened the mining bureaucracy's administrative autonomy and injected partisanship and secrecy into decision-making under ZANU-PF ministers, fomenting elite-supervised pilfering. The tracking of diamond production and revenues was strategically disrupted, and state institutions overseeing diamond mining contracts were compromised by ministerial interference. These problems were amplified by complex systems for collecting diamond sector taxes, which involved several institutions with varying capacities and diverse political patrons (Sibanda and Makore 2013; Sibanda 2014). These structural weaknesses, paired with the complicity of the international diamond trade, opened pathways to illegal trading, tax evasion and the illicit export of earnings (Global Witness 2012a, b; Mailey 2015). In 2017 Parliament's Public Accounts Committee reported that there had been no audited accounts of state-led mining operations in Marange since 2013 (*The Standard* 2017). Independent experts estimated that USD 2 billion in diamond earnings was unaccounted for between 2008 and 2012 (PAC 2012). A sustainable DRM strategy for Marange, one official report found, required the strengthening of the state's administrative, oversight and security institutions, and greater public scrutiny of executive decision-making (Parliament of Zimbabwe, Committee on Mines and Energy 2018). Others pointed to the renewed need for greater information transparency, state accountability and civil society participation (USAID 2016).

Inclusion and Sustainability: The AIDS Levy

Since its first diagnosed case of AIDS in 1985, Zimbabwe has been one of Southern Africa's most-affected countries by the HIV/AIDS pandemic. By the late 1980s government had initiated a National AIDS Co-ordination

Programme, and in the following decade, its efforts intensified and became more diverse as rates of infection, illness and mortality rose sharply (SADC 2008). In the mid-1990s, the government undertook extensive consultations in the process of formulating a comprehensive National AIDS Policy, launched in 1999 (Government of Zimbabwe 1999). It established the National AIDS Council (NAC) as a statutory body to coordinate the work of government, non-governmental organizations, the private sector, donors and other stakeholders, in alignment with the National AIDS Policy and National HIV and AIDS Framework (SADC 2008). A key issue in the management of the pandemic involved funding: low and unstable external support for HIV/AIDS had undermined government interventions in the late 1990s and early 2000s, and sustainable, predictable interventions would require domestic funding (NAC 2014).

To support the NAC and the state's HIV/AIDS interventions, in 1999 the government established the National AIDS Trust Fund, commonly known as the AIDS Levy. A 3 per cent tax on personal and corporate income, the Levy was a unique innovation in a region at the epicentre of the pandemic, where its performance was closely watched and soon became recognized as a model for best practices (Bhat et al. 2016; SADC 2008). The success of the AIDS Levy provided important lessons for revenue mobilization strategies aimed at funding social services. Key among them were the importance of building a relatively autonomous and capacitated institution to serve as the focal point for multi-stakeholder relations and bargaining, and the consolidation of stakeholder and taxpayer trust through efforts to enhance transparency, accountability and public education around the collection and distribution of revenue.

The process surrounding the Levy's establishment underscored the importance of stakeholder inclusion at an early stage. The Levy was preceded by intense lobbying by civil society organizations, non-governmental service organizations and health professionals. Through public consultations, demonstrations, supportive research and other means, stakeholders pressured the government to situate the HIV/AIDS crisis as a national political-economic priority. This engagement process resulted in the embedding of governance principles in the NAC that evoked its multi-stakeholder origins.

A statutory body with a diverse executive appointed by the President, the NAC both enjoyed considerable administrative autonomy and was bound by rules designed to ensure its accountability.[17] Clear guidelines stipulated the NAC's programme expenditure targets and implementation was closely monitored.[18] Annual audited accounts were produced and made publicly available. By the NAC Act, diverse stakeholders were mandated to participate at national and subnational levels via AIDS Action Committees, structures critical in the drawing up of plans and disbursing of funds (SADC 2008).[19] Investment in public awareness-raising around the benefits of the Levy helped to win broad acceptance of the tax, while the encouragement of robust debate within the NAC's administrative structures and with civil society stakeholders served to consolidate the NAC's legitimacy. A key innovation was the democratizing of access to finance for AIDS interventions, which enabled diverse groups and activities to obtain funding, enhancing a sense of community ownership.[20]

The significance of the AIDS Levy for Zimbabwe's national AIDS interventions was reflected in the NAC's accounts (Table 12.3). While the economic crisis and hyperinflation of the early 2000s sharply limited the impact of the income tax-based Levy, the post-2008 recovery period underscored the Levy's importance. In 2009–2013, the Levy's contribution to NAC's revenue exploded from 26.8 per cent to 85.7 per cent, alongside a sharp fall in donor support and dwindling government grant contributions over the same period.

For expert observers, the AIDS Levy represented a viable DRM strategy for financing a critical health care response (ZEPARU 2015). In the context of unpredictable donor contributions and government's limited

---

[17] The NAC was established by the National AIDS Council Act of 1999 [Chapter 15: 14], while the AIDS Levy was established under the Finance Act [Chapter 23: 04] the following year.

[18] For example, NAC rules stipulated that 55 per cent of revenues be allocated to purchasing antiretroviral medication. Spending targets could be revised, but only with the approval of NAC structures (SADC 2008).

[19] The Act stipulated that Action Committees include representatives of ministries, Chiefs and Local Authorities, HIV-positive people, non-governmental organizations, faith-based organizations and the business sector.

[20] For example, the Levy funded the domestic production of antiretroviral medications, specialist training and employment of nurses, provision of food for AIDS-affected communities, and payment of school fees and other expenses for school-going AIDS orphans.

Table 12.3 Sources and contributions of funds to NAC (2009–2013) (USD millions)

	2009		2010		2011		2012		2013	
Total NAC funds (USD millions)	21.29		39.8		34.57		37.57		39.10	
of which	USD m	% Total	USD m	% Total	USD m	% Total	USD m	% Total	USD m	% Total
AIDS Levy	5.71	26.8	20.52	51.5	26.46	76.5	32.54	86.6	33.53	85.7
Government grant	1.26	5.9	1.25	3.1	1.39	4.0	0.43	1.1	0.81	2.1
Development partners	14.31	67.2	17.43	43.7	5.57	16.1	3.89	10.4	4.21	10.8
Investment income	0.01	0.1	0.65	1.6	1.11	3.2	0.68	1.8	0.54	1.4
Profit on disposal of assets	0.01	0.03	0.01	0.04	0.01	0.04	0.12	0.03	0	0.0
Other income	0	0.01	0.01	0.04	0.02	0.05	0.02	0.05	0.02	0.1

Source: ZEPARU (2015) based on data from NAC (2014)

resources, and against the backdrop of weak state administration and transparency in the management of revenues, the AIDS Levy seemed to offer opportunities for dependable long-term financing of health and strengthened policy autonomy and stakeholder inclusivity (AUC and GF 2016). Yet the Levy's sustainability and long-term viability were cast in doubt by its underlying fiscal structure, which remained dependent on a weak and stagnant formal sector. A critical source of economic growth, the informal sector, continued to suffer low rates of tax compliance and comparatively higher costs of collection. The sustainability of AIDS efforts funded primarily by formal sector income taxes therefore remained a matter of concern.

Conclusions and Recommendations

While Zimbabwe has typically enjoyed a high tax effort and performance relative to many of its neighbours, it has also experienced multiple obstacles that have hindered the effective translation of revenue growth into improved social services and protection. In seeking to understand these contradictory circumstances, this chapter explored the evolution of state-citizen relationships. It found that the positive engagements in the first years of independence were eroded by a neoliberal development framework and worsened sharply in the 2000s during a period of heightened political contestation, economic crisis and sharply contracting fiscal space. As state transparency and accountability weakened in the context of elite state capture and increasing militarization of the political space, governance and state-citizen relations frayed and sharply undermined resource bargaining. The collapse of social protection in the early 2000s provoked a fiscal and social emergency and set the stage for a new period of DRM innovation under a changing political dispensation.

However, the effectiveness and sustainability of government's revenue raising efforts were called into question by the unresolved problem of high recurrent expenditures, primarily involving the civil service and state-owned enterprises. With further revenue growth via new or expanded taxation measures unlikely to keep pace with government's spending increases, donor and stakeholder engagement with government in the 2010s focused more closely on issues of fiscal discipline and transparency, and the strengthening of local business and investor confidence amid continuing weak flows of new capital. In this context, tax bargaining processes remained constrained by the contradictory dynamics of the state's short-term financial needs, stakeholders' developmental ambitions and the faction-ridden political elite's concerns over political expediency and rent-seeking.

Zimbabwe's revenue mobilization experience raises questions about the impact of institutional capacity and suggests the need for greater nuance in understanding the differentiated nature of stakeholders' bargaining access to the state. A compounding element has been the deepening of state capture, reflected in administrative militarization and elite rent-seeking, which diminished and refocused state capacity and autonomy. In important sectors like mining, this resulted in significant revenue losses due to rent-seeking, weak deal making and poor enforcement, and enabled companies to heavily influence the outcome, if not the principles, of policy reform in the sector. More broadly, the critical importance of institutional autonomy for improved revenue flows was underscored repeatedly in the 2000s by the success of DRM innovations like the AIDS Levy. In such cases, improved transparency, legitimacy and tax compliance were closely associated with stakeholder participation and administrative autonomy. While tax decentralization also posed challenges, including multiple overlapping tax burdens and poor accountability, public oversight emerged as a critical corrective factor in achieving strong outcomes. In this context, the importance of democratic strengthening of state institutions, policy processes and oversight practices became clearer, and raised questions about imbalances in stakeholder access to, and effectiveness in, bargaining with the state. This implied the need to identify forms of institutional engagement which could support more inclusive, effective and enduring resource bargaining outcomes.

The findings suggest several mutually reinforcing steps which might be taken to strengthen DRM and social outcomes in Zimbabwe.

First, there is a critical need to address state capture by strengthening bureaucratic capacity and autonomy and facilitating integration of policy at national and local level. The experiences of the AIDS Levy underscore these factors' importance for revenue gains and improved social spending. In the post-Mugabe era, the strengthening of the bureaucracy's professionalism and independence will be vital in re-establishing strong foundations for constructive state-society relations and citizen's trust.

A second challenge involves state fiscal discipline. In the 2000s the government repeatedly failed to contain expenditure due to the ruling party's political objectives. As a result, recurrent expenditure consumed a rising proportion of revenue and left significant social spending dependent on donor support. Firm and verifiable commitments to control spending were needed, along with the prioritization of vulnerable social sectors. Without strengthened fiscal discipline, the social benefits of Zimbabwe's expanded DRM efforts will remain in jeopardy.

A third priority emerging from the findings is the need to improve tax equity. Rising tax inequity in the 2000s contributed to worsening tax compliance and produced sharply negative impacts on the livelihoods of poorer households. As the relative contribution of income tax declined, revenue increasingly came from indirect taxation. VAT and a suite of new taxes on communication and transport services diminished the disposable income of poorer Zimbabweans. Despite demands from leading civil society actors, there was little evidence of significant shifts by the state on this issue.

A fourth obstacle for DRM involved the hierarchical pattern of resource bargaining, which emerged in the 2000s. The findings suggest that the restructuring of state institutions through state capture, the continuing fiscal leverage of established business interests and the political elite's recurring instrumentalization of civil society and popular constituencies in state-society policy engagements, contributed to uneven stakeholder influence on DRM bargaining, policy formulation and policy implementation. Power imbalances, reflected in the chequered experience of the TNF, suggested measures were needed to improve the effectiveness of civil society participation.

Finally, the challenge of balancing taxation with developmental outcomes remained. Since 2009, questions of tax fairness, linked social benefits and administrative transparency were a recurring focus of government-citizen engagements around the funding of services and infrastructure. However, the positive lessons from the development of successful DRM innovations were slow to be taken up in the elaboration of a broader DRM state strategy.

References

African Union. 2009. *African Mining Vision*. Addis Ababa: African Union.

AUC (African Union Commission) and GF (Global Fund). 2016. *Innovative and Domestic Financing for Health in Africa: Documenting Good Practices and Lessons Learnt*. Addis Ababa: African Union.

BCZ (Business Council of Zimbabwe). 2011. *Indigenisation and Economic Empowerment*.

Bebbington, Anthony, Abdul-Gafaru Abdulai, Denise Humphreys Bebbington, Marja Hinfelaar, and Cynthia A. Sanborn. 2018. *Governing Extractive Industries: Politics, Histories, Ideas*. Oxford: Oxford University Press.

Bhat, Nisha, Peter Kilmarx, Freeman Dube, Albert Manenji, Medelina Dube, and Tapuwa Magure. 2016. Zimbabwe's National AIDS Levy: A Case Study. *SAHARA: Journal of Social Aspects of HIV/AIDS* 13 (1): 1–7.

Bond, Patrick, and Richard Saunders. 2005. Labor, the State and the Struggle for a Democratic Zimbabwe. *Monthly Review* 57 (7): 42–55.

Dansereau, Suzanne. 1997. Rebirth of Resistance: Labour and Structural Adjustment in Zimbabwe. *Labour, Capital and Society* 30 (1): 90–122.

Dube, Godwin. 2014. Informal Sector Tax Administration in Zimbabwe. *Public Administration and Development* 34: 48–62.

Dzirutwe, MacDonald. 2018. Zimbabwe's Mnangagwa Names Ex-banker Mthuli Ncube Finance Minister. *Reuters*. September 7.

Financial Gazette. 2017. Statutory Funds to be Included in Budget. October 5.

Githahu, Mwangi. 2018. How is Zimbabwe Faring since the Arrival of President Emmerson Mnangagwa? *Leadership*. June 12.

Global Witness. 2012a. *Diamonds: A Good Deal for Zimbabwe?* Report.

———. 2012b. *Financing a Parallel Government?* Report.

———. 2017. *An Inside Job - Zimbabwe: The State, the Security Forces, and a Decade of Disappearing Diamonds*. Report.

Government of Zimbabwe. 1991. *Zimbabwe: A Framework for Economic Reform (1991–1995)*. Harare: Government of Zimbabwe.

———. 1999. *National Policy on AIDS for Zimbabwe*. Harare: Government of Zimbabwe.

———. 2011. *Indigenization and Economic Empowerment (General) Regulations: Minimum Requirements for Indigenization Implementation Plans Submitted by Non-indigenous Businesses in the Mining Sector.* General Notice 114 of 2011. Harare: Government of Zimbabwe.

———. 2013. *Draft Minerals Policy.* Official Policy Document. Harare: Government of Zimbabwe.

Government of Zimbabwe and World Bank. 2017. *Zimbabwe Public Expenditure Review 2017*. Harare: Government of Zimbabwe/The World Bank.

Government of Zimbabwe, Commission of Inquiry into Taxation. 1986. *Report of the Commission of Inquiry into Taxation*. Harare: Government of Zimbabwe.

Government of Zimbabwe, Ministry of Finance and Economic Development. 1985–2016. *Data on Revenue Performance and Contribution*. Harare: Government of Zimbabwe.

———. 2017. *Annual Budget Review for 2016 and the 2017 Outlook*. Presented to Parliament 20 July.

Government of Zimbabwe, Ministry of Mines and Mining Development. 2019. *Fiscal Incentives in the Mining Sector*. Accessed 22 March 2019. http://www.mines.gov.zw/?q=mpd/56.

Hammar, Amanda, Brian Raftopoulos, and Stig Jensen. 2003. *Zimbabwe's Unfinished Business: Rethinking Land, State and Nation in the Context of Crisis*. Harare: Weaver Press.

Hawkins, Tony. 2009. *The Mining Sector in Zimbabwe and Its Potential Contribution to Recovery. Comprehensive Economic Recovery in Zimbabwe*. Working Paper No. 1. United Nations Development Programme (UNDP) Working Paper Series. Harare: UNDP Zimbabwe.

———. 2014. *Mining Policy in Zimbabwe*. Mimeo.

Jourdan, Paul, Gibson Chigumira, Isaac Kwesu, and Erina Chipumho. 2012. *Mining Sector Policy Study*. Harare: Zimbabwe Economic Policy Analysis and Research Unit.

Kanyenze, Godfrey. 2014. *Fiscal Mobilization for Social Development in Zimbabwe*. LEDRIZ Working Paper. Harare: Labour and Economic Development Research Institute of Zimbabwe.

———. 2017. *Background to Social Contract in Zimbabwe*. Presentation to Zimbabwe Congress of Trade Unions Social Contract Preparatory Meeting, Harare, 27 March.

Kanyenze, Godfrey, Timothy Kondo, Posper Chitambara, and Jos Martens, eds. 2011. *Beyond the Enclave: Towards a Pro-poor and Inclusive Development Strategy for Zimbabwe*. Harare: Weaver Press.

Khan, Mushtaq. 2010. *Political Settlements and the Governance of Growth-Enhancing Institutions*. SOAS Working Paper. London: School of Oriental and African Studies.

Mahove, Christopher. 2018. Labour Wary of Mnangagwa's 'Zimbabwe Is Open for Business' Mantra. *Africa Portal*, 20 August.

Mailey, J.R. 2015. *The Anatomy of the Resource Curse: Predatory Investment in Africa's Extractive Industries*. ACSS Special Report No. 3. Washington, DC: Africa Center for Strategic Studies.

Mate, Rekopantswe. 2018. *Social Policy and Social Spending in Zimbabwe: 1980 to 2015*. PDRM Working Paper No. 2018-8. Geneva: United Nations Research Institute for Social Development.

Matyszak, Derek. 2011. *Racketeering by Regulation*. Research and Advocacy Unit Report. 2nd Edition, May 2011.

Mawowa, Showers. 2013. *Community Share Ownership Trusts (CSOT) in Zimbabwe's Mining Sector: The Case of Mhondoro-Ngezi*. Harare: Zimbabwe Environmental Law Association.

McMahon, Gary, Rene Hochreiter, Robinn Y. Kearney, and Brandon Tracy. 2012. *Zimbabwe: From Economic Rebound to Sustained Growth*, Growth Recovery Notes, Note IV: Zimbabwe's Current Potential for Mining Growth.

Moore, Mick. 2013. *Obstacles to Increasing Tax Revenues in Low Income Countries*. Working Paper 15. International Centre for Tax and Development/United Nations Research Institute for Social Development/Swiss Agency for Development and Cooperation.

Moyo, Sam. 2011. Land Concentration and Accumulation after Redistributive Reform in Post Settler Zimbabwe. *Review of African Political Economy* 38 (128): 257–276.

Moyo, Theresa, and Manasa Hwenga. 2010. *South African Mining Companies Corporate Governance Practice in Zimbabwe: The Case of Zimplats and Murowa*. Johannesburg: Southern Africa Resource Watch.

Mupamhadzi, David, Lymann Mlambo, and Isaac Kwesu. 2014. *A Critical Review of the Mining Fiscal Regime in Zimbabwe: Towards an Optimal Structure*. Paper for Chamber of Mines of Zimbabwe, March. Mimeo.

NAC (National AIDS Council). 2014. Financial Reports. Accessed June 2015. http://nac.org.zw/funding/.
Ndimande, Jefferson, and Knowledge Moyo. 2018. 'Zimbabwe Is Open for Business': Zimbabwe's Foreign Policy Trajectory under Emmerson Mnangagwa. *Afro Asian Journal of Social Sciences* 9 (2): 2229–5313.
Newsday. 2018. Panic as Prices Soar. 4 September.
PAC (Partnership Africa Canada). 2012. *Reap What You Sow: Greed and Corruption in Zimbabwe's Marange Diamond Fields*. Published Report.
Parliament of Zimbabwe, Committee on Mines and Energy. 2018. Second Report of the Committee on Mines and Energy on the Diamond Sector in Zimbabwe for the Period 2009–2016. S.C.
PBO (Parliament Budget Office). 2016. *Statutory and Retention Funds: What Is the Way Forward? An Analysis of the Retention Fund*. Harare: PBO.
Prichard, Wilson. 2015. *Taxation, Responsiveness and Accountability in Sub-Saharan Africa. The Dynamics of Tax Bargaining*. Cambridge: Cambridge University Press.
RBZ (Reserve Bank of Zimbabwe). 2008. *Annual Report*. Harare: RBZ.
Rutherford, Blair. 2012. Shifting the Debate on Land Reform, Poverty and Inequality in Zimbabwe, an Engagement with *Zimbabwe's Land Reform: Myths and Realities*. *Journal of Contemporary African Studies* 30 (1): 147–157.
SADC (Southern African Development Community). 2008. *The Zimbabwe National AIDS Levy Trust (The AIDS Levy): Report in the SADC HIV and AIDS Best Practices Series*. Gaborone: Southern African Development Community.
Saunders, Richard. 2000. *Never the Same Again: Zimbabwe's Growth Towards Democracy, 1980–2000*. Harare: Edwina Spicer Productions.
———. 2017. *Contestation and Resource Bargaining in Zimbabwe: The Minerals Sector*. PDRM Working Paper No. 2017-13. Geneva: United Nations Research Institute for Social Development.
———. 2018. *High Value Minerals and Resource Bargaining in a Time of Crisis: A Case Study on the Diamond Fields of Marange, Zimbabwe*. PDRM Working Paper No. 2018-1. Geneva: United Nations Research Institute for Social Development.
Scoones, Ian, Nelson Marongwe, Blasio Mavedzenge, Jacob Mahenehene, Felix Murimbarimba, and Chrispen Sukume. 2010. *Zimbabwe's Land Reform: Myths & Realities*. Oxford: James Currey.
Sibanda, Mukasiri. 2014. *Analysis of ZMDC'S 2012 Audited Financial Statements*. Harare: Zimbabwe Environmental Law Association.

Sibanda, Mukasiri, and Gilbert Makore. 2013. *Tracking the Trends: An Assessment of Diamond Mining Sector Tax Contributions to Treasury with Particular Reference to Marange Diamond Fields*. Harare: Zimbabwe Environmental Law Association.

The Standard. 2017. Marange Gems Plot Thickens. 18 June.

UNDP (United Nations Development Programme). 2008. *Comprehensive Economic Recovery in Zimbabwe: A Discussion Document*. Harare: UNDP Zimbabwe.

USAID (United States Agency for International Development) 2016. *Gap Analysis of Mineral Revenue Disclosure and the Information Needs of Various Stakeholders*. Report Authored by Mukasiri Sibanda and Gibson Makore for the USAID Strategic Economic Research and Analysis – Zimbabwe (SERA) Programme, Contract No. AID-613-C-11-00001. Harare: USAID.

Whitfield, Laurence, Therkildsen Ole, L. Buur, and Anne Mette Kjaer. 2015. *The Politics of African Industrial Policy*. Cambridge: Cambridge University Press.

World Bank. 1985. *Zimbabwe Country Economic Memorandum Performance Policies and Prospects*. Report No. 5458-ZIM (October 28). Country Programs Department, Eastern and Southern Africa Regional Office. Washington, DC: The World Bank.

———. 2014. *Doing Business: Understanding Regulations for Small and Medium-Size Enterprises*. Washington, DC: The World Bank.

———. 2018. *World Bank Overview on Zimbabwe*. Washington, DC: The World Bank. Accessed 19 April 2018. http://www.worldbank.org/en/country/zimbabwe/overview.

ZELA (Zimbabwe Environmental Law Association). 2012. *An Outline of the Mining Taxation Regime in Zimbabwe*. Harare: ZELA.

ZEPARU (Zimbabwe Economic Policy Analysis and Research Unit). 2015. *Domestic Resource Mobilisation: The Case of Zimbabwe*. Harare: ZEPARU.

ZIMCODD (Zimbabwe Coalition on Debt and Development). 2014. *Zimbabwe's Tax System: Opportunities and Threats for Enhancing Development in Zimbabwe*. Harare: ZIMCODD.

———. 2018. *ZIMCODD Position on Tax Dodging Practices by Individuals and Private Companies*. Harare: ZIMCODD.

ZIMSTAT (Zimbabwe National Statistics Agency). [Various Years]. Data on Growth Rates of Real Gross Domestic Product. http://www.zimstat.co.zw/.

13

The Politics of Domestic Resource Mobilization for Social Development: Conclusions

Katja Hujo

The different chapters in this volume have approached domestic resource mobilization (DRM) for social development through the lens of a political economy analysis focusing on bargaining processes, changes in key relationships and institutional development in a context of asymmetric power relations, diverse historical legacies and boom-and-bust cycles in the international economy. The studies show how important successful revenue mobilization is for state building and state capacity, as well as for state-citizen and state-business relations. DRM is also of paramount importance for achieving globally agreed development targets such as the Sustainable Development Goals (SDGs), which the international community committed to in 2015. This agenda commits governments to apply a holistic and integrated approach in their development strategies and to design and implement policies that are transformative, defined as attacking root causes of poverty, inequality and unsustainable practices

K. Hujo (✉)
United Nations Research Institute for Social Development (UNRISD), Geneva, Switzerland
e-mail: katja.hujo@un.org

K. Hujo (ed.), *The Politics of Domestic Resource Mobilization for Social Development*, Social Policy in a Development Context,
https://doi.org/10.1007/978-3-030-37595-9_13

(UNRISD 2016). In the introduction to this volume we have therefore argued that in order to raise the necessary funds to implement the 2030 Agenda for Sustainable Development, it is not enough to increase the quantity of resources, but the quality or transformative potential of resource mobilization needs to improve in tandem: in order to contribute to transformative change, financing policies themselves need to be sustainable in economic, political, social and environmental terms, and they need to be based on fair, inclusive and transparent political processes (UNRISD 2016).

A key analytical category framing the studies presented in this book is the concept of resource bargaining. It designates a process of contestation and negotiation around revenue policies and related social development policies, connecting resource mobilization and public spending. Such an integrated analysis of revenue and expenditure policies has been missing from mainstream economic literature on financing development until recently (Hujo and McClanahan 2009; UNRISD 2010).[1] In addition, the political nature of fiscal policy is also largely absent in studies and reports of international organizations and donors, although it features prominently in the academic literature.[2]

These two omissions in mainstream approaches towards finance for development and DRM result in a lack of understanding of what drives revenue mobilization, in terms of political and economic factors, and what the obstacles towards progressive fiscal reform are, which reforms are most appropriate in which contexts, and why implementation of reform blueprints or best practice policies is often not producing expected results in developing countries.

The thematic, comparative and in-depth country studies presented in this volume provide us with a more complex narrative about DRM for social development, including both the national and international context, past and present, and the political and economic drivers of revenue extraction. Indeed, the analytical framework, which guided the studies in this volume, has proven to adequately describe the reality in the different

[1] This gap is addressed in some of the more recent literature related to Finance for Development in the context of 2030 Agenda for Sustainable Development. See for example UN (2019).

[2] Levi 1988; Brautigam et al. 2008; Moore 2008; Martin et al. 2009.

countries analysed, contributing important insights to a debate that hitherto has been biased towards technical and siloed approaches to finance for development.

A set of findings and implications for policy emerge from the different chapters and country studies presented in this book.

Contestation, Bargaining and Outcomes

The different studies in this volume show that DRM is a political process of contestation and bargaining over who pays and who benefits. This process is marked by differences and asymmetries of power at different levels, from the local to the global, which are in turn shaped by historical legacies and economic and political contexts.

Resource bargains struck with donors usually display power asymmetries lopsided towards the creditor side, while there tends to be little engagement with civil society (beyond consultation which is mandatory in some debt negotiations such as those related to Poverty Reduction Strategy Papers—PRSPs) as negotiations tend to be held behind closed doors between technocrats and policy makers from donor and recipient countries. To the contrary, DRM processes linked to tax reform or extraction of mineral rents are often important public policy issues and can provoke contestation, social mobilization and even violent conflict. Clear examples of this are the tax riots of police and military personnel in Bolivia after the announcement of the International Monetary Fund (IMF)-supported personal income tax proposal (Chap. 9), the opposition to coercive enforcement practices related to the informal sector tax in Uganda (Chap. 11), the local social movement that opposed mineral extraction in a rural community in Nicaragua (Chap. 10) and the opposition from business groups in Argentina to a further rise in export taxes on agricultural commodities (Chap. 7). Power asymmetries also loom large between state and business actors/capital owners regarding bargains about levies on productive activities, profits and capital rents. In Chile, strong and coordinated business organizations have successfully lobbied against raising corporate taxation beyond moderate increases during the democratic transition, while fragmented business interests in Argentina allowed politicians, at least temporarily, to increase tax rates on the corporate sector, in particular commodity exporters (Chap. 7). In Uganda, the tax system relies heavily on a small number of taxpayers, mostly multinational companies, with around 35 top taxpayers accounting for 50 per cent of revenues collected by the Uganda Revenue Authority (URA). Big business players are hence not only more visible in negotiating tax reform, they are also more likely to successfully promote their interests and negotiate exemptions or other favourable treatments, of which multiple examples exist (Chap. 11 in this volume; Kangave and Katusiimeh 2015).

How resource bargains unfold, who the actors are and what outcomes can be observed regarding revenue yields and social development are shaped by historical legacies and structural drivers of revenue performance. Several chapters in this book point to the fact that revenue collection changes little over relatively short periods of time, given the complex governance tasks involved in taxation as well as the structural determinants of tax takes, such as per capita income level, urbanization, the size of the non-agricultural sector and international trade (Moore 2013; Chaps. 4 and 5 in this volume). In addition, tax performance depends on historical legacies, which is for example visible in the former labour reserve economies of Southern Africa, which display higher tax takes based on direct tax, compared with, for example, Western African cash-crop economies with lower tax takes and reliance on trade taxes, a legacy from colonial times (Mkandawire 2010). In addition to higher tax takes, the labour reserve economies also present a fairly consistent welfare regime cluster that is distinct from the rest of Africa: as shown by Mkandawire in this volume, labour reserve economies not only have high "tax effort" regimes but high social expenditure regimes as well (both at the aggregate level and at the sectoral level, e.g. in the health sector), both attributes related to legacies of colonialism (Chap. 5).

In the case of Zimbabwe, for example, the liberation struggle against Colonial Rhodesia resulted in post-independence demands for access to land, education, health and economic participation, and these needs were situated at the heart of the new Zimbabwe African National Union-Patriotic Front (ZANU-PF) government's development agenda. This new social bargain and associated revenue strategies were, however, constrained by the priorities of international donors, the fragile foundations of the post-war Zimbabwean economy and the limited capacity of the state to raise and administer new revenue, resulting in uneven development outcomes. Social progress in the first years of independence underpinned by donor support, a strengthening tax system and mining rent, was eventually eroded by a neoliberal development framework and worsened sharply in the 2000s during a period of heightened political contestation, economic crisis and sharply contracting fiscal space (Chap. 12).

Resource bargains related to natural resource rents analysed in this book have been linked with improved social development outcomes in some cases, such as in Bolivia. This was aided by booming commodity prices between 2000 and 2014, which allowed mineral-rich poor countries to become less dependent on aid and expand their policy space (see also Chap. 11 for the Uganda case). However, using natural resource rents as a key financing source for development encounters several challenges: before revenues from the extractive sector can be spent through public policies, they have to be captured by the government; revenues from natural resources accruing to governments need to be distributed among producing and non-producing regions, which requires negotiations between different state levels (Chap. 8); and in order to contribute to sustainable development, these revenues have to be allocated in ways which result in positive economic and social outcomes while minimizing negative environmental impacts.

The different case studies in this volume show the diversity of development outcomes associated with a strategy of mineral-led and -financed development. While in the case of Bolivia, successful capture, distribution and allocation of hydrocarbon rent has resulted in unprecedented social and political achievements based on a broad popular base which claimed national ownership of hydrocarbons (Chap. 9), the picture is different in Nicaragua where interests of mining companies and the government are in opposition with local communities who see their traditional livelihoods under threat (Chap. 10). In the case of Zimbabwe, a highly contradictory development path in what has been coined an anti-developmental model is observed (Chap. 12). Despite a promising start after independence and some innovative experiments in taxation and revenue generation in the midst of economic crisis in the 2000s, mineral-rich Zimbabwe was simultaneously witness to excessive rent-seeking by elites, spiralling debt dependence and severe decay of social services, eventually undermining state-citizen and state-donor relations as well as institution building (Chap. 12). In Uganda, greater policy space through the mobilization of domestic resources including oil revenues has had a limited impact on social development spending, which despite having some electoral appeal competes with other government priorities such as economic and infrastructure investments and political spending (Chap. 11). All cases seem to confirm our initial hypothesis (Chap. 1) that successful revenue bargains reduce donor influence in policy-making processes of recipient states. However, while improved fiscal capacity in recipient states has the potential to reduce dependence on foreign aid, this new autonomy is often time-bound, and the need to access external credit can re-emerge in times of crisis or structural shifts in the world economy. No compelling evidence can be found that successful DRM encourages donors to provide more aid to countries.

Finally, resource bargains are not only negotiated between the state and citizens, donors or the business sector but also between different state levels, the topic of Chap. 8 by Arellano-Yanguas and Mejía-Acosta in this volume. Extractive industries (EIs) are by nature enclave industries, which is not only problematic in terms of economic diversification and linkage effects but also for income (in)equality across regions, an important equity indicator for sustainable development. In contexts where fiscal governance is decentralized and specific revenues are raised at subnational levels, revenue-sharing arrangements that equalize the receipts from mineral rents across regions can redress these tendencies. However, political factors such as the nature of the relationship between national and subnational political actors, and the related degree of bargaining power of subnational actors, shape the outcomes of bargaining processes between different state levels about rent distribution (Chap. 8). In Bolivia, with the introduction of the Direct Tax on Hydrocarbons (IDH) in 2005, the government adopted a distribution formula that devolves 63 per cent of revenues from EIs to subnational actors such as municipalities and prefectures in tandem with sharing resources across producing and non-producing districts (Chap. 8). However, one precondition for positive development effects of fiscal decentralization rests on state capacity at the local level, which in the case of Bolivia continues to be highly disparate, with poorer districts having lower implementation and revenue-raising capacity compared to richer ones (Chap. 9 in this volume; Jiménez Pozo 2017).

Key Relationships

The quality of meso- and macro-level social relations is a marker of social development and democratic governance. As a result of DRM processes, we observe changes in key relationships between state, civil society, donors and business actors. These changes are not only driven by DRM processes but also determined by key features of governments and political leaders and how they relate with key stakeholders. Whereas external actors such as donors and foreign investors often have disproportionate influence in resource mobilization processes (as shown in the cases of Nicaragua, Uganda and Zimbabwe), lobbying of national business actors and competition between different state levels can result in suboptimal revenue yields and regressive distributional outcomes (e.g. in Uganda, Zimbabwe and Nicaragua; see also Chaps. 6, 7 and 8 in this volume).

Changes in key relationships can be analysed through the lens of changing citizenship regimes and their relationship with tax capacity and DRM (Chap. 6). Citizenship regimes create links between governments and certain social actors or groups by establishing them as legitimate participants in political processes and as claimants vis-à-vis public resources and authorities (Chap. 6). These groups are more likely to be included in fiscal compacts.

In the case of Brazil, both middle classes and popular sectors were incorporated into a new social contract during the successive governments of the Workers' Party (Partido dos Trabalhadores—PT) since 2003. The coalition of previously excluded working class, popular sector and middle-class actors provided a social base that gained legitimacy in the struggle for democratization and oriented a political cleavage in opposition to neoliberal stabilization during the 1990s. When growth returned in the 2000s, these actors established stable linkages with the state through social policies and institutions that used expanded revenues to share some of the benefits of commodity-led export growth. Despite this stable cross-class coalition, economic and political elites have blocked efforts to reverse patterns of inequity in the tax system such as regressivity and a lack of universality. While in Brazil the tax burden increased for all sections of the population from 1996 to 2004, this increase was generally greater for the poor (Chap. 6).

In the case of India, low tax take is associated with political coalitions that largely favour middle classes and internationally dynamic economic sectors, limiting the redistributive capacity of the state. The result has failed to produce a coalition in support of increased revenues, with middle classes particularly opposed to using tax to redistribute the benefits of growth driven by the technology and service sectors in which they are central players (Chap. 6).

Bolivia is another example of a new citizenship regime which has successfully incorporated the historically excluded indigenous majority population under the government of the first indigenous Bolivian president, Evo Morales. The 2009 constitution—defining Bolivia as a representative, participatory and communitarian democracy—formally recognized citizens' right of contestation, and accountability regarding electoral promises has been strengthened. The constitution also established a new social contract, which created a space for direct citizen participation as well as access to public services and income transfers. Social rights and social provisioning have since been strengthened and expanded, funded mainly through the nationalization of gas and oil resources but also through a variety of tax reforms: a series of measures that aimed to broaden the tax base and fight tax fraud and smuggling have contributed to increasing tax revenues since 2006 (Chap. 9).

Nicaragua's key relations have evolved differently in response to policy approaches adopted by different governments in the time period analysed. Similar to experiences in other countries analysed in this volume, the neoliberal reforms implemented in the 1990s reflected a new configuration of actors and of economic and political power, which deeply impacted state-society relations in post-revolutionary Nicaragua. Large business actors, some of which had been expropriated during the revolution, re-emerged as influential and well-organized actors. Social tensions and political contestation increased, while Nicaraguan civil society became a highly diversified and fragmented player. In this period, mass organizations and grassroots movements were weakened, though they also gained autonomy from the revolutionary party Frente Sandinista de Liberación Nacional (FSLN), while non-governmental organizations (NGOs) rapidly gained influence (Chap. 10).

Nicaragua's state-citizen relations have recently deteriorated as a result of violent confrontations between the government and social movements protesting against particular reform projects (pension policy) as well as against state repression and lack of transparency and accountability in politics (Chap. 10). Tax policy reforms and new tax legislations implemented over the past decades have not succeeded in creating a sustainable and equitable fiscal contract in support of social policy reforms which would move the country's social system towards a more comprehensive and universal system of social provision. While several social assistance and productive livelihood programmes have strengthened government ties with particular groups of civil society, others such as parts of the NGO sector and women's organizations have been increasingly alienated. Relations with investors and business have been surprisingly harmonious, taking into account the historical legacy of the current leadership under President Ortega as a revolutionary socialist party. However, relations with traditional donors have soured as a consequence of "bad" governance, while new donor alliances with Venezuela and China are affected by political and economic instability, in particular in Venezuela (Chap. 10).

In Uganda, the National Resistance Movement (NRM) government enjoyed high legitimacy after the end of the civil war. With the introduction of competitive elections in 1996, it has been increasingly responsive to citizens' demands for social service delivery such as universal primary education and abolition of health user fees, as well as regarding the elimination of the unpopular Graduated Tax levied on the informal sector, which in turn deprived local governments of an important revenue source, increasing the power of the central government. Over time, civil society has become more diversified and vocal, staging protests when fundamental rights of certain groups are concerned.[3]

---

[3] Such as the Domestic Relations Bill or the Anti-Homosexuality Act in 2014, although in the case of the latter the strongest contestation came from the international community and donor countries; see Kangave and Katusiimeh (2015).

While citizens are less concerned with the funding of social policy through general tax policy or contributions (which rather than a sign of lack of interest or technical expertise of the public might be due to the fact that the incipient social contract in Uganda continues to be heavily externally funded), the business sector is said to have considerable influence on tax bargains: big national and international enterprises wield considerable structural power as they contribute disproportionally to a narrow tax base and can therefore credibly threaten with disinvestment and instrumental power through political lobbying and influencing activities. Small- and middle-sized firms are able to put pressure on governments through public protests as the example of the strike of import-export traders against the introduction of value added tax (VAT) in 1996 demonstrates (Chap. 11). As regards state-donor relationships, Uganda has gone through different phases, described by Kjaer and Ulriksen as moving from consensus to contestation (Kjaer and Ulriksen 2014): erstwhile harmonious relations in the context of the first donor-supported poverty eradication action plans and the Highly Indebted Poor Countries (HIPC) initiative in the 1990s were followed by several conflicts with the donor community, while new revenues (oil) and donors (China) expanded the government's policy and bargaining space.

Key relationships in the context of DRM policies in Zimbabwe show some similarities with Uganda as regards the post-conflict, post-independence legitimacy and credibility of the ZANU-PF government vis-à-vis civil society, business actors and external donors during a first state-building period characterized by strong social investments and adverse impacts of economic crisis and structural adjustment policies which were implemented in the 1990s, strengthening further the role of external donors, international financial institutions (IFIs) and private business. The neoliberal turn marked a profound rupture in the consensus around post-independence social redistribution, alienating labour unions while private businesses and donors showed strong support (Chap. 12). Civil society started to mobilize under union leadership, and with alliances of NGOs, grassroots movements and networks focused on issues of socioeconomic rights and public sector accountability. In response to the failure of structural adjustment, political contestation and economic crisis, a new political opposition party emerged, the Movement for Democratic Change (MDC), which was formed in 1999 under the leadership of the labour movement and civil society representatives. As the economic and political crisis worsened, and donor relations soured in the context of the contested fast-track land reform, ZANU-PF turned increasingly to militarization and repression of civil society and local business actors, which eventually led to a donor boycott with devastating effects on the Zimbabwean economy, a defeat in the elections and the formation of a power-sharing arrangement with MDC in 2008, paving the way for re-engagement of ZANU-PF with civil society, donors and business.

Regarding specific revenue sources, the study reveals that state-citizen bargains have been weak in the mining sector, especially in the 2000s when the sector evolved into the key contributor to GDP, exports and fiscal revenue, though bedevilled by state capture, lack of transparency, and secret bargains struck with powerful mining companies. Other financing instruments such as the Aids Levy displayed greater stakeholder inclusion, citizen engagement and oversight, effectively contributing to finance important health interventions in a period of continuing fiscal constraints and volatile donor support (Chap. 12). This confirms our initial hypothesis that resource bargains that yield improved revenues to governments and social benefits to citizens require effective state engagement with citizens (see Chap. 1).

Finally, business power and the way business actors organize and interact with the state is important to understand the extent to which governments in Argentina and Chile have managed to implement progressive taxation and social and labour market policies in recent decades (Chap. 7). Encompassing business associations in Chile have successfully exercised political influence to maintain their privileges and push back against higher taxes and universal social policies, whereas a more fragmented business sector in Argentina allowed left-leaning governments to increase business taxes, especially during the commodity boom in the 2000s, funding that was channelled into redistributive social protection reforms. The analysis emphasizes firstly that the understanding of historical trajectories is important, as both countries experienced a transition from business-oriented military dictatorships to democracies, which resulted in new sets of competing claims towards government and redefinition of key relationships, and secondly that in order to reach a broad-based consensus for a more egalitarian policy and political mix, positive incentives for business actors, either through a positive growth context or industrial policies, are needed (Chap. 7).

Institutional Development

The third theme explored in this book is institutional development—or capacities for revenue mobilization and service delivery. It examined the extent to which the politics of domestic resource mobilization generated pressures not only for creating new or better institutions to effectively raise revenues but also for upgrading the institutions entrusted to deliver services, reflecting a resource bargain which provides social services and benefits in exchange for financial contributions by citizens, business and donors.

One key finding emerging from the various studies in this volume is that upgrading institutions for DRM and service delivery goes beyond technical approaches to capacity building, typically promoted by external donors who, however, have usually targeted technical capacity to the neglect of state capacity (a broader concept which includes ability to reach political settlements with domestic actors in defining public policies next to fiscal and administrative capacity; see Bangura 2006 and UNRISD 2010). As mentioned above, fiscal capacity is strongly path-dependent and influenced by historical legacies such as colonial history (Chap. 5). Nonetheless, policy and institutional reforms, including strengthening tax administration or social policy institutions, as well as changes in contextual factors, can increase fiscal space and state capacity. The chapters in this volume show that political state capacity needs to underpin technical reforms to make them work, an argument which is endorsed in Chap. 4 by Moore and Prichard who argue that strong and competent tax institutions can help confront political resistance (e.g. to tax the rich) and increase trust and compliance by taxpayers. Another lesson emerging from this collection refers to the implications of external funding for institution building. As Chap. 3 by Cherrier shows, donors have been able to catalyse social protection reforms in sub-Saharan Africa (SSA) through providing initial funding for social assistance programmes while being aware of the fact that sustainability and ownership of these programmes would be reflected in an increasing share of national budgets allocated to these schemes, making DRM a necessary condition for the long-term viability and institutionalization of social policy.

One example of the technical and political nature of institutional reforms is the introduction of independent revenue agencies, an institutional innovation that gained traction in SSA in the 1990s to increase tax collection. As the case of the Uganda Revenue Authority (URA) shows, institutional strength and organizational performance are ultimately a function of linkages with political leadership, because such links guarantee greater financial and political support (Chap. 11). A similar finding emerges from Chap. 8 by Arellano-Yanguas and Mejía-Acosta. It shows that in countries with more generous patterns of revenue sharing from EIs, such as Brazil, Bolivia and Peru, subnational governments obtained a greater share of EI revenues based on the specific nature of their political processes and historical circumstances. Political alignment of subnational governments with the central government as well as the strength of subnational actors (e.g. capacity to mobilize stakeholders at the local level) tends to be associated with higher revenues for subnational governments, whereas the level of fiscal decentralization, a formal institutional characteristic, is not a clear determinant.

Zimbabwe's post-independence experiences with revenue mobilization raise questions about the impact of institutional capacity on resource strategies and social delivery. While state programmes were weakened by resource constraints in the 1980s, neoliberal austerity and state cutbacks in the 1990s and a full-blown economic crisis in the 2000s, the effectiveness of state institutions was also undermined by evolving elite domination and state capture. This affected the policy and administrative autonomy of state institutions and limited public oversight and accountability, with highly negative impacts on revenue performance, especially from the mining sector, and public services (Chap. 12).

In Nicaragua, revenue mobilization and social development performance have been volatile and uneven in the country's recent history, which is also reflected in its institutional development. Much of the social policy architecture and new participatory institutions created under the rule of the Sandinista government post-1979 was dismantled under subsequent neoliberal regimes in the 1990s; public institutions were partly replaced by market mechanisms, with adverse consequences for access to and quality of social services, as the example of the health sector shows. The entry of for-profit institutions and a disempowerment of the Ministry of Health resulted in a highly fragmented and unequal system which now depends on external funding and has lost its focus on prevention and community services (Delmelle and Mendoza 2017). Institutions tasked with revenue mobilization, service delivery and monitoring of private actors are considered lacking transparency and accountability, in particular new institutions and programmes that were created in the context of Venezuelan funding through the Alternativa Bolivariana para los Pueblos de Nuestra América (ALBA) (Chap. 10). ALBA funds are not accounted for in the national budget and information about amounts, spending and impact is unavailable.

Finally, the Bolivian case is an example of both positive institutional spillovers from successful DRM strategies in a context of deepening democratization and state-citizen relations as well as less successful attempts to overcome administrative capacity constraints at the local level, which undermine service delivery in poorer localities, reinforcing existing inequalities in a context of ambitious governance and institutional reforms (Chap. 9).

In general, our initial hypothesis—that institutional development in revenue generation sectors has spillover effects on institutions in social sectors as the links between resource generation and social provisioning become established in the strategies of governments and citizens—could not be clearly confirmed, although there are signs of a positive association of institution building and fiscal space, in particular domestic resources, for social provisioning. In general, institutional legacies, administrative capacity constraints and political factors have a strong bearing on the performance of state institutions and social delivery.

Policy Implications

Based on the findings of the studies presented in this book, the following policy implications emerge:

Actual and potential taxpayers and other relevant stakeholders need to be involved in transparent and inclusive revenue bargains that establish links with social policy. They need to hold governments to account for the agreed distribution and allocation of resources. The links between revenue mobilization and social spending are most visible in taxation and social contributions. Taxation can embody a purposeful and mutually accountable state-citizen relationship where public services are provided in exchange for the payment of taxes by citizens and corporate actors. Earmarked taxes as well as social contributions maximize this contribution-benefit link, which can be beneficial in terms of increasing compliance with contributory obligations. Bringing more citizens into such bargains with defined benefits is therefore crucial for strengthening state-citizen relations. Resource bargains enhance transparency and legitimacy in the use of revenues, which can yield positive governance returns and claims making on public policy. Such resource bargains can also raise tax collection through building a tax culture and expanding the pool of taxpayers, and they provide incentives for citizens to hold governments to account on revenue distribution and allocation, contributing to greater budget transparency and spending efficiency.

Countries should diversify the financing mix and move towards sustainable instruments. The different financing instruments implemented at the national level, while context-specific and shaped by historical legacies and economic structures, can be diversified in view of minimizing negative environmental or socio-economic impacts. Taxation systems, if progressively designed (so that tax rates increase with income level), can contribute to redistribution and improve equality, including gender equality. They can be used to provide incentives for more sustainable consumption and production patterns, and they contribute to inclusive growth and human rights by financing income guarantees and universal social services. Mineral rents provide resources for developing countries which are often stripped of other types of funding sources.

However, mineral-led development poses risks and challenges with regard to structural change, employment, gender equality and environmental protection. While improving the governance of rent distribution and allocation is crucial for harnessing the transformative potential of these resources, the ultimate recommendation is to diversify away from mineral dependence, in order to avoid revenue volatility, to develop more dynamic economic sectors with greater employment and innovative potential and to safeguard the environment.

National resource bargains need to be complemented by global bargains such as official development assistance and improved global governance. While there is no conclusive evidence whether aid undermines efforts to raise taxes, it can have a catalytic effect on mobilizing additional domestic resources for social policies, especially in low-income settings. This has been the case where foreign aid actors supported national actors in investing in social policy and helped upgrade public institutions entrusted to deliver social services. Whether aid has a transformative effect depends on how sustainable and reliable it is, how it is distributed and allocated and whether it enhances state accountability and institution building. Global governance is furthermore important to guarantee macro-economic stability and crisis prevention, curb illicit financial flows and promote developing countries' access to external finance and markets.

Public policies need to support an enabling environment for DRM. While many revenue sources have the potential to contribute to social and sustainable development, realization of this potential depends not only on the specific design of policies but also on whether financing strategies are supported by an enabling policy environment, which is often a challenge in low- and middle-income countries. Enabling factors at the national level include economic policies which support labour-intensive growth, are conducive to structural change and lead progressively to higher rates of formalization, household income and equality. Other enabling factors are investments in state capacity—both in terms of capacity to create political consensus and support for progressive reforms and to broker investment deals with transnational corporations that are favourable for the country—and administrative capacity to implement reforms and enforce compliance with tax laws and regulation, especially by high-income earners and big corporations. And last but not least, democratic, transparent and accountable institutions and political processes provide an environment where citizens, business actors and donors are most likely to collaborate effectively and to deliver on their commitments.

References

Bangura, Yusuf. 2006. Fiscal and Capacity Building Reform. In *Public Sector Reform in Developing Countries: Capacity Challenges to Improve Services*, ed. Yusuf Bangura and George A. Larbi, 131–160. Basingstoke: Palgrave Macmillan and United Nations Research Institute for Social Development.

Brautigam, Deborah, Odd-Helge Fjeldstad, and Mick Moore. 2008. *Taxation and State-Building in Developing Countries: Capacity and Consent*. Cambridge: Cambridge University Press.

Delmelle, Guy, and Mendoza, René. 2017. *Reformas Estatales, Fortalecimiento Institucional y Políticas de Movilización de Recursos en Nicaragua: El Caso del Sector de la Salud*. PDRM Working Paper No. 2017-9. Geneva: United Nations Research Institute for Social Development.

Hujo, Katja, and Shea McClanahan, eds. 2009. *Financing Social Policy: Mobilizing Resources for Social Development*. Basingstoke: Palgrave Macmillan and United Nations Research Institute for Social Development.

Jiménez Pozo, Wilson. 2017. *Movilización de Recursos Domésticos, Desarrollo Social y Cambio Institucional: Descentralización y Autonomías Municipales en Bolivia*. PDRM Working Paper No. 2017–1. Geneva: United Nations Research Institute for Social Development.

Kangave, Jalia, and Mesharch Katusiimeh. 2015. *Tax Bargains: Understanding the Role Played by Public and Private Actors in Influencing Tax Policy Reform in Uganda*. PDRM Working Paper No. 2015-2. Geneva: United Nations Research Institute for Social Development.

Kjaer, Anne-Mette, and Marianne Ulriksen. 2014. *From Consensus to Contention: Changing Revenue and Policy Dynamics in Uganda*. PDRM Working Paper No. 2014-21. Geneva: United Nations Research Institute for Social Development.

Levi, Margaret. 1988. *Of Rule and Revenue*. Berkeley: University of California Press.

Martin, Isaac M., Ajay K. Mehrotra, and Monica Prasad, eds. 2009. *The New Fiscal Sociology: Taxation in Comparative and Historical Perspective*. New York: Cambridge University Press.

Mkandawire, Thandika. 2010. On Tax Efforts and Colonial Heritage in Africa. *Journal of Development Studies*, 46(10): 1647–1669. Accessed 23 February 2016. http://eprints.lse.ac.uk/31211/.

Moore, Mick. 2008. Between Coercion and Contract: Competing Narratives on Taxation and Governance. In *Taxation and State-Building in Developing Countries: Capacity and Consent*, ed. Deborah Brautigam, Odd-Helge Fjeldstad, and Mick Moore, 34–63. New York: Cambridge University Press.

———. 2013. *Obstacles to Increasing Tax Revenues in Low Income Countries*. International Centre for Tax and Development and UNRISD Working Paper 2013–15. Brighton: ICTD at IDS/UNRISD. Accessed 6 November 2015. http://www.ictd.ac/en/publications/obstacles-increasing-tax-revenues-low-income-countries.

UN (United Nations). 2019. *Financing for Sustainable Development Report 2019*. Inter-agency Task Force on Financing for Development, 235–260. New York: UN.

UNRISD (United Nations Research Institute for Social Development). 2010. *Combating Poverty and Inequality: Structural Change, Social Policy and Politics*. Flagship Report. Geneva: UNRISD. Accessed 16 March 2016. http://www.unrisd.org/poverty.

———. 2016. *Policy Innovations for Transformative Change. Implementing the 2030 Agenda for Sustainable Development*. Flagship Report. Geneva: UNRISD. Accessed 29 August 2019. http://www.unrisd.org/flagship2016.

Index[1]

[1] Note: Page numbers followed by 'n' refer to notes.

K. Hujo (ed.), *The Politics of Domestic Resource Mobilization for Social Development*, Social Policy in a Development Context,
https://doi.org/10.1007/978-3-030-37595-9

K

L

M